ADVENTURE IS IN MY BLOOD

ADVENTURE IS IN MY BLOOD

Volume III

(1957 - 1964)

Russell Annabel

Illustrated by
Louise Lopina

SAFARI PRESS INC.

Annabel, Russell

Second edition

Safari Press

1997, Long Beach, California

ISBN 1-57157-065-9

Library of Congress Catalog Card Number: 00689375

10 9 8 7 6 5 4 3 2

Readers wishing to receive the Safari Press catalog, featuring many fine books on big-game hunting, wingshooting, and sporting firearms, should write to Safari Press Inc., P.O. Box 3095, Long Beach, CA 90803, USA. Tel: (714) 894-9080 or visit our Web site at www.safaripress.com.

TABLE OF CONTENTS

	Foreword	vii
Chapter 1	Fiesta of Fins	1
Chapter 2	Life in the Big Frost	13
Chapter 3	Horse Hunt in Caribou Land	25
Chapter 4	Adventure with Makos	35
Chapter 5	Buck Fever Can Happen to Anybody	45
Chapter 6	Trophy Hunt in *Mañana* Land	57
Chapter 7	Grudge Grizzly	65
Chapter 8	Big Luck at Cuyutlan	75
Chapter 9	Trouble at Erickson Creek	85
Chapter 10	Death of a King Wolf	95
Chapter 11	Pete's Educational Bear Hunt	105
Chapter 12	Adventures of a Mexican Mutt	115
Chapter 13	Long Hunt for a Water Dog	129
Chapter 14	Captain Sharkbait's Triumph	139
Chapter 15	The Curse of the Chonchos	151
Chapter 16	The Mysterious *Onca*	161
Chapter 17	The Shootingest Characters	169
Chapter 18	The Craziest Cat Hunt	181
Chapter 19	Ladies . . . with Guns	191
Chapter 20	*Chubasco*	203
Chapter 21	When the Fish Went Nuts	217
Chapter 22	Storm Ducks with Crocs	227
Chapter 23	The *Tigre* of Santa Rita	237
Chapter 24	The Damnedest Duck on Earth	247
Chapter 25	Hell in Catskin	255
Chapter 26	Coyote-Wolverine War	265
Chapter 27	Mad Coyote	275

Chapter 28 The Gotch-eared Bull of Toonakloot 285
Chapter 29 Kill or Starve 295
Chapter 30 Snowblind! 305
Chapter 31 Waiting for the Caribou 315
Chapter 32 Long Hunter, Alaskan Style, Part One 325
Chapter 33 Long Hunter, Alaskan Style, Conclusion 337
Chapter 34 Joys and Sorrows of a Wrangler 349
Chapter 35 The High Price of Moose Meat 359
Chapter 36 In the Moon of the Drunken Bears 371
Bibliography 383

FOREWORD

Years ago, when I was managing editor of the old *Anchorage Daily News*, I first ran across Russell Annabel's incredibly vivid fishing and hunting stories in *Outdoor Life* and *Sports Afield*.

I found something especially compelling and unique about everything he wrote. Sometimes I'd read an Annabel story four or five times, captivated by the way he used words.

A passage that started " . . .the ground squished underfoot and the trees dripped like patented sprinkling systems. . . ." was wordsmithing of a quality I had never encountered before.

"Rusty"—Alaskans always called him "Rusty"—and I became good friends. When he had to take a long trip, he "loaned" me his dog, "Punkins." I have been an admirer of Rusty's ever since.

Some of the best war reporting in World War II is contained in Rusty's United Press dispatches from the Aleutian Islands. But it was his accounts of hunting and fishing in the incomparable Alaska wilderness that drew from him his finest writing.

Annabel's genius is such that he can effortlessly "beam" readers into Alaska's darkest, bear-infested wilderness. Through the sheer imagery, almost wizardry, of his words, the reader sees and experiences Alaska's magnificent landscapes the way Rusty saw and experienced them.

Annabel was at his best in describing wilderness conflict—the attack of a grizzly, the predatory assault of wolves on a helpless moose. This passage was typical of his prose: " . . . pandemonium broke loose in the dark strip of timber yells, snarls, howls, screams—an indescribable blood-chilling racket that echoed and re-echoed among the white hills. It sounded as if every wolf in the region was engaged in a free-for-all battle to the death."

It was a sad day for Alaskans who knew Rusty and treasured his work when, for reasons of his own, he decided to leave this vast, game-rich wilderness, never to return. When he left, Alaska lost a powerful spokesman who loved Alaska and conveyed that love in everything he wrote.The Alaska Rusty portrayed in all its awesome beauty is doubly meaningful to those of us who live here.

Since he left us, decades ago, nobody of his stature has come on the scene to take his place or to depict with such grasp the rawness and grandeur of outdoor Alaska. In my own case, as a writer of five books on this great outdoor empire, I still feel a sense of mourning not only at Rusty's passing from the earth but also because he chose to leave Alaska at the peak of his power as a writer.

There's no Mt. Rushmore, of course, devoted to outdoor writers, but if there were, Rusty's lean, weather-beaten, intense face would be there mountain-high.

I urge readers enjoying this book to recognize that this is not just another outdoor book but the work of a truly great American writer who never received the recognition he so richly deserved.

Cliff Cernick
May 1996

Fiesta of Fins

Tony was just back from the war and aching for a billfish with the kink in its brain that makes it crazy on the end of a line. We found him one at the Fiesta of Fins.

It was one of those sun-stricken Mexican noons that you get in August, and we were off Tiburon Island in the Sea of Cortes, specifically, at a legendary angler's heaven called the Fiesta of Fins. Just ahead of our charter boat was a flotilla of seagoing fishing dugouts manned by ex-cannibal Seri Indians. The canoes were anchored, slim hulls, dove-gray against the blue blaze of the water and heavy hand lines out. Their occupants lolled on the thwarts. Above them and above us whirled a million sickle-winged seabirds—a guarantee of the presence of plenty of fish, big and small.

Young Tony, my fishing compadre, was trolling a twelve-pound dolphin bait. Since morning we had sighted enough billfish to unhinge a man's senses, but with one exception they had been striped marlin or sailfish. We wanted a black marlin. There was a reason.

"Maybe we're here too early," Tony said, "Or too late. Or maybe—" Then it happened, right on cue.

The great fish rocketed up in a blind strike. A marvelous blind strike. I suppose he had started from deep down near the bottom, for he came so high out of the water, Tony's dolphin in his mouth, that his tail cleared the surface by a good eight feet. His head actually was higher than the outriggers. He seemed to hang there, motionless and metal-gleaming against the blue-hot sky, as if the scene were on a movie screen and the film had been stopped. It was a thing to make your hair stand on end, to make your heart hammer like a bop drum. Then he arched his body, half-somersaulted and came down with a tremendous splash, sledging the water with his tail, a sound like a salvo of gunfire.

He was a black marlin, a silver-and-blue apparition with a spear as long as a boarding cutlass, a sea-brute to lure an angler halfway around the world, as this one had Tony. I told myself that he would go 400 pounds, and as I did so I heard somebody hollering, and presently realized it was me. But I wasn't the only one. By this time everybody was sounding off like inspired lunatics. It was a time for hollering. Anybody who wouldn't have hollered, shouldn't have been here. I mean, there ought to be something in the game laws preventing calm, collected anglers from hanging black marlin. They miss most of the fun. It's a waste of good fish.

With the heavy Norwegian hook set solidly in his jaw, Tony's marlin jumped into the sun, then tailwalked toward the Seri canoes, shaking himself like a mambo dancer full of peyote and leaving a wake like a speedboat. He was on a collision course for the largest of the canoes. It was the canoe of Vaquero, the Seri chief, a notably grim customer whose unsavory reputation provides conversation in tequila joints from San Blas to the mouth of the Colorado. I figured that in about ten seconds there would be a crash to write home about, and brother Vaquero would wind up in the water with a lapful of black marlin and canoe splinters. But he was lucky. Just before the fey marlin reached the craft it disappeared beneath the surface, to come out again in a spectacular, truly magnificent jump—over the canoe.

I wish every angler in the world could have witnessed it. Gripping a stanchion, voiceless now, I saw Vaquero hurl himself to the bottom of the canoe, losing his straw hat overboard as he did so. I saw the marlin soar through the space the chief had so recently occupied, and plunge into a cobalt wave on the farther side. There were outraged yells from the Indians, and fist-shaking. A screwball man-o'-war bird dived hopefully on Vaquero's hat, banking away when he decided it wasn't edible. The deck quivered as Gabriel Aldrete, our skipper, gunned the twin diesels to chase the departing marlin, and young Tony turned to me with his eyes bugged out and his mouth hanging open.

"H-holy f-frijole," he said in a voice that didn't sound like his, "we've latched onto a broncho."

I will explain later what a broncho marlin is, or try to. Right now some new action was developing. A knife flashed in the sunlight. It was held by Vaquero, who was leaning forward to slash the line whizzing across the gunwales of his canoe. He should have known better. He had the wrong script. Mexican charter-boat captains are a rugged breed, and they take a dusty view of such acts as the chief was about to commit. Gabriel must have anticipated what Vaquero would try to do. Otherwise I don't see how he could have dealt himself a hand as fast as he did.

"Don't cut that line!" he bellowed in Spanish.

Looking up, I saw him leaning off the flying bridge with a .30-30 Winchester all ready to go. Vaquero swiveled around and gave Gabriel and the gun a basilisk stare, and if I read his expression correctly he was thinking that the skipper would look good in a roasting pit, Tiburon style. But he changed his mind about cutting the line. Instead, he lifted it carefully over the stern of the canoe with a paddle shaft. No doubt he lost face in doing so, but his hide remained unpunctured, which obviously was his major concern of the moment.

Latching onto this fish began one afternoon when Tommy Jamison and I were sitting on the front porch of the fishing office at Miramar. We were doing no more than enjoying the shade, listening to the honey-sweet cooing of pitaya doves in the laurel de la India tree across the way and waiting for the sun to drop below the yardarm. Tommy is sports-fishing director for two resort hotels here, operating fourteen boats and playing host to around 10,000 anglers a year. I had just made another check on the altitude of the sun, when a taxi came barreling down the road from the airport. The driver pulled up with a show-off flourish and a screech of brakes. Out jumped Tony.

Maybe you've experienced the wonderful, heart-warming surprise this was to us. We hadn't known he was coming. So far as we knew, he was still in Korea doing his part in the police action. The kid hadn't changed much. A mustache had been added, he was a little heavier, and there was a certain look in his eye that hadn't been there before. Otherwise he was still the same laughing, curly-headed Tony who had left here two years ago. Tommy's brother-in-law. My best fishing friend.

"I yearn," Tony said, after he had shaken hands around, "to go fishing. Been dreaming about fishing for quite a spell now. I'm way behind with it. Got any black marlin you want caught?"

Tommy had the answer to that, and it added up to a swell homecoming gift to a veteran. "Tomorrow I'll send you and Rusty out on the *Nautilus*—to the Fiesta of Fins," he said. "If you can't catch up there," he grinned, "yours is a hopeless case and you'll have to take it elsewhere."

The Fiesta of Fins . . . as yet the place was only a name to us, but a potent one. Most of Tommy's charter-boat captains had been far-roving commercial fishermen before they came to work for him, and they had kept telling us about finding a reach of water twenty miles north of Tiburon, where billfish actually gathered in schools during August and September. Fins sticking up everywhere, they said. Nothing else like it on this coast, maybe nothing like it in the world. As the fish had seemed to be in a playful mood, leaping and cavorting, the captains referred to the spot with Latin felicity as the Fiesta of Fins.

No sport fishermen, so far as we knew, had ever visited the place. Tommy and I had long planned to, but had never got around to it. The chief reason was that Tommy had only one boat capable of the 280-mile round-trip cruise from Miramar—the forty-eight-foot, twin-diesel, seagoing *Nautilus*, and usually she was under charter far in advance. How he intended to make her available tomorrow, I had no idea. It was none of my business. The important thing was that Tony and I were going to pioneer what promised to be a great new fishing ground, and that it was practically certain to be the angling adventure of our lives.

"Have fun," Tommy said wistfully at the pierhead next morning as we cast off. He couldn't go. He had business. We could tell him about the Fiesta of Fins when we returned, he said.

The fun began two days later. It was midafternoon. Ahead loomed the broken violet peaks of Tiburon, sinister since the time of the Conquistadors as the home of wild men. Only once during the voyage north had we put out a line. That was when we got into a school of flashing emerald-and-green dolphin and caught one of these superb fish for the galley. We had been in such a sweat to reach the Fiesta of Fins that we hadn't wanted to slow the boat to trolling speed. But now Gabriel had told us that we would anchor for the night at the south end of Tiburon, which gave us the rest of the afternoon to fish. So Tony baited up with a frozen mullet, and Gabriel cut the revolutions to four knots an hour.

We went in across the mouth of Wild Dogs Bay, where clouds of seabirds were working over a vast school of sardines. We sighted the blue tail-lobe of a good-sized mako shark and offered him the bait, dragging it within feet of his snout, but he wasn't interested. Maybe he was full of sardines at the moment. Or maybe he just didn't like mullet. Anyway, he slid into the side of a wave and disappeared. We passed a basking sea turtle that, I'll swear, would have weighed close to 250 pounds. We sighted a barnacle-backed gray whale. We watched a "flight" of sierra mackerel skitter across the water on blurring tails, with something big and hungry torpedoing after them just under the surface. We gazed at the grim topography of Tiburon and wondered if cannibalism had really been stamped out there. Then Gabriel, steering topside, stamped on the overhead for attention.

"*Vela*—sail!" he shouted above the muttering of the diesels.

The sailfish was on our portside, loafing along through the sun-spangled waves with his paneled dorsal and the top half of his tail showing. As we passed him he dived, to come up behind Tony's bait, his spear, head and hump out of the water. As always, it was a tense moment. Would he, or wouldn't he, strike? He was a sporting fish. He struck. He shot ahead half his length and whacked the skipping mullet with his spear, a solid blow that drove it under, knocking the line free of its clothespin clip on the outrigger. Gabriel threw out the clutch. Tony let a few yards of line spin off the reel. The sailfish was convinced. He thought he had killed the mullet, so he grabbed it between his jaws and turned away. Whereupon Tony set the hook, and things began to happen.

I mean, things really began to happen.

You couldn't reasonably have asked for a more fight-minded sail. It set out to give Tony a lot of trouble, and was big enough to do a fair job of it. Around ten feet. Maybe 110 pounds. He jumped six times, then took off in the general direction of California. I am reliably informed that a Pacific sailfish, when genuinely trying, will travel up to sixty miles per hour. This one apparently was trying. Line melted off the reel. Tony screwed the drag down some more, looking worried. Then the fish turned back in a wide circle, and Gabriel cut in at full throttle to close the gap. I figured the pyrotechnics were about over. He was a good sailfish but he'd had it. Six jumps are a lot of jumps, and it had been a long, sizzling run. I was about to say as much, when I saw something. It was our snooty friend the mako shark, or one of his relatives. He was after Tony's sailfish. A mako is fairly fast for a shark, and the tired sailfish was handicapped by the couple of hundred yards of line it was still dragging. Watching with my binoculars, I saw the mako make three passes, each closer than the one before. The sailfish was staying on the surface. I suppose he thought he was going to have to do some more jumping or start losing chunks of his anatomy, and was keeping in position for it.

We had a .30-30 Winchester in the cabin. I went forward and got it. By the time I had stuffed shells into the magazine, the sailfish was 100 feet astern and the mako was coming in for another pass.

I tried a snap shot and the slug ricocheted. I tried again and missed. The sailfish had now gotten himself rolled up in the cable leader and was virtually helpless, with a third of his dorsal torn off. The mako, kill-crazy, paid no attention to the .30-30 bullets. As he finished his run he lunged half out of the water, and this gave me my chance. I never made a better shot. The slug plowed into the shark where head and body joined. You could hear the whoomp it made, and see the sudden spurt of blood. Veering off, out of control, the mako skidded over the water in a crazy spiral, and I got two more into him. He was sinking slowly into the glimmering amethyst depths when Tony brought the sailfish alongside. We had no idea whether or not the crippled fish would survive, but we cut him free anyway and pumped him up and down a few times to work some water through his gills. He skulled off presently, an honest-to-gosh beat-out sailfish. I hope he made it.

Tony wiped sweat off his forehead. "Few more shows like that," he declared, "and I'll forget I ever left home."

The sun slid down the Aztec-blue sky, a breeze came up cool and sweet out of the west, and the eye-piercing glitter of the water softened to radiances of copper and turquoise. We stood into Wild Dogs Bay, looking for an anchorage. In a cove ahead were four sailing canoes, the canoes of turtle fishermen. I put my glasses on the occupants. They were dark, broad-faced men, naked to the waist, with long hair tied in ponytails: Seris. North America's most primitive people, the Stone Age savages who had little use for fire, whose religious rites had required the use of genitals slashed from boys, whose marriage ceremony consisted of a footrace between a nubile girl and the bachelor men of the tribe.

At the bow of one of the canoes stood a harpooner who apparently had sighted a turtle. His two paddlemen eased the canoe forward in response to hand signals he was giving them. Suddenly he raised his harpoon. It was about twelve feet long, with a thick octagonal wooden shaft and a single, barbed, metal point. The paddlemen backed water as the harpooner thrust powerfully, straight down. He scored. The turtle, as big around as a washtub, allowed itself to be hoisted aboard without protest. Then the three Seris did something that I had heard about but had hardly believed. Wrenching the harpoon head out of the turtle's barnacled carapace, they took turns sucking blood from the wound. When they'd had their drink, they drove a wooden plug into the hole as one would hammer a bung into a beer keg.

We were alongside the canoe now, and Gabriel asked the Seris if they would sell the turtle, offering the current price in Miramar, forty pesos. The Seris stared up at us, their obsidian eyes hostile, but after a moment the harpooner nodded. So Gabriel told them to butcher the turtle and deliver the meat to us when we had anchored. We moved deeper into the cove and dropped the hook off a white sand beach curved like a Moslem moon, and were sitting at the stern watching the sun wallow down through whorls of pure color, when the canoe came with the meat. There was a heap of it, and you could see why the Mexicans claim there are four kinds of meat in a turtle—beef, pork, veal and chicken. Not until the meat had been paid for and we were stowing it in the icebox did Gabriel discover that we had been cheated.

"They kept the liver," he gritted. "The thieving *cabrones*."

I asked Tony why the liver was so important, considering that we had more turtle meat than we could possibly eat. Medics are welcome to the information this got me. All Mexican fishermen, Tony said, believe that sea-turtle liver, eaten any way you like it, is the best of eye medicines. And since eyestrain is an occupational malady out here, due to the quicksilver glitter of the water, I guess Gabriel had a right to be sore.

We ate turtle steaks for dinner. Then, as the yellow Seri moon floated into a clear pearl sky, we had guitar music and singing. The two mates, Raoul Ramos and Panchito Morales, could do pretty things with a guitar and had voices to match, and in this wild place on such a beautiful night the music was straight enchantment. But it didn't last. Competition arose. From the beach came a swelling high-pitched chorus, the wild Seri dogs howling their wrongs to the moon and the stars. How the dogs got here, only the Seris know. There are scores of the animals, all sizes and colors, and since the bay is uninhabited they must have a rough time finding food. I suspect that they could be dangerous. At any rate, they were miserable, off-key singers. So we put aside the guitars, and Gabriel told us a story.

It was a true story, the story of something Gabriel had seen a splendid striped marlin do not far from here. All of us except Tony had heard of the episode, but none of us had heard the whole tale from Gabriel himself.

Two years ago, Gabriel related, a chap named Ed Davis had arrived at Miramar from Indianapolis with a party of five, and had chartered the *Nautilus* for a week's fishing trip. They cruised up toward Tiburon. On the way, Davis heard one of the mates and the cook talking about broncho billfish. Never having heard the term before, he asked Gabriel to explain it. The request was tough, but Gabriel did his best. A broncho billfish, he told Davis, is a marlin or sailfish with a kink in his brain that makes him different from normal billfish. He is a berserker. He does wild, unorthodox things. He may, when hooked, jump toward the horizon in a sustained all-out blast of energy, keeping it up until his heart quits and he falls dead on a wave. Or he may dive to the bottom and fight there, and sensing defeat, wedge his spear under a ledge or in a crevice, or even drive it into mud, to prevent you from bringing him to the surface. Or, recognizing you as his enemy, he may try to sink your boat and kill you.

Davis, impressed, said he wished earnestly to encounter a broncho billfish. He was a mild, Mr. Peepers sort of guy, but apparently he craved action. He got it.

They were trolling through a tidal drift of tiny red crabs. Birds and small fish were gorging themselves on the crabs, and Gabriel figured there ought to be some nice billfish around, too. At the north edge of the drift, his hunch panned out. The low, sloping dorsal of a striped marlin showed astern, closing in fast on Davis' mackerel bait. The fish was "glowing," the word used by sports-boat crews to describe the change of color that takes place in marlin when they are ready to strike. Probably the change is caused by the fish's frenzy to kill. In any case, this marlin as it came in was an unearthly luminous dark blue, with his thirteen vertical stripes shining like bands of burnished silver. He grabbed the bait, savaging it, and Davis socked the 10/0 hook into his jaw.

After jumping twice, the marlin slammed out northwestward. He was a good fish and made a pretty run, taking out nearly 300 yards of line before he turned. There had been nothing to indicate that he was a broncho. But when he burst out of a wave crest 400 feet distant and came greyhounding straight at the *Nautilus*, Gabriel knew what they had tangled with. Gabriel spun the wheel, trying to bring the boat's bow around to face the oncoming fish, but there wasn't time for the maneuver. The marlin was really pouring on the coal.

With beautiful timing, the fish planed beneath the surface at the last instant, and came out again in a long, flat jump that covered at least forty feet. He crashed into the rail just behind Davis' fighting chair. The *Nautilus'* rail is two inches thick, made of jungle maple, which is a very hard wood. Yet the marlin's spear went through the rail, with five inches of it sticking out on the inboard side, and broke off as the stunned and dying fish fell to the water. There was no question in anybody's mind that the attack had been deliberate. When they reached port, Davis asked Tommy if he could buy the section of rail in which the spear was embedded. Tommy had it sawed out and gave it to him, commenting that he was delighted the spear was in the rail and not in Davis.

"Maybe that's the best way to find a broncho marlin," Gabriel said, winding up his story. "Just wish for one, like Davis did."

"I'm wishing for one right now," Tony said. "A broncho broncho marlin. Find me one, *please*."

We set night watches and turned in. At daybreak one of the mates awakened us with the information that we were getting under way, and that within four hours we would arrive at the Fiesta of Fins. This prospect, together with the growing dawn, would have made any fisherman run a temperature. At first the morning was all blue air and sea wind. Then color exploded like the Apocalyptic Vision over the Tiburon peaks as the sun boomed up behind them. During the run north, Tony and I put out feather jigs, figuring we were going to need a large supply of fresh bait. We caught sierra mackerel, skipjacks and another dolphin. Tony snagged a turtle and lost his jig and some line. We saw several billfish but didn't try for them. We were in a hurry. Sportfishing history beckoned.

Tiburon was a mirage-warped pastel silhouette behind us, and we had sighted eight striped marlin and seven sailfish, when Gabriel, chart in hand, called down to us, "We're heading in, and we're going to have company."We went topside, and had our first look at Vaquero's flotilla of sailing canoes.

The canoes were anchored in the middle distance, a cluster of slender dark shapes dancing on the knife-bright swells. Judging from the storm of seabirds over them, the Seris had dropped their carved stone anchors at the hottest spot the Fiesta of Fins offered today. Gabriel told us that the twenty-mile cruise out from the island was nothing for the Seris. These people ranged the whole of the Sea of Cortes, he said, fishing, trading, hunting and pearling. We ran toward them across the blue, blue water. We sighted another striped marlin. Then we saw twelve sailfish strutting in a circle, in what looked like a mating ritual. That is, if it wasn't a mating ritual, I have no idea what it could have been, unless they really were having a fiesta.

Tony was all set, an eager beaver in plaid shorts and rope-soled sandals. We had rigged what is known on this coast as medium-heavy tackle—twelve-ounce rod tip, sixty-pound-test Dacron line, 9/0 reel and 9/0 hook, with twenty feet of plastic leader. For bait we used the dolphin we had caught on the way in, put on New Zealand style. It was a twelve-pound fish, just about the right size for a good black marlin—if there were any black marlin hereabouts. Tony got into the fighting chair and buckled on the harness. I slid the dolphin over the stern and the mates put out two hookless teaser plugs. Gabriel let go with a couple of blasts on the airhorn. The Fiesta of Fins was no longer virgin of sport fishermen.

Our first customer was a sailfish.

We were working through a mess of floating weed when the fish surfaced in the wake and came in slowly for a look at the skipping dolphin. We didn't want him. We had passed up a squadron of better sailfish. So nobody was disappointed when we snagged a sizable chunk of weed which all but enveloped the bait. We figured the sailfish would now go away. But instead, while Gabriel was reversing the boat, the fish struck the weed several times with his spear, knocking it off the bait. He then gazed at the exposed dolphin a moment, turned and disappeared.

"Decided he wasn't hungry, after all," Raoul said.

"Or he was just trying to be helpful," Tony said.

Twenty minutes later we sighted a fair-sized striped marlin, but he was boat-shy. The moment we turned toward him to present the bait, he took off. Gabriel shrugged, and headed back toward the Seri canoes, where the congregation of birds was still working over a school of either sardines or anchovies. I was watching the pelicans dive, marveling as always at the clever way the grotesque cusses half-rolled, braking their forward speed, a millisecond before they hit the water, and wondering how they managed to keep their eyes on the target. Suddenly Panchito let out an ecstatic yell. "*Pez espada Negro*—black marlin!"

There he was, fifty yards off the starboard bow. You couldn't mistake the peaked dorsal with its serrated trailing edge. Beneath the sun-shot waves you could see the mass of his body, blue-black in the blue water. I felt that old pounding in my chest. He was a good one. Sighting one of these huge brutes always does things to you, no matter if you've stalked scores of them. Gabriel hit the throttles to pass the fish and offer him the bait. Panchito held up both hands to show that his fingers were crossed. Raoul rolled his eyes heavenward. Tony braced himself like a fighter waiting for the bell.

Then the worst happened. The marlin quit us. He sank beneath the waves and was gone. For a moment or two I thought he might reappear in the wake. When it was obvious that he wasn't going to, we looked at one another with the special brand of resignation common to disappointed fishermen everywhere.

Tony broke the silence: "Like the Mig pilot said to the Saber jet pilot," he said, "a guy can't win all the time."

We trolled on toward the Seri canoes, with the birds swirling about us like brown and white confetti, and our propellers making hash out of thousands of the small fish on which the birds were feeding. We were opposite Vaquero's canoe when we got the blind strike I told you about at the beginning. Maybe it was the same black marlin who had so thoroughly ignored us a few minutes ago. I wouldn't know. But he was a sure-enough, grade A broncho, as Vaquero and his tribesmen would testify. It took Tony two hours to fight him down. As the marlin lay gasping alongside, I decided again that he would go 400 pounds. We could have killed the handsome monster and taken the carcass back to Guaymas, where smoked black marlin and fresh marlin steaks are highly thought of; or we could have given him to the Seris.

We did neither. If you are a grand kid like Tony, you don't kill the fish you have dreamt about the past couple of years. So we cut the leader and watched the big marlin right himself and swim wearily down into the non-sensically blue depths. Then we baited up and went searching for another one.

Right here is as good a place as any to give you some information about the Sea of Cortes and how to reach the Fiesta of Fins. The sea, known also as the Gulf of California, is rated by ichthyologists as one of the world's greatest natural aquariums. Fish of many species migrate up the coast of Mexico from perhaps as far south as Panama, find themselves hemmed in here with no exit to the north, and either return south or remain to do what comes naturally. Like all wild creatures, they seem to have favorite gathering spots. For the billfish, this apparently is the Fiesta of Fins. Probably a combination of tidal currents, depth and available food attracts them. Or it may be that the place is a spawning ground. Marlin containing eggs have been taken near Tiburon.

At any rate, there is no question that the Fiesta of Fins offers some of the finest billfishing to be found on the planet. To date, nobody knows the extent of the area or how much time the fish spend here. I envy the anglers who will complete the exploration of the place.

Well, the beautiful day wore on. We hung a striped marlin and released him. We hung a mako shark and killed him. Toward sundown we hung another black marlin—no broncho—and lost him when the hook cut out. Then the radio began squawking, and it was Tommy at the hotel calling Tony.

In the course of the conversation that followed, I heard Tommy ask, "You got that Korean frost thawed out of your bones yet?"

And heard Tony reply happily, "Where's Korea?"

I guess that ties it up. See you next year at the Fiesta of Fins.

Life in the Big Frost

There are so many strange, humorous and terrible stories to be told about cold— real cold that can turn a man to ice.

Once upon a winter night I was a guest at the cabin of a gray-thatched little Yukon trapper whom the sourdoughs called the Professor. While we sat drinking tea and smoking at the plank table, my host came up with a highly original theory about the cold. It was a bitter night in February, around fifty below. The frozen dooryard birches were popping like pistol shots, the Yukon ice hooted and growled and through the frost-flowered windowpane you could see great multicolored aurora curtains flapping among the brilliant stars.

"A thought occurs to me," the Professor said solemnly. "I believe that I understand at last why the white northern tribes were so fierce, and why they were able to dominate the earth."

He wanted me to ask him, so I did. "Why?" I asked. "Because," the Professor grinned, "when a man has lived through a succession of these godawful icebound winters, he no longer fears anything. He knows that he has already experienced the worst. So the sword-swinging northmen with frost in their beards had a cinch. They couldn't miss."

Buy it or not, the little guy had an idea. Up here in the boondocks, near the top of the ladder of the latitudes, the summers are warm and wonderful, but the winters are plenty cold, and cold is a human-conditioner with a wicked wallop. Abetted by snow, ice and polar winds, it becomes a hostile force that you have got to battle, or at least plan against, seven days a week, from freeze-up until break-up. Of course I am not, I hasten to add, referring to the cold encountered in our northern cities, where a man can always duck into a tropically warm saloon if he feels frostbite coming on. City cold was long ago rendered practically harmless by militant chambers of commerce, thermostat-controlled radiators, electric blankets and such. The cold we will deal with here is the old primeval cold that waits back among the giant silver peaks and along the forlorn spruce-fringed wilderness rivers—the cold that lays grim, and often bizarre pitfalls for the careless, the unwary and the inexperienced.

Consider what happened to the Kerosene Kid, who was no amateur. The mistakes he made one morning could have cost him his feet and legs. That they didn't was straight smokehouse luck.

The Kerosene Kid once had a proper name, I am told, but probably nobody in Alaska remembers it today. The nickname the boys gave him was too apt, sticking with him like a burr on a siwash blanket, from Ketchikan to Barrow and back. So I will use his nickname while I explain how he earned it. A bull-shouldered 220-pound veteran musher, he operated for more than a decade as a dog-team freighter in the Susitna-Matanuska country, and we liked him because he was hustling and dependable, but I never heard that he had any bosom pals. One reason, I suppose, was that he possessed a crazy temper that exploded in all directions when things didn't go to suit him, which quite often they did not. Knowing him, you could imagine how he must have cussed and bellowed on this particular occasion when he broke through the ice of the lower Matanuska into overflow water.

As we got it later, he had freighted in a load of grub and tools for some stampeders who planned to make their fortunes mining placer gold up Metal Creek Canyon. He was returning with an empty sled when the mishap befell him. His Malamute leader didn't detect the masked overflow, nor did the Kerosene Kid himself. The only warning he had was a sullen crash, and then he was standing there knee-deep in the black, rushing water. This was in January, a pretty azure-and-silver morning, with a handful of sundogs flanking the sun, and the bright circle of Chugach peaks sheering up bold and sharp-cut in the luminous air. The thermometer on the porch of Phil Allen's roadhouse, over at the railroad junction, registered eighteen below, which wasn't especially cold for these parts in January, but cold enough when a man had wet feet.

Actually the Kerosene Kid wasn't in serious trouble, not at first. He had no difficulty getting ashore, and there were windrows of flood-deposited driftwood along the bars. In a matter of minutes he could have built a fire and changed into dry socks and moccasins. But he took a chance. A mile across the valley he could see smoke rising from a homesteader's cabin, and, sore at himself, the dogs and everything connected with freighting, he headed for it. To give him his due as a woodsman, it would ordinarily have been a quick, easy run to the cabin with the light sled. But things went wrong. Fate pulled the plug out of the situation. Partway to the cabin he got into a mess of spruce blowdown, and lost five minutes finding a route around the stuff. Then the Malamute leader, rattled by the bawling out he was getting, misjudged the steepness of a slough bank and fell back with the other dogs in a wild, uproarious tangle. More minutes lost.

What with these unwanted delays, the Kerosene Kid's feet were frozen when he reached the cabin, and he was fit to be tied. The homesteader, a gallused Scandinavian sodbuster from Minnesota, known hereabouts as Stuttering John because that was what he did when he talked, heard the dog team highball into the clearing and came to the front door. After taking one look at the grim-faced Kerosene Kid stumbling up the snowdrifted path, he stood hastily aside to let him enter.

"Ya got any kerosene?" the Kerosene Kid demanded. "If ya have, I need it right now, in a hurry."

"Yah. I g-got f-five g-gallons," Stuttering John said, eying the musher's ice-sheathed moccasins and pants legs. "B-but m-maybe s-snow and w-water—"

"Get the damn kerosene," hollered the Kerosene Kid, "and keep the advice." He knew from experience that while water chilled with snow made an excellent thawing bath for frozen parts, kerosene was better because it also acted as a balm. Limping to a bench as far as possible from the glowing cabin stove, where his feet wouldn't be exposed to direct heat, he drew his belt knife and slashed the strings of his moccasins. "And if ya can spare the time, cut the top outa the can, please. I wanta put m' feet in it. They're froze. Savvy?"

Still sputtering about snow and water, Stuttering John disappeared into a back room. When he returned he had a five-gallon can of kerosene with the top cut out, into which the Kerosene Kid at once plunged his bare feet. For some time the big musher sat there, resentful as a slug-singed grizzly, awaiting the agony that would come when circulation started again in his feet. But instead of his feet, it was his knee joints that began to ache, and he could have sworn that they were stiffening. Then, to his horror, he saw a telltale whiteness creeping up his legs. In a flash of comprehension, he understood the cause of the phenomenon. Stuttering John had gone out the backdoor and brought the kerosene from his cache. As kerosene freezes only in extreme cold, this had remained liquid although its temperature was that of the atmosphere, eighteen below. Jerking his feet out of the can, he swiveled to face Stuttering John.

"Ya crazy squarehead," he sailed, "ya've rooined me. This kerosene is colder'n God's death. I think it's froze m' legs plumb to the knees."

"W-well," Stuttering John said contritely, "I t-tried to t-tell you that w-water and s-snow—"

Which is how the Kerosene Kid got his nickname, and if the tale has a moral I guess it is that a man should be very careful what he puts his feet into when the mercury is below the zero mark. Or maybe that one should make a practice of giving a stutterer time to speak his piece. The chap might have something important to say.

In the specialized business of keeping alive and reasonably efficient in brutally low temperatures, even the Eskimos and sourdoughs give the Armed Forces credit for being expert. The Army and the Air Force conduct winter survival schools on the polar rim, hold snow maneuvers under the most rigorous conditions and maintain laboratories for the study of cold and its effect on men and materials. Together they have developed what is probably the finest cold-weather gear in existence. If war comes to the high North, they are prepared for it. But there was a time when they weren't. Back in the anxious days following Pearl Harbor, Major General Simon Bolivar Buckner, commanding the Alaska Defense Command, believed it was an even bet that he would have to fight the Japanese on the Alaska mainland, possibly in winter. This was not a happy prospect, for the Army then had virtually no equipment suitable for a winter campaign in the kind of weather and temperatures it could expect. Nor had it decided yet what types of gear it wanted.

As could have been expected, Buckner was getting advice from a wide assortment of pioneer wonders whose firsthand knowledge of cold had been gained chiefly within city limits. Not much more helpful was a cold-weather experiment board he had set up, which was tinkering with some of the weirdest gadgets and garments ever designed for use by man in a northern winter. One handy-dandy brainchild was a sleeping bag with sleeves and legs, in which, presumably, a soldier would be expected to fight as well as sleep. Another, for the Air Corps, was a handsome sheepskin flight boot, warm and easily pulled on and off. So readily did these boots come off, in fact, that the first time a pilot bailed out wearing a pair of them, they parted company with him when the parachute snapped open, and the hapless throttle-jockey landed in deep snow, miles from anywhere, in his stocking feet.

One winter evening at Anchorage I was having a bourbon-and-water with Buckner and several members of his staff, and he was recounting his winter-equipment troubles, hitting all the blue notes. As the payoff, he said, "I would be delighted to know what the authentic sourdough—if such exists—wears on the trail. I mean to say, I wonder if it would be possible to capture one of the gentlemen in his native haunts and bring him in for study by my hardworking experiment board."

Maybe it was the bourbon, but at this point I had a scintillating idea. "You could send up to my place at Goose Creek," I said, "and have Starvation Smith waylaid." Starvation was then trapping wolves on the creek, making his headquarters at my cabin. I really believed that he might be of assistance. Probably he couldn't have told you the difference between Fahrenheit and Centigrade, but he had been successfully combating cold in the North for nearly half a century.

Buckner had heard about Starvation, and apparently the suggested project intrigued him. In any case, a day or two later Lieutenant Ed Johnson was dispatched by plane to Goose Creek to bring Starvation in, by special invitation from the general. Johnson's orders were to deliver Starvation at headquarters dressed exactly as he found him on the trail, which he did, but in a way this was a mistake. Because when he caught up with him, the old-timer was not running his trapline. He was snowshoeing to the railroad flagstop at Montana Station, bound for town to sell some pelts and buy a stock of grub. Surrounded by an aura of bay rum shaving lotion, he was resplendent in a blue serge suit, a topcoat with racetrack checks and a Kelly-green cloth cap complete with ear flaps. Inside a pair of beat-up felt overshoes that somebody had given him, he wore yellow dress shoes with natty bulldog toes, circa 1920. Since he was heading for Anchorage anyway, he willingly accepted the general's invitation and made the trip by air instead of by rail.

He must have been a four-bell sensation at OST headquarters. Anyway, Buckner was still laughing about the episode many months later when we crossed trails for the last time, on Okinawa. One of his treasured memories, he declared, was the bulge-eyed astonishment of the experiment board when the elegant and sweet-smelling Starvation was dropped into its lap. But, he said seriously, ideas and sketches that Starvation gave them would result in new and vastly improved snowshoes and sleeping bags for the Army. So it had turned out all right. The venerable wolf-peeler had done some good for the country.

"If he had been twenty years younger," Buckner said, "I might have made him head of the experiment board."

Sourdoughs have a joke about gauging cold in camp on the winter trail, and one September evening old Tex Cobb sprung it on a new schoolmarm at Matanuska. The town was giving a get-acquainted dance in the schoolhouse, with a box supper to follow. The teacher was making the rounds, introducing herself. She was a well-assembled green-eyed redhead, a production, a real pleasure to look at. The way I heard it, the men on the school board had voted unanimously for her on the basis of a photograph she had submitted with her application for the job, and obviously they had made no mistake. As the saying goes, the gal couldn't have fallen on her face if she'd tried.

Getting around to Tex, she took his hard-knuckled paw, welcomed him to the dance and remarked that she had heard that he had just come down out of the mountains. "Wasn't it terribly cold up there?" she asked.

That was opening enough for Tex. Holding onto her hand, he began filling her in on the cold, both domestic and foreign. Around here, he told her, even in the coldest months—January and February—the temperature usually stayed above zero, except for spells when it would drop down to maybe forty below for a week or so. "But shucks," he said, poker-faced, "I bet'cha we don't even have a two-dog night until after Christmas."

"Two-dog night?" she said, puzzled. "What is a two-dog night?"

Tex explained, gazing admiringly at her red hair and still keeping possession of her hand, that because mushers seldom bothered to carry thermometers, they judged cold by the number of sled dogs they had to drag onto, or into, their sleeping bags at night to keep warm. A two-dog night was only moderately chilly. But when a man had to use four or five dogs, why it was getting good and cold, no fooling. One night on the upper Tanana, he said, he'd had to sleep with eight long-haired huskies, and even then had dang near froze to death. It must have been colder that night, he said, than anything the Roosians ever shivered through at the Pole of Cold over on the Verhoyanski River in Siberia, where they claimed it had once been ninety below. But then of course the upper Tanana was a notoriously cold region, not like here on the Matanuska, the banana belt of the territory.

"I believe I would almost rather freeze," the schoolmarm said, retrieving her hand by an effort, "than sleep with a pack of savage wolf dogs."

"Don't worry, ma'am," Tex chuckled, manifestly thinking that the chances were remote indeed that such a beautiful creature would ever have to bed down in a snowbank on the trail. "You won't never have to sleep with dogs to keep warm. You jest ain't the type, believe me."

Tex wondered for days why the teacher abandoned him so abruptly. The only theory he had, he said, was that she plain wasn't in the mood for compliments.

Back in my flowering youth I once made a fur-buying trip by dog team along the Arctic Coast, in the course of which I learned a prime lesson about cold and cold-weather pants. With me was a lad named Clarence, who had been a swimming instructor at a Seattle pool. He was personable and willing, but one of those kids that things happen to. The day before Christmas we were camped with a band of Eskimos on a coastal lagoon, east of the Halahula River, buying white fox pelts. It was the usual Eskimo temporary fish camp, tents walled around the blocks of snow and heated by primus stoves and seal-oil lamps, if you could call that heating. Over everything hung the odor of human urine, which these Eskimos still used as soap and to make their hair shine. It was cold. The wind whining across the ice pack gave you the feeling that warmth was a myth, that it had been lost forever from the world.

Clarence came down with a dire case of Yuletide fever. There was a whaling ship in the ice some ten miles distant, and all of a sudden he was smitten by an overwhelming desire to spend Christmas Eve aboard her. "The crew will have a big party," he said. "There'll be Christmas music and songs, and we'll get something to eat besides whitefish and skinny boiled caribou. Maybe even pudding with brandy sauce. Come on, let's go."

So we went, all duded up in fancy clothes we'd had made by Eskimo seamstresses at Dease Inlet and were wearing for the first time. They were something. Stylish short caribou-fawn parka jackets with white-wolf ruffs and five kinds of fur in the trimming. Squaw-catcher mukluks and beaded gauntlet mittens. And the purtiest pale-gold, baby-seal pants a man ever laid eyes on. The Eskimos wore their skin clothes fur side in, and the seamstresses wanted to make ours so we could do likewise, but we had vetoed the suggestion. We aimed to look sharp, and boy, we did. When we set out afoot for the whaling ship, we were the best-dressed travelers on this hyperborean coast, and knew it.

Jog-trotting through a wilderness of shattered pressure ridges, we had covered perhaps half the distance to the ship, when Clarence asked me to wait a moment. He stepped behind an uptilted slab of ice, and I lit my pipe and waited. Time passed. Then I heard him cussing. Laughing and cussing at the same time. I asked him what the joke was, and he replied that he was in a heck of a fix, his doggone pants had frosted on the inside and, worse, he couldn't get them buttoned. If I didn't mind, he said, he needed some help. He sure did need help. Although neither of us realized it at first, he was in bad trouble. He had worked up a sweat—a mistake of which we were both guilty—and the handsome baby-seal pants, hair side out and no underwear beneath them, had absorbed the moisture and become coated with frost on exposure to the air. The frost must have been mighty uncomfortable until it melted, but the main difficulty was with the buttons of the fly. They baffled us. We struggled with them for fifteen minutes and got nowhere. Our hands were too cold, or the buttonholes were frozen or too small, or all three.

When he had to give up, Clarence said there was no feeling left in his fingers. I looked at them, and they were frozen, all right, stiff as sticks and dead-white to the knuckles. Hoping to prevent Clarence's groin from freezing, too, I took off the light shirt I wore under my parka and rigged it around his waist like an apron. Then we headed for the ship, bucking the razor-edged wind. An hour later we were aboard, and the captain, a bearded Scot from San Francisco, named Wallace, was working over Clarence in his cabin. While he was no medic, the captain said, he thought it was likely that Clarence would lose two fingers of his right hand, as they were frozen to the bone. This should have been devastating news to a swimming instructor, but Clarence barely listened to it. He was worried about something else.

"How about—uh—the rest of me?" he asked, gulping.

"Well, if you mean what I suppose you mean," the captain said, his eyes twinkling, "there is some frostbite, and I imagine it'll be painful, but I doubt that any amputation will be necessary."

"Thanks, Santa Claus," Clarence sighed with the relieved look of one who has weathered a major emotional experience. "And a merry, merry Christmas to you, too."

Without intending to, I played a dirty trick on my trapping partner, Baldy Harris, one subzero night. Because of me he got messed up in the snow on a spruce-bough bed that—I'm not kidding—could have made him an invalid for the rest of the winter. We were in the Yellowjacket country, south of the plateau, trapping foxes, and had run out of fresh meat. So Baldy, getting fed up with sow-bosom, said he guessed it was time for him to fare south and kill a couple of sheep. There was a band of twenty-odd sheep across the valley—rams, ewes and young stuff—stooging around on a whale-backed summit that the winds had blown clean of snow. But they were high, and Baldy wasn't sure he could reach them and return to camp in one day. He had a logistics problem.

"I hate to carry a sleeping bag," he said. "But on the other hand, I'd hate worse to make a siwash camp, with no bedding."

This was where I should have kept my mouth shut, but didn't. I asked Baldy if he had ever heard of the Injun method of sleeping warm with only a thin tarp for covering. He said no, he had not, and that it sounded impossible but also interesting, so tell him about it. The trick was simple, I said. Nothing to it. First you scooped the snow off a spot seven or eight feet long by around five feet wide. Next you built a fire on the exposed ground. After letting the fire burn a while, you removed the coals and covered the heated ground with a thick mattress of branch tips. All that remained was to lie down, cover yourself with the tarp, which would hold in the rising warmth, and enjoy a comfortable night's sleep.

"Now that's a smart stunt," Baldy asserted enthusiastically. "If I get caught out tonight I'll use it, by gosh."

Only after he had departed did I realize that I had neglected to impress upon him that it was important, when making the kind of bed I had described, to use deciduous branches for the mattress. I don't know how cold the day was in degrees, but nailheads inside the cabin were frosted white, and when I threw out the dishwater it hissed in the air as if it had hit a hot stove. The whisky-jacks were sitting around in the trees with their feathers fluffed out, looking sorry for themselves and refusing even to come down and forage. The air was so full of ice dust that the diamond glitter hurt your eyes. Thirty below anyway. Maybe colder.

Baldy had to make a long, hard climb for the sheep, he subsequently told me. He toiled up the bed of a boulder-choked ravine that brought him out on the high point of the sumit, above the band, in position for what should have been a certain kill. But at the last critical moment, as he was inching across a wind-stiffend drift, sliing his rifle and a snowshoe ahead of him and trying to spot the two likeliest meat critters, something went wrong. A wind shift probably. At any rate, the sheep spooked, and fled out of sight around an outjut of rock before he could get in a shot. It was growing dark before he again caught up with the band and succeeded in killing two young rams. By the time he got the carcasses down to timber and had gutted them, he was tired out and half frozen, too weary to come on to the cabin. So he roasted some liver and ate it, then made a spruce-bough bed on fire-heated ground, covered himself with a balloon-silk tarp he had brought along and went to sleep smiling over how easy it was to outsmart cold if you knew how.

But early next morning when he came hobbling into the cabin he was one of the angriest men I ever faced. Dropping his pack, he pointed a shaking finger at me and burbled incoherently for a quarter of a minute before he got a word out.

"I made one of your blasted Injun-method beds," he managed to say at last, "and I know now that you never slept in one, and neither has anybody else. Listen. There's pitch in spruce boughs, ain't there?"

I said there was.

"And there's turpentine in spruce pitch, ain't there?"

I said maybe there was, or something like turpentine, I was no expert. And as I said it I was wishing that I was somewhere else. Anywhere else.

"It's turpentine," Baldy shouted, "and last night I had one helluva turpentine steam bath. I'm scalded all over like a packinghouse hog, and I think I'm gonna die. So don't just stand there gawking. Get all the salve we got, and help me rub it on."

There are so many strange, humorous and terrible stories to be told about cold. One winter I went to Barrow to do part of a story for Kate Smith. A Navy oil-drilling outfit was stationed there, the officers of which decided on a Saturday night to have a party for me at their club. They sent an enlisted man to the stores department with a sled to bring back materials for the party, and on the way back the guy just happened to lose a bottle of booze off the load. Finding the bottle later with remarkable ease, he upcapped it there in the snow and gulped down a good three fingers before pausing for breath. It was his last drink in this life. The temperature of the whisky was minus fifty degrees, and its effect on his throat and stomach was approximately that of boiling water. I have no idea what was given as the official cause of death, but the episode was one that I did not radio to the States for use by Kate Smith.

Then there was the time a pair of new residents came up to Goose Creek for their first Alaska moose hunt. They killed a bull on the opening date of the winter season, and did a meticulously workmanlike job of skinning and quartering the carcass, after which they stacked the chunks of meat in a neat pile and covered it with the green hide. Several days later, ready to return to town, they discovered to their dismay that the meat and hide had frozen into a rocklike unit. Unable to break it apart even with pry-poles and the camp ax, they resorted to fire. Starvation Smith dropped in on them during the operation, and told me afterward that it looked and smelled like the biggest barbecue ever held north of Texas. I have often wondered how the pair explained the charred meat to their families and friends, and what they would have done if they had made their kill out on the tundra, with no fuel available.

And there was the time Kobuk Watson, a trapper, doped out a marvelous scheme to prevent potatoes from freezing. Kobuk was going to fly to Sky Lake for marten, and as that is high, treeless country, he would have to pitch his tent on at least ten feet of snow and dig green alders for fuel, if he could find any. Yet he was taking with him a full sack of potatoes. When I asked him on the airstrip at Talkeetna how he expected to keep the potatoes from freezing, he replied that he was going to cut a hole in the ice of Sky Lake and sink them at the end of a rope. They couldn't freeze in the water, he said, and any time he wanted them all he'd have to do would be to haul up the sack. It sounded reasonable, but it turned out there was a hitch, an unexpected one. I met Kobuk in town the following spring, and remarked that he must have enjoyed the luxury of potatoes away up there.

"Didn't get to eat a damned spud," he growled. "There were beavers in the lake. Seems as if beavers like spuds, too."

I guess that about winds up this piece about the cold, and I hope I haven't disturbed the northern chambers of commerce or worried any prospective settlers. Alaska really is a wonderful land and I know people who have lived there for years and years without suffering too much from cold, and who have no intention of ever living anywhere else.

It's swell in the summer.

Horse Hunt in Caribou Land

Pitchfork was the travelin'est horse I ever did see. When he led my packstring into the migrating caribou herd I was in for a horse hunt in Caribou Land.

"I hate every horse in the world," I said. "Also I hate bears. And if I ever catch up with Solo Swanson, I'm going to take him apart cell by cell and scatter the pieces."

"Keep yer shirt on," Tex said.

Shaggy, iron-maned, old Tex Cobb and I had greeted Alaska dawns under a variety of circumstances, but this particular September morning near the headwaters of Yanert River took the cake. Fifteen miles from camp, unarmed, we were roosting in the windy top of a timberline spruce. We had been here an hour. We were cold, tired, wet and hungry. Moreover, I was so sleepy I was half afraid I would doze off and fall out of the tree, which would have been an unfortunate thing to do, because the mountain grizzly who had chased us up here was still waiting for us to come down. It began to look as if he intended to make a permanent project of us.

At the moment he was a biscuit-toss distance in a scrap of redtop meadow, crouched over the carcass of a barren-ground caribou, feeding. I don't believe I ever saw an uglier grizzly. His pelt was the color of a dirty burlap sack. He had a grotesquely high hump, a lean alder-splitter snout and legs that looked too long for the rest of him. As he crunched bones and ripped off mouthfuls of flesh, his flat wicked eyes were alert to every move we made. True, it seems to be against the modern grizzly code, so to speak, to get all-out tough with humans, except in cases of direst provocation, but apparently this bear hadn't received the word. Or else he was simply a hard case who didn't give a damn. He really didn't have so much to be sore about. All we had done was try to share his breakfast, which in the circumstances wasn't as crazy as it may sound, as I will explain later.

"If we perch here much longer," I said, "we won't have to worry about our AWOL horses. They'll be so far away nobody could find them. Over in Canada maybe."

"Take hit easy," Tex said. "I got a scheme to fix the dang bear's wagon fer him. Be ready to light outa here."

Here I'll have to cut in to give you the background of this treetop drama. It began with one Solo Swanson and a horse named Pitchfork. In June, when the passes opened, we had set out with our long-time client Gunn Buckingham of Memphis, Tennessee, to make a packhorse jaunt along the north slope of the Alaska range, the trip to end with a caribou hunt. As planned, it was to be a pleasant gypsy summer and autumn. But at Healy station, the jumping-off place, while Tex and I were absent from camp, Buck bought this Pitchfork horse from Solo for $300, having heard us say that we needed another pack animal. Solo guaranteed the horse to be sound, gentle and willing, and stated that the only reason he was selling him was that his brother in the States desperately needed money for an operation. Whereupon he disappeared with the cash, and our troubles began.

Tex and I had never met Solo, but were looking forward to the pleasure. It was said that he made his headquarters somewhere in the Yanert country.

As for Pitchfork, I will give him credit for being the best-looking horse in our string of ten. He was a proud-cut, coyote-dun gelding, six years old, 1,250 pounds, intelligent dark eyes and clever as a mountain goat with his feet. But if he had any other good points, we missed them. Being proud-cut, he at once established himself as boss of the other horses, to whom he was a horrible example. He threw his packs. He would work only in the lead, and when he got there he refused to hold the trail. His worst habit, however, was straying at night, and when he left he took the rest of the string with him. He didn't hit the back trail, which would have been understandable as most horses occasionally commit this sin. Instead, he invariably took off deeper into the peaks, heading for heaven knew where. As a result, Tex and I did a lot of horse hunting. We did a lot of walking before breakfast.

What with one thing and another, we had stored up some passionate grievances by the time the cottonwoods flamed yellow and the hunting season was upon us. So it wasn't unexpected, one golden morning, when Tex abruptly swung our course toward the passes leading to the Yanert. The Yanert was as good a place as any, he said, to meet the caribou migration. Besides, he added, he figured it was time we had conversation with Solo Swanson—about $300 worth.

The day before, at purple dusk, we had slanted down into the glacier-gouged valley and found a campsite on a jack-spruce flat bordering the river bars. We had covered thirty up-ended miles since daybreak, and the horses were wooden-legged, beat out. While Tex and Buck pitched the tents and started supper, I shoved the hobbled animals back onto a good pea vine flat I had spotted coming off the mountainside. We always liked to hold a pack string on pea vine at night. The stuff is the equal of grain when frost has ripened its seed pods, and horses are so fond of it that usually they do not wander. We ate our supper by firelight, turning in as soon as we had finished. Buck remarked that it was a fine, large night for sleeping.

Which it absolutely was. Only not for Tex and me. Around 1 A.M., at moonrise, something woke me. I sat up, listening. A slow wind whined down the valley, bringing the sound of river music. On a black ridge behind us a wolf cub was broadcasting the brand-new discovery that it was good to be alive. Otherwise nothing. But I kept listening. Our association with Pitchfork had made me as suspicious as a brush Indian playing cutthroat poker. Presently the wind flawed, and in the sudden lull I heard it—the clink of shod hoofs traveling steadily up the waste of gravel bars. There was another sound, an odd muted rumble, a vibration in the air, but I didn't try to identify it. It didn't seem important just then. I reached over and shook Tex.

"Guess what," I said. Tex didn't have to guess. "I swear that Pitchfork must've been raised on straight loco weed," he groaned, surging out of his fawnskin robe. "Allus tryin' to make a gitaway, an' never knows where he's gittin' to."

We pulled on our pants and pacs, and I put fresh batteries in the flashlight while Tex found a *riata*. We hadn't kept a wrangling horse at camp because in these mountains, to stay in working condition, a horse needs plenty of time and freedom of movement at night to stuff his belly. He can't do it on a picket line; or anyway he won't. He gets lonesome and paws and shatters the night with raucous protests. And next day on the trail he is a major headache. He can't keep his mind off the nearest clump of grass. So, being afoot, the sooner we caught up with our departing transportation, the less walking we would have to do. Buck heard us and wanted to know what was going on. Tex told him.

"If you run into Solo Swanson out there," Buck said "invite him over. Tell him we've got a sound, gentle, willing cayuse to sell."

It didn't occur to either of us to take a rifle, since it was unlikely we would be gone more than a few minutes. The moon had now floated well above the summits, and the horses' trail was easy to follow. Half-a-mile above camp we sighted the animals. They were in a huddle against the shine of the river, staring toward the timber. In a moment we saw what the attraction was, a band of caribou. There were perhaps 100 in the band, and they were over at the rim of the spruces, drifting up the valley through the pointed moon-cast shadows. With the silvery light picking out their polished antlers and the snowy capes of the bulls, they looked very glamorous. As we stood watching them, we began hearing other caribou back in the timber, brush cracking, ankle joints clicking, antlers knocking together. The soft drum-thunder of their hoofs, I realized, was the curious sound I had heard from camp.

This was the autumn gathering for the long migration north, and we had hit it right on the nose, which was professionally gratifying.

But horses, whatever the reason may be, are always fascinated by caribou. The presence of the splay-footed wanderers gives them screwball notions. They try to get into the act. They'll be so weary under their packs that you'd swear there wasn't another mile left in them, yet they'll go lumbering joyously out to meet a herd of caribou as though hoping to follow it clear to the Arctic Ocean. The fleet caribou lead them on. They seem to get a kick out of it. They'll circle a packtrain, swooping in and out, rearing and snorting, putting on a terrific show. Then they'll slam off at high speed for the horizon, while the poor bemused horses whicker idiotically for them to wait, please. Between Pitchfork and these caribou tonight, it was small wonder our string had lost interest in pea vine.

"If hit ain't one doggone thing," Tex declared, "hit's seventeen others. C'mon, let's go catch one o' them delooded jughaids. With the caribou here, we gotta have us a wranglin' horse."

Pitchfork had ideas about that. Wheeling in phony alarm at our approach, he took the hobbled string in pell-mell, kangaroo-hopping flight across the ribbon of bar and into the timber. It was typical. It was as if he knew he was hell in horsehide and enjoyed demonstrating the fact. Our next move was to get ahead of the horses, if we could, and keep them between us and camp until we were able to tie onto one of them. So we sprinted up the bars a couple of hundred yards, then cut into the spruces. The strip of timber was narrow here, a mere fringe between the river and the pitch of the valley wall, and was broken by a moon-dappled opening with a game trail running through it. Panting, we took up a tactical position where the trail emerged from the blackness under the trees. Tex shook out a brush-popper's loop. I had the flashlight ready. Minutes passed. Then, through the sounds of wind and water, came the unmistakable scrape of a hoof against rock.

"Get set," I whispered.

"I ought to strangle him, not just catch the critter," Tex whispered back.

We should have known better. It was too easy. Out of the shadows, cross wind, moved deeper shadows. Tex crawled forward, whirling the Manila hard-twist, and I clicked the flashlight on. Tableaux. Caught in the beam of light were two caribou, a gaunt heavy-antlered bull and a trim young heifer. They stood stone-still for an instant, ears strained toward us, heads jerked high, gazing in what must have been shocked disbelief. Then the bull uttered a hoarse blat, and the two lunged past us. As they did so, we saw that the bull was crippled, his right hind leg drawn up and useless. The result of a gunshot wound, perhaps. Or maybe wolf work. Anyway, he was a tragedy. With a ruined leg, striving to keep up with the hard-traveling herds and trying to hold a debutante heifer with the woods full of competition, he had too many troubles. The pair vanished upvalley, and we resumed waiting.

More minutes passed. Then Tex touched my arm as, close at hand in the gloom, a hobble chain jangled. "I know dang well that ain't no caribou," he muttered.

Suddenly there the horses were, crowding one another on the narrow trail, blowing as if spooked by the darkness and the unfamiliar place. This time Tex suffered an attack of the eagers. Before I could turn on the flashlight, he made his throw at the nearest horse. It was good. Tex had grown up with a *riata* in his hand, roping discouraged dogs and goats, and was no more likely to miss with one than he'd miss his mouth with a fork. But he should have waited. Ten horses to choose from, and he had roped the only one we had never ridden and maybe couldn't ride, the ineffable Pitchfork. The rest of the string was stampeding with great abandon in what seemed to be the only interesting direction tonight, upvalley. I tried to turn them, but no luck.

"Well, anyhow, we got ol' Pitchfork," Tex said with forced heartiness. "Ya wanta go back to camp fer a saddle, or try him bareback?" He had tied a war bridle and was fitting it to the big dun's head.

I said I would try him bareback. The fact was, I never was any great shakes as a bronc-stomper. Given the breaks, I could sit up there and rattle after a fashion. But to tackle a serious job of hard riding, in a form-fitting saddle, at night, in heavy timber and on stony ground, was my idea of asking for a busted skull. Bareback, you'd have a gambler's chance if the horse tried to scrape you off on a limb or smash your leg against a boulder. You could at least unload on approximately your own terms. So I said the blazes with the saddle, I would do the best I could Injun-style.

Unbuckling Pitchfork's hobbles, I cinched up my belt, pulled down my hat, took a short hold on the *riata*, and swarmed aboard. To nobody's surprise, I guess, it didn't last long.

By Tex's count, I stayed with the dun five jumps. The salty cuss was an operator, you couldn't take that away from him. He bogged his head, let out an airhorn bellow and went fence-railing across the opening like a rodeo hotshot. I lost track of him the second jump, and after that was all over him, hanging on with both hands. The next thing I knew, the sky was underneath, which is a dismaying phenomenon. A split-second later I made a sweet three-point landing, both shoulders and the back of my neck, in a clump of snowbush. By the time I stopped seeing comets, Pitchfork had taken leave of us, and Tex was worrying about whether my neckbone was still connected to my backbone, and so on. The way the situation currently added up, we weren't doing so well. Not only had Pitchfork made off with our *riata*, but he was now footloose, no hobbles to handicap him, if they ever had.

"I purely despise that horse," I said.

"We would o' done better," Tex said brokenly, "with the bull caribou."

Having no valid excuse to return to camp, we spent the next four hours slogging drearily up the valley, fording sloughs, stumbling over rocks, emptying ice water out of our pacs, wringing out our socks. Fragments of the caribou migration ghosted past us. The knife-sharp wind felt like winter. Our wonderful horses, led by Pitchfork again, had left the timber for the open bars and were traveling into new country as though they knew exactly where they were going. The tracks showed that Pitchfork was crowding them, like the stallion he imagined himself to be. Sunrise found us at timberline. On our left was a tall granite cliff, with a point of skinny spruces reaching from it to the river. If I had known what awaited us beyond those trees, I would have called the night's work off. I would have found a nice pile of leaves and conked out on it until the raveled sleeve of care was really knitted up. But instead, innocently, we mushed on in the new light, neither of us talking, covering ground like a pair of somnambulists.

The thin belt of spruces yielded to a small meadow. Just as we plodded into the grassy space, a wild and savage sound froze us in our tracks. It was the roar of an angry grizzly, a full-throated *wagh-h-h*, loaded with threat and decibels. It had come, as nearly as I could tell, from a tangle of scarlet dwarf birches directly across the meadow. I submit that every person should, at least once, hear a grizzly roar at close range. It does things to your nervous system. I mean, it brings you up on your toes. It is a sure tonic for that tired feeling. Still, we didn't expect trouble. What the heck, we had lived for years at a time in some of the earth's most populous bear pastures, and most of our bruin neighbors had bent over backward to keep the peace. If this bear had a morning grouch, that was his business. The thing to do was to be diplomatic and give him room for it.

"Sounded real hostile," Tex said. "Y' reckon he was roarin' at us?" "He wasn't just practicing," I said.

After stalling around until we felt certain the bear had gone elsewhere, we angled across the meadow toward the river, the direction the horses had taken. Tex continued speculating as to why the bear had sounded off. In a moment we found out why. The bear had been warning us away from a kill. Wading through the waist-high, frost-killed grass, we practically stumbled over the carcass of a caribou so recently pulled down that it was still warm, still bleeding. It was a bull, and his neck was broken. The claw marks of the sledgehammer pawstroke that had broken it were an inch deep through hair, hide and muscle. Of interest was the healed scar of a crippling wound above the hock of the right hind leg. Presumably the bull was our trouble-beset acquaintance of a few hours back. He had been a cinch for such an end.

Tex gave the birch thicket a careful scrutiny, then drew his belt knife. This I could have predicted. The sight of downed meat would make Tex hungry if he had just finished a ten-course dinner. "Might as well git the liver," he said. "Hit's been a spell since we ate."

"If the grizzly is still hanging around," I said, "I hope he's the charitable type."

He wasn't. We cut out the liver and wrapped it in grass. I was thinking it would go mighty good roasted over willow coals, even without salt, when there was a windy snort behind us. We swiveled about as one man. It was the bear, all right. He had circled to get our scent, and here he came. He wasn't charging. He was just pigeon-toeing arrogantly toward us, rolling his shoulders, back hair all rucked up, lips curled to show his fighting teeth. The nearest likely-looking tree was a branchy, dead spruce over on the riverbank, 100 feet distant. Leaving the liver hanging in the air, we reached the tree neck-and-neck, and were still making an even heat of it when pencil-size limbs near the top stopped us. The bear had halted at the caribou carcass.

So here we clung, forlorn and disgusted, in the dawn's early light. As stated at outset, an hour dragged past. Then Tex came up with his scheme quote to fix the dang bear's wagon fer him unquote.

It was a novel plot sure enough, an authentic flash of the Cobb genius. Nobody else could have thought of it. The tree had been gnawed by generations of porcupines, and the scars were heavily coated with resin. Grinning, delighted with himself, Tex sliced off long shavings of this pitchwood with his knife and tied them into a bundle with a piece of pack string. Up to this point I hadn't caught on. But when he reached for his match safe, all was clear. He was going to put the grizzly to flight by firing the meadow. To give the old gent his due, it seemed a sound idea. The wind was right, the grass looked dry enough to burn and there was no possibility of starting a forest fire, not at timberline in September.

So optimism prevailed as Tex touched off his torch and tossed it out into the meadow. But it seemed that the grass wasn't as dry as we had figured. It smouldered and smoked in a slowly widening circle about the blazing pitchwood. The wind fanned up a few sparks, the bear whuf-whuffed and retreated warily but not far enough, and I told myself that our score was holding up beautifully, nothing had gone right yet. Then came the payoff, fate's final kick in the groin. The sickly circle of fire reached the litter of resinous twigs and bark fragments under our tree. Anybody who has seen flames swoosh up a pitch-coated dead spruce will understand what happened. Through my mind shot the ghastly thought that we were about to achieve the distinction of being the only horse wranglers ever to self-incinerate themselves in a treetop with a bear as a spectator.

"Gawdamighty," Tex yelled, as the blast of heat enveloped us, "let's git outa here."

Nobody ever offered me better advice. Bailing out of the tree by the hard expedient of sliding down the branch ends, we arrived on the ground with only minor burns and bruises, and fled upstream. I don't know what the bear did. We never saw him again. When it seemed safe, we slowed to a walk, blowing like draft animals. Downstream the smoke of our fire had thinned to a thread against the wildrose sky. Automatically I picked up the horses' trail and began following it. I felt as though I had been doing it all my life. Tex halted, pointing.

"There's Solo Swanson's cabin," he said. "An', by gad, there's the horses."

About a quarter of a mile distant, with Pitchfork in the lead, our ever faithful companions of the trail were straggling up the bed of a plunging alpine streamlet toward a pretty flat on which stood a peeled-log cabin. Pitchfork looked fresh and full of stuff and vinegar. He carried his head high, his dark mane and tail blew handsomely in the wind; he was almost dancing. By contrast, the other horses were caricatures of themselves. After the night's trek with hobbles, they'd had it. They moved as if their joints were fused and their heads weighed 500 pounds apiece. A sorry lot of pelters. We hastened after them, insofar as we were capable of hastening, that is.

The cabin door swung open and out stepped Solo, shading his eyes against the sun. From Buck's description, it couldn't be anybody but Solo. He was tall and pink-bearded, shitepoke lean, in waist overalls and a red-flannel undershirt. He stood motionless a moment, like one of those statues of an old-time buckskin scout, then stuck some fingers in his mouth and whistled, a shrill birdlike whistle with a lilt at the end of it. What happened thereafter I still don't believe myself except on rainy days. Pitchfork gave a high, happy whicker, unlike any whicker he had ever uttered when he was with us, and went up the remaining slope like a cat, the *riata* snaking behind him.

Here and there, at one time and another, I have witnessed some affectionate reunions between men and pet animals who had been separated for a while. This one topped them all. I mean, it was special. It was a thing to make you envious. The implication of the scene, Solo with his arms around Pitchfork's neck, and Pitchfork nuzzling Solo, nipping at the red undershirt, exploded on Tex and me at the same instant.

"Holy sufferin'," Tex said in a voice that didn't sound like his. "The miser'ble knothead is a one-man horse. Onliest one I ever knew." Then another thought struck him, with visible impact. "Been tryin' to leave us an' git back home fer the past three months, the pore so-an-so."

Thus the baffling behavior of Pitchfork, his orneriness and repeated desertions, all at once made sense. The idea was going to take some getting used to, but it appeared that the big dun was after all an admirable horse in his own way, and that Solo Swanson was no part of a backwoods swindler.

It was past noon of the brilliant autumn day when we got back to camp. Buck was sitting on a rock, binoculars glued to his eyes, watching a band of caribou across the river. He lowered the glasses as we rode in through the spruces, sized up our mud-plastered, smoke-grimed clothes and the gaunt horses, and shook his head.

"What did you do with Pitchfork?" he asked.

"We—uh—sold him back to Solo Swanson," Tex explained. "Sorta on time. After payin' his brother's hospital bill, seems like Solo is plenty broke."

Buck looked puzzled. Then he laughed. "Well, I hope Pitchfork is as happy to be rid of us as we are him." He slid off the rock to help us put the hobbles back on the horses. "Some Pitchfork," he said. "Some Solo Swanson."

Adventure with Makos

Caballeros! *It doesn't come any crazier than a* Cordonaso *hurricane and a surf full of cannibal sharks. Come along on a Mexican adventure with makos.*

It was the softly radiant hour of the pearl, 8 A.M., with a breeze that could have been jugged and sold as pure tropical elixir. There were four of us. Tom and I were doing the fishing, Juanito was our guide. The fourth member of the party, uninvited, was Horace the tobacco-eating burro, a moth-eaten beast who looked old enough to have campaigned with Pancho Villa. Out front the world's heaviest surf was crashing endlessly. Behind us, the beat-up Hotel Guadalajara squatted defiantly on a barren dune. Most of the rest of the town had been knocked down some years ago by a combination of hurricane and tidal wave. Tom had just hooked an acrobatic mako when Juanito began sounding off.

"*Señores*, the sky snake is coming. *Favor de Dios*, run!"

"Cut that out," I said over my shoulder. Juanito is sixteen, the youngest saltwater guide in Mexico, so far as I know. He is a pleasant, competent brat and I would unhesitatingly recommend him to any angler adventuring to the rich, little-known sea pastures of this southwest coast of Old Mexico. But it is true that during the past ten days Tom and I had gotten somewhat teed off with him, for reasons that will appear. "We're busy," I said.

We really were busy, or at any rate Tom was. The silver-and-blue mako, in three wild seaward runs and a series of spectacular lunges, had stripped Tom's reel to the final critical yards. Complicating the matter, the fish's clan relatives were now closing in on him for an easy cannibal breakfast. I counted eleven of the streamlined brutes knifing through the green swells beyond the surf, dorsals and upper tail lobes gleaming like burnished gun-steel. I was telling myself that Tom was a cinch to lose not only the mako but also a reelful of line, and wondering if I could sucker him into making some book on it, for a new sombrero, say, when Juanito started hollering again, panic in his voice.

"But *señores*, please. It is a big, big sky snake. Only look."

This time we looked. The sight would have scared Genghis Khan.

I'll explain presently what the sky snake was and what it did. First I've got to give you the background of this unusual fishing expedition. I had jolted into Cuyutlan in company with Tom and assorted members of his family, male and female. Tom is a lean, cigar-puffing cotton buyer from the Snuffy Smith country, who a month ago said the blazes with business and headed south for an extended angler's holiday. It could be that he had invited me to come over the mountains from Jalisco with him because he was worried about blowgun Indians, *tigres*, crocodiles in the stream crossings and other unreliable jungle fauna. Anyhow, the purpose of the trip was to take mako sharks in the Cuyutlan surf. I am aware that the mako is not considered to be a surf fish. But there was a widespread story, almost a legend, about these Cuyutlan sharks.

In substance, the tale goes that each October 10 the surf here becomes mountainous. Mollusks, crabs and other small creatures churned out of the sand attract hordes of fish—corbina, roosterfish, sierra mackerel, sardines and whatnot. These fish in turn attract packs of mako sharks. Then, punctually on October 15, the mighty hurricane called the *Cordonaso de San Francisco*, the Sash of St. Francis, blasts in. Theologians and meteorologists may be interested to know that the hurricane gets its name from the belief that St. Francis personally brings it about. Hoping to make fishermen penitent, he takes off his rope sash and, using it as a whip, strides across the ocean beating sin and seven bells out of maritime things in general.

That's the way the boys tell it. So we checked in at the hotel on October 11, and marked time for ten days. No makos. No *Cordonaso*. Not even any small fish until yesterday. Which explains in part why our Juanito was sort of in the doghouse.

Yesterday noon Tom and I were sitting glumly on the hotel gallery drinking *WCTU* cocktails (coconut milk spiked with orange juice), when our first break occurred. Close inshore a vast school of sardines suddenly darkened the swells. At once a screaming cloud of seabirds gathered above the fish, diving and diving. Then, on all sides of the school, I began seeing white surges. My pulse jumped. Only one fish in these waters makes such a commotion on the surface when feeding.

"Roosterfish," I said, and as one man we departed for our tackle.

They gave us some action. Tying on Jap feathered jigs, we waded out until the surf was lifting us, and began casting. I saw two roosterfish arrow along the green, nearly vertical wall of a wave, like fish behind an aquarium window. They struck at almost the same instant, solid all-out smashes. Although roosterfish seldom jump, they are admirable fighters, and when taken in the surf are a delight indeed. I beached mine ten minutes or so after he took the lure. He went thirty inches and was bulge-bellied from the sardines he had eaten. His curious dorsal, for which the species is named, stood nearly a foot high and consisted of soft black, unconnected rays, with a broad slash of Indian yellow angling across it. I killed him for dinner, then went over to see how Tom was making out. He had let his fish run as far as it would, and now was battling it back in through the hills and valleys of water. Juanito and Horace the burro were behind him, rapt spectators.

"Son, this is too much fun to enjoy without a smoke," Tom said to Juanito. "So fetch me a cigar and some matches from my tackle box, hey?"

Juanito meant well. He peeled off the cellophane wrapper, stuck the cigar politely in Tom's mouth, and scratched a match on the seat of his jeans. But as he leaned forward, holding the match, cupped Mexican fashion in both hands, Horace got into the act. Begging for a bite of the tobacco, he thrust his bony, flop-eared head unexpectedly over Juanito's shoulder. Tom had been feeding him cigar butts since our arrival here. Juanito, shoved off balance, stumbled, and the match flame touched the taut line. There was a twang like a tired guitar string giving up. Tom stood motionless a moment, probably counting to ten, then turned with ominous plantation dignity.

"I will destroy you two jackasses later," he said between his teeth.

But it was a grand, golden afternoon. For a welcome change, the sea was full of life. A squadron of whales went past. Bonitos were jumping. Several great sow sea turtles were stooging around outside the surf, waiting for nightfall so they could come in and lay their eggs in the sand. We took eight roosterfish and released them. Then the corbina, or sea trout, hove on the scene, and we beached six. They were good corbina, the type called *cavallo cuchi*, averaging about four pounds. Toward evening a school of sierra mackerel burst out of a wave top to run skittering on their tails, a gleaming gust of fish, with something huge pursuing them beneath the surface. Whatever the latter was, it refused to strike. We knocked off and went back to the hotel.

Sundown brought a strange sight. As the red disc was dropping through a cloudless coppery sky, a mirage formed across its setting. That is, I guess it could be called a mirage. It showed the silhouette of a flat island with palm trees and several buildings. One of the buildings had a gabled roof. The only comparable place I had ever seen in these latitudes boasting a gabled roof was a fishing station I once visited near Macao.

"It means that the makos and the *Cordonaso* are coming, pronto," Juanito said with conviction when the scene had flickered out.

"I'll bet you believe in the Hindu rope trick, too," Tom said.

Our cook did himself proud in the matter of dinner. We had roosterfish fillets, jungle quail broiled Mexican style, corn- and squash-blossom fritters and apple-bananas candied in wild mangrove honey. A meal to charm a gourmet's society. Afterward somebody broke out a radio and tuned in on KRLD, Dallas, Texas, for dance music. Naturally, the first voice to come blaring out of the air was that of brother Elvis Presley giving with the rock 'n' roll. I said the hell with it and went to bed. It had been a busy afternoon.

But it was going to be a busier night.

Waking up around two o'clock, I went out on the gallery to check the weather. No change in that. But the ocean was something to behold. It was loaded with greenish phosphorescence, and myriad fish were streaking about in it like fire-arrows. Some of them looked plenty big, eight feet and better. Directly in front of the hotel a school of sardines, or maybe mullet or *pajaritos*, formed a wide coruscating wheel of light, and the big fish were slashing into it. I guess I must have stood here a couple of minutes gawking at the show before comprehension struck me with the impact of a sandbag. Whereupon, as excited as the chap who first found paydirt on the American river, I hastened back into the hotel.

Since Mauricio, the manager, thriftily shuts off the electric plant at midnight to save gasoline, the patio was illuminated only by the ghostly flicker of a coal oil lamp whose chimney hadn't been washed, I figured, since the day the joint opened. I caromed off a table and some chairs, did a stem-Christy at Tom's door, and knocked with both fists. When Tom stuck his head out, looking like a dyspeptic owl and grumbling that he didn't give a damn if the Injuns were off the reservation, I said in a conspiratorial whisper, "Don't breathe a word of it, *amigo*, but the makos are here."

"Huh? Whatcha say?" he said foggily. Then, coming out of the ether, "The makos!" he bellowed. "Lord love a flounder, how does a man get some light in this place?"

With that, the hotel woke up. The lighting problem was solved when Mauricio emerged from the goblin gloom of the kitchen with an armload of fat ocote pine torchwood. In the time it takes a tenderfoot to build a corn shock cigarette we were on the beach, blazing torches stuck in the sand, baiting up with fresh mullet. A dozen or so hotel guests gathered around. A *vaquero* on a spotted pony loped down from the road. Some turtle-egg hunters with buckets, shovels and flashlights joined us. Thus, taken by and large, Tom and I had quite an audience when we waded out to try our luck.

The makos were cooperative. At my second cast one hit with the force of a runaway truck. I now began to learn some things about these sharks. In deep water, with plenty of room to maneuver, they are superb fighters. But in the surf they surpass themselves. At the stab of the hook they apparently go berserk trying to get back to the open ocean. This one vaulted and swapped ends, rolled and ran and hammered the water with his tail, splashing up fountains of green sea fire. I don't know how big he may have been, but he was one of the good ones. I have never fought a better fish with my feet on land. Probably I worked him too hard. Anyhow, I lost him. The hook sliced out. Our audience was silent as I reeled in. They were disappointed. They had wanted a dead shark. I felt like a matador who had bungled the moment of truth.

While Juanito was rigging another bait for me, Tom got his first mako strike. It was a thing to see. His mullet was a luminous dot skidding down the slope of a swell. The line, curving with the tide, was a thin pencil-stroke of fire. Then this shark torpedoed a full fifty feet along the wave top, scattering gouts of luminescence, and grabbed the bait before it fell into the trough. He was another good fish. With the hook in his jaw, he came out high and handsome. Three times in fast succession. He ran seaward, turned and blasted back, busting through the glowing school of sardines.

Tom was winching in line desperately, when all of a sudden there were two sharks instead of one. They leaped together, side by side, and when they came down one appeared to be sledging the other with his tail. I suppose that the newcomer had cannibalistic ideas. In any case, he found himself in a situation. As nearly as I could figure it, he struck the line and got a turn of it around his tail and couldn't get it off. The result was inevitable. Tom didn't have a prayer. The two tandem-hitched fish simply headed west and kept going. After a moment Tom's reel was empty and the line broke at the knot with a pop like a Gene Autry cap-gun. Our audience remained considerately silent.

"If this keeps up," Tom said, "somebody is gonna have to make a quick trip to civilization for a shipment of gear."

Before I could say Amen to that, I caught a whiff of Chanel. At my elbow a finishing school voice said, "Does anybody mind if an amateur tires?" It was Tom's niece, name of Stafford, a twenty-one-year-old canary-wing blonde. Any way you look at this young lady, she is a connoisseur's item. Not only is she assembled like a Swiss watch, but also she is a considerable heiress. But for the past several days she had been in what used to be called a pet. Yesterday she had declared that if Tom continued to hang around in these forlorn boondocks she was going to start walking to a place called New York.

"In fact, if I ever consider getting married," she had added bitterly, "the first thing I am going to ask the candidate is 'Do you fish?' If the answer is affirmative, the deal is off."

I handed her my rod and wished her well. I am a guy who believes in keeping the peace where temperamental blonde heiresses are concerned. Wading out until the surf was creaming about her hips, she made a cast. She was no amateur. Somebody, somewhere, had logged some hours teaching her to use casting gear. And I don't mean a Girl Scout instructor. The mullet sailed out over the surf and landed just this side of a cruising mako. He made a run at it, missed for some reason, and turned back. But the next cast scored. It was the same mako and he shot in like a rocket and made a high-speed turn with the mullet in his mouth. The princess hit him three times, leaning into it, and the battle was joined. He was a fair mako. He put on a swell surface show, and naturally our audience applauded. But not for the shark. A Mexican *caballero* would applaud an American blonde if she were knitting mittens.

What happened next wasn't Stafford's fault. A king wave roared in. Having started probably somewhere in Polynesia, it had plenty of momentum. It broke higher than the gal's head and rolled her under. Tom and I went in after her fast, but Juanito was faster. Juanito is amphibious. The backwash was taking her out when he found her in the smother of water and got hold of her blouse collar. She still had the rod and the mako was still on. Tom and I had arrived in time to be tumbled by the next wave, so that the four of us were swept ashore in a heap. Stafford's hot-weather blouse hadn't been equal to the occasion. Juanito held what was left of it in his hand. With her hair in a witch's tangle over her face, plastered with sand and with a lei of seaweed around her neck, Stafford looked like an "I dreamt I was fighting a mako shark in my what-you-call-it bra," illustrated by Salvador Dali.

But she beached the fish. Twenty minutes after she socked the hook into him, he was on the sand. While he turned flip-flops, popping his jaws in a sort of Russian commissar grin, I clobbered him with a length of driftwood. I didn't seem to be getting anywhere. Then the *vaquero* stepped down off his pinto, hauled out an ancient .45 Peacemaker, and with a deferential, "*Con permisso*," let go six shots into the shark's head, which took care of the matter. Our audience was cheering wildly. You got the impression that there hadn't been such a show in Cuyutlan since St. Francis' big wind scrambled the town. Stafford sat down and began giggling. In my ignorance I thought she was hysterical. I guess Tom did too. But apparently the younger set isn't what it used to be.

"I take back what I said yesterday," she declared between giggles. "Introduce me to some surf fishermen, uncle, please."

Deciding that we'd had a large workout, we went back to the hotel and turned in. Tom and I were up at first light. As the cook didn't have his charcoal fires going yet, he gave us an emergency breakfast—six raw turtle eggs apiece in glasses, seasoned with lime juice and red chili powder. The technique was to shut your eyes and gulp. But the eggs were very nourishing, the cook assured us, and a sovereign specific for flagging male potency. We expressed our gratitude and headed for the beach. Tom was limping. When I asked him how come, he said his corns hurt. Must be going to rain or something, he said. The makos were still with us, fins everywhere. We had landed two small ones when Juanito and Horace came down from the hotel. Horace crowded against Tom, wistfully eying his morning cigar. Tom grinned at him. "Beat it," he said. "I think you're a Republican in disguise." I hooked another small shark and lost him, then we moved up the beach toward a gap in the surf.

An educational experience awaited us. We were walking single file along the water's edge when a mako made a run straight at us from 100 feet out. He grounded, threshed frantically and returned to deep water with the backwash of the next wave. A few minutes later another shark repeated the performance. I told myself that they had been pursuing small fish, but didn't believe it. I recalled that last year at Santiago Beach, twenty miles north of here, a shark, species unknown, had hurled himself onto the sand and killed a woman bather. Her fiancé was one of the witnesses. When I thought of how we had floundered around in the water last night, a chill jittered up my spine. I wouldn't have gone out there this morning, for fishing purposes, if I had been offered an interest in Fort Knox.

We cast into the surf gap, and Tom hung a nice one. After a fifteen-minute fight, he got the fish started in on the crest of a comber. Eager beaver, he threw his half-smoked *panatela* into the water, planted his feet and horsed the shark with everything his tackle would stand. As the mako headed in, carried by the onrushing wave, Horace bounded after the cigar butt. It could have been his last act this side of burro heaven. The shark hit the sand, stood on his tail and flopped forward. His jaws banged shut, inches from Horace's front legs, like a sprung bear trap. Fortunately this morning I wasn't depending on any driftwood club for dispatching sharks. I had borrowed a purty new .38 Colt from Mauricio. The mako was giving us his politburo grin when I shot his tiger eyes out. We measured him. He went nine feet.

Tom parked himself on a log and took his shoes off. "Doggone corns still hurt," he said. "Weather's gonna change."

He could have said that again.

By now the sun had climbed into a brass-dust sky. A migration of dragonfly-like insects was overhead, making for the jungled peaks. There were no birds in sight. Despite the breeze, I was sweating. We moved back in front of the hotel where some sizable fins were showing, and resumed casting. Tom presently hooked the air-minded heavy-weight mako mentioned at outset. The fish had taken most of his line, and was in imminent danger of being eaten alive by a pack of its *compadres*, when Juanito began giving us hi-fi about the sky snake. "Only look, *señores*," he pleaded.

So, as I said, we looked.

The sky snake was a waterspout. Black and funnel-shaped, it was whirling in from the south-southwest. Its head was in a boiling wrack of cloud and its foot in a welter of wind-lashed water.

Behind it was a solid front of plum-colored murk, shot through with lightning flashes. The whole hair-raising setup had formed in less than five minutes. You didn't need a surveyor's eye to see that it was aimed directly at Cuyutlan. Being hit in the face by several hundred tons of high-velocity water wasn't my idea, believe me, of a proper ending for this pleasant morning's fishing.

"Cut your line," I yelled.

"But it's the last one I've got," Tom yelled back. "Maybe—"

It was too late then. It had been too late anyway. The waterspout swept in, swaying and curtsying, making more noise than the surf. A gust of rain-filled, sand-laden wind belted us. I cut Tom's line when the mako was at the top of a pretty, twisting jump, and we sprinted for the hotel. Before we made it, the waterspout plowed across the beach, picked up a palm-rib fence and the roofs of two thatched huts, and disintegrated in the middle of a coconut plantation. I remember thinking that nobody would have to pick those coconuts. Then we were on the hotel gallery, boosted along by the first screaming onslaught of the *Cordonaso de San Francisco*. Aided by Mauricio, we got the big front door open against the weight of wind. Tom, panting as if he had just loaded sixteen tons, stood his rod in a corner and shook Juanito's hand.

"Congratulations, son," he said. "St. Francis finally took you off the hook."

Buck Fever Can Happen to Anybody

In folklore it's always the tenderfoot who suffers from buck fever, but plenty of experts don't agree with that. And "Two-Squaw" Riley maintains that a man has never really lived until he's had it at least once.

Old "Two-Squaw" Riley, up on the Yukon Flats, had a unique and highly personalized theory about buck fever. Two-Squaw was a tough, cockeyed little flannel-mouth Irishman who had batted around in the northern wilds since the brave days when Swiftwater Bill, the Malamute Kid, and Gordon Bettles were heroes up here. I don't know how he got his nickname because he never explained it twice the same way. It was a different story every time and always a good one, of course ribald. Two-Squaw really was quite a yarn-spinner. So when he explained buck fever to a bunch of us over a jug of Hudson's Bay one winter night in his trapline cabin, it was bound to be a pretty dramatic and memorable explanation.

Two-Squaw said he was guiding a cheechako bear hunter named B. S. Hartman. This was an autumn hunt for mountain grizzlies, and they had backpacked into the snow-patched peaks above Bowstring Lake, in the Talkeetnas. The pilgrim was sulking, Two-Squaw said, because he had been talked out of bringing his pet rifle, a sleek little pump-action .32 that might have been all right for sheep or caribou but was short of the kind of authority needed for grizzlies. In town Two-Squaw had issued a ukase—leave the peashooter behind or hire another guide.

So, probably because no other guide was available, B. S. Hartman reluctantly consented to leave for the grizzly country armed with Two-Squaw's spare .405. The .405 wasn't a handsome weapon, Two-Squaw admitted, and it kicked like a mule because the breech mechanism was worn, but when you hit a bear with it the bear stayed hit. The slug would practically skid the critter backward.

"I do hope nobody sees me carrying this piece of junk," B. S. Hartman bellyached. "My gawd, haven't you ever cleaned it?"

"Shore I have," Two-Squaw replied with assumed indignation. "I remember the day, too. Lemme see now, it was back in the fall o' '97 or the spring o' '98, one o' the two."

Leaving camp at daybreak of a winey gold-and-turquoise morning, they battled their way up through a mess of brush and blowdown to a blueberry meadow under a line of cliffs. As they sat down and got out their binoculars, a pair of whistling marmots suddenly began sounding off on their right. Then they heard rocks rolling. Big rocks. Quarter-ton boulders that nothing in these peaks save a grizzly could have budged. Two-Squaw shoved his glass inside his shirt and motioned for silence and caution. Then he and B. S. Hartman tiptoed over the turf toward the source of the disturbance. There was a grass-bordered streamlet, then a steep green ridge with shale spines skylined on its crest. The crash and pound of rolling rocks seemed to come from just beyond the ridge. Maybe fifty yards distant. B. S. Hartman, hot-eyed and pale, was walking in the lead.

"Now listen," Two-Squaw whispered. "That's gotta be a grizzly over there. So when ya open up on him, keep shootin' till I tell ya to stop. I mean, git all the lead ya can into him."

B. S. Hartman didn't reply. He was walking like a man in a trance, his gaze fixed on the ridge crest.

They passed among huge boulders patterned with strange lichen growths arranged in broad concentric rings like rifle targets, and came out on a steep ramp of wind-scoured rock, with the two silver-gray whistlers scuttling for safety ahead of them. Then Two-Squaw sighted the bear. Or anyway, sighted its rump. The animal was 100 feet below them, digging into the rim of a talus pitch. In the hope of obtaining a few pounds of fat whistler meat, it had excavated a couple of tons of rock and earth and was still digging industriously. Two-Squaw touched B. S. Hartman's arm and pointed. But as he did so a shadow fell across the bare rock at their feet. And at the same instant, from some twenty-five feet above them, came a hoarse, inquiring grunt. Two-Squaw said he was afraid to look. He said he felt a deep freeze start both ways from the pit of his stomach and knew doggoned well his hair stood up straight and stiff as the bristles on a brush.

After what seemed like a weekend of paralysis, he said, he swiveled his head around and took a popeyed look up the slope. If the animal standing there wasn't the biggest grizzly in the world, he said, it was at least the biggest one he, Two-Squaw, had ever seen. It apparently had emerged from behind one of the boulders and now was standing erect on its hind legs, front paws extended to maintain balance, weaving a little as grizzlies always do when on their hind feet.

The sunlight glinted on its polished, curved, stevedore-hook claws and the mountain wind was winnowing its mahogany pelt. Its nose was beginning to curve up to show its fighting teeth and that was bad. Two-Squaw said it stood about twelve feet net altitude, and since it was above them on this steep pitch it towered as high as the roof of a bungalow.

B. S. Hartman made a sound like air escaping from a punctured tire. Then he muttered desperately, "Gottakillhim! Gottakillhim!" and began running cartridges through the .405. Only he neglected to pull the trigger. He was just working the lever, flipping the cartridges down the hill. As the last one hit the shale, the grizzly concluded it had urgent business elsewhere and departed at top speed around the mountain. The other bear, also alerted now, lit out with equal haste in the same direction. Two-Squaw and B. S. Hartman stood looking at each other. The pilgrim was trembling so violently he seemed about to come apart.

"N-nobody'll ever believe it," he said in a marsh-bird croak. "You'll have to give me an affidavit. Four shots dead center with a .405 at t-twenty-five feet, and the brute takes off like a gazelle."

But the guy was happy even if he had lost a trophy. He'd had a wonderful experience. As Two-Squaw declared over another round of hot buttered rum, the hunter who hasn't had a good, honest-to-gosh, bone-rattling case of buck fever hasn't really lived. The steely nerved gents with ice water in their circulatory systems, he said, who drop dangerous game as casually and unemotionally as if breaking clay pipes in a shooting gallery, just don't know what they are missing—and moreover probably are doggoned liars.

I'll ride along with that. And I claim buck fever is nothing to be ashamed of. Once I saw an Indian chief come down with a beautiful attack of it. Of course, he had an alibi, but then what buck-ague victim hasn't produced one?

This noble redskin's name was Wasilla. He was a Susitna-Denna, venerable and rawboned, tall for a canoe Indian, smiling and easygoing but with a chief's eyes, the kind of eyes Sitting Bull, Crazy Horse, and Cochise had according to the old prints you see, and he lived the year-round in a log-walled tent three miles upriver from my homestead and had been a friend of mine since I was knee-high to a fleshing block. In summer he subsisted on salmon and in winter on moose meat. It was coming on winter now and Wasilla was meat hungry. He hadn't made a kill yet because the moose herds were on the other side of the mile-wide Susitna, waiting until the ice was safe to cross. You could see them over there, milling like cattle in the brush. Wasilla couldn't stop watching them. The thought of fat juicy ribs, sweet tongue and broiled gut stuffed with kidney fat was driving him batty after three months of straight fish.

So on this particular gray, freezing early-winter day as I was sitting in his tent dickering with him for a pair of snowshoes, he stood up for anyhow the tenth time and opened the door for a look across the river. A second later he whirled and snatched up his parka, cap, and rifle.

"Here comes one," he whispered as if the animal could hear him at three-quarters of a mile. "A black bull. Dat's best kind o' bull, too."

We laid an ambush in some naked scrub willows at the head of a bar where we figured the bull would make his landing. Then we had a long wait and this didn't do Wasilla any good. He was too fine a hunter to fidget, but his breath came faster and faster and his jaw muscles were ridged as if he was trying to bite a spike in two. I suppose that in his time he had killed upward of 200 moose, yet this wait was getting under his skin. He wanted the bull so desperately he could taste it.

And the bull's actions didn't help. The animal was afraid of the ice. He would start across a slick spot—one of those black places with the white frost flowers where you can almost see the deep, fast current rushing underneath—and would snort and backtrack, searching for a safer spot. Several times he turned and glanced toward the bank he had left, as if he regretted the whole project and would return if only he wasn't more scared of the ice behind than of that ahead. Each time he did this, Wasilla gripped his rifle and started to rise on his elbows. And he was shaking now, not much but still shaking.

When the bull was 200 yards distant our plot against him went spectacularly haywire. He was catfooting toward us in the wan wash of cold sunlight, a big, black, high-humped, thick-maned, wonder-anterled, long-snouted old settler with shoulders like a Percheron and a neck like a beer barrel, when the ice started to let go under him with a series of gunshot reports. He swirled back at the first sharp crack, managed to reach safe ice, and turned upstream, away from us. At once Wasilla groaned in Denna, "I'm going to lose him," and stood up and opened fire.

It was a sorry exhibition. Wasilla carried a .30-30 and normally was a fair shot for an Indian, but this time he couldn't have hit a heifer in the rump with a frying pan. He emptied the rifle so fast that I'll swear he had a couple of cast hulls in the air all the while. And he never touched the bull. But the slugs smacking the ice and whistling off toward the horizon so confused the animal that it turned back toward shore—and in a moment broke through into the water.

"Don't shoot any more," I said. Me advising a chief of the Moose-Eater Denna. "Give him a chance to get ashore if he can."

"How could I shoot anymore?" Wasilla wailed between clenched teeth. "I got no more shells."

With that Wasilla dropped the .30-30, grabbed his butchering ax, and sprinted toward the floundering bull. By this time the animal had got his feet on the bottom and was lunging at the shelf ice, raring to strike it with his front hoofs, trying either to get onto it or break a lane to shore. Wasilla dispatched the bull in the bloody manner of his ancestors. He came in from the side, wary of the lashing hoofs and the sweep of the spiketined antler, and began chopping at the bull's spine. It was unpretty and it took some doing, but he accomplished it. The bull went over on its side, supported by the edges of the narrow ice channel it had broken, and died. Wasilla came back ashore, panting, and we went up to his tent to get the material for a Spanish windlass with which to drag the great carcass out onto the bar.

"I dunno what's matter with me," he said. "I never shoot dat bad before."

"You had buck fever, that's all," I said.

"Yeah?" he said wonderingly, obviously never having heard the term before. "Dat's somet'ing new. Goddamit, us Injuns catch more t'ings from the white man."

In any clinical discussion of buck fever such as the boys and I were having with Two-Squaw, I always try to get in a few hundred choice words regarding my own prize experience. This was in the big-timber country of Washington, where my father was a boss logger. Cougar, bear, and deer county. Giant trees so tall the clouds raveled on them. Salal and huckleberry undergrowth so dense that, as the loggers said, when you got into it you couldn't find your rump with both hands.

I was eleven and we lived in a log house on a piece of gravelly hilltop land which my father fondly hoped would someday be a farm. In this latter respect he didn't have a prayer, but he was trying. As a start he had built a cedar-shake chicken coop and bought twelve Rhode Island red hens and two roosters. I don't know why he thought two roosters were necessary. Probably it was just his typical lumberjack's flair for overdoing things.

Anyway, Dad felt he was embarked upon the dream venture of loggers, long-trappers, tall-water sailors, and rough-barked characters generally—a chicken ranch. And he could prove to you with a pencil stub and piece of paper that from this modest beginning would develop a business that would enable him to retire and would support us handsomely in his old age. The one thing that disturbed him was the presence hereabouts of numerous chicken-hungry varmints. Skunks, weasels, mink, marten, an occasional fisher, and worst of all, an outsized cougar that seemed to have the curiosity of a hotel detective and the instincts of a burglar.

This cougar had followed Dad home at night through the timber several times and had been sighted prowling near the house. Dad was convinced that the animal had sinister designs on his chickens. In consequence, being a forthright guy, the old man got hold of an 8-gauge shotgun, the only one I ever saw, and handloaded shells for it. I don't know what he put in those shells. In view of what happened I didn't care to ask. But he was playing for keeps. I mean to say, all he wanted was one broadside at the animal.

Came a September night, clear and frosty, with a huge smoky moon riding above the fir-rimmed clearing, and a keen little wind whining in from the Pacific sea pastures. I was sleeping on a couch in the front room. Around midnight I was jerked awake by a tremendous disturbance at the chicken house. A frenzied squawking and fluttering. The thump of chickens flying against the shake walls. Of course I knew the cougar was there. And since nobody else in the house had heard the uproar, this was my chance to become a hero and I seized it.

I slipped out of bed, took the 8-gauge down from its deer-foot rack, and headed down the moonlit path to the chicken house, feeling like a composite of all the famous big-game hunters in history.

At the chicken coop, I climbed onto a pile of lumber and peered in through the open window—and felt an icy shiver of fear ripple up my spine. Six feet distant, glaring unwinkingly, was a pair of great luminous eyes. They were on a level with my own eyes, so I figured here was the grandfather of cougars, a cat the size of a Shetland pony. Certain that I had only the merest fraction of a second in which to save myself before the brute launched himself through the window at my throat, I tried to let go a blast with the scattergun. But my muscles were on strike. I was shaking so badly I could barely keep my balance on the lumber pile. At last I got the side hammers back on full cock, but when I raised the weapon it wavered about as if it, too, had the quaking meemies.

Somehow, eventually, by a herculean effort, I leveled the barrel at the pair of menacing eyes, and pulled both triggers. I never heard the shot. The last sound I was conscious of was the squawking of the chickens. Then a great quiet descended, out of which Dad's voice aroused me. He was in his nightshirt, carrying a lantern and a stick of stovewood he had picked up as the handiest weapon available.

It appeared that the battering-ram kick of the 8-gauge had flung me backward off the lumber pile and I had landed on my head on a pile of rocks. Knocked silly. All the 206 bones in my frame hurt. I felt as if I had been through a Pawnee sun dance. I stood up, still shaking, and gibbered something about the cougar, warning Dad, as I recall, to take no chances on account of the ferocious marauder might only be wounded.

Whereupon Dad yanked me into the chicken house and pointed out, in logger language, what a four-bell boner I had committed. The evidence was there and it was incontrovertible. It seemed that a hoot owl had flown into the chicken house through the window and alighted on the long pole roost. He probably had been all set to start murdering chickens when I arrived on the scene. I have got to give myself credit—I made a clean sweep of the situation. Apparently all the chickens were back on the roost in line with the owl when I pulled the 8-gauge off. Except for a few fragments here and there, I had blown the lot of them through the back end of the coop. Dad was out of the chicken business.

"I ought to beat the holy old Mackinaw out of you," he raged, "and I would, too, except I think there's a law against whipping idiots. And anybody who can't tell twelve hens, two roosters, and a hoot owl from a cougar, sure as hell ain't very bright."

In the folklore of the American frontiers it is always the tenderfoot, not the old-timer, who suffers from buck fever. The pilgrim shakes himself loose from his hobnails and misses an easy shot and, boy, does he get kidded. The hired help hooraws the hide off him and the poor guy hangs his head and takes it, resolving to take vitamins or eat raw meat or something in the hope of developing foolproof nerves such as rugged professional outdoorsmen traditionally possess. But if there was any way to get at the truth, I would make a little book that every buckskin mountainman and timber-runner from Dan'l Boone to Kit Carson came down with buck ague on occasion, so completely he couldn't have hit a barn door with a handful of gravel.

Once, for example, I saw green-eyed, iron-maned old Tex Cobb, Alaska's senior working woodsman, tremble like an aspen leaf in a typhoon, and miss a shot he had waited years to get.

Tex and I were trapping in the Friday Creek country, east of Matanuska. One bitter day a month after freeze-up, when the ice was hooting and banging and a cluster of pale sundogs hung in the hard sky, we climbed a snowpeak and killed two fat mountain goats. We made the kills so late in the afternoon that it was impossible to sled the carcasses to the cabin. So we rolled them down the mountain and hung them in a gaunt hangman's cottonwood at timberline. While we were mushing home, kicking our siwash webs through the powder-dry snow in the multicolored flare of the aurora, a wolf howled on the ridge above us. Tex jerked around as if he had been struck. The vocalizing wolf was a personal enemy of his. You could recognize its howl as far as you could hear it because something was cracked in its throat—the result of getting into a snare Tex had set for it, and which the animal had somehow broken by lunging against it.

Tex hates all wolves, but he especially hated this one because it had consistently outsmarted and humiliated him. It had avoided so many traps, snares, deadfalls, and ambushes that I think he was becoming superstitious about it. He called the wolf Ol' Whitey, and usually appended a string of blistering adjectives ending with, "An' I'll git the bastard yet."

"Your friend's talking to you," I said.

"Yeah, but I'll talk last." Tex gritted. "Some day I'll git m' sights on that lousy, yodeling, slant-eyed— "

Early next morning we necked a pair of hand sleds up the snowshoe trail to get our goats. Dawn was breaking when we reached timberline. In case you haven't seen a winter sunrise in the far-northern mountains, there was a tall, eerie, spreading peacock trail of radiance above the southeastern peaks—silver and rose and saffron—which seemed to be giving a lot of light but actually wasn't. We rounded a clump of snow-hooded brush and there fifty yards ahead was the hangman's cottonwood—and Tex suddenly halted and crouched, motioning me to do likewise.

Over his shoulder I beheld a dramatic sight. Standing in a circle about the base of the tree, staring up at the two goat carcasses, were seven timber wolves. They must have been there for hours because you could see they had padded the snow to ice. One of the seven was Ol' Whitey. I had watched him at least a dozen times through glasses, but had never realized how large he was. He made the other six adult wolves look like pups. His coat really was slight gray, but in this tricky half-light he was white as a polar bear. A ghost wolf.

Tex whispered, "Now, damn yer hide, I gotcha."

He slipped the loop of the frozen babiche towline off his shoulder, yanked his right mitten off with his teeth, and thumbed the safety latch off his rifle. The rifle was a beautiful Waffenfabrik Mauser .30-06 with a long, thin, ribbed barrel, which Tex recently had fitted with a micrometer receiver rear sight. It was a good rifle and Tex could shoot it. In fact, Tex is one of the best shots on big game I have ever known. But this time hard luck overtook him.

Tex had the white wolf dead to rights, but strangely nothing happened. He lowered the rifle and raised it again. He shifted his position to the right, then to the left. He shrugged his shoulders as if his parka were too tight. Suddenly I saw that he was trembling. It was hard to believe, but there it was. He had it. Old Tex Cobb, the North's top hunter, was experiencing a monumental case of buck fever.

He braced himself visibly, shook his head like a fighter trying to throw off the effects of a blow, and tried a snap shot. The bullet smacked into the goat carcass, a foot above the wolf's head. Before he could chamber another cartridge, the wolves vanished like shadows into the snowy brush. Tex's alibi was a honey, and so pat that he must have used it before.

"What a miser'ble shot that was," he said in a burst of ersatz candor. Then he added, "Hit's this newfangled receiver sight. Jest as I was about to shoot, danged if a particle o' atmosphere didn't git stuck smack center in the hole."

In the interest of accurate reporting, I called upon a Johns Hopkins neurologist the other day and asked him to please explain buck fever in language that even I could understand. The learned medico, jettisoning polysyllabic Latin by a supreme effort, allowed that buck fever was akin to stage fright, mike fright, the trembling jitters a prize fighter gets when he steps into the ring, and the wonderful shaking fumbles a lad experiences when he first tries to swipe a kiss from his best girl. In short, it is compounded of anxiety, overeagerness, and fear of failure, abetted by too-enthusiastic functioning of the adrenal glands. The doc said it could happen to anybody regardless of experience, and that it couldn't be anticipated and there was no cure for it.

But I've got to disagree with that last. I once saw a truly majestic case of buck fever cured in two seconds flat. It was a pretty rough cure and I don't recommend it, but it worked.

This was in Sonora during a hunt I made with Pete Dunham, a likable blond, overweight broker from the Deep South. We were after dwarf Sonora white-tailed deer and we weren't doing so well. In the first place Pete wasn't built for riding cow ponies in upended country, and in the second place the dwarf whitetail is one of the smartest, most elusive animals that ever gave a guide a bad time. I don't claim he will actually get down on his belly through an arroyo to escape, or dive into a hole or anything like that, but he's got tricks just as effective.

You'll sit on your horse looking at a trophy buck maybe 100 yards distant, right out in the open, plain as a smokehouse on a raft. And then you'll ease your hand down to sneak your rifle out of the boot—and swish! he's gone. Like a magician's prop. Usually gone for keeps, too.

So on this particular molten, sun-stricken morning we set out from an abandoned ranch site known as Chupi Sonora, heading for a maze of brushy canyons said to be densely populated with dwarf whitetails. It turned out to be some expedition. The region was supposedly uninhabited, but before we'd covered a mile assorted characters began joining us. First a lean *vaquero* with a toothpaste-ad smile materialized on a hilltop and slid his horse down to us and latched on. Then two ancient, grizzled *mescaleros* who must have been around since the Alamo spurred out of a cactus thicket, inquired politely about our health and state of grace, and joined up.

Next we came to an open-faced thatched hut beside a creek where a middle-aged man and his wife and a neat, high-breasted brunette who looked like Dolores del Rio ten years ago were barbecuing a *borrego*—a castrated sheep—over a bed of black-walnut coals. Without hesitation the housewife shoved the sizzling *borrego* into a sack while her man and the girl saddled three sleepy-eyed broncs. Before you could roll a corn-husk cigaret they also were in the procession.

Pete couldn't speak any Spanish. "Listen, ask 'em what the hell they think this is—a picnic?" he said.

"I already asked," I said. "They think we're bandits going over the hill to liberate the next town."

They were nice people, generous, friendly, and kind if you met them halfway, like all the back-country relics of Montezuma's empire you find south of the border. They knew from the mountain grapevine that we were hunters, and since they themselves possess firearms, a chance to go hunting was an occasion, and in this case it was doubly fascinating because they had a couple of Yanquis to observe. We gave them a show. In fact, I'll bet they are still arguing about it, trying to decide exactly what happened.

The *vaquero*, whose name was Nacho, was the hero of the day. He helped us look for game, and he didn't need glasses. He had eyes like a condor.

"*Venado!*" he said suddenly, pointing down the slope. "*Venado toro!*"

It was a dwarf whitetail buck all right. He had a good head and he was about 300 yards distant and he had seen us. He was standing in a little open space surrounded by boulders and smoke brush, poised and motionless, ready to pull that famous disappearing act. Pete jacked a cartridge into his .270 while everybody froze and held his breath. Then Pete began to shake. He had a grade-A, blue ribbon case of it. It had hit him all of a sudden and I don't think he even knew what his trouble was. He was shaking so wonderfully that even the conchose on his chaps were dancing. I told him to sit down and try it that way, thinking it might help. I also told him that if he flubbed this shot the good-neighbor policy would be shattered so far as these people were concerned. I told him a lot of things. I was trying to talk him out of it. But I needn't have bothered.

Just as Pete sat down the buck took off. Instantly Pete leaped up, yelled, "*Yeee-owww!* and snapped the .270 to his shoulder. The yell halted the buck just long enough. Pete wasn't shaking now. And with the crash of the shot we heard the sharp smack of the open-point 130-grain slug smashing home. The buck went down and stayed down. It was a performance to make you toss up your hat and cheer. As could be expected, our Mexican friends were deeply impressed. They stood there with their mouths open, giving Pete the admiration treatment. The chesty del Rio babe murmured, "*Que hombre!*"

I said, "Yelling at the buck to stop him was a real smart deal, brother."

"Whaddya mean 'yelling at the buck'?" Pete groaned. "For crisakes, I sat on a cactus."

Well, as I was saying some pages ago, there we were in Two-Squaw Riley's cabin on the Yukon Flats and Two-Squaw was holding forth on the subject of buck fever, which started all this. So I think Two-Squaw ought to have the last word. As he measured rum, sugar, butter, and cinnamon into the glasses for another round, he said, "I'll tell ya men, ya jest recall the things ya most wanted to do, an' were scared maybe you couldn't but finally did—an' I don't care whether it was killing a grizzly, sellin' a pretty gal an idea, or beatin' the ears off a guy who was good with his hands—if ya claim ya didn't get any buck-fever shakes at the start, then I say ya wasn't int'rested enough to have any real fun when ya got there."

Trophy Hunt in *Mañana* Land

We were after onca *— rarest cat of them all.*
But we wound up with a wild croc on the end of a rope.

"Relax Horse," I said to Blue as we came ashore on the sand bar in the middle of the gray-green river. "That thing over there is just a dead crocodile. Nothing at all to get snorty about."

Blue snorted emphatically, flattening his ears.

This was in Nayarit. The river was the jungle-fringed Santiago, and I was hunting with Tom and Don Dionicio. Several minutes ago we had spotted the croc here on the sand bar, looking like something from a "Lost World" set. Tom, using a telescope sight, put a .270 slug through its head, and I swam Blue out to get the carcass. For Blue this should have been old stuff. The big roan was a veteran of many a crocodile hunt. But, surprisingly, the moment he saw the kill, he spooked. He rolled an eye at me, and under the wet saddle I could feel the quivering gun-spring tautness of his muscles. Poised to take off like an antelope, he was telling me that the seven-foot croc was bad medicine, and that caution was in order.

I should have heeded him, because Blue is a smart horse, maybe the smartest, toughest, and most companionable horse I have ever ridden. But I was in a hurry.

It was getting late. Already the November sun was trying to spear itself on a peak, and Don Dionicio's Golden Skull Ranch headquarters, where we intended to spend the night, was ten miles distant. Riding through heavy riverfront jungle after dark is an aging experience. Ten miles of it would, I'll bet, give even a Cora

Indian the creeps. So, ignoring Blue's objections, I spurred him up the bar. The croc lay draped across a drift log. I pitched a loop over it, behind the forelegs, and reined back into the river. I was feeling pretty good. I told myself that we rated merit badges for this kill, not only because the croc had an evil reputation, but because its hide would make a swell trophy.

At which point, abruptly, the situation curdled.

Tom and Don Dionicio, over yonder on the palm-plumed bank, appeared to have suffered a mysterious seizure. Waving their arms and pointing, they were shouting something about the croc. I looked back but didn't see anything unusual. Just sun-gilded water, wind ripples, and odds and ends of drift. Then—a thing to make your pulse stutter—the rawhide *riata* yanked powerfully against my leg, and I swiveled around again in time to see an armored tail lift up and bang the water. Staring bug-eyed at the spot, I managed to accept the ghastly fact that our "dead" croc hadn't been so doggoned dead after all. As I was to learn, it had surfaced a moment earlier, and Tom and Don Dionicio had been trying to warn me that it was still alive. Blue strained toward the shore. He was plenty spooked now, and believe me, so was I. A wounded Mexican crocodile can be a nasty customer. If this one attacked, out here in deep water, it was bound to be a rough show, with the odds anyhow five-to-one in the croc's favor.

"Turn him loose," Tom yelled.

"No! Keep him fighting the *riata*," Don Dionicio bellowed.

I had a .45 in a shoulder holster. I got it out and waited, wondering why the croc hadn't bitten the *riata* in two. "Horse," I said to Blue in a voice that sounded strange to me, "it's been wonderful knowing you."

Here I've got to splice in some background. With Don Dionicio's aid, which included the use of horses and gear, Tom and I were building ourselves a hunting lodge on the giant Golden Skull, at a beautiful spot where the Laguna Santiago thrusts a green arm back against the shaggy upsweep of the Sierra Nayarit. Tom is a retired cotton buyer who chews cigars and argues that the whole trouble with modern man is that he doesn't spend enough time hunting and fishing. As we planned to have our lodge-warming party in December, our efforts had been divided the past couple of weeks between construction and the exciting business of collecting some trophies for decoration purposes. By now we were beat out and saddle-stiff, and short on sleep, but matters had progressed famously. I mean, luck had given us a great big neon smile.

It began with the temple-blossoms buck, fifteen days ago.

We were riding to the ranch to pick up the Ramirez family, whom we had engaged to help out at the lodge, when we cut the buck's sign. His tracks, the largest we had seen this autumn, led toward a brushy hillside scar that had been a cornfield before the soil played out. Tom got down for a careful look, following the trail until he lost it on hard ground. When he returned there was a glitter in his eye, and he was chewing his cigar with unwonted enthusiasm. You never have to ask Tom what his sentiments are. You can tell by the angle of the cigar and the energy he devotes to mangling it. Currently he was all steamed up.

"We jumped him," he said. "But he won't go far. He's still around here. If we take a stand on that hilltop early tomorrow morning—"

So the Ramirez family, packed and ready to go, had to wait. Rising next morning while the ranch roosters were still prophesying another day, we rode to the hilltop stand and sat down to sweat out the buck. Or rather, I sweated him out. This kind of hunting never was my long suit. I haven't got the patience. Time drags. A flight of emerald parrots circled to look us over. Somewhere a guaco hawk was laughing itself silly over a private joke. Down at the bottom of the hill, against the gaudy backdrop of temple blossoms, some pale-blue, four-inch butterflies were doing an aerial dance. All very peaceful and Paul Gauguin, but I wished to hell the buck would show up if he was going to. Tom just sat there with his rifle across his knees, looking contented. Tom could outwait an Indian. In fact, it wouldn't surprise me to learn that he is part Indian. Piute maybe. He hunts like one. Which, in a way, is a compliment.

Three hours passed. The sun had climbed into a polished turquoise sky and it was getting hot. Then, with no warning, Blue busted things wide open. *Whaaa-huh!* he bawled. Following this, there was a rattling crash as he pulled over the dead huinole sapling to which he was tied. Whatever he had seen or winded, he had communicated his fright to Tom's horse. They both looked ready to stampede. Tom stood up, registering disgust.

"Some fun," he growled. "If there was a deer within a mile of here, it's gone now."

He started to add to the statement, but the words got lost. Because, as the old-timers used to say, events were transpiring.

Mind you, we had sat here all this time, mouse-quiet, taking the brush-grown clearing apart foot by foot, without seeing a flicker of animal life. Not even a rabbit. Not even a bumbling bug-hunting armadillo. But now, thanks to the uproar Blue had created, the place had begun to jump.

"Wh-what's that thing?" he stuttered as a cat streaked out of the center of the clearing, heading for the jungle.

Fast as the shadow of a swooping bird, the cat was reddish-brown, stocky, weighing maybe sixty pounds, with a long white-tasseled tail. As I tried to find it in the scope of my .30-30, I thought, "It's an *onca*—it couldn't be anything but an *onca*," and was thrilled clear through because in this country the *onca*, a subspecies of jaguar, is the trophy of trophies. I didn't get a shot. The cat was too clever at keeping brush between itself and us. With a scattergun I think I could have scored, but with the .30-30 I didn't have a prayer. Not looking back once, the cat flashed into the green shadows at the jungle rim, and was gone. Meanwhile, Tom had opened up. Turning, I saw the buck highballing out of the other side of the clearing. Tom missed twice, overshooting, but his third shot caught the buck at the top of a soaring bound. Shoulder-hit, it came down hard on its knees and head, turned a half-cartwheel, and crashed into the pink-and-white cascade of temple flowers.

"An *onca*," I said, answering Tom's question.

We went over and untangled Blue from the sapling. As nearly as we could second-guess from the rapid-action drama that had taken place, the *onca* had been stalking the buck, which must have been bedded down out of our sight, when Blue winded it. You couldn't blame the roan for sounding the alarm. *Oncas* eat horses. They have eaten men, too.

"If this cayuse had some training," Tom declared, slapping Blue's rump either in forgiveness or apology, "he'd be a number one hunting horse. He's got brains. Stays wide awake like a third baseman."

As if I didn't know it. I had been trying for a month to buy him from Don Dionicio. Each time I brought up the subject, however, Don Dionicio stalled. He claimed he thought he had promised the horse to a timber scout in San Blas, or anyhow to somebody. His memory was getting bad, he said. Maybe he was kidding and maybe he wasn't. With Don Dionicio it is hard to tell. We dressed the buck, stuck some temple flowers in our hatbands, and rode back in the noonday heat to the ranch house.

Don Dionicio was sitting on the gallery with a pitcher of lemonade and was wearing a glum expression. If you were a Wallace Beery fan, you know what the guy looks like and how he talks. He shouted through a window for extra glasses, and got busy telling us his troubles. He was losing stock. He suspected a *tigre* was responsible, but the buzzards hadn't revealed the presence of any carcasses, which was baffling. This morning the payoff had occurred. His foreman had reported a prized yearling Brahman bull missing. So it was time to do something. But the question was, what? We told him about seeing the *onca*, and he thought it over.

"He might be the guilty one," he admitted. "But if there were carcasses, what is wrong with the buzzards?"

Unable to answer that, we helped him drink the lemonade. Presently he reached a decision.

"All right," he said. "I will send my daughter Carmen to borrow dogs from my uncle. She knows how to work them. Kill me this *onca cabrone*, please, and we will see what is in his stomach."

Next morning when we went down to the kitchen to forage breakfast, Carmen was there ahead of us broiling venison steaks. Carmen is special. Eighteen, nice but potentially explosive, she is a ranch brat who rides like a Comanche and who, somehow, has escaped the iron duenna custom of the country. After eating, we made the acquaintance of the dogs. There were two of them. They were old and sad-eyed, probably mixed Walker and blue tick, and after one look you knew where they would have won fame—in J. R. Williams' *Out Our Way*. But they bore cat scars, which gave them prestige with us. We rode into a prairie-fire sunrise and, at the old clearing, showed the dogs where the *onca* had vanished into the jungle. Tom assured us cheerfully that it wouldn't be long now. What a dreamer he was. Either yesterday's sun had largely destroyed the cat's scent, or the dogs were loaded with the true *mañana* spirit.

They cast this way and that, they held conferences, they pondered. They took turns experting the project. In four hours we covered less than three miles. I decided that our *onca* hunt was a bust and was deeply disappointed because, of the known species of cat here on the west coast, the *onca* is by all odds the rarest.

We spent two more days with the dogs, still hoping to come up with the *onca*. But no *onca*. No nothing. On the morning of the third day we informed the Ramirez family that we were ready, at long last, to transport them to the lodge. This proved to be a colorful undertaking. The family consisted of three adults and four children, and they had a large assortment of baggage, which included two crates of chickens, a caged parrot, and a six-foot boa constrictor named Pancho. The boa, we were told, was harmless, a household pet who earned his keep catching rats and mice. He didn't look so harmless to me. At the moment he was being coiled into a wicker pack-pannier. Don Antionio, the head of the Ramirez clan, had a Strangler Lewis grip on his neck, while his son Arturo took care of the coiling-in job. The snake didn't like it. When they closed the lid on him, he struck it with his snout, hissing like a popvalve letting go.

"I got a feeling," Tom said thoughtfully, "that nightmare and I are never going to be buddy-buddy."

By midmorning we had the fourteen-horse string lined out for the lodge. Partway there, Don Antionio spurred alongside me. Don Antionio is a blue-eyed Mexican with a white beard. A character. To give you an idea, local gossip had it that when his mango trees didn't bear to suit him, he beat them with a club.

A week later, when we returned to the ranch for supplies, Don Dionicio had intelligence for us. The stock-killer, he said, wasn't a *tigre* or an *onca*, but a crocodile. One of his *vaqueros* had found the spot where it had killed the Brahman yearling. In this area many wide dry washes run down from the grasslands to the river, and the cattle like to gather in them, to feed along the rims and to stomp flies. They have favorite watering holes at the river, and apparently the croc had been hanging around them, picking off a calf or yearling whenever it got the chance. Since a croc always drags a kill underwater, storing it there until it becomes ripe, there had been no carcasses lying about to attract buzzards. Thus a mystery was solved.

Don Dionicio told us, further, that the croc had been spotted, and that it was a big one, one of the few big ones hereabouts that had survived the war waged against the species by stockmen and hide hunters. The best way to kill it, he opined, would be to catch it basking on a sand bar in the river. That was where Tom came in with his .270 and its telescope sight.

"Tomorrow, if you are willing to help," Don Dionicio said, "I would like to start hunting for this crocodile, and keep hunting until we find and kill him.

It took three days. As I said at outset, when we sighted the croc it was taking its ease on a sand island. Tom shot it, and now here

Blue and I were out in deep water with the wounded saurian struggling at the end of a forty-foot *riata*. Not knowing what else to do, I began blasting .45 slugs into the water between us and the croc. Anything to keep it from closing in and coming up under us. Blue touched bottom, got into swimming water again, then found a submerged bar and lunged for the shore. The croc was throwing itself end over end, lashing at the *riata* with its tail. Then Tom's .270 crashed again, and the matter was finished.

When we got a look at the dead stock-killer, it was clear why it hadn't bitten the *riata* in two. Its biting equipment was out of order. Tom's first shot had hit its upper jaw, shattering it and, obviously, knocking the croc temporarily cold. Maybe the water revived it. Or maybe it just naturally recovered consciousness in time to protest against being towed ashore. Anybody's guess is as good as mine.

Don Dionicio ran a hand along the big roan's neck. He had been meaning to tell us, he said, deadpan, that his memory was improving. For instance, just now he had remembered that they had not, after all, promised Blue to the San Blas timber scout. It must have been me, he said, who he had in mind. So naturally, if I still wanted the horse, he was mine as of this moment, provided we came across with an invitation to our lodge-warming party in December.

Louise Lopina ©96

Grudge Grizzly

"In case you're interested, this prospecting trip has turned into a bear hunt. No jug-headed, peanut-rumped, shanty-backed grizzly can claw up my horse an' get away with it!"

My introduction to this mountain drama was a spray of earth being thrown out from behind a boulder fifty feet above us. Something was digging there. Obviously a bear—you didn't have to be an Alaska Daniel Boone to know that. Jack Filce, my current partner, sidestepped fast, checking the chamber loading of the .40-82 he insisted on carrying. The rifle was so old there wasn't a speck of bluing on the octagon barrel, and to get ammunition he had to write wheedling letters to gun editors, gun collectors and rifle clubs all over the country. But for its purpose, in its day, I guess, it was a heck of a gun. It made noise enough, anyway. I got clear of the .40-82's probable muzzle-blast path just as the bear swaggered into view and stood up.

It is a fact, dismaying to magazine illustrators, that a grizzly or brown bear does not look big when it is on all four feet. The reason is that bears are short-legged, and we humans are accustomed to looking at cattle and horses who really have altitude when on all fours. But, gentlemen, this I will declare, when a mountain grizzly stands on his hind feet, above you on a forty-five-degree slope, he looks tall. He looks tall and big. Also formidable. This particular bruin actually was no giant of his species. I would give him 700 pounds. But he was in autumn pelage, so that his wind-rippled, silver-yellow hair made him appear broader than he was, and the slope distance gave him the illusion of being as tall as a telephone pole.

We didn't want any trouble with him. Jack and I had come into the Wood River country to spend the summer prospecting. I had figured it might be profitable because Jack was lucky. He and Lymer Cox were among the first white men on the Yukon, and had made some fine strikes, the Stewart River, diggings included. This afternoon we had spotted a likely looking dike crossing a mountain slope and had climbed up to gather some float and maybe take a pan or two. Now here we were face to face with a grizzly who didn't appear to be at all friendly. He was a long-snouted cuss, with dirt all over his face and chest, and as he stood regarding us, weaving to keep his balance, he kept making little come-on gestures with his paws. He had been doing a lot of digging for Indian potatoes and such because his claws were blunt, but they were still a good three inches long and looked as dangerous as chisels.

"G'wan, beat it," Jack said to him: "You ain't gonna prove anything except that a dead grizzly is plenty dead."

I don't know what was the matter with that bear—there aren't any good books on bear psychology, none that I ever read anyhow. He should have beat it. He should have flagged his hump over the nearest ridge and taken out his grudge on a black bear, or maybe a caribou. Instead, here he came. In such moments you don't really remember doing anything. At least I don't. I heard the awe-inspiring boom of the .40-82, and took a snap shot at the grizzly's neck with my .270. I saw hair, meat and blood spurt out like a gunk from a hose. Then the bear veered off to the right like a bobsled rounding a bend and jumped over a willow-fringed bank. I heard him hit the brush below the bank. But I didn't dash up to see how he was getting along. Not me. I have lived among grizzlies for thirty-odd years, I am still alive and in one piece, and whatever this particular grizzly was doing at the moment was, so far as I was concerned, strictly his own business. For all I cared, he could be growing a beard, having a baby or writing a letter to his congressman.

Jack felt the same way about it. "You suppose we kilt him?" he asked. "If you're so curious, go on over and take a look," I said. "I will do that," he replied with dignity, "as soon as I've had a smoke."

Well, it wouldn't have done any good anyhow. The slope below us was studded with house-sized boulders and was covered with alders thick as quills on a porcupine's back. We found where the bear had landed on his feet and made a twenty-foot bound downhill. There was some blood on the brush which I figured had come from his neck or head. But he wasn't a dying bear. I mean, he was on his feet and traveling, and plenty dangerous because he was hurt and in thick country which he probably had known intimately since he was a cub nuzzling his mother's teats. The odds of sorting him out of that mess of brush and rocks without getting smacked down were anyway twenty to one. I didn't want a grizzly pelt that bad. Neither did Jack. And, remember, we hadn't started the trouble.

Jack had with him on this trip a venerable piebald mare named Maud. I do not know how old Maud may have been, but she was crowding the maximum age that horses attain. She had been with Jack so long that she no longer regarded herself as a beast of burden, but as a full-fledged member of any expedition in which she took part, vested with authority and full of privileges. Jack nightly went through the motions of hobbling Maud—that is, he would knot a bandanna around her fetlocks, give her detailed advice as to where the best forage was to be found, warn her against getting into bogs and threaten ferociously to beat the living whey out of her if she strayed during the night. Maud would bare her teeth at him and head for the most barren piece of wild pasture in sight. It was a routine. All the old-timers knew it by heart. Maud could have gotten a membership in the Sourdoughs Club any time simply by pawing at the door.

Tonight she didn't do so well.

Maybe there is such a thing as premonition. Anyhow, I couldn't sleep. It was a night of brilliant moonlight, and I was lying there watching swaying branch-shadows of the tent roof when I heard Maud let out a bellow as if mortally stricken. Which, it turned out, she almost was. Jack and I caromed through the tent flaps neck and neck, both of us barefoot and making painful progress over the flinty talus on which we were camped. Out yonder in the green glimmer of a meadow I could see Maud. She was down. Beyond her a shaggy shadow bounded toward the timber, paused once to look back, and vanished silently. It was a bear. A grizzly. In the morning we found his tracks, also the bloody half-scab of a wound torn off on a bush. But meanwhile we had the problem of patching up Maud, keeping her in the land of the living. She was a surgery case. Surgery case! We could have used the services of the Veterinary Corps. The bear had swiped her across the neck, knocking her down, and then had taken a sizable bite out of her paunch. The pink guts were bulging out.

"Gawdamighty," Jack said, "stick them tripes back in an' hold her down whilst I get a buckskin needle an' some sinew. Sit on her head, dammit. If she stands up, everything'll fall out."

I sat on Maud's head while she groaned and bled and tried to bite me, and Jack got his equipment and did a fairly neat job of suturing, all things considered. In the morning Maud wasn't feeling so pert, but she was alive, which was more than I had expected. Jack finished his breakfast and got busy oiling up the .40-82. "In case you're interested," he informed me, "this here prospecting trip has temporarily turned into a bear hunt. On account of I am gonna kill that damn grizzly if I have to foller him to Yesler Way, Seattle. No jug-headed, shanty-backed, peanut-rumped, long haired, would-be-tough grizzly can claw up my horse an' get away with it. I been in the country too long."

Prospectors are not, of course, ordinarily classed as sportsmen. But they develop a priceless feeling for terrain. Jack could just about read the wounded grizzly's mind. He knew that the animal, bad hurt and feverish, would want to lie in cold, mucky ground, downwind from camp and above it, with brush between him and us. Also that he would by this time be stiffened up plenty and wouldn't travel far. After explaining this, he spent close to an hour looking the slopes over with his glasses. Finally he gave a grunt of satisfaction and pointed with gnarled forefinger. Half a mile upstream a small creek, snowfed, plunged down from the lip of a hanging valley. It passed through a dense stand of second-growth birches and willows, then wound through a small triangular flat before it entered the river. At the upper end of the flat was a slanting fire-killed spruce snag. In the snag sat a raven.

"Maybe it's a caribou, or maybe it's another bear," Jack said. "But there's something about making a professional stalk. I had been guiding for a number of years, and meat hunting and trapping for a lot more. I figured that when the going got technical, I was entitled to sit up in the front row with almost anybody. But I learned a few items from old Jack. Anybody would have. We mushed half a mile downstream to fool the raven, then went up a draw and out across a high swell of tundra that sloped toward the creek bed in which our grizzly was supposed to be cooling his injuries. Shoving the battered .40-82 ahead of him, wriggling along on his knees and elbows, his worn caribou shirt almost the same color as the turf, Jack was an authentic part of the scenery. We actually crawled right up on a red fox cub sunning itself against a boulder. The big-eared youngster was so startled that it fell over trying to make up its mind which way to run. But of course the raven was the key to the situation. It was still with us, but in another snag.

Probably as old as Jack, and plenty smart or it wouldn't still be around, the bird inevitably spotted us when we came over the break of the tundra hill. It turned on its perch, cocking its head this way and that, adding up the situation. I knew doggoned well that when the bird spooked the bear would too, assuming the bear actually was there. Presently it did spook. Having concluded that we weren't peaceful, it took off on whooshing wings, and uttered a mellow bell-like *bonk, bonk* as it banked overhead. We were about 150 yards from the head of the creek flat, with a reasonably clear lane of fire. Jack stood up and snicked back the hammer of his rifle. As he did so, there was movement between a big boulder and clump of frosted willows. A bear stepped into view, head up, snuffling the wind. *Blowie!* went the .40-82. I hadn't had a chance. I was waiting for a target. Old Jack had simply cut loose, or else his sighting reflexes were a lot faster than mine.

He scored, but I don't know how he could take credit for it, and I hope that's not sour grapes.

With a smack like a double-jack hitting a drill, the heavy soft bullet struck the aforementioned rock and made a beautiful one-cushion billiard into the bear's chest cavity just behind the right shoulder. I mention this clinical detail because I saw hair fly and that was where the wound was when we clambered down the hill and found the bear lying dead. I doubt that the animal had taken a step after being hit. The old-fashioned lead had spread so extravagantly upon hitting that rock that it had practically torn the heart out of the grizzly. A pompom projectile wouldn't have done more damage. Jack blew the smoke out of his rifle barrel, an act that always seems to give the old-timers great satisfaction, shoved in a new round and reached for his pipe.

"Big devil would claw up a pore defenseless horse, huh? Thought he was jest too dang tough fer words, did he?" By this time he had his pipe stuffed with something called Master Workman, and was scratching a sulphur match to light it. Suddenly he soliloquy broke off on a sour note. He stared at the dead grizzly, let the match burn his fingers, and began cussing bitterly. "We been double-crossed," he almost hollered. "That there bear aint' the same bear. He ain't got a mark on him, except the one I jest put there. Take a look for yourself."

It was a fact. Our grizzly was a prime specimen, an admirable trophy bear, one that any sportsman would have been proud of. But he wasn't the culprit we had been seeking. All innocently, he had paid for the sin of a tribal relative. We took off the pelt, doing a good job of it. I mean, we even skinned out the claws and opened up the lips so they could be used for a head mount. The raven came back and watched us. He was no dope. He knew now that we weren't collecting ravens, and the meat we would leave behind would fatten him for a whole hard winter of cold and snow. Jack didn't have much to say, and I didn't comment. After all, it was his horse that had got worked over. But finally the old chap filled his pipe again and delivered himself of an opinion.

"I allus did wanta try to be a sportsman," he said, "ever since one time over at Aishak Lake when I seen a Limey duke wearing a red-checkered vest an' choke-bore pants, an' carrying a gun that musta cost him anyhow five ounces of dust. So now, by gosh, we're sportsmen, even if we ain't got the gear that goes with it."

I gathered, I said, he meant we were still after the grizzly who had tried to chew out Maud's gizzard. He allowed that I was quite correct. The project could take years, he said. But what was time? Besides, he said, he might even get fond of being a sportsman. You couldn't tell. Everybody had some secret little ambition. He had once, on the upper Yukon, he said, known a successful bank teller named Bob Service who actually wanted to be a poet, the poor guy.

We found Maud still down and looking mighty poorly. Jack carried some water to her, examined her wounds and told her she was good for anyhow another ten years on the trail. He thought she needed an enema but be doggoned if he could figure out what to use for equipment. Which was maybe just as well. Later we lashed the grizzly pelt in a frame and put it in the sun to dry, because we had only a few pounds of salt with us, just enough for ourselves and Maud. In the morning we made a big hunt for the wounded grizzly that got us nothing. Jack tried everything he could think of, and so did I. We didn't find a track, a drop of blood, or a scab-encrusted hair. Nothing. We figured the bear had stiffened up plenty and was hiding out where even the birds hadn't found him. But I had a hunch about the animal, a good honest hunch, and it paid off. I hereby take credit for it.

Upon occasion I have heard learned persons discourse formally and informally on the subject of hunches. The consensus seems to be that a guy sees more than he thinks he sees, knows more than he realizes he knows. When all of his senses and buried knowledge get together and crystallize—*wham!*—just like that, he has a hunch that tells him what is going to happen. So I had a hunch about the wounded grizzly. It came to me while we were trying to rig some mosquito netting to keep the flies off Maud's injuries. The bear had tried once to kill her. He had smelled her sweat on us up there at the mineralized dike—when we shot him—he blamed her equally for his troubles, and was less afraid of her than of us because she didn't carry a gun.

So he would come back and try again. To believe that, you had to believe that he was a killer bear. But then, he had charged us without provocation, and the same night had tried for Maud, which made it not so hard to believe. There have been plenty of killer bears in the North, more than ever got themselves publicized. You could ask the few remaining old-timers, only they probably wouldn't talk. Anyway, I was as sure that the bear would try to finish off Maud as I was that the sun would come up tomorrow morning. So I cut the few clumps of brush between her and the tent. I drank a couple of quarts of high-powered coffee so I wouldn't sleep. I took the .270 apart and cleaned it, and went to bed with my clothes on.

"Expecting company?" Jack asked. "Just trying to make like a sportsman," I said. "They take their boots off when they go to bed," he said, "I think."

We didn't need anybody to stand watch. We had Maud. It was a cinch she wasn't going to get any sleep, and also it was a cinch that no bear was going to come anywhere near without her letting us know about it. The moon came up, sailing through a pretty cloud-flecked sky, and the spruce shadows reached across the clearing and began to shorten. Jack was snoring. At this point Maud gave a scream that should have been recorded on tape. Hollywood could have used it. All I had to do was roll over and put my hands on the cold breech of the .270. I didn't make any other move. None was necessary. I had that moon-flooded delta pan under the muzzle, just right. Maud was trying to get to her feet, still pleading for help. I was hoping that Jack's buckskin-needle hem stitching would hold, when I saw the bear. He played it cute. He stayed in the timber as long as he could, then followed the dark finger of a spruce shadow until he was ready to start his rush.

I caught him at the top of his first jump, and heard the 180-grain bullet break bone. He landed on his chin, bawling, came around fast as a big cat, and charged the tent. Maybe he was so hard hit he didn't know where he was going. I'll give him the benefit of the doubt. A .270 bullet is fairly small, but if you have a little luck, if it hits right, if flying bone fragments help a bit, it's a thing that will discourage and confuse the toughest that exist. Thus perhaps the bear wasn't actually charging the tent. But the effect was the same. Here he came, stumbling and wobbling some, trying to roar but not having much luck due to a wind shortage, straight at us. In the moonlight, the way I was set up, I could have hit him with my hat. But I knew I had only one shot coming, and I urgently wanted it to stop him before he landed on my prone carcass. So I waited. I figured to break his neck, or try to, and then beat it due south out of the tent door, where maybe I would be able to spend some time cussing the unfortunate slowness of the Mauser's bolt action and the variants thereof.

Something cold and heavy slid across my shoulder, and an instant later what seemed the biggest noise since the top blew off Vesuvius exploded in my right ear. Jack was in action. Having grasped the situation immediately, the varmint had brass-bound nerve to use me for a rifle rest. He didn't stop shooting. Unhampered by a bold action, he just kept blasting rounds through the .40-82 while I lay there and took it. The bear didn't have a prayer. I won't say that the hail of fire skidded him backward, as Jack later claimed, but I will take oath that he lost momentum very suddenly. He didn't need four-wheel brakes. He didn't need anything. When he hit the ground he was as dead as any bear this far north.

Jack was shouting something at me but I couldn't hear him. I figured my eardrums were ruined from here on in. "Should of woke me up, dammit," he yelled in my face. Then, "What'sa trouble? You gone deaf or something?"

We got Maud on her feet a week later, and when she was able to take on a little nourishment, we headed back over the passes. Jack and I carried the outfit, of course. All Maud carried was the two grizzly hides, and that was because Jack had lashed them around her to keep off flies and gnats. At the top of Cody Pass we met a party of eastern sportsmen we'd encountered fifteen days or so earlier. By this time they had whiskers and dirty shirts and were squinting at the peaks with that five-mile professional look that Stewart Granger tries for and almost achieves. They'd taken some fair Dall sheep, a couple of caribou and a wondered-antlered old bull moose who must have been lost, to have been caught in these peaks. They didn't have any bear pelts. All of them, including the head guide, whom I irrationally did not respect too much because I could remember when he had been a saxophone player down at salt water, rallied round Maud to look.

This was when Jack got his accolade. Probably he has never recovered from it. "You know, I'll make a confession," said the biggest and whiskeriest gent of the party. He had the dirtiest shirt and therefore must have been paying for the hunt. "When we met you chaps before, I thought Rusty was just knocking around in the hills with some old prospector. Never had any idea, Mr. Filce, that you were an ace grizzly hunter." I stepped on the guide's toe and that shut him up, so I guess Jack still rates as a very sporting trophy hunter, in some quarters anyhow.

The last I saw of Maud, she was doing all right. As for the bear, I believe that he was a veritable killer. My first shot at him on the mountainside had taken a divot out of his skull, and I think he was just plain nuts, in agony and out to kill. But he started it, and he sure got what he asked for. I mean, Maud wore his hide home.

Big Luck at Cuyutlan

We tangled with a surf full of sharks, a wild marlin nicknamed "The Acrobat," and a sawfish that would have scared Dracula to death. I tell you it was quite a stay.

"Craziest thing I ever saw," Tom declared one copper-rose morning as we were baiting up to begin another day of surf fishing. "These people must be tired of living, by gosh!"

With our "teenage factotum" Juanito, we were on the black volcanic beach of Cuyutlan, Colima, the west coast of Mexico. This was during Holy week, one of the few seasons when the place isn't a ghost camp. There were anyhow 100 bathers in the water, men, women and children, all Mexicans. Just beyond them, at the edge of the high-breaking combers, some thresher sharks and a couple of huge white sharks were systematically cutting a school of sardines to pieces. As usual the threshers put on an exciting show. Their technique was to plow at high speed through the school, at the surface, hammering the water with the scythelike upper lobes of their tails. Then they would return to pick up the sardines they had killed or stunned, and make another foray. The bathers saw the sharks but were not visibly alarmed. It gave me the cold creeps. It was the raw stuff for a Charles Addams masterpiece.

"But nobody has been eaten here yet," Juanito told us, shrugging. "Not right here, that is."

We waded out and began casting into a rising wind. After a score of fruitless tries, Tom at last got the distance he wanted, and plunked his mullet squarely in front of a trailing thresher. Without hesitation the shark clamped his jaws onto the bait, and Tom socked the hook into him. He was a good shark, around eight feet.

He sounded, came up in a fast, slanting lunge that knocked the top off a wave, and headed north, paralleling the shore. At this point Mauricio, manager of the charmingly beat-up Hotel Guadalajara, our home away from home, came down the beach carrying the establishment's one sunshade umbrella, an outsized candy-striped number with tassels. Sticking it upright in the sand, he joined us to watch Tom battle the thresher. Mauricio is a wiry, mahogany-faced gent, crowding sixty, who likes Americans, hates shoes, and specializes in deadpan humor. Also he is smart. I have never seen him in swimming.

Tom was horsing the shark, digging his heels into the sand and pumping line for all he was worth, when two other threshers shot in with cannibalistic intent. One leaped full length out of the water to tail-sledge the hooked shark, while the other savaged a chunk out of the luckless brute's back. That ended the fight. To the manifest disappointment of the two cannibals, who continued to chop and slash until the water got too shallow for them, Tom brought the wounded shark in, skidding it on the crest of a white-maned breaker. As it lay banging its jaws and pounding the sand with its grotesque tail, I clobbered it over the head with a length of driftwood. It subsided, and prying its mouth open, I reached tentatively for the hookshank with a pair of pliers. While I was thus occupied, an especially hard gust of wind whistled along the beach. Juanito touched Mauricio's arm, pointing.

"Your umbrella, *Señor*," he said, "is leaving."

No question about it, it really was. It had blown over and was now coming toward us over the sand, bouncing and rolling, gathering speed at a great rate. Tom, Juanito and Mauricio sprinted to intercept it, but only Tom scored. By dint of fast footwork and good timing, he got a two-handed hold on the wooden staff of the thing, and went tearing down the beach with it in ten-foot bounds, hollering, "Powder River," at us over his shoulder. He was having fun, I guess, but it didn't last long. Ahead, at the base of the dune, was the storm-cut *arroyo* that serves as the hotel's garbage dump. In it, prowling hopefully among rotting green coconut shells, bottles, bones, the sun-dried carapaces of turtles and other debris, were some dogs, a couple of red pigs and a flock of buzzards. Tom, unable to see past the umbrella, sailed grandly over the rim to crash-land in the midst of the scavengers. When we arrived, he was chuckling merrily to himself as he scraped part of a spoiled banana off the side of his head.

"I don't know why you do such things," Mauricio complained, panting as if he had used up all the oxygen in Cuyutlan. "We try to take good care of our guests, and then you decide you are in an airplane, and dive headfirst into the garbage. Suppose you had broken your neck?"

"You people just don't understand the thrill of living dangerously," Tom said, gazing over the *arroyo* rim to where shark fins knifed the peacock water within fifty feet of the unconcerned bathers. "Me, I'm a reckless, umbrella-rassling, son-of-a-gun of a Yankee fisherman," he stuck out his chest, "too doggoned fearless for my own good."

Tom and I have spent almost a year fishing at Cuyutlan. Tom is a retired cotton buyer. He chews cigars, is lean and tough as a winter shitepoke, and has discovered a talent for screwball adventures. Until his retirement, he informs me, he carried responsibility from the day he was old enough to work. Now, footloose and carefree, with all the fish and game in Mexico to work on, he is like a lad in a toy shop. I mean, he has a lot of accumulated steam to blow off. Cuyutlan could have been created for the purpose.

Admirable fishing companions they are, Tom, Juanito and Mauricio, but lousy weather prophets, rating no prizes and not to be trusted. We had been hearing good reports about the night spearfishing at Armeria Lagoon, five miles south, and one afternoon Tom suggested that we walk down there and try our luck. I asked Mauricio if he thought it would rain. Thunder had boomed over the jungled sierra since morning, and the horizon was ringed with murk and tall cumulus clouds. Mauricio shook his head. There wasn't a chance of rain, he said. The rainy season wouldn't start for at least a month. Tom, in a voice of authority, said his corns didn't hurt, so absolutely it wasn't going to rain. Juanito put in his two-bits' worth. The pelicans, he said, always flew to inland waters before a storm, and look where they were now, diving for mullet in front of the hotel. No rain, *Señores.*

So the three of us slogged down the beach to Armeria Lagoon. Mauricio didn't go. The hotel's plumbing system was haywire again, he said. Besides, his rheumatism was bothering him.

At the Rancho of the Parrots, with whose owner we had fished several times, we borrowed a skiff, a gasoline lantern equipped with a reflector and a spear. The sun went down, a fiery six-sided crystal—it often assumes this startling shape before dropping behind the sea horizon when a storm is due in these latitudes—and instantly the light left the sky, as if a master switch had been pulled. With Juanito at the oars and Tom up front with the spear, we fared forth onto the black tidal lagoon, adventure bound. Schools of pargo and mojarras flashed through the clear, shallow water, seemingly flying. A ray scuttled out of the light. Once a shark surfaced beyond spear range, his eyes shining like a cat's. On the shore, among witched-tangled mangroves, birds made eerie sounds, and nations of tree frogs were practicing choral croaking. It was mysterious and fascinating, a world apart from the daytime world.

But the thunder still growled and the lightning flashes were coming at closer intervals.

We had killed two pargos, and made a pass at a turtle, when Tom poised the spear again, motioning urgently to Juanito for more speed. At the rim of the light a section at the bottom seemed to be moving. Then, as Juanito strained at the oars, a vast dark shape came full into view, a sawfish. Tom made his cast. The spear, a four-tined affair with an eight-foot wooden handle, hissed into the water, and I heard the muffled chug as the barbed points drove home. Hit just behind the head, the sawfish planed to the surface, making a splash like a tree falling into the water, and fled toward the lagoon's mouth. We had 100 feet of stout cotton line tied to the metal shank of the spear, and within seconds the sawfish had taken it all and was towing us. I congratulated Tom, who had struck a Captain Ahab pose, but soon wished I hadn't. Because, as thunder salvoed like the bombardment of Attu, rain suddenly sluiced out of the spooky darkness.

"Be doggoned. Looks like we're gonna have a little shower," Tom said with forced heartiness. "It'll be—uh—pleasant after such a hot day."

Some shower. It was a cloudburst, a Niagara. It streamed down with increasing force until the shore was blanked and I had no notion whither we were being towed. I hope it wasn't to sea. Juanito bailed, Tom stared silently ahead, one hand on the taut line, and I sat at the stern listening for breakers. Thirty minutes passed. Then Tom said he thought the sawfish was weakening. It was putting less strain on the line, he said. As my experience with sawfish was limited, I didn't know whether or not one would attack a boat. But we took a chance. We hauled in line, and presently made out the ripple-blurred shape of the fish in the light. He was no giant as sawfish go in these parts. Five hundred pounds maybe. After several flurries, one of which caused the boat to take water over the side, and a wicked raking cut across the bow that ruined a new paint job, he allowed us to hoist him to the surface.

I hastily put two .45 slugs into his head. Whereupon, behind us, startlingly close, a dog barked. I recognized the dog's voice. Happily, we were back at our starting point, the ranch. We towed the kill ashore, and Juanito went up to the house in quest of an ax. When he returned with one, I chopped out the fish's saw for a trophy. It was a good one, with fourteen heavy teeth. We then returned the items we had borrowed, managed to refuse the offer of a night's lodging, and set out in the continuing downpour for the hotel. Arriving there, bone-tired and wet as drowned seals, we found Mauricio in the kitchen enjoying a late snack.

"Nice shower," he remarked, shouting to make himself heard above the roar of the cloudburst on the tile roof. "Good for the crops."

"Just what we needed," I said, "after such a hot day."

Because you can't launch a boat at Cuyutlan, we once worked up a powerful grudge against a certain husky black marlin who, for reasons of his own, demonstrated every morning at sunrise out in front of the hotel. No sooner would we settle down on the gallery with a pot of coffee, in a mood to appreciate the seabirds, the changing jewel colors of the water and northward march of cloud formations, than the marlin would appear, to jump, tailwalk and wallow about on the surface like a seagoing hog. He was a showoff marlin, strictly from Smithfield, and so almighty big and beautiful that he sort of diluted the pleasure of taking surf fish. Juanito named him *El Maromero*, "The Acrobat."

One afternoon we drove Mauricio to Manzanillo, the seaport city forty miles north, to buy groceries. It was a blistering day, and when the shopping was done, we repaired to a sidewalk cantina to cool off. The cantina was known as the Amorous Octopus, and in it we met one Miguel, a piratical-looking turtle fisherman who owned a boat, and who frequently, he told us, cruised down past Cuyutlan. One thing led to another, as will happen in a seaport cantina on a hot day, and almost before I realized what was going on, it had been arranged that Mauricio would drive the car back and Miguel would take Tom, Juanito and me south to catch, *El Maromero* the black marlin. Only, Miguel said, we would have to swim ashore, as naturally he couldn't land at Cuyutlan, and would be unable to bring us back to Manzanillo on account of pressing business farther south at his turtle-hunting grounds. It was, all present declared, a truly masterful plan. Salute to the marlin fisherman, amigos.

Yeah. We chugged out of the mountain-girt harbor at midnight in an ancient tub, which, for untidiness and smells, couldn't be matched, I'll bet, this side of the Yangtze Delta. Dawn was breaking over the sierra when we stood into Cuyutlan. Miguel had a rod, battered but serviceable, and we put out a ten-pound dolphin bait. Tom did the fishing. On the beach a small crowd had assembled, and Mauricio was waving from an upstairs window of the hotel. Some burros and the village dogs completed the audience. We had trolled past the hotel five times with a brassy coral light, when a black marlin slammed into the wake and spear-whacked the skipping dolphin. Miguel hit the clutch, and Tom thumbed his reel to freespool. Satisfied, the marlin took the bait. Forty minutes later, after a dramatic, action-filled fight, Tom brought the fish in to the gaff. I estimated he would go 200 pounds. We gave him to Miguel, who said he had a market for marlin steaks.

"All Cuyutlan passengers ashore," Miguel now intoned. Obviously he thought it was funny. It wasn't.

We were in shorts, barefoot, Mauricio having brought our clothes back to the hotel. Miguel put the boat in as close as he dared, shook hands around, and wished us a happy landing. No sharks were in sight. If one fin had showed I would have signed on to hunt turtles, believe me, for the duration. As it was, we went over the side and headed ashore, riding the swells. Juanito, who is amphibious, set the pace, and eventually a comber tossed us, winded and grateful, onto the sand. It had been a brave experience and we received plenty of plaudits. But, sitting on the gallery presently with our morning pot of coffee, we weren't as pleased as we might have been. Something was missing. Somehow the day wasn't beginning right. Juanito was lounging on the top step eating a slab of papaya. Suddenly, he stood up, gazing seaward, and laughed. Out front, a black marlin was jumping. The fish greyhounded and walked out on his tail. He wallowed and splashed, waving his spear at the sky, a showoff fish if ever one swam.

"It is *El Maromero*, Juanito hollered, "We caught the wrong marlin."

Everybody thought it was a swell joke. So did we. We settled back to watch the new day grow. It was now starting according to the script.

We were eating lunch one sunstricken noon when a flight of brown pelicans appeared from nowhere and began diving close inshore. Gulls and terns joined them. The birds were plunging into a dark shadowlike area that could have been a school of sardines or mullet, except that there were no silvery flashes such as those fish would have made. Juanito, after some study, said that it was a mass of migrating sea snakes, and that certainly game fish were out there preying on them. He was so right. Hardly had he finished speaking when, beyond the cloud of whirling wings, a torpedo-fast something, at least five feet long, unzipped the green shoulder of a wave, leaving a wake of foam. I had no idea what kind of fish it was. I didn't even care. Any fish that big and fast was a welcome visitor indeed. In no time at all we were on the beach with our gear.

It proved to be one of those golden, marvelous days that you treasure forever. We took sierra mackerel, roosterfish and yellowtail. Tom hooked a monster, species unknown, that took off seaward and simply kept going, breaking his line at the reel knot. The sea snakes moved slowly north, staying inshore, and together with the birds and killer fish, we moved with them. Juanito told us that the snakes came in each year at about this time, probably to mate. Often, he said, you will find them in pairs at the sand. If you tried to handle them they would strike, but were nonvenomous and had weak teeth. To the seabirds and predatory fish they were apparently a delicacy. Beachcombing dogs and cats also ate them, when they could. By late afternoon, wave-battered and weary, our eyes smarting from spray and sunglitter, we'd had enough.

"Get me one of those snakes," Tom said to Juanito as we plodded back to the hotel. "I want to make a sketch of it and say thanks, friend." "*Si, Señor*," Juanito said.

At dusky, violet twilight we sat in the car awhile listening to the radio. The world was loaded with troubles, according to newsmen, but then we got Rosemary Clooney and Bing Crosby and that was grand. Fireflies were winking among the dunes when we went to our room and turned in. Along in the black tailings of the night Tom awakened me. "Do you hear something in here?" he asked.

I sat up, listening. Over in a corner there was a rustling sound, followed by a thump. Metal rattled. We had no lights since Mauricio, to save gasoline, shuts off the power plant at midnight. But we had a candle stub. Tom lit it and pussyfooted across the room. I figured the intruder was one of the land crabs that sometimes prowl through the hotel at night. I was wrong.

"Damned if it don't sound like it's in my tackle box," Tom said. With that, he lifted the lid and stooped to peer into the box. Something lashed out at his hand, and wriggled to the floor.

"Halleluja!" Tom bellowed. "A snake!"

I did a broad-jump off the foot of the bed, and we left as one man, nearly tearing the door off its hinges. Tom dropped the candle, and of course it went out. While we were working toward the open spaces through a diabolical maze of tables and chairs, Mauricio appeared with a kerosene lamp in one hand and a .38 Colt in the other. He asked where the snake was, and Tom pointed mutely to our room. Mauricio closed in cautiously, the lamp held high. By this time other guests had arrived, everybody excited and full of questions. *Blowie!* went the Colt. "Got him," Mauricio said with satisfaction. Somebody brought a broom and swept the snake out where we could get a look at it. Two feet long, dark green, it had a vivid orange stripe along each side, ending on its curiously flattened tail in perfect Greek feet patterns. A light dawned on me. Looking around for Juanito, I saw him coming down the stairs.

"Did you put that thing in Tom's tackle box?" I asked him.

"*Si, Señor*," he said. "He wanted it, and I didn't know where he was, so I put it in the box where it would be safe. If you wish," he said, "I could get you a sackful tomorrow."

"D-don't bother," Tom said weakly. "P-please."

One morning we were helping Mauricio search the laundry room for a scorpion that had been seen there, when the cook's pretty sixteen-year-old daughter Panchita came up from the beach looking disgusted. There were so many fish of some sort in the water, she said, that she couldn't swim. They kept bumping into her. Thousands of them. They—But Tom and I didn't wait for the rest of it. Leaving Mauricio to deal with the scorpion by himself, we departed at jet speed for our tackle. The fish turned out to be *cuahtetes*, saltwater catfish, averaging about two pounds. Something, probably barracuda or roosterfish, had given them such a scare that they seemed about to come ashore.

"Man, if we can catch enough of those beauties," Tom said, "I will throw such a southern catfish fry as nobody ever attended south of Lost River, Louisiana."

With the help of hurriedly rounded up recruits we got the fish. The little cusses hit willingly, on both meat scraps and pieces of fish, and unlike most freshwater cats, they fought. Before the day was over, they had gained my admiration.

True to his promise, when nightfall came Tom put on a sure-enough Dixie fish-fry with tropical trimmings. While the moonlit surf thundered in and palms curvetted in the wind, we sat barefoot on the sand with villagers and the hotel guests, eating catfish and hushpuppies, and wondered why nobody had ever thought of this before. Guitars, an accordion and a finger drum backed up singers in a rollicking ballad about a fisherman who fell in love with a mermaid but had to abandon her because she slept in the water and couldn't eat the chilis of old Cuyutlan. Panchita and another girl, with flowers of Cortes in their hair, whirled and stamped in a Spanish dance.

"Straight out of a Fitzgerald film," I kidded Tom. "Practically plagiarism."

"Phooey," he jeered. "Nobody from Hollywood ever fried catfish like these." He leaned back against a palm bole and watched the moon-silvered breakers creaming on the black sand. Then, serious, he said, "A year ago I didn't know there was such a place as Cuyutlan. Now it's practically my home, by gosh, and that's so terrific I still can't believe it's happened. Fisherman's luck. . . ."

Trouble at Erickson Creek

It was the worst breakfast I ever ate in my life.
Watery owl soup. You try it sometime.
It sounds funny, but it wasn't. Not at all.
Unless that cabin showed up in a big hurry we were
in trouble—all kinds of. . . .

It was, I maintain, a brain-twister of a backwoods puzzle. All the clues were visible, begging to be recognized, but Tex and I had to admit that we were baffled. We stayed baffled until, one storm swept night, I got out of bed and climbed a tree. . . .

Morning had come in bitterly cold, the air filled with a diamond drift of frost crystals. Spruces were popping and the snowbirds sat around with their feathers fluffed waiting for the sun to warm them. We breakfasted on wolf stew, and followed by our trail-weary Malamute pup Hyak, struck out across the riffraff of broken ridges south of camp. Yesterday we had cut the trail of a lone moose here. The trail had been old then. Today it was ancient. But we got a break. As if fate had decided it was time to encourage us a bit, we had traveled less than an hour on the wind-drifted days-old trail when it led us into a moose yard.

The sourdough who discovered the Klondike couldn't have been more grateful. No moose were in sight, but the animals were here. Plenty of them. The abundance of fresh sign was proof of it.

"Our troubles end right here," Tex said in a voice like a raven's croak, as he checked the wind and his rifle sights. "The jinx has laid off us, we ain't gonna starve after all, an' hit don't make no difference now if we never find that doggone lost cabin."

I hoped. Big, iron-maned old Tex Cobb and I were no strangers to ordinary garden-type hard luck, but the miserable deal we had been getting in these frozen boondocks took the Academy Award. I mean, it was special. It had angles nobody ever heard of before, and which I still don't believe myself except on lonesome nights when I can't sleep. Easing our six-foot Susitna webs through the powder snow, we entered the yard. It was a burned flat thickly grown to willows, maybe eighty acres in area. Deep-wallowed trails crisscrossed it in all directions, and over the place hung a good, warm smell like that of cattle bunched on a blizzard drifted range. There was meat enough here, I told myself, to feed all the hungry trappers between Nome and Kootenai Crossing.

"Keep an eye on Hyak," Tex whispered. "We don't want him to git excited an' bollix things up."

Hyak was a canine waif, seven months old, that we had rescued from the dog pound down at Anchorage. We bailed him out for $5, just in time to save him from becoming a municipal statistic, because he showed promise and we liked to have a dog in camp. He was big-boned, smart and stubbornly independent, with a silver-gray coat and comically mismatched eyes, one pale blue, the other brown. We held high hopes for him, but probably he wasn't so optimistic about us. Our talents as woodsmen, during the brief time he had been with us, hadn't exactly burned with a clear, gemlike flame.

"Don't worry about Hyak," I whispered back. "He hasn't got strength enough left to get excited."

We were only a biscuit-toss into the yard when brush cracked noisily off to one side. Swiveling fast, shedding our right mittens, we saw a cow step into view. She was a Walt Disney moose, a herd dowager, grotesquely ribby and sway-bellied. With her big ears stiffly erect and her back hair lifting, she stood regarding us belligerently. You didn't have to be a student of moose psychology to know what was going on in her mind. She was trying to decide whether to stampede hellbent across the flat, spooking every moose present, or stick around quietly and find out what we were up to. We tiptoed past her—if you can tiptoe in snowshoes—heading for the center of the yard. I had my fingers crossed. Cow moose had played some dirty tricks on me, and I hated having one behind us and downwind during this critical operation. But I couldn't think of anything to do about it.

Ahead we could see the shine of an opening. Dark forms were moving in it. Antlers glinted. You could now hear the sound of heavy teeth biting off frozen twigs. But there was no chance yet for a shot. Too much brush. *Give us a few seconds more*, I thought, thumb on the safety latch of my .270. *Only a few seconds more.* We didn't get them. Behind us the quiet was shattered by a snort like an airhose breaking. Hoofs pounded through the snow. Brush cracked. I took a quick look over my shoulder. Of course it was mamma, the keg-bellied cow. She had thought it over, and come to the conclusion that she was scared. And she wanted all her friends to know that she was. I tried to cut down on one of the bulls in the opening, but there was still too much brush between us. He was as safe as if he'd been behind a stone wall. By this time moose were plowing through thickets all over the flat.

"Gawdamighty," Tex hollered. "We're licked ag'in."

Here I've got to splice in some necessary background. We were in the high Talkeetnas, sixty miles east of the government railroad. Shortly after the first big snows we had bought a trapline, sight unseen from one Blueberry Jack, an old friend who was abandoning the fur trails forever, he trusted, on account of having struck a placer paystreak over in the Iditarod country. We paid $1,500 for the line, the bill of sale listing a twelve by fourteen cabin, traps, sundry tools and utensils, and a four-month grub supply for two men. The cabin was located in a short canyon near the headwaters of Erickson Creek. We knew how to get to the canyon. As for the cabin, Blueberry Jack assured us that we would have no trouble finding it. No trouble at all.

"Only thing is," he said, "it might be snowed in a little. She drifts kinda deep there in the canyon some years."

As understatements go, this proved to be a collector's item.

We went in with seventy-pound packs containing trail grub, personal gear and a battery-powered radio. No doubt some woodsmen would have omitted the radio and taken more food, but Tex and I were fond of radio entertainment, keeping up with world events was said to be educational, and why carry grub to a grub cache? On the afternoon of the fourth day, ten miles or so from Erickson Canyon, we killed a bull caribou. We had halted in a stand of cottonwoods on the shore of a loon lake to eat some bannock sandwiches, and Hyak and a family of whisky-jacks were mooching from us when we saw the caribou coming toward us across the ice. I took hold of Hyak's ruff to keep him quiet. He was so fascinated by the caribou that his blue eye had turned white, and the brown one, green. Nothing, however, could be done about the whisky-jacks. At sight of the caribou they had begun to scream and chatter in spasms of collective hysteria.

"Should we or shouldn't we?" Tex asked, referring to the bull.

"We should," I said.

Later we would string traps down this way, and a cache of meat would be an asset. You'd always know where you could come to chop off a meal. The bull was now 200 yards distant, plodding through a brittle windcrust, his hoofs scattering it like broken glass. He was very light in color, and carrying small, curiously deformed antlers. With the sun on his snowy cape, and his breath trailing behind him in cottony white puffs, he made a picture to remember. Suddenly he halted, gazing straight at us. Since we had the wind, either he had sensed our presence or, more likely, the screwball clamor of the whisky-jacks had warned him. As he turned to flee, Tex's long-barreled Sauer Mauser crashed. The bull went down with a broken neck, hoofs hammering a tattoo on the ice. Wishing there was more daylight left, we dragged the kill back into the timber and got busy dressing it.

Surprisingly the carcass was fat, most caribou being rawhide lean after the rut. In a moment we discovered the reason for the animal's fatness, his deformed antlers, and the fact that he had been traveling alone. It wasn't the carcass of a bull at all, but that of a steer. Probably a wolf had castrated him for sport, a playful thing wolves sometimes do when meat is plentiful and they become bored with plain killing. We had never eaten caribou steer meat, but the Tena Indians had told us about it, claiming it was wonderful. Saving out the liver and a chunk of suet, we hoisted the carcass into a tree and tied it there with snowshoe babiche. The whisky-jacks, silent now, were busily airlifting meat scraps back among the cottonwoods, and Hyak had stuffed himself with various parts of the caribou's internal gear.

"Ain't much of a cache," Tex said, "but hit'll gave to do fer now. Tomorrow or the next day, when we're settled in the cabin, I'll come back with some tin, canvas an' nails an' fix hit right."

We arrived at Erickson Canyon after dark, in the teeth of a mountain windstorm that had threatened since morning. Toiling over huge drifts, parka hoods masking our faces against the blowing snow, we made our way upstream until we found shelter in a little postage-stamp cover. Here we camped. I pitched our balloon-silk fly and cut boughs while Tex went after wood. Tex was gone quite a spell, and was cussing when he returned, dragging the tops of two snags. He had never known it to fail, he growled. If you had shelter there was no wood, or else it was the other way around. He'd had to claw his way a quarter of a mile upstream, he said, before he found anything dry enough to burn.

As we had figured it would be today, our trail grub was about finished. For supper we fried most of the caribou liver, sharing it with the ever-hungry Hyak, and used nearly all the remaining flour and rice. This left us barely enough food for breakfast. But shucks, there was nothing to worry about. Tomorrow we would be snugly established in our new cabin, with a whole winter's supply of grub at hand. Storm wind bellowed past the cove, its back eddy fanning the fire and making the flames dance. The radio brought us Bing Crosby and Judy Garland doing pretty things with some new show pieces. Everything was swell. We thought.

Morning broke calm and cold, tidal waves of color spilling over the peaks. Tex was up ahead of me, a fire built and the tea bucket on, thawing his moccasins. "Jest lookit the snow that has drifted into this canyon," he said. "Musta been blowin' here, by gosh, since freeze-up. Only the tops o' things are stickin' out."

I looked, and didn't like what I saw.

After eating we searched for the cabin. The canyon was three quarters of a mile long and 400 yards wide, and the snow in it was at least fifteen feet deep. We traversed it six times, end to end, without finding a trace of previous human occupancy. I mean, wherever the cabin stood it was plenty snowed in, the stovepipe included. I don't recall ever putting in a more frustrating day. The situation was ridiculous, like an idiotic joke. I kept thinking that we would stumble over the cabin at any moment, and have something to kid about the rest of the winter. But we didn't. At sundown we drank tea for supper, sweetened with the last of the sugar. It only made me hungrier.

Hyak, realizing that he wasn't going to be fed, foraged on his own. A colony of adventurous field mice had left a tracery of trails here in the cove, and the pup seemed to believe that the tiny animals would make good provender. Anyhow, he began digging industriously. By full dark he had excavated a hole behind the lean-to that would have held a piano, and hadn't caught a mouse to show for it. Aurora banners flamed across the sky, the wind blew again, and somewhere to the south we heard the baritone howling of timber wolves. I turned on the radio, but all I could get was Basil Rathbone in a mystery play so I turned it off. We had a mystery of our own to solve.

"This here damn predicament we're in," Tex said judgmatically as we were going to bed, "wouldn't happen ag'in to anybody, I'll bet, in 200 years."

"We've still got the caribou carcass," I said. "In the morning I'll go after a load of it."

I started well before daybreak, taking Hyak with me. For a change it was easy snowshoeing, the packed trail having frozen hard as iron. Sunrise was painting the valleys when I sighted the lake below me. As I slanted down to the ice, a great horned owl rose heavily from a brush clump ahead, carrying what looked like part of an ermine. When the bird alighted in a snag, Hyak started after it, yelping joyously. He didn't get far. So loose was the snow that he bogged to his ears, and practically swam back to the trail. It was funny and I laughed at him. In view of what lay ahead, I needed a laugh. Partway across the lake I cut the trail of five or six wolves. They had been made early last night, during the wind. Nobody would have needed a crystal ball to know what had brought the animals here. I ran the rest of the way to the cache tree.

The scene there wasn't pretty. Bloody, padded-down snow. Caribou hair, bone splinters and yellow urine stains everywhere. Beds where the wolves had slept off their gorge. Of our fat caribou steer carcass not one edible ounce remained. As nearly as I could figure it, the wolverine had got here first, and had climbed the tree and chewed through the babiche tie-strings, tumbling the carcass to the snow. Later the wolves had taken it away from him. Probably they had killed him for his trouble. There was evidence of large activity out through the timber, but I didn't investigate. I didn't feel so good. I was just beginning to realize how beautifully we had been clobbered. Because now, unless we found the cabin or made another kill, we were in more trouble than we could handle. I doubted that we could make it back to the railroad. Sixty miles on an empty stomach, in deep snow and subzero cold, is a far, far piece.

On the way back to camp I was delighted to see Hyak's owl still perched in the snag. I shot the bird, and it spun crazily to the snow, a wing broken. Hyak lunged after it, determined this time. He learned something about wounded owls. When I caught up, the bird had the talons of both feet sunk into the pup's muzzle and was energetically shredding his ears with its beak. I killed the owl with my belt knife and tied it to my packboard. Hyak, bleeding copiously, was so outraged and humiliated that his blue eye had turned green, and his brown one red. We met Tex scouting through the timber at the canyon mouth. He hadn't found the cabin. When I told him about the loss of the caribou carcass, and how a wolverine had made the wolves' banquet possible, he was fit to blow a fuse. Like me, he had counted on juicy roasted ribs for supper.

"Absolootely wouldn't happen ag'in in 200 years," he said.

At camp we put the owl on to boil. It didn't weigh much, and I judged it had been one of the elder inhabitants in these parts, but who cared? It was meat. Tex informed me that he had been trying the Sherlock Holmes method, hoping to deduce the cabin's location, but it had only got him more confused. For instance, the best green timber for cabin building was down at the canyon mouth. But, on the other hand, all the deadwood suitable for fuel was upstream. And our cove, the only wind-sheltered spot in the canyon, was midway between the two. In short, the cabin could be almost anywhere.

When the owl was cooked, we dined. Hyak, more fastidious, didn't want any owl. He foraged again. First he got interested in a red squirrel's nest which, wind-torn and long abandoned, hung in a spruce beyond the fire. Then, having convinced himself that it wasn't alive, he resumed digging for mice. Tex told him that he was nuts, that he ought to save his energy, but the pup pretended not to hear. Later, when we had turned in and I was lying half-asleep in my robe, I found myself gazing at the squirrel nest. For a moment I had the curious feeling that it might somehow be important to us. But it was an elusive thought and made no sense. I attributed it to boiled hoot owl, and slept. During the night the wind blew again, and once I heard wolf song lift from the dark ridges.

Next morning, after the worst breakfast I ever ate in my life—watery owl soup—we held a conference. The thing to do, we decided, was to forget about the cabin, write it off for the time being, and concentrate on trying to kill some meat. This was not a caribou winter range. Only an occasional small herd drifted through. But there had to be moose in the area. The presence of wolves guaranteed it. As Tex pointed out, the shaggy killers weren't hanging around because they enjoyed the scenery. He figured they had located a moose yard, and was betting that we could find it too. With moose down, he said, our problems wouldn't amount to much. We could live under trees and take fur in deadfalls, if we wanted to, until spring. Straight moose meat wasn't a bad diet at all, he said, once you got used to it.

I said I would like to get used to it, starting any time.

If I make myself clear, it was no surprise to us, the way things had been going, when today's meat hunting project took a surprise twist. We hunted south of the canyon. Toward noon we struck a moose trail, the first since leaving the railroad. It wasn't fresh, but we followed it anyway. There was meat at the other end of it, wherever that might be. The trail led over a series of steep, tumbled ridges, and after a couple of hours I was bushed. I knew that if we failed to make a kill, today was the last day of hard snowshoeing left in me. Tex was no ball of fire either. He kept stumbling, and breathed as if there was an oxygen shortage. We topped another high ridge, dragging our webs through the sugar snow, and sat down to rest. You could see the moose trail for a full mile in the next valley. Tex shrugged. We didn't have a chance.

Came the surprise.

Hyak, lying at my feet, bounded up snarling. It wasn't a puppy snarl, but one that would have done credit to a hard-case team leader. He had winded something down the ridge slope. Presently a ptarmigan squawked. Then a flock of the snow-white birds rocketed up the 150 yards below us, to fly out across the valley. I was trying to spot whatever had flushed them when, at the rim of a half-buried alder thicket, shadows moved. It was a pair of black wolves. Outsized brutes, they were wallowing badly, and seemed to be making for the moose trail, as if they had scented it. Tex and I fired at the same instant. The foremost wolf went down stone dead, blasted off its feet. We had both held on the animal. The other made a tremendous, straining bound downhill, gaining the shelter of a brush-bordered wash, where it vanished at sputnik speed.

"You ever eat wolf meat?" Tex asked. I said I hadn't. "Me neither," he said. "I sure hope hit's nourishin'."

It was. The wolf, a male weighing close to ninety pounds, must have been living high, for it was in good flesh. I built a fire while Tex took off the pelt and cut some loin steaks. Roasted on sticks, the meat wasn't bad. Better than boiled owl, at any rate. We ate the entire loin and part of a ham before approaching sundown broke up the feast. Hyak didn't join us. He wanted no part of the wolf, roasted or raw. At purple twilight, with the pelt and carcass on our packboards, we took a shortcut back to camp. When we had dragged in wood, we sliced up the liver, heart, kidneys and some shoulder meat of the wolf for a sourdough stew, and put the mixture on to cook during the night. Tex thought of something, and chuckled. He had forgotten to tell me, he said, that he had found caribou hair in the wolf's entrails.

"He musta been one of the cusses that et our steer carcass," he said. "An' now here we are, holy smokes, eatin' him. Could be a moral to hit, huh?"

At first light next morning, feeling better, we went back and took the moose trail again. As related at outset, we found a moose yard, only to get fouled up by brush and a scatter-brained cow. But the old warlock's act backfired. Apparently none of the other moose had heard, seen or winded us. Anyhow, here came three of them barreling toward us through the brush, behaving as if they didn't know where they were going but were in a sweat to get there. Two were bulls, the third a stilt-legged heifer. I don't remember using the sights. The rifle bucked against my shoulder, I heard the whiplash bang of Tex's Mauser, and then the two bulls were down kicking in the snow.

"Oh happy day," Tex said.

Midnight had come, and the wind was roaring again, by the time we finished butchering and got four packs of meat to camp. I should have slept like a dead man, but didn't. Maybe I dreamt about the squirrel nest. Or maybe a surfeit of moose meat stimulates thought. Whatever the cause, suddenly I was sitting upright in my robe staring at the nest, and wondering how I could have been so dumb. I'd had plenty of exasperating experiences with red squirrels. I knew where they liked to build their nests, and why. Getting hastily out of bed, I pulled on my pants and moccasins.

Tex turned over and wanted to know what was going on. I told him I had an uncontrollable desire to climb a tree, that was all. So I climbed the tree, got the nest and brought it over to the fire. Ripping the top off, I shook out its contents. It was an interesting jackpot. Out fell bits of torn paper, pieces of string and part of a sock. Of course the squirrel had pilfered the items from the cabin. Tex dressed and sat cogitating deeply, sort of like a man in a trance. I guess I was doing likewise. Matters were beginning to add up, fast.

"You know why there ain't no dry wood around here?" Tex said. "Because Blueberry Jack cut hit all down, that's why." "Sure. And you know something else?" I said. "I don't think Hyak was digging for mice." "If he wasn't," Tex said, "then what in hell—? Holy Pete, ya reckon he could smell the cabin? Ya mean we're camped right on top o' hit?"

We cut a pole and took soundings. Five feet down we hit something solid. Then something that rattled—tin. "Ya hear that holler klonk?" Tex said. "That was the stovepipe, by gad." Hyak, too full of moose meat, was watching us. He yawned. In the firelight both of his eyes were green. Perhaps he was thinking that, given time, he would have uncovered the cabin without help. As I said, he was a smart pup. Worth the $5 we had paid for him. Leaving the snow-shoveling job for morning, we propped some roasted ribs beside the fire to heat. We had to build up our energy. The weeks ahead held a lot of hard trapline work.

"I tell ya," Tex said bemusedly, "hit wouldn't happen ag'in in 200 years."

Death of a King Wolf

"Don't care how many there are," Tanana said.
"They'll pay for it. Let's flag that airplane." My blood was up too.
One thing I wanted, that was the death of a King Wolf.

Tanana was hollering from the next room of the cabin, "Wake up, Rusty. Wolves in the clearing." He sounded plenty excited—for him, that is. This guy is a gaunt, jerky-tough, old-timer with an almost supernaturally low boiling point. I mean, he isn't the type to shout "Wolf!" in the middle of the night unless something special involving wolves is occurring.

I came awake fast. Wolf-song filled the night, the blood-chorus of a running pack outside in the clearing, high, staccato and thrilling, like no other sound on earth. It smashed at your senses. You could feel the vibrations in your bones. It was a big pack, an almighty big pack, and it wasn't there on any social visit.

This last became too apparent when I at last got organized and joined Tanana on the snowdrifted doorstep.

Out there under the blazing low-hung, blue-and-gold stars, a thing of primeval savagery was taking place. We had on the homestead what we regarded as our private herd of moose, around twenty head of bulls, cows and young stuff. They wintered here. They fed from our slash-piles, accepted our protection, loafed in the dooryard, got tough with us on occasion, and patently considered themselves members of the family. Tanana and I had been out in these Toonakloot boondocks better than twelve months, and our moose were just about the only company we'd had. We had named them all and were fond of the big grotesquely ugly brutes. Maybe, in their way, they were fond of us too.

Anyhow, they stuck around. Now the whole herd was in breakneck flight down through the naked cottonwoods toward the creek, the wolves hazing them. Of course the pack was trying to separate the calves and heavily-pregnant cows from the dangerous fighting bulls. The ancient deadly routine.

But the wolves' operation went abruptly haywire when, 300 yards from the cabin, our moose refused to cross the creek and came stampeding back toward the clearing. Maybe there was open water. Or maybe an ice jam. Who knows? I had been trying to estimate the size of the pack, and didn't believe my own guesses. One wolf can sound like half-a-dozen when it wants to. This pack sounded like a honey to me. Tanana came up with the answer.

"Holy suffering gawdamighty," he said, "it's a king wolf making a sweep of the countryside. Dozens of the varmints. Get set, feller."

He didn't have to tell me. I was really set. I had my favorite close-range weapon, a venerable beautifully made .401 auto. It holds six shells, and you can blast them out with great celerity when necessary. Also, if you know the gun, you can place them with reasonable accuracy even in bad, tricky light such as we had now. Tanana was armed with a 12-gauge double-barreled shotgun, and he sometimes is wont to claim in campfire bull sessions. To help you get the picture, the Toonakloot cabin is on the brow of a thirty-foot bank which yields to a timbered stream flat. Behind the cabin extends a reach of level ground containing our clearing. There was maybe three feet of snow. As Tanana finished speaking, the moose and the wolves came busting up the bank, scattering drifts, crashing through frost-brittle brush.

First into view came a bull. I recognized him. We had named him U.S. Special. Beside the bull, running easily in the loose snow, was a lean apparition that he at first mistook for another moose. It was that big. But to my startled eyes, in starlight, it appeared blue. Then I saw that it was slashing at the hamstrings of U.S. Special, and knew that it was a wolf—the biggest wolf I had ever seen in my life, and the only blue one, if it really was blue. How could you be certain in starlight? I lost my chance. The two animals were past me before I could begin to react. But things were still altogether active in our dooryard.

Next up the bank lunged a big-bellied cow, with a wolf having fun working on her throat. I gave this wolf the treatment, but it took some doing because the cow's legs were flying in all directions and I wanted the wolf, not the cow. I got the first one into him.

He went down on a shoulder, and after that I just kept the barrel lined on him and kept touching the trigger of the wonderful old .401. The muzzle flare had me half-blinded but that didn't matter. I mean to say, I purely sprayed slugs at the wolf until the hammer clicked on an empty chamber. My intention was to keep him down, and he stayed down. When the moose-wolf procession had passed the cabin, he lay stretched out on the snow, the deadest wolf south of Pt. Barrow.

"Varmints asked for it," Tanana said in the sudden pear-shaped quiet. He was reloading his 12-gauge. I now recalled having heard the gun boom twice. "Got one myself," he declared. "Right over there by the woodpile. . . . But did you see what I thought I saw—a blue wolf as big as a horse?"

I said I thought I had seen the animal too.

Naturally the pack had vanished, and the moose were gathered at the far end of the clearing, the bulls snorting and stomping about as if they alone, by their sagacity and prowess, had saved the dire situation. Tanana and I, too wide awake to go back to bed, dragged the two wolf carcasses into a back room where they wouldn't freeze before we got around to skinning them tomorrow morning, built up the fire and put on a pot of coffee. Tanana went into my bedroom and scraped frost off the windowpane with a thumbnail. He took a long look at the huddle of moose—the moon was up now—and stiffened suddenly as if he had been stabbed in the liver.

"Moose down out there," he announced grimly, "and it sure looks like Jenny. You couldn't hardly mistake them skinny legs."

With that I joined him. We scraped some more frost off the window and I took a long critical look. And here I've got to fill in a few words of background. Tanana and I had been out here on the west flank of the Talkeetnas too long—trapping, prospecting and cruising a stand of magnificent white birch timber that a certain government agency claimed was absolutely necessary to our national welfare. We had cabin fever, and we had made a pet of a stilt-legged, sparkling-eyed, orphan moose heifer, some eight months old, that we had named Jenny.

Jenny was quite a gal. She followed us around and often slept on the doorstep, and we cut down choice birches and willows for her to feed upon, and held her spellbound, we trusted, with long-winded dissertations concerning our hopes and ambitions and theories anent life and the universe. The things that heifer must have heard. But she was our friend and we were sentimental about her, and if that should be difficult to understand, try living in a wilderness moose pasture for a year, some 100 miles from the nearest town clock.

Now, peering through the frost-flowered window, I agreed with Tanana. The downed moose out yonder in the starlight and moonlight looked like Jenny. Hastily and without comment, we pulled on parkas and mittens, lit a gasoline lantern and went out to investigate. It was Jenny—in bad trouble. She was hamstrung on one side and her paunch had been slashed open. Several yards of her intestines, frozen and snow-encrusted, were wound around her threshing hind legs. Her eyes were wild in the lantern light. I didn't know whether or not she recognized us. But she was beyond help. Only one thing could be done for her. I put the muzzle of the .401 behind her big ears and tripped the gun.

"All right," I said. "Comes now a payoff wolf hunt. I am going to call in an airplane and gun down a few of our noisy, bold-murdering visitors."

"If we have to foller them to the North Pole," Tanana said in hearty agreement, "or even to Siberia."

Feeling too mean and vengeful even to cuss, we two cabin-fever cases put out the emergency signal for aircraft. We snowshoed a fifty-foot circle in the back yard and darkened it with ashes from the heating stove. Then we drank coffee, cleaned guns and thought dark and violent thoughts while awaiting daybreak. In the North there is an extraordinary, very husky young bush pilot whose first name is Leon. I helped bring him up and I am proud of him, in most respects, that is. I believe that he began flying at about the age of twelve. Anyway, to hold a license, he was twenty-one for so long that the whole North was beginning to chuckle about it. At present he had a freighting contract that brought him twice a day over the homestead, flying something classified to some restricted place for certain mysterious gentlemen upriver. We were waiting for Leon.

Dawn was a vast peacock-fan of cold color above the snow peaks when Tanana cocked his head to one side and said, "Here he comes."

Engine-roar racketing among the frozen cottonwoods, the small red monoplane came in low from the south. Leon saw the emergency signal as he passed overhead and turned and came drifting back. Fifty feet above us he stuck his head out the window, cut the throttle, and yelled, "What's wrong with you guys down there? You sick or something?" He was taking a pilot's chance, of course, and I hope nobody writes me about carburetor ice. I know about carburetor ice. I know about Leon, too. I waved him in, and he put the ship down among the stumps, brushpiles and spooked moose.

Tanana and I explained what had happened, and stated that we wished to charter him for a wolf hunt of indefinite duration.

Leon, broad, blond and blue-eyed, smelling of gasoline and purty in an Eskimo-made sik-sik-puk parka that had cost him plenty unless he had a seamstress friend in the Arctic, which no doubt he had, grinned tolerantly.

"Been wondering," he said, "even made a couple of bets, as to how much longer it would be before you two sourdoughs got birds on your aerial, out here all alone. How many wolves did you say came through last night?"

"Dozens. Maybe 100," Tanana snarled, shoving his neck out like a banty rooster, "Who cares? You gonna fly us or not?"

"Yes," Leon sighed, "I know better but I will. Only first I have freight to deliver. On the way I will take a look at the trail left by this tree-mendous pack of wolves."

Purple peak-shadows were pointing across the valley when Leon kited in from the north and eased his skis into our cluttered clearing. For the first time in our association, excepting maybe once when he really was a teenager and met a brown bear face to face while picking blueberries, he looked impressed. "Found them in a jackspruce thicket fifteen miles upstream," he said. "It's really an old-time, king-wolf pack, the kind Pappy used to talk about. And the king wolf is blue, the biggest, handsomest wolf I ever laid eyes on. Sky blue and big as a pony."

"How many?" Tanana demanded belligerently.

"Dozens. Maybe 100," Leon said soothingly. "Who cares?"

We took off next morning at first light. There was no wind and the plane was overloaded. I feel that I should declare that I have seen most of the masters lift a ship off in difficult circumstances—Hap Arnold, Jimmy Doolittle, Nate Twining, Gorden MacKenzie, Bob Reeve and others—but Leon rates a salute for this performance. The snow was sticky and she wouldn't lift. The wall of timber came rushing toward us. The engine was screaming its metal heart out. Then Leon rocked her over on the left ski and came back on the stick, and we were in the air, clearing the frozen carcass of Jenny, clearing stumps and brushpiles, an onery bristled-up bull moose—and the treetops.

"Hallelujah," Tanana said reverently.

Below us now in the blue-hazed snow was the trail of the pack. Gun-scared, the wolves had been in flight, not traveling single file but scattered a bit. The trail could have been that of a small band of caribou. It was the trail of a veritable king-wolf pack. For those not acquainted with the term, such a pack is one assembled by a wolf of superior power and ability, able to rally his clan relatives from maybe fifty miles around to join him on a foray through an area. True the wolf social system is matriarchal, rigidly so, but when a great dominant male arises the old females will follow him with their families—so long as he leads them to meat and not into too much trouble. The wildly spectacular king-wolf sweep, once common, is now almost nonexistent. There aren't enough wolves, for one thing. For another, the land is ringed and crisscrossed with traplines and batteries of snares, and the human inhabitants possess high-powered rifles and covet the government bounty paid for a dead wolf. But somehow this blue king wolf had arranged a sweep. Except for the airplane, it seemed like old times.

Then below our wings was the jackspruce flat Leon had mentioned, triangular, perhaps ten acres of slender snow-plastered green javelins aimed at the sky. The main pack trail led into it, and a few trails went out of it. But there were wolves remaining under the spruces. Leon put the plane down on the treetops and circled at stalling speed. Tanana was up front, window rolled down, scattergun ready, a look on his face like that of an elder prophet pronouncing doom. I was in back with the .401 and a pet 12-gauge Parker.

Out of the timber, nerves unable to endure the threat from the sky, streaked a brown wolf, maybe a two-year-old. He didn't know where he was going, I guess, only wanted to be away from where he was. He achieved that desire. If there is a Wolf Valhalla that is where he ended up. Tanana, who knew about as much about deflection shooting as I know about the theory of least squares, hit him with both barrel charges of buckshot.

At this juncture I saw a flash of sky blue deep in the timber. I said to Leon, "Put me down, and let Tanana cover from the air."

Leon floated her in against the timber and banged off again within seconds after I had piled out. He wanted to be certain that the blue wolf stayed where he was. The propwash blew my muskrat cap fifty feet distant and hammered enough snow under my parka collar to cool a case of champagne. I stepped into the siwash hitches of my webs, checked the .401, and headed into the patch of spruces, the wind in my favor. By this time Leon was overhead, and suddenly he tipped the plane over on one wing and began burping his engine. He had sighted a wolf—the blue king wolf, I hoped—and was pointing a wing at the animal, telling me where it was. Trying to watch in seventeen directions at once, I moved toward the indicated area. There were wolf tracks everywhere, and one particular track, close to seven inches long, almost had to be that of the king wolf. I don't recall ever having seen a larger wolf pawprint.

Directly above me the plane's engine was burping again, and I wondered why, if the king wolf really was in view, Tanana hadn't opened up. In a moment I found out why. Ahead was a high piled tangle of windthrown timber. The enormous wolf tracks led in under it. The wolf was hidden from the air, and was at bay, making his last stand. He was playing it the only way he could. Now I have never been accused of being a gutless wonder, but I freely confess that at the moment I felt a chill not due to the atmosphere. It could be that there are man-killing wolves. I have heard tales, but personally I wouldn't know. However, I was aware that I was within feet of a desperate and most formidable antagonist, more dangerous if he wanted to be than any grizzly or brown bear. Leon was working the engine again, trying to tell me something, and I could see Tanana's whisker-stubbled face peering anxiously out the right window above the twin barrels of his shotgun.

Then, and maybe you know how it is in wild circumstances, I experienced a surge of confidence. When you get that feeling, you are going to win, regardless. I said to myself, "This one is for Jenny." Aloud I said, "Come and get it, killer, or I'm coming after you." Nothing happened, so I took off my webs and, pockets deep in snow, started under the jackstraw pile of windfalls. What happened occurred so fast and was so bizarre that I'll be doggoned if I know exactly how to describe it. There must have been anyhow ten wolves under the fallen timber, hiding from the airplane. Apparently the rest of the pack had scattered, the matriarchs having decided that the adventuresome hotshot blue king wolf would only lead them into more trouble, and that there was enough trouble in the world without going around looking for it. But ten were enough, or however many there were. They wanted out of there, and I was in the way. I submit that everyone, at some time in his career ought to find himself crawling under windfalls, in deep snow, with close to a dozen wolves coming at him.

All I remember is that I looked for blue and saw it, and started shooting. Above me a shotgun boomed twice. Leon was now practically down among the trees. If I were blessed with a son his age, I would wish him to be Leon. I hear from fairly reliable reports that Leon is no angel, but he flied like one. I shot the .401 empty, saw wolves wallowing past me on both sides, and was reaching into my parka pocket for another clip when I realized the show was over. The king wolf was down, fifteen feet from me. He died with his lips turned back, showing his teeth. I had hit him with all six shots. Leon landed, and he and Tanana dragged the huge shaggy carcass into the open. I didn't help. The truth is I was kind of shaky. I needed to sit down and have a smoke.

Leon stood looking at the blue wolf. "You know what?" He said. "I'm gonna fly you two characters to town. Because there is just one cure for cabin fever—asphalt."

Louise
Lepina

Pete's Educational Bear Hunt

The best time to kill a bear is when you are twelve years old. But I'll tell you something. That boy wasn't the only one learning things on this *bear hunt.*

"Put yer glasses on the farthest bear," Old Jack Filce said when we had topped the high shale buttress. "If that ain't a medicine pelt, I never saw one." He sounded excited, for him.

I was busy at the moment. I was making certain that our guest, coonskin-capped, wondrously freckled, twelve-year-old Pete Edwards III, didn't start any rocks rolling. We were on a frost-tinted mountainside between Knik Glacier and the mossy landmark known as One-Sleep Cabin. It was late afternoon. The two black bears we were stalking were over yonder at the margin of a belt of huckleberry thickets, 700 yards distant. An hour ago, when we tied the horses and started climbing for them, the animals had been a quarter of a mile apart and in heavy brush. Now they were on open ground, moving together. It was the first real opportunity we'd had to look them over.

With Pete safely settled, I got out my glasses. Presently I was excited too. The 16X prisms revealed that the bear had a truly strange and beautiful pelt, the almost-shaggy hair so silky that it winnowed in the breeze, and so glossy that it shone like polished jet. It was the second medicine bear I have laid eyes on in close to forty years of living in the world's most populous bear pastures. These bears are, so far as I know, simply ordinary blacks who have grown extra-special coats of hair. But the Denna Indian shamans set great store by the freak pelts, claiming that they were loaded with magic properties. Jack had lived with the Denna in the brave, bygone days and obviously was most eager to kill this present fancy looking bruin. It was going to take luck. Between us and the bears there was not a scrap of available cover. Nothing but weathered shale and caribou moss. Worse, the sun was already sliding down against the peaks.

Pete, wide-eyed beside me, wanted urgently to know what a medicine pelt was. I told him to keep his shirt on, please, and Jack would explain at a better time, probably in rich detail. This Pete had a king-sized bump of curiosity, and when he wanted to know something he wanted to know it right now.

We were trying to figure some way to get within shooting range while we still had light, when, dramatically, the bears themselves solved the problem. They came face to face on the near side of a huckleberry thicket, and the next second were disturbing the peace. Maybe it was a dispute over feeding rights. Or perhaps they just felt ornery. Anyway, they began circling and feinting, back hair rucked up, lips curled to show their fighting teeth. At first it was strictly a demonstration. I expected that, like other black bear controversies I had witnessed, it would end with both of them walking away as if nothing had happened. Only it didn't. They sprang suddenly together, and went down biting and slugging, each trying with the claws of his hind feet to disembowel the other. Holding the glasses on them, fascinated, it seemed to me that the medicine bear, the smaller of the two, was taking a bad mauling. Actually, as we were to discover later, he was being killed.

"I dunno what in heck we're waitin' fer," Jack said. With that, he stood up and sprinted toward the bears. Lean and shaggy, costumed in mackinaw pants that he had worn two years that I knew about, and a fringed buckskin shirt that could have dated back to the Klondike rush, he looked like a composite of all the mountain men who ever lived. Although twenty years younger, I had to put out plenty to catch up with him. Even Pete was being left behind. We managed to cut the distance to the bears in half before the embattled animals saw us. They bounded apart, stared, and fled. The medicine bear headed down toward One-Sleep Cabin, dodging among boulders and ledges, while the other took to the brush, climbing. Since the medicine bear was Jack's by right of discovery, I followed the latter animal with my sights. He was a mere shadow-shape in the screening thicket until he emerged into a little opening. Here he committed a tactical error. He halted to look back. I squeezed off the shot, and the 220-grain .30-06 slug went through him, kicking up rock dust on the other side. He spun, bit at his ribs, and sagged against the mountain, dead.

Meanwhile Jack was endeavoring to get lead into the medicine bear, with no luck. Due to the wildly broken, boulder-strewn ground below us, he had an almost impossible target. The ancient and treasured .40-82 he insisted on carrying would boom, and the bullet would ricochet, howling out over the valley. Finally the rifle was empty, and the bear, again beyond range, was galloping into the timber.

I said to Pete, forestalling a barrage of the boy's questions, "You can't really hold it against the poor guy. The sun was in his eyes."

"No, it wasn't," Jack said with dignity, as he thriftily gathered up his cast hulls for reloading. "The fact is, I'm learnin' to be a sportsman. I decided to spare that bear till next time, to give him an honest, sportin' chance."

Pete grinned. He said he knew, golly grasshoppers, when he was being kidded. At this point I'd better splice in some background to explain what sort of hunt this was and how Pete happened to be with us. Jack and I had been partners off and on for years, and it was our pleasant custom each autumn, if we could find the time, to ride into the mountains and put up a supply of smoked black bear meat. It made a good vacation. Moreover, cottonwood-smoked bear quarters, tenderloins and bacon-sides yield breakfast fodder of superior quality. Usually we hunted the huckleberry thickets here at the head of Knik Valley. Not only were black bears uncommonly plentiful in the area, but the berries on which they fattened for hibernation gave their meat a fine flavor. We would take in rock salt and waterproof canvas bags, kill two or three bears, pickle the meat a few days in strong brine, then smoke it under a tarpaulin until it could be transported home for further smoking.

Last week, however, when I rode over to Jack's homestead with five horses and my outfit, ready to head upriver, I found the old-timer busy shepherding Pete. It seemed that Pete was the son of a friend, an engineer working for the government who had been called unexpectedly to Barrow on business. In short, Jack was baby-sitting.

"I sure would like to go with you," he said wistfully. "But you see how it is."

I saw, so I said what he wanted me to say. Bring the kid along, I said. I had an extra sleeping bag he could use, and exactly the right horse for him, a gentle 800-pound palomino filly named Flossie.

Pete couldn't learn to hunt bears any younger, I pointed out. Besides, his presence would enliven the hunt, lend it sparkle. It would give us a new and uncritical audience for a lot of hoary campfire yarns, and a chance to display our shining talents as woodsmen. As for the so-called matter of roughing it on a mountain bear hunt, the worst that could happen to the kid would be that he'd get lost playing Davy Crockett on the camp flat, and we'd have to sort him out of the bushes.

Just like that, innocently, I said it. Nobody can tell me that a man doesn't have prophetic flashes.

When Jack had gone through the formal pretense of thinking the suggestion over, he allowed that a bear hunt might, everything considered, be a wonderful experience for the lad. Educational, healthful too. Whereupon, with no more palaver, we got together some additional gear, packed up and hit the mountain trail. Thus began the doggonedest bear hunt we ever made together. We camped at a pretty spot a mile below the glacier, where there was pea vine and clear water. Next day we encountered the medicine bear and made our first kill. Two days later, in the berry thickets close upvalley from One-Sleep Cabin, where Jack seemed to think the medicine bear was hanging out, we scored again. The bear killed was a run-of-the-woods black, but the circumstances of his demise were special. They convinced me that adventure had young Pete by the hand.

We sighted the bear toward midafternoon. It was a hazy, copper-skied day, with a huge cold front hanging in the east that certainly was breeding a Knik windstorm, and we were hoping to get some more meat in camp before it broke. We had been five hours in the saddle, scouting the timbered moraine hills and watching a dozen square miles of mountainside, when I spotted the animal poking lazily along through a huckleberry patch on the brink of a rimrock cliff, less than 500 yards distant. Hastily we rode up a creek draw as far as we could, tied the horses and climbed afoot to intercept the animal. It was Pete's turn to make a kill, or try to.

"The main thing is, don't get rattled," Jack advised the kid when we had found a suitable ambush. "Jest put the sights on that bear's shoulder, hold 'em there good an' steady, an' ease the shot off. Keep shootin' till I tell ya to stop. Savvy?"

Pete nodded that he savvied, and Jack handed him the .40-82. The bear was 150 yards distant now, upwind, still moving toward us along the cliff rim. He was hog-fat, so fat that his sides bulged, and no doubt was wishing that freeze-up would hurry and arrive so he'd have an excuse to dig in somewhere and sleep till spring. Pete thumbed back the hammer of the heavy rifle, and rested its octagon barrel across a rock. He was taking it big. He had no buck fever shakes, but below the coonskin cap his brow was furrowed in grim concentration, and he was so pale that his freckles stood out as though they had been daubed on with a brush. The bear inadvertently made things tough for him. Each time he got his sights lined, and was taking up the trigger slack, the animal would go out of view behind a rock or bush. After five minutes or so of this, I found myself getting a case of sympathetic nerves.

At long last, when the bear was directly above us, he reared up among the tall huckleberry bushes, gathered a double armful of branches to his chest and began stripping off the purple, frost-sweetened berries. I thought, "Now is your chance, boy. Burn him down." I didn't realize what this could lead to. It wasn't my afternoon to be bright. Jack did a little better. He saw the trouble coming and tried to prevent it, but by then it was too late.

"Hold it, son," he whispered hoarsely. "Wait'll he—"

Baloom! went the .40-82. Davy Crockett, if he had still been around, couldn't have made a better shot. But it caused violent things to happen. The softnosed bullet whacked home, and the bear stepped forward into space. He fell forty feet, striking several ledges, landed on loose shale slabs at the base of the cliff and came tumbling down the steep pitch. Rocks dislodged by his fall followed him. He busted through bushes, caromed off boulders and sailed through the air, gaining momentum with each foot of slope distance. Pete got off another shot. The kid was carrying out instructions, you couldn't take that away from him. In fact, he was working the rifle's action to try again, when the bear and his accompanying shower of rocks whizzed past us—into the draw in which we had tied the horses.

"Gawdamighty," Jack groaned.

He took the gun from Pete and we hurried down the draw to assess the damage. A bizzare scene awaited us. We had tied the horses to a slanting wind-thrown spruce under a vertical bank. They weren't cheechako horses, and not especially spooky. I mean, they were tolerant of dead bears, blood and gunfire. But they had never before experienced anything like the avalanche that had just landed in their midst. Maybe they thought more rocks and bears were coming. At any rate, they had departed, taking the windfall with them, all fouled up with it, their tie-ropes and one another. The creek bed was mucky here, and when they slammed into it they bogged. My horse Piecrust was now down on his brisket in the attitude of a praying pilgrim at Mecca, with Jack's Pilot sitting on him, the windfall snubbed between the latter's forelegs and slanting over his shoulder like a flag standard. Flossie, Pete's little palomino filly, had a tie-rope sawing under her tail, and was bellering piteously for help.

The bear lay piled up against an aspen, quite dead, as he had every right to be.

In due time, by dint of main strength, threats and cajolery, we got the situation in hand. Except for the loss of a few divots of hide here and there, none of the horses were hurt, which was a minor miracle. Pete went over for a look at his bear. He was so manifestly proud of himself that I half-expected him to put a foot on the carcass, beat his chest and let out a Tarzan yell. I envied him. The best time to kill a bear is when you are twelve years old. There are few thrills like it, believe me. Pete asked how old the bear was, how much it weighed, what it had eaten when there weren't any berries, and whether we thought he ought to spend his savings to have the skin tanned. He was a question-asking kid sure enough. We told him maybe four years, close to 250 pounds, vegetation and salmon, and he'd have to use his own judgment.

"Well, I want to say," he said, "that this bear hunt is turning out to be even more interesting, golly hoppergrasses, than I expected."

"Yeah," Jack said heavily. He scraped some muck off the side of his face, and examined a rope-burned hand. "I was jest now thinkin' the very same thing."

The main event was yet to come. Reaching camp in the menacing flare of a blood-red sunset, we put the bear meat in brine, then Jack started supper while I attended to the horses. I picketed Flossie on some grass behind the tent for use as a wrangling horse, and hobbled the rest of the string and shoved it several hundred yards downvalley into a pea vine meadow. After a good mountain supper of bear chops, bannock bread, meat-juice gravy and stewed dried apples, Jack and I smoked a while and Jack told Pete a story. It was an old one I recalled having heard as a youngster at Denna campfires. Probably it had been told in prehistory by members of the Bear Society before that group migrated from the Altai Mountains in Asia to the New World, and by the Sanskrit-speaking people among whom shamanism originated.

It was the story of Knife, a Tyone lake shaman who became the first space traveler by virtue of owning a medicine pelt. Like other professional men before and since his time, Knife had gotten so disgusted, what with a nagging wife and a swelling list of ungrateful, tight-fisted clients, that he decided to try his luck elsewhere. He waited for a clear night when the moon was full. Then he ceremoniously spread his medicine pelt on the ground at the village center, and with all the people watching, sat upon it and issued flight instructions, so to speak. Instantly the medicine pelt rose into the air, like a flying carpet, and carried him to the moon. There Knife sits today, looking down at the earth and shaking his fist at the Tyone Denna, a constant reproach to them and a reminder of the powerful magic contained in a medicine pelt.

"An' if ya don't believe it," Jack said, "take a look fer yerself next time there's a full moon."

We turned in, Pete asking questions about medicine pelts and Denna magic until he fell asleep in the middle of one. The windstorm, threatening all day, held back until five o'clock in the morning. Then it swooped down across the glacier to pounce on us like a screeching gray lynx. The tent ballooned, yanking at its pegs, trying to take off. I went out to check on things. Gravel was rattling across the ground, and the air was full of blowing sand. Somewhere a tree crashed down. From the open river bars out front came a steady roaring, braying and shrieking. The Knik windstorms, I should explain, are notorious. They blow at all seasons, may last anywhere from a day to a week, and sometimes attain gale force.

Jack joined me, hitching up his suspenders. "One thing about this country," he said, "it don't get monotonous." He cocked an ear to the wild wind sounds coming from the bars. "We better bring the other horses in afore they drift, if they ain't drifted already."

I got a flashlight and we went out through the straining cottonwoods, leaning into the weight of the wind, hat brims pulled down against the driving sand. We didn't use Flossie because we figured we could finish the chore in the time it would take to saddle up. A mistake. Boosted along by the broadhanded slaps of the storm, we came to the pea vine meadow, and I swept it with the beam of the flashlight. The four horses were in a huddle across from us. They had our scent, and knew who we were. But when we started toward them, they stampeded hellbent downwind into the timber. Of course the mounting fury of the storm had made them nervous. But sometimes I think all horses are nuts. We ran after the knotheads, thinking they would soon get tired of rattling their hobbles through the brush. They didn't. We caught up with them three quarters of an hour later, and then only because they had got themselves thoroughly bollixed in a mess of alders and down timber.

Daybreak was a wan glow in the east when we arrived back at camp. We tied the would-be deserters to some young green spruces that the wind couldn't blow onto them and which they couldn't pull over. Jack said he thought some coffee would go good. I thought so too, and began building a fire. I was touching a match to a twist of dry grass tucked under a strip of pitch-bark, shielding it with my hat, when I thought of something. I hadn't heard Flossie whicker at the other horses. When the fire caught, I went around behind the tent for a look. Flossie wasn't there. I think I knew then what had happened. Parting the tent flaps, I put the beam of the flashlight on Pete's sleeping bag. The kid wasn't in it. I shouted for Jack. Investigating, we found that Pete's saddle and bridle were missing from the rigging pile. We stood looking at each other.

"This is a hell of a note," Jack said somberly. "It absolutely ain't no mornin' fer a green kid to be foolin' around in the timber."

"If you ever hear of an understatement of the month contest," I said, "don't fail to send that one in. It's a natural."

When eight o'clock came and Pete hadn't returned, we climbed the mountain behind camp, found a sheltered spot in the lee of a boulder and got busy taking the countryside apart with our glasses. The wind was still howling like a thousand wolves, and plenty of sand was blowing, but you could see down through the stuff better than I had hoped. Half-an-hour passed, then Jack said, "Take a look at the old One-Sleep layout. See if ya notice anything queer." I picked the place up with the glasses. The squat, sod-roofed cabin, once a trapline headquarters and gold-rush way camp, hadn't been used for years. The stovepipe was capped with a tin can, and the bearproof window shutters were shut. The dooryard was empty. Wondering what Jack thought he had seen, I brought the cache into the field of the glasses. It was an old-time cache, twenty feet high, shake roof, rusted tin varmint guards on the four supporting posts, a ladder slanting up to the plank door. I shoved the glasses back inside my shirt.

"Let's go," I said. "I don't get it, it's mysterious, but our Pete is down there."

Here I'm going to give you Pete's account of what had happened, as Jack and I got it from him. The kid's trouble wasn't only that he was lost. He also believed that the medicine bear had him trapped. The whole thing began at camp when he heard Jack say that we'd better bring the other horses in before they drifted. Wanting to go with us, he hurriedly dressed, but by the time he was ready we had gone. He then pulled his very own personal prize boner of the hunt. He saddled Flossie and rode after us. Within minutes, confused by the banshee wind, the darkness and the blasting sand, he was hopelessly lost. At full daylight he found himself in the One-Sleep Cabin clearing. Flossie, traveling with the wind, had brought him here, which was natural because she knew the place and it was only a pistol shot off the main valley trail. Pete didn't know where he was. Not really scared yet, the thought struck him that if he climbed to the top of the cache, he might be able to see camp. On the ground beneath the cache was a pole ladder. Tying Flossie, he succeeded in standing the ladder against the cache, and climbed to the platform.

He was clinging here, his coontail flying in the wind, afraid the swaying, creaking cache was going to blow over but trying to spot a familiar terrain feature, when he saw the medicine bear. It shouldered out of some flame-yellow willow brush fifty yards distant and came angling across the clearing toward the cabin. He recognized the animal because he'd had a good look at it four days ago on the mountain with Jack's glasses. But it was behaving far differently now. Its gait was stammering and crabwise, and as it drew closer Pete could hear it uttering deep moans. Its jaws were covered with froth. Like a mad dog, Pete thought. When it was abreast of the cache it halted, staring at Flossie. Then it looked up at Pete. Probably there had never been a stranger tableaux in the decades-old clearing. Suddenly Flossie bawled, fighting her tie-rope, and this broke it up. The bear ran, stumbling, across the clearing to a grass-shaggy knoll, which it climbed. At the top it lay down, half-hidden by the grass, facing the cabin.

What the kid did next is hard to understand unless you make full allowance for the fact that this was his first trip into the wilds. A youngster brought up in the backwoods would have stepped aboard Flossie and thumbed his nose at the bear, knowing that the filly could outrun any bruin in the North. But to Pete, safety lay in the cabin. He climbed down, unbarred the splint-log door, and went inside, taking Floosie with him.

That was where they were when Jack and I came down through the cottonwoods, crowding our horses. I was still trying to comprehend the setup, knowing the kid was here or had been here, but wondering what he had done with Flossie and why we hadn't seen her from the mountainside, when the filly shickered.

Jack hailed the place, and Pete opened the door a crack, then swung it wide. Flossie was looking over his shoulder, wanting to join our mounts. We had questions to ask, a lot of them, but Pete started talking first.

"The medicine bear is up there on that little hill," he said, pointing. "I think he's crazy. Do bears go mad like dogs? Do they foam a the mouth? What makes them—"

Jack and I had swiveled as one man. Behind the tall wind-bludgeoned red-top grass on the knoll-crest a black shape was visible. It stirred, went out of sight, then reappeared on the down-wind slope of the knoll. Jack slid the .40-82 out of its saddle boot. Despite his previous performance, he could shoot the venerable rifle. It boomed, and the bear came rolling. Jack put another slug into it for insurance before it came to rest at the foot of the knoll. If the bear had been crazy, it had good reason. When we turned the carcass onto its back for skinning, we saw that it was horribly claw-raked from chest to pelvis. A fold of intestine bulged through one gash. The fight at the huckleberry thicket had been as savage and deadly as it looked. But the bear's pelt was perfect. Jack ran his fingers through the silky hair, his bearded, windburned face splitting in a wide smile. No doubt he was remembering yarns the Denna shamans had told him, some of them probably even gaudier than the one about Knife's flight to the moon.

"What I would like to know, golly-hoppers," Pete said, kneeling beside the bear, his Davy Crockett coontail whipping in the wind, "is how you found out where I was when I didn't know where I was myself?"

"The ladder was standin' up against the cache," Jack said. "No—uh—growed up woodsman would've gone away an' left it there. An' if he was stayin here, he would've taken the cap off'n the stovepipe so he could cook himself somethin' to eat. Simple, huh?"

Which, I guess, does it. See you on a mountain black bear hunt.

Adventures of a Mexican Mutt

My scruffy little mite of a pooch may well be the best hunting dog south of the border. Join us on a few hunts, amigo, and you'll see what I'm talking about.

"He is a black-hearted profanity of a *coati solitario*, truly a bad one," my farmer host Primitivo told me for anyhow the fifth time as we ate breakfast by ocote pine firelight at the kitchen end of his grass-thatched home. "It will be a miracle if he does not kill your small dog."

"Take it easy," I said. "You'll frighten Chica. She'll think we're going after a dog-eating *tigre*."

Chica was under the plank table enjoying tortillas smeared with chili sauce. We had arrived here at the Michoacan hill village of Todos Santos yesterday by auto from the coast, our mission being to collect the skin and skull of a *coati solitario* for a naturalist friend in the States. If we could find one of the surly brutes, that is. Grapevine information indicated that Primitivo was the man to see. So I looked him up, and it appeared that we were in luck. For the past week, it seemed, Primitivo's cornfield, on which he and his family depended for a living, had been systematically raided by a *solitario*. The animal came out of the mountain forest in the early morning hours, Primitivo said, to eat and destroy disastrous quantities of the young spring sprouts. It had proved too crafty for traps and too tough for dogs, and Primitivo did not own a gun.

As to exactly what a *solitario* is, you'll have to ask the naturalists, and they don't agree. Some maintain that he is simply a coati, genus *nasua*, related to the raccoons and ring-tailed cats, who for some reason turns rogue and is outcast from his kind. Others hold that he represents a separate species. In any case, he is larger and more powerful, and has heavier jaws and teeth, than the common run of coatis. His record for killing and mangling dogs is a gaudy one. The Tarascan Indians tell you he is crazy. They may have a point.

"My own dog Pedro fought with him," Primitivo said. "He came home dragging his guts. And Pedro was a big dog." "You're scaring hell out of Chica," I said. "She's the sensitive type."

Breakers of flamingo and saffron light were silhouetting the black volcanic peaks when we headed down the almost perpendicular trail leading to Primitivo's cornfield. We passed a spotted cow standing on her hind legs to graze. We passed a stone fence-corner gay with yellow orchids that smelled like a keg of perfume with the bung out. Near the bottom of the trail was a weathered shrine, and to the left of it, beyond a boundary hedge of hog plums, was the cornfield, tilted and green-glimmering. You still couldn't see much, but we had the wind. Out in the field, 150 yards distant, was a dark blob that could have been a rock, except that I thought it was moving. Chica said it wasn't a rock. She stood with her shoulder against my knee, trembling nervously. Chica had never met a *solitario*. She was all revved up. As the light strengthened, the suspected object took color and form. It was the *solitario*. He was moving away from us, pulling up corn sprouts with both paws.

I told Chica to get busy, and warned her not to get close with the animal. If she did, I whispered, he would unzip her from north to south. I like to think she understands when I give her orders like that. Anyhow, nobody, me included, can prove she doesn't.

She went across the rough field like a black shadow. When the *solitario* saw her coming he let out a coughing snarl and began bouncing up and down on stiff legs, very hard-boiled. Imagine an underslung Airedale with monkey paws, raccoon-type tail and a thin, mean snout, and you'll know what he looked like. Chica whipped past him, raking hair from his hip. She spun, trying it again, but had to veer off when he reached for her. In a foaming, tooth-popping rage, he no more reminded you of an ordinary coati than a hostile ocelot reminds you of a tabby cat. The *solitario* fights like a baboon, holding an antagonist with his paws while he bites out chunks. That is what this one yearned to do to Chica, but he wasn't fast enough. They went in dizzy circles, Chica feinting, keeping him so busy that he was getting his legs braided. Then she

began giving him openings, retreating toward me each time he charged. It was one of her better performances.

When I was sure of him, I laid my sights on his chest and pulled. He died before he hit the ground. Chica came back to me, and I picked a red hog plum and gave it to her. Chica likes plums. In fact, she likes anything that is even approximately edible. Primitivo's brown Indian face was creased in a wide grin. It could be he hadn't been so excited since Paracutin erupted in a Michoacan cornfield.

"If one may inquire," he said, "of what breed is this Chica?"

He had me there.

Her father looked sort of like a golden retriever, and her mother vaguely resembled a poodle. Chica looks like a fox terrier, except for her black coat. I acquired her at Guaymas when Tommy Jamison, who operates a fleet of sport-fishing boats there, stealthily deposited a packing box on my porch one morning containing six puppies. At the time I considered this a dirty trick, especially since in giving the pups away I ran out of sympathetic friends and found myself stuck with the female runt of the litter, namely Chica. But today, two years later, I claim that the guy did me a whopping favor. Chica may not be the best all-round small hunting dog south of the border, but I have yet to meet a more interesting one. Among other assets, she has an awesome flair for creating dramatic situations, which makes her most valuable in my business. At times, however, I've got to admit, she kind of overdoes this.

As an example of what I mean, take a hunt we made for chachalacas, the superb green Mexican jungle fowl. We had drifted down into the San Blas country, and were staying with Jesus (pronounced *Haysoos*) Hernandez, an amiable 250-pound tobacco planter. Haysoos, with a carved-mahogany face like a Toltec laughter mask, a startling basso profundo voice, and a magnificent pair of drooping mustachios, was a character straight out of a Cisco Kid TV show. He and Chica at once became fast friends, partly no doubt because he liked to feed her pieces of comb honey, of which she is passionately fond. He got a kick out of her efforts to chew the stuff while keeping it from sticking to her teeth. His little honey dog, he called her.

From such apparently innocent things a man's troubles too often arise.

Haysoos had told me where we might find some chachalacas, so this morning Chica and I drove out to try our luck. Several miles from the plantation, on a cart road that tunneled through a brute of a jungle, we parked under a shaggy oil-nut palm and sat listening. Echelons of emerald parrots buzzed us. A rhino iguana with wattles and a ringed tail bowlegged across the road, gave us the lidless antediluvian stare and fled into a ditch. A brown little saltaparedes wren alighted on the radiator ornament, the wren that is said to spy on wives when their husbands are absent and report later to the husbands. Chica whuffed indignantly at it. Then, back in the jungle, we heard what we had been waiting for, the harsh three-noted calls of some chachalacas having a discussion about something or other.

I picked up the 12-gauge and told Chica to put the birds into a tree for me. Also I requested her to please remember to let me know where she was when the chore was accomplished, on account of my radar wasn't working. A few days earlier she had let me blunder hopelessly around in a thorn thicket looking for both her and a flock of chachalacas after she had found the birds and treed them.

She gave me a sardonic look and disappeared into the greenery. I envied her. The sane way for a man to tackle one of these Tarzan's nightmares is to have a helper up ahead with a machete cutting trail. Lacking one, I plowed into it the hard way, and believe me I had my eyes peeled for snakes. You keep hearing down here about a ghastly leaping adder (*Bothrops mummifera*) that lies in ambush on a limb and launches itself at you. If one launched itself at me, I wanted to see it first. Chica began barking. I busted through a tangle of coral vine, removed a garroting loop of liana from around my neck, and saw her looking up into a gigantic anona tree that seemed to have anyhow a quarter acre of top foliage. Overripe fruit still hung from its branches, among which bees and bright-winged butterflies were having a fiesta.

According to Chica, the chachalacas were up there too. I should explain that the chachalaca is a pheasantlike, long-tailed bronze and green-gold *Ortalis*, peculiar to this hemisphere. Handsome and sporting as well as being an excellent table bird, it is sometimes, the Mexicans assert, bred with domestic fowl to produce superior lightweight fighting cocks. Personally, I am a chachalaca fan, but hinting it in heavy jungle can be a headache. I circled the tree. No luck. But as I was about to make the circuit again, one of the birds betrayed himself. He squawked at me, shifting his position, and I caught the movement. The beautiful beggar was partway out on a lower-level limb, crested head cocked sidewise, tail jerking, poised for flight.

"Take off," I hollered.

He obliged instantly, and I fired. At the impact of the No. 6s he somersaulted in a shower of feathers, and fell to the leafy surface of another limb. A whole gang of chachalacas burst out of the opposite side of the tree, raucously sounding the alarm. I didn't even get a look at them. Chica, who had been all set to pounce on the dead bird, registered disgust. She didn't have anything on me. As there wasn't a rock within five miles that I might have used to dislodge the bird, I was faced with the miserable job of climbing the tree. I hope I never have to climb another like it. Unnoticed until now, bugs, lizards, small birds, iguanas, a fancy looking macaw and something that possibly was a black squirrel crawled, flitted and leaped about me as I clambered laboriously toward the limb on which the chachalaca rested. Bees were everywhere, and as they seemed to be getting warlike, they worried me.

But I reached the chachalaca, and after admiring it, dropped it to the ground. At which point I beheld a dismaying sight.

Chica had climbed one of the tree's buttresses and was digging and gnawing at the rotten wood of an ancient scar. Out of a hole in the scar bees were pouring. They swarmed about her in glittering veils. So many were crawling on her that her back looked brown instead of black. By this time scouting squadrons had located me, and it was time to move. I made a disorderly descent, falling the last six or eight feet, snatched up the chachalaca, yelled at Chica, and headed for the car. This trip I didn't need a machete-man, and the hell with the leaping adders. I was moving so fast one couldn't have hit me anyway. Bees were all over me, in my hair, inside my clothes, batting against my face. Yet, I was astonished to note when we were safe inside the car, not one had stung. Chica appeared to be likewise unscathed. I concluded we were just naturally loaded with luck.

Driving back to the plantation, I ignored Chica. Our little honey dog was really in the doghouse. We found Haysoos sitting on the porch with a pitcher of lemonade, mopping his big face with a bandanna, looking hot but comfortable. I told him about Chica's incredibly dumb katzenjammer with the bees and my narrow escape. "Treed as I was," I said, "the damned things could have killed me. There were millions of them."

"*Si*, I know the place," Haysoos rumbled, taking Chica onto his lap. "The bees are from one of my hives. I bought the stock in

Sinaloa. They are," he grinned, sinking the harpoon into me gently, "Kualmeca bees, the stingless variety."

But although she is a tough and crafty witch, Chica bought herself a package during a quail hunt we made one blistering topaz-blue autumn day among the Aztec pyramids near Santiago Ixcuintla, in Nayarit.

We were foregathered with some of the local sporting gentry in a little adobe *cantina* know as The Misfortunes of Pearl Harbor, eating iced Camichin oysters with lime juice and a novel "salt" composed of red chili powder and ground maguey worms, and listening to Bing Crosby on the juke box, when I first heard about the quail and the pyramids. It seemed there was plenty of both. Furthermore, our new-found friends assured me that few if any outsiders had hunted the former or examined the latter. So of course the thing to do, as all present agreed, was to organize a shoot. There were four gringos in town, one a chestnut-blonde steno from Kentucky, name of Anne. In the morning we rounded them up, borrowed some shotguns, loaded two cars with personnel, ice and provisions, and set forth. Such things happen in Mexico.

The day was hotter than $75 worth of Tabasco.

Beside the road the machete-shaped leaves of banana plants hung limp and dusty. Heavy waves shimmered over the fields as the hammering sun drove even the lizards to shade. My self-appointed guide for the day was a personable lad named Rafael, who had planned to be a bullfighter until a bull tore his shirt off one day, persuading him that his future lay elsewhere. He now had his own business, selling bat guano from a cave he had found, and was doing all right, he informed me with satisfaction. When we had been driving for maybe an hour, he abruptly wheeled the car off the road and made a dramatic stop at the rim of an arroyo.

"There are the pyramids," he announced.

As quail cover goes, in Nayarit or anywhere else, the place was unique. There were around thirty pyramids scattered over an area of about one square mile, all of them covered with earth and shaggy with sun-seared weeds. The quail were on the shadowed sides of the pyramids, obviously seeking shade, which showed how smart they were. Rafael, Chica, the blonde from Kentucky and I angled off by ourselves. At the base of the pyramid that we came to a covey of six got up. The gal didn't shoot. I did, and missed with both barrels, but I had a reasonable alibi. I was using a Victor Sarasqueta 16-gauge, made in Spain, that didn't fit me, and Italian shells dating back, I'll bet, to Garibaldi. The birds had looked like Gambel's quail.

Rafael, as I was reloading, picked up a beautifully flaked razor-sharp obsidian knife-blade and handed it to the young lady. From this moment on, my shooting really suffered. There was more interesting pre-conquest Aztec stuff lying around underfoot than you'd find in some museums. A single got up on my left. It was my shot, and I missed again.

"Don't be discouraged with me," I said to Chica, "I'm just confused. I don't know whether I'm quail-hunting or archaeologizing."

Another covey rocketed out of the weeds. The gal made a double. I missed one and killed one. They were Gambel's quail, all right, plump little characters with pert topknots. I wished they weren't. Gambel's quail is an admirable bird in his way, good to eat and providing sport in places where often there is no other sport, but the more you hunt him the deeper becomes your affection for the bobwhite. These birds were giving Chica a terrible time. Her tongue was hanging out and her temper was frayed. She had learned that to flush a bird was a sin, and now plainly felt it was somehow her fault when the coveys ran from her, to flush over in the next forty. I was sorry for her. But she couldn't learn about Gambel's quail any younger.

"What was the name of this city?" I asked Rafael. "Who knows?" he said, shrugging. "We just call it The Pyramids. Why don't you give it an Americano name, to commemorate our hunt?"

I thought this flattering proposal over while we beat the weeds around some more pyramids. In two hours we covered at least three miles, sweated plenty, and killed eight birds. The rest of the party, after some desultory bang-banging off yonder in the heat haze, had trooped back to the cars. I was about to suggest that we follow suit, when I saw that Chica had quit us. Backtracking, we found her. She was making camp. On the whole sunburned flat there was one green bush, and she was under it, digging wearily, trying to find cool earth. Conscience-stricken because manifestly she was close to sunstroke, I picked her up. As I did so, I noticed that she had uncovered some brightly painted pottery shards. Although my pockets were already sagging with trophies, I selected a piece of the ancient busted pot, olla or whatever, and took it along.

At the cars, where lunch was spread in the welcome shade of a tree, Chica was soon sufficiently recovered to eat a hamburger, a custard apple and two roasting ears. I reached into my shirt pocket for a cigarette, and brought out the piece of pottery. The Bluegrass blonde steno, sitting beside me, glanced at it, did a fast double take, and gasped. Pointing at the red-and-cream design on the fragment, she said, "Those old Aztecs weren't so primitive. Look what it says there. That's shorthand for 'Dear sir.'"

"There's your name for the place," I said to Rafael. So if you are ever in Nayarit, and the boys invite you to shoot quail among the pyramids at a place called Dear Sir, don't let the name throw you. Chica dug it up.

As a rabbit dog Chica is passing fair. She gets the job done. But there was a period when her rating was mighty low. She had a curious fixation, being convinced that rabbits lived in trees.

I first became aware of this during a rabbit hunt we made with Policarpio Sanchez near the seacoast village of Concha, north of Banderas Bay. Policarpio, an old friend, is a husky charcoal-burner who sports a Jalisco sombrero so wide that you wonder how he gets through a door with it, and who has been studying English for years because he hopes some day to move to the United States where, he had heard it rumored, a man is buried with shoes on. Due to his occupation, Policarpio spends a lot of time in the forests, and consequently knows a great deal about game and where to find it. So when he told me one day that the cottontails near his place at Concha were the largest and fattest he had ever seen, he had two guests on his hands as of that moment.

"Your dog Chica has had much experience trailing rabbits, no doubt," he said as we bumped over a range of dunes to his thatch and palm-pole house. "Any dog will trail a rabbit," I said. "It comes naturally."

Yeah.

Bright and early next morning, with surf thundering behind us and the jungle breeze so charged with flower fragrances that you could have sold it by the bottle, we went up a stock trail to a pretty spread of green pasture land. It was a place to make you homesick. Except for some long-legged tree ducks sitting idiotically in the tops of coquita palms, and an army of pale land crabs scuttling about in the fence rows, you could have kidded yourself that you were back in the dairy country of western Washington. A cottontail hopped out of a thicket, took a critical look at us, and started for other parts in a hurry. I killed it. It was a sure-enough big cottontail, around seventeen inches long and close to four pounds.

Some minutes later, as I was crawling through a barbed-wire fence, a second rabbit lined out in front of us. I was handicapped, but Chica wasn't. Yelping joyously, she pursued the cottontail past a group of startled cows, around a dugout canoe doing service as a watering trough, and into a small clump of huinole trees. Here the cottontail gave her the old razzle-dazzle and disappeared. Instead of taking its trail, she halted and looked up into the trees. Among the branches were some clusters of chinese-red mistletoe, and I thought at first that she had mistaken them for larger and more interesting game. But I was forced presently to the conclusion that she actually believed the rabbit was up there hiding in a treetop.

"I never before in my life," Policarpio said, trying not the laugh, "saw a dog do that."

Probably nobody else had. It bothered me the rest of the day, as Chica was hardheaded about the matter. She kept on trying to locate rabbits in trees. Finally, on the way home, I recalled an incident of last year, which explained everything. I told Policarpio about it because I didn't want him to think that Chica was completely off her rocker. For the same reason I'd better pass it on here, together with a related background incident. It will get a bit complicated, but hang on, it'll come out all right.

Cut to the hot country, on the Santiago River, where Chica and I were occupying a large isolated plantation house. It was one of those velvet-black tropic nights, sweltering and overcast, with not one of the 3,000 stars certified for the *mañana* latitudes showing in the jungle sky. I was sitting in the living room absorbed in a novel of cloak-and-dagger intrigue, while Chica lay on a palm mat eating sugar cane. Suddenly she bounded up, snarling, her back hair on end. She was staring at the door. A typical hot-country door, the lower half was wood, the upper half screen. Something was nudging it from the outside. It would swing open a couple of inches, then the spring would pull it back with a bump. Considering the kind of boondocks that surrounded us, any of a number of unpleasant varmints could have been trying to get in.

I was deciding what steps to take when, so help me, just outside the door there arose a wild outburst of maniacal laughter, a tenor wha-a-a hya-a hya-a! with a bourbon rasp, sort of. I sprinted for the scattergun, Chica at my heels.

"Just keep out of the way," I advised her as I dropped buckshot charges into the chambers of the gun. "Whatever that thing is, with the voice it's got it's bound to be dangerous."

When we eased back into the living room, the door was being pushed open again. I slipped the safety latch. Chica was showing her teeth. She was putting on a good act anyhow. At this juncture our visitor entered. It was a bulge-eye giant tropics toad. While Chica and I gazed at him, fascinated, and my blood pressure gradually subsided, he ambled across the floor and began picking up flies, victims of my last spray job. As he seemed right at home, he had probably been in here before. In the morning I made inquiries and learned that the critter was known locally as a laughing toad, and that his tribe was numerous hereabouts. I have since heard their nerve-jangling outburst many times, and submit that somebody ought to come down to the Santiago River country and make a recording of it. It would be a killer on a midnight mystery program.

What with this experience, Chica and I were ripe for the payoff episode, which took place a few nights later. I had turned in, and was enjoying a thunderstorm cannonading over the sierra, when Chica asked to be let out. Her motive, however, wasn't what I expected. The instant I opened the door she streaked out into the black walled compound, barking her head off. So I hastened for the shotgun again, and this time a flashlight as well. A margay cat had been reported in the vicinity, and I earnestly hoped that it had paid us a visit, because of all the trophy cats in Mexico I particularly wanted to come up with the mysterious margay. I found Chica growling at the dark tower of a guava tree that dominated one end of the yard, which was promising.

Holding the flashlight in my left hand, I swept the tree with its beam. Some vampire bats, who had been pirating guavas, flapped away into the blackness. A tree frog croaked querulously. Overhead a thunderclap let go like a bangalore torpedo. Then, high in the tree, the light reflected from a pair of eyes. Only they didn't belong to a margay. Perched there against the sky was a huge owl. Disappointed, and because owls were on the outlaw list here due to their tireless raids on turkey roosts, I fired a barrel at him. There was a muffled squawk, a beating of wings, and something thudded to the ground. Chica was on it in a flash. But when I put the light on her it wasn't, surprise, the owl she had. The owl had planed halfway across the yard and was dead in a coffee bush. What she had was a baby cottontail. I assume, and trust I am right, that the owl had scooped the rabbit out of the yard and flown into the tree with it. Otherwise I don't know how to account for the fact that I shot at an owl and knocked a rabbit out of the tree too.

"So that must have been when Chica got the notion that rabbits inhabit trees," I said to Policarpio as we plodded homeward. "It was a very rare happening," Policarpio said. "But, then, maybe next time—who can tell?—it really will be a margay cat in the tree."

But mostly, when Chica tells me about game, it pays to believe her. For a dog her age, she has been around a good deal and learned a lot. As the windup of this chronicle of her adventures, take the time I disputed her judgment regarding a band of javelinas.

We had ridden up to a place called Venados, on the western flank of the Sierra Madre, in Sonora, to make a pig hunt with Geronimo Valdez, a whiteheaded, warp-legged little *vaquero* who manned a line camp there for a cattle company. Geronimo was a card, one of a vanishing breed, who wore spurs with three-inch rowels, thought Americans were ill-informed because none had been able to tell him how many days it took to ride a horse to New York, and honestly believed that a man's virility was likely to suffer, perhaps permanently, if he didn't stuff himself with bull beef at least once a month. As Chica had been stung on a front paw by a scorpion, she arrived in state in a pack pannier toted by a burro, occasioning some astonishment. After unsaddling, I asked Geronimo if he was hopeful that we would find some good pigs. It was getting along toward winter, and I was afraid they might have cleaned up the acorn crop here and departed seeking other provender.

"But of course we will find pigs," Geronimo said. "We will simply ride to where they are, and hola! there they'll be." Put that way, it sounded like a cinch.

Turning out next morning with the cactus birds, we rode into the fire-opal flare of the sierra sunrise, climbing a rocky trail that led through a sahuaro forest to the rim of a deep barranca, the sides of which were dotted with oaks. Here we dismounted and began scanning the countryside for pigs. Chica was using her own legs this morning. The effects of the scorpion poison had about worn off, and besides, her burro had gone AWOL during the night. Possibly the animal wasn't *sympatico* to carrying a dog. From where we sat we could see, a mile or so distant, a camp of Tarahumares, the shy half-tamed Indians of Sonora's vast unexplored canyon. Smoke from their breakfast fires made blue brush strokes in the luminous air. You could almost smell the roasting tortillas.

Chica had found a deer antler, old enough in appearance anyhow to have been shed in the time of Folsom Man, and for lack of anything else was gnawing it. Abruptly she dropped the antler and stood up, sniffing the wind. At the same instant Geronimo touched my shoulder.

"Javelinas, *señor*," he said. He was pointing down the slope to a stand of oaks, 200 yards distant.

After a moment I spotted the animals, but to me they didn't look like javelinas. Six or seven of them, they were in a mess of grass and low brush just beyond the trees, apparently feeding. The javelina has a blackish-brown coat, weighs about fifty pounds, and stands about sixteen inches at the shoulders. These animals seemed to be light brown, hardly darker than the sun-scorched brush about them. The smallest looked heavier than fifty pounds. But Chica said they were javelinas. She had hunted pigs a couple of times before, and was excited. She was Geronimo. But I hesitated. Then an idea struck me.

"Those things are domestic hogs," I said. "Probably from the Tarahumare camp."

Geronimo gave me a startled look, and burst into silent mirth. "But the Tarahumares do not keep pigs," he said. "They believe that pigs are Spaniards in disguise. Go ahead and shoot, *señor*."

It was two against one. So I rested the .270 across a rock and cut down on the nearest animal. With the crash of the shot it went over on its side, rolled and fetched up against a sapling. The others ghosted into the grass, and that was the last we saw of them. Chica, forgetting her scorpion-stung paw, went down the slope like a whippet, and when Geronimo and I caught up had her teeth set in the dead animal's ear, trying to shake the carcass but only shaking herself. It was a nice javelina boar. It even looked like one now. The color and size were normal, and how I could have thought otherwise beat the heck out of me. Usually I can come up with an alibi of sorts, but this time I was stymied.

"You should have trusted Chica," Geronimo laughed. "She kept telling you they were javelinas."

I should have, no question about it. A smart hunting dog like Chica would never mistake a trophy boar for a Spaniard in disguise.

Long Hunt for a Water Dog

Perro de agua *the Mexicans called it.*
It swam like a seal, ate frogs and snakes, and crossed with camp dogs. But nobody knew what they were.
That's what sent me on a long hunt for a water dog.

Policarpio nudged me with a sharp elbow. "Listen. They are coming," he whispered. "The *perros de agua*, the dogs of the water." I listened but didn't hear anything unusual. A million tree frogs were practicing choral croaking, and somewhere a sparrow-size pygmy owl was trying squeakily to sound big and dangerous. I listened some more, real good. Nope. Policarpio's Indian ears were sharper than mine. We were on the jungled bank of the wild Rio Tarogua, in Colima. Out front was a wide-swinging eddy that reflected starlight and the shine of a misty half moon. The surface of the water was dimpled by rising fish. They were chacal, a minnow-like species, which are served hard-fried in the cantinas of western Mexico as pretzels and salted peanuts are served elsewhere. These fish were also, I had been informed by practically everybody lately, the favorite food of the mysterious *perro de agua*.

"Find the chacal and there you will find the *perro de agua*," the jungle folk asserted. "That is, if crocodiles are not plentiful. Because the crocodiles eat the *perro de agua*, you understand."

Presently I will identify the *perro de agua*. But first I want to tell you about some of the adventures we had on this notably adventure-filled hunt. One was about to begin.

"Be ready," Policarpio said impatiently. "Surely you hear them now." I heard something. Coming faintly down the hot, humid night wind, blurred by the frogs and the burbling of the river, the sounds were elfin, musical, perhaps best described as resembling flute notes. I had been expecting barks or howls. These liquid sounds were so different that it was hard to imagine them being made by any member of the canine tribe. I shifted to an easier position and wiped the sweat off my hands. Policarpio was sitting as motionless as a stump, holding the mooring line of a little dugout canoe in which he was supposed to retrieve my *perro de agua* if I succeeded in shooting one. Suddenly the school of chacal broke up in panic, skittering across the moonlit water. As this took place, three heads rose above the surface forty feet out, shining like silver in the soft light. They were dog-size. I had one split-second look at them and then they were gone. I hadn't even had time to raise the 12-gauge buckshot-loaded shotgun I held across my knees. Policarpio didn't say anything. He didn't have to. We just sat there, waiting. The chacal had vanished. Fifteen minutes passed and a wisp of cloud moved across the moon. I glanced at Policarpio and saw that he was sitting very erect, with his sombrero tilted forward, registering sorely tried patience. Lately he had been doing some unwarranted bragging about my prowess with a scattergun. As a result he felt betrayed. He figured I should have gone into action faster than Jimmy Robinson at his best and killed all three *perros de agua* bang! bang! in one brilliant bombardment.

Our vigil dragged, and I was thinking that I would give a pocketful of *centavos* for a smoke, when I saw movement in the mooncast shadow of a vast kapok tree. A dark object came into view, traveling against the current. It was close in against the bank, and formless. Certain that it was one of the *perros de agua*, I tripped both barrels and grabbed for the flashlight clipped to my belt. With the twin blasts the eddy erupted in fantastic fashion. Something huge was struggling on the surface, sledging the water, creating a disturbance that could have been heard, I'll bet, half a mile distant. I put the beam of the light on the center of the commotion and saw a lashing armored tail, a greenish-brown saurian body and a long, ugly, tooth-popping snout. Getting stiffly to my feet, I reached for shells. But before I could reload, the uproar on the water abruptly ceased. The eddy was again empty and peaceful, all moonlight, current ripples and tree shadows.

"The animal you shot," Policarpio said in the voice of a man who has just counted to ten, "was a crocodile."

"So I gathered," I said. "Unlovely cuss. Active, too."

Policarpio ignored that. "I will tell our people at camp that the light was bad," he said, "and it was a mistake anybody could have made."

Policarpio is a three-quarters Aztec character, tall and dignified, who believes that American sportsmen are erratic geniuses who should never venture farther than two blocks from town without a guardian. At the moment I could have pushed him into the river, but I needed him. We were hunting for what promised to be the rarest animal of them all, an amphibious dog. I had heard about this improbable beast for years. Its Aztec name was Ixcuintla, and you were told that it was web-footed, that it swam like a seal, made its den in a bank with the entrance underwater, and subsisted on fish, frogs, and snakes. It could be tamed, everybody said, and would cross with domestic dogs. But the species was scarce because crocodiles tirelessly raided its dens.

Then last month, visiting at the university of Colima, I was assured by the senior professor of biology, one Dr. Juan Rangel, that the *perro de agua* actually exists and is, in fact, a true canine. As proof he showed me a natural history book in which the animal was listed, its Latin name given as *Canis genuinus*. That was enough for me. I telephoned *Sports Afield* and got an assignment to make an all-out hunt for the *perro de agua*. In consequence here I was, to heck-and-gone the other side of nowhere, prowling the tangle of streams in the great Armeria River system with four men, five horses, one mule and a donated truck which I daily expected to lose in quicksand or a bad crossing.

My strategy was to visit as many as possible of the riverbank villages and offer a 500 peso reward to the man who spotted a *perro de agua* and brought word to us, provided the information resulted in a kill. I explained most carefully that I wanted to make the kill and do the field taxidermy myself, because if the animal actually turned out to be of a new species it was imperative that the specimen be in proper condition for shipment to a museum. Everybody said that he understood. So eager in fact were the villagers to be helpful that by the end of the first week I had notebooks full of data, legends and anecdotes concerning the *perro de agua*. Some of the stories were lulus.

One, which I expect to remember in nightmares, was related in a torch-lit, palm-thatched cantina-restaurant by an elderly fisherman named Pedro Domingo. Pedro said that he was sitting on the riverbank one evening repairing a torn net when he saw a snake swimming toward him. It was a ten-foot tilcuate, one of the blue-black semiaquatic constrictors common in these western rivers. The snake was heading ashore, and was now some thirty feet out, swimming lazily, its thick body gleaming in the late sunlight. Pedro reached for a rock to throw at it. He knew that the snake wasn't venomous, but still he didn't want it to make a landing right at his feet, which apparently it intended to do.

Before he could spook the snake away, however, there was a boil on the surface as a swift brown shape rocketed up from the bottom. It was a *perro de agua.* The animal lunged half out of the water and grabbed the snake behind its head. Pedro said that he had heard that the water dogs and the tilcuates fought mighty battles, but that he had never before been fortunate enough to witness one. The snake at once began throwing coils around the *perro de agua* and trying to set its teeth in the water dog's muzzle so it would have leverage to apply its deadly squeeze. Fighting on the surface, they drifted down into shallow water and on the point of a bar. By this time, Pedro said, the snake had three or four turns around the body of the dog but still hadn't been able to get a fang hold. It was hissing loudly, a gargling sound, and lashing the mud and water frantically with its tail. As for the *perro de agua*, it was just hanging on, chewing toward the snake's spine.

The battle ended as abruptly as it had begun, with victory for the dog. The snake's coils relaxed, its threshing tail went limp, the desperate hissing ceased. Still maintaining its original hold, the *perro de agua* dragged the reptile's feebly writhing carcass farther out onto the bar. At this point two dog pups appeared. They simply materialized in the shallow water, Pedro said, and went ashore and also fell upon the dying tilcuate. They were yellow and perhaps three feet long. Apparently the adult *perro de agua* was their mother. At any rate, it was willing to share the snake with them. Pedro said with a shudder that it was a gruesome thing to watch the three feed hungrily from the body of the still-living reptile, but that he was proud and happy he had observed the episode because now the people in the United States would know how the *perro de agua* and the tilcuate fight.

At Cuyutlan, down near the river's mouth, municipal president Eduardo Michel told me about a wildish experience he once had with a *perro de agua.* A wiry, blue-eyed little chap, Eduardo was a cattleman before he entered politics. One morning he rode out with two *vaqueros* to scout the riverbank for some strayed yearlings. The three had slid their horses into a dry wash and separated to look for tracks when Eduardo's mount, a half-broke sorrel pinto, snorted and shied violently. The cause of the horse's fright was a *perro de agua*. A dozen or so yards up the wash, cut off from the water, the animal was crouched behind a brush clump, obviously trying to make up its mind whether to try to break past Eduardo or climb the bank and flee into the jungle.

Eduardo carried a pistol, but typically of the Mexican cattleman he reached for his forty-foot rawhide *riata* instead of the gun. As he built a loop, the *perro de agua* made up its mind and came streaking hellbent for the water. Eduardo let it pass him, then flipped the loop out expertly and yanked it tight around the animal's belly, whereupon the unexpected occurred. Just as Eduardo opened his mouth to call in the *vaqueros*, with the idea of doing a little justifiable bragging about being the only man hereabouts ever to rope a *perro de agua*, the beast whirled and attacked. It was a sizable *perro de agua*, Eduardo said, maybe five feet long, and it moved like greased lightning.

The sorrel pinto wanted no part of the animal. Cold-jawing the bit, it uttered a terror-stricken bawl and tried to climb out of the wash. It picked a bad place. The top of the bank caved and the pinto and Eduardo fell back in a cloud of adobe dust. Eduardo confesses that he is somewhat vague as to subsequent details. For a time he, the pinto and the *perro de agua* were all mixed up with one another and trying to get unmixed. When the dust cleared, he found himself sitting in a wickedly spined thornbush with his pistol in one hand and the pinto's reins in the other. The *perro de agua* was no longer with them. It had bitten through the *riata* and presumably escaped to the river.

"Did the animal look like a dog?" I asked.

Eduardo scratched his head. "There are so many kinds of dogs," he said. "Big dogs, little dogs, shaggy dogs, hairless dogs. This one looked like a dog of the water."

Came a morning that I would just as soon forget. Actually it could have been right pleasant as there was a pretty sunrise, the breeze was loaded with flower fragrances, and some singing quail and a flock of black Colima robins were providing background music. But I was having a blazing row with the cook because he insisted on putting cinnamon in the coffee. He drank chocolate himself and liked it flavored with cinnamon, and so he had the stubborn conviction that anybody with a really cultivated palate ought to enjoy coffee doped with cinnamon. We had reached the point where I was running out of Spanish cusswords, when I heard a horse arriving at a high rate of speed. The rider was our Policarpio. He pulled up just short of the campfire, his horse squatting on its haunches, and hit the ground, talking excitedly.

What he was saying sounded at first like lines from the "Hut-sut Song," but presently getting himself in hand, he managed to declare, "An Indian, *señor*, is coming in. He is bringing a dead *perro de agua*."

Hallelujah! Of course the White Hunter of the movies and TV is always calm in such momentous moments, completely self-possessed. He lights a cigarette, reaches for his sun helmet and says something offhand like, "Prepare some food for the man," or, "Please move that horse, it seems to be standing with a hoof in the water bucket." Stewart Granger does it beautifully. But not me. Anyhow, I was still hostile on account of the cinnamon-flavored coffee. "Well, where is this Indian?" I hollered at Policarpio. "Why didn't you stay with him? He might not find the camp. He might change his mind about coming in. Sweet hoozis, what a pack of knotheads I picked for this job."

"Tranquilize yourself, *por favor*," Policarpio protested. "The Indian comes. Behold him with your own eyes."

Emerging from the emerald shadows of the jungle was a weazened Indian mounted on a moth-eaten burro, carrying a muzzle-loading, percussion-cap shotgun. Tied behind the sawbuck saddle he was riding was a bulging gunny sack. I recognized him as a man I had talked with back at a river village named Madrid. He was one of the fishermen who go out at night with a dried-cactus torch and a dip-net for chacal—a chacalero—and he had given me his solemn word that if he saw a *perro de agua* during his nocturnal activities he would take our trail with all haste to inform us of the fact. His name was Primitivo.

"One hears that you have killed a *perro de agua*," I said.

"Yes, of a truth," Primitivo said complacently. "Since it was a big one I thought I had better shoot it myself—to make certain, you understand."

With that he dismounted, took his time about untying the gunny sack, and dumped its contents onto the ground. It was a skin, shrunken out of shape and sun-dried to the stiffness of sheet-iron. No skeleton. No teeth with which I might have made a stab at establishing that the animal was a bona fide member of the canine race. There is no use trying to explain how I felt. It couldn't be printed anyway. The skin was six feet, three inches from tip to tip. The paws were webbed, their pads rough and cracked. The claws were white, weak for an animal of this size, and showed evidence of much recent digging in rocky soil. The head seemed to have been about as large as a spaniel's but had been equipped with very undoglike whiskers, four inches long, white and stiff. The pelt was rich brown, with glossy guard hairs and soft blue-gray underfur. It didn't look like any dog fur I had ever seen.

Crossing my fingers, I asked Primitivo what he had done with the carcass. I was hoping that the buzzards and other scavengers might have left something helpful.

"Why, I threw it into the river," he said. "Because nobody eats the flesh of the *perro de agua*, you understand. It is not our custom."

Here it's better to draw a veil over the morning's little drama. We continued upstream, following stub roads, open bars and the remaining traces of the ancient cobble-stoned Spanish *camino real*. I spent a lot of time scouting ahead on a fast-walking black mule named—I wouldn't fool you—Pony. We saw some curious sights, had some rare experiences. One blazing sun-stricken noon we came upon a wild plum tree full of coatis, a dozen or more of them, and watched the long-tailed, long-snouted creatures troop headfirst down the trunk of the tree, a feat that I considered impossible even while watching them do it. Another time, in ambush above a rock-walled pool in which chacal were rising, we were startled when a cottontail rabbit dashed past us making a great racket in the fallen leaves. I was laughing at Pony, and lighting a cigarette when an ocelot whipped past in pursuit of the rabbit. The cat was in view such a short space of time that I probably couldn't have hit it even if I'd had the shotgun in my hands.

Still another time, a full day ahead of the outfit, I made camp after dark and inadvertently rigged my hammock under an *incha vevo* tree. The *incha vevo* is the Aztecs' tree of death. Camp under it, they assert, and you will be dead by morning. When I woke this morning, eager to take a stand near some slack water that looked made to order for chacal and *perro de agua*, and saw the thorny, white-flowering tree towering above me, I had a bad moment or two. Medics had told me that a toxic substance falling from the tree's leaves at night could be truly dangerous. But I felt fine.

When the outfit caught up with me I took pleasure in informing Policarpio that I had spent the night under an *incha vevo*. He looked me over critically, and shrugged.

"Perhaps the tree didn't recognize you as a Christian sportsman," he said. Which I suspect was a crack, but if so it was too subtle for me.

We were approaching the great blue-green wall of the Sierra Madre, and the valley was narrowing, when I got my first good look at a *perro de agua*. Our camp was in a nice place, a natural opening surrounded by orange and mango trees gone wild, and we had decided to spend the day here because the long-suffering truck needed attention. Toward midmorning my partner Roberto Gomez strolled down to the riverbank. Roberto, a lean hawk-faced gent, is a state official. As such he always carries a .45 automatic with ornate grips stuck in his waistband on the left side. Around these parts a purty .45 so worn is the insignia of authority, taking the place of a uniform and badge. Roberto had been gone from camp only a few minutes when he came hurrying back.

"Something down here I want you to see," he said. "It is a curious animal and you should know about it."

The animal turned out to be a bulge-eyed giant tropics toad as wide across as a plate. While it regarded us impassively, Roberto told me about something he had seen a Huichol Indian *brujo*—medicine man—do with one of the toads. The incident occurred on a *tigre* hunt, during which the paying guest, an American sportsman, came down with such a severe attack of rheumatism in both legs that he could neither walk nor ride. When it began to appear that the man would be a litter case, one of the Huichol machete-men announced that he was an accredited *brujo* of his tribe, and that if everybody would please bear with him, he would soon cure the suffering sportsman. He then disappeared into the jungle, to return after a while with one of the outsized toads. Without any of the drum beating, chatting or rattle-shaking that most medicine men consider essential to their art, he rubbed the rheumatism victim's legs with the living toad, after which he released the toad at the edge of camp and declared that all was well, the cure was effected.

"Four hours later the American was walking, free of pain," Roberto said. "I saw it myself and I am no credulous Indian. I graduated from a university. I—what in hell was that?" A liquid whistle had come to us across the water. It was the same sound Policarpio and I had heard the night I shot the crocodile.

We hastened to the water's edge. Swimming toward us at an angle was an animal that could only be a *perro de agua*. Its head was prick-eared, sleek and short-muzzled, and the sunlight shone on its bristle of white whiskers. You couldn't tell what its body was like. If we had been anywhere near salt water I might have guessed that that animal was some kind of seal. I didn't have a gun. The only firearm between us was Roberto's duded-up .45. Now I have nothing against the .45 automatic. It is a respected weapon, and in my time I have known two or three master sergeants who could shoot it quite accurately. Roberto tried. He got off two rounds before the *perro de agua* departed. The first, a noble miss, hit the water under the animal's belly and perhaps stunned it momentarily. The second made a fine splash off yonder.

"Took me by surprise," Roberto said defensively. "I wasn't myself. I had my mind on toads."

We hunted three days in the vicinity without sighting another *perro de agua*, then took off again upstream. Pony and I prowled ahead. One day we got into a flock of wild turkeys and I killed a fat gobbler. Another day we spotted a *tigre* sunning itself on a rock high above us, but the *tigre* had seen us too, and went away. Finally, on a day of wind and thunderclouds, I got my chance at a *perro de agua*. We weren't far ahead of the outfit. I could hear the truck groaning across a bar, and imagined I could hear Policarpio threatening the horses with a variety of punishments if they tried to roll in the sand with their gear. I halted on a grassy bank to wait for the party.

I was carefully scanning the water, a habit which I believe will stay with me the rest of my life, when I saw a wave that wasn't being made by wind or current. Out in the middle of the pool below me, some fifty feet distant, something was swimming underwater. The unseen creature was too big for any of the local fish, and we had climbed above crocodile country. As I slid the shotgun out of its boot, a head broke the surface. It was a *perro de agua*. This time I was ready. I fired both barrels, saw the buckshot make a pretty pattern, and knew that I had scored. The *perro de agua* tried to dive, then lay over on its side, drifting with the current. I hung my spurs in Pony's ribs and lifted him with the reins. He didn't hesitate. He was a mule in a thousand. He soared off the bank, went completely under with me, and came up swimming like a champion.

The *perro de agua* had sunk, but there was a blood trail in the water, and at the end of it I saw him, a brown shadow, deeper down than I could reach from the saddle. I dived for him, got hold of a leg, and came up to make a grab at Pony's tail, and missed. We went down through a current chute below the pool without getting maimed on a rock or snag—a minor miracle—and came ashore on a bar that struck out from the bank. Pony had water in his ears and was sore about it, and my camera, binoculars and current notebook were in the saddlebags and probably ruined. But I had a *perro de agua*. I sat down in a mud hole, without caring a damn that it was mud, to examine the animal. It was as familiar as an old friend and with good reason. In Alaska I had trapped or snared a good many of its brethren. But it was hard to get used to the fact that the species existed down here in the tropics. Especially it was difficult considering the buildup I had received concerning *perros de agua* at the university. *Canis genuinus*, my eye. It would cross with domestic dogs, my aching back. Here came the truck, slamming up the bar. In a moment everybody was embracing me Latin fashion and shaking my hand. I was a seventeen-gun hero, they thought.

"Of a truth, it is a fine *perro de agua*," Policarpio said. "Not the largest, you understand, but a splendid specimen." (The animal was 5 1/2 feet long.) Roberto gave me a searching look, and said, "You do not seem much excited. Is it because you are tired—or disappointed?"

"Make it just wet," I said. "But listen. If anybody ever comes to you gentlemen again for information about the *perro de agua*, you tell him that it is the largest, fattest, most elusive, hard-to-get and geographically misplaced of the world's veritable otters."

Because that's what the animal was, a huge otter. One of a giant race. It was its size and altered tropical pelt that had prevented me from guessing its identity. Which, I guess, winds this up. See you on a jungle hunt.

Captain Sharkbait's Triumph

Sharkbait pointed to a color picture of a luxury cabin cruiser tacked to the adobe wall.
"Being chicken never got anybody that."

"If you gents will take some good advice, cut that line and let's beat it to port," I said to Sharkbait and his customer Don Pedro when the first gust of stormwind came in across the purple-cobalt water. "Try for the fish some other day. Because who wants to get blown to Tehuantepec?"

Sharkbait flashed his brightest professional smile and said to take it easy, please, we still had plenty of time. Don Pedro didn't say anything. A 250-pound cattleman to whom the ocean would forever be strange territory, he was just hanging onto his rod, beginning to look worried and half-seasick. We were in a beat-up open boat under the Primavera cliffs, a couple of miles from the palm-shaggy village of Barra de Navidad, Jalisco. Half-an-hour ago, drift-fishing a mackerel bait here, Don Pedro had hooked something huge and mysterious. The fish had stayed on the bottom, savagely bulldogging and busting about, until it managed to foul the line, probably around a rock. I had no idea what kind of fish it was. Sharkbait admitted reluctantly that he didn't know. But it had tremendous weight and power. It had towed the boat when Don Pedro screwed the drag down.

"Plenty of time, hell!" I said. "Take another look."

You didn't have to be a weather prophet. Out to the west nervous lightning flickered among mosques of high-piled clouds, and below the clouds was the dark line of a squall moving toward land. Sharkbait pretended he didn't hear me. For the dozenth time he gunned the boat around the spot where the line seemed to be hung up. Nothing happened. I knew what Sharbait's feelings were. The kid was eighteen, a savvy saltwater Mexican brat dominated by a wonderful golden dream that I will presently tell you about, and it griped his soul to think of turning the unknown fish loose. Moreover, Don Pedro was a person of influence, loaded with loot. The kid needed him. So he did what he thought he had to do. He kicked off his cowhide huarache sandals, which left him clad only in shorts, and motioned for me to take the handle of the outboard.

"Don't go away and leave me," he kidded, and flipped over the side. As he did so lightning blitzed a tree on the sierra and there was a thunderclap that should have been heard in Omaha.

"*Valgame Dios*," Don Pedro gulped. "Naturally I would like to take this monster, but I wonder if the boy had considered that it might be a dangerous fish? Perhaps a giant octopus, or the grandfather of sharks, or who knows what?"

I didn't have any answer to that. We watched the kid go hand over hand down the heavy monofilament line. The roundabout was an azure desert, sun-dappled, fanged with pinnacles of black rock, across which schools of brilliant small fish were moving. Sharkbait went out of sight behind one of the upthrust rock formations, to reappear working at the line. He was close to thirty feet down. I was holding my breath sympathetically, when back against the dim loom of the cliff base, I saw a vast form materialize among the shadows. It was our hooked fish. I had only fleeting glimpses of it because the boat was now pitching in all directions, but it appeared to be reddish brown, deeply built and about the size of a garage door. It was opening and shutting its mouth, and I could make out the taut line leading to it. I still didn't know what kind of fish it was. But with the exception of a few manta rays, it was the biggest I had laid eyes on in these parts.

"That thing could swallow a man whole," Don Pedro said when he spotted the fish. "Why doesn't the boy come back up to the boat? I don't like this. I don't like it so much that I think maybe I am going to be sick."

"He hasn't seen the fish," I said, spooky myself, "and he'll rejoin the party when he runs out of air, I earnestly hope and trust."

Apparently the outsize creature was watching Sharkbait, and had concluded that he meant no good. At any rate, it suddenly shot seaward in a blur of speed, and hit the end of the line slack with a runaway-truck jolt that ripped the hook out. I saw the mangled remains of the mackerel bait swirl in the fish's wake and settle to the bottom. Then came Sharkbait, clawing for the surface and oxygen. I helped him aboard, after which I leaned over Don Pedro's shoulder and cut the line. I didn't give the kid the I-told-you-so treatment, but I felt like it, because we had waited too long. A barrel of water came over the bow as we roller-coasted into the first whitecapped waves. Before I could bail it out the initial onslaught of the squall struck, rain, screaming wind, lightning stabs and a continuous roll of thunder like the bombardment of Tarawa.

Sharkbait's guardian angel was on the job. I mean, we made port, and you couldn't logically place credit for it anywhere else. When we turned into the sheltered lagoon at the village the boat was only partly swamped and the motor, which had been repeatedly drenched by following seas, was purring valiantly. Don Pedro stumbled ashore, his face a lovely shade of hunter's green, and reached for Sharkbait's hand.

"I know that you took those risks only because you wanted me to catch the big fish," Don Pedro said emotionally. "Be assured that I will not forget it. When the weather improves," he added as he took off through the solid sheets of rain, "we will try again, *capitán*."

Later, changing into dry clothes at Sharkbait's house, I said, "You keep crowding your luck that way, sucker, and sooner or later you'll wind up in a real sweetheart of a jam." Sharkbait pointed to a four-color print of a luxury cabin cruiser tacked to the adobe wall, outriggers set and a marlin flag flying, uniformed mate at the wheel on the flying bridge. "Being chicken never got anybody a boat like that," he said. "Me, I intend to own one."

That was the kid's dream. He was in love with boats, blue water, and big-game fishing. When he looked at a pretty boat, he was like a lad watching his best girl coming down a springtime street with a rainbow behind her. But lacking money, the only boat he had to work with as yet was the primitive craft in which we had just tempted Davy Jones. So he was doing his fighting best to acquire a bankroll. Excepting today's affair, it was a pleasure to watch him work. Last fall when I was going out with him as supercargo we latched onto a visiting angler from Michigan, name of Harvey. This Harvey was a lean, likable chap, white-headed, who told us that the biggest fish he had ever caught was a five-pound bass. Now, thanks to an inheritance, he was out for whoppers. Sailfish and marlin. Yo heave ho, and a whole tropical ocean to fish in.

"If you don't mind," he said when we pushed off the first morning, "I'd like to rig my own baits. I've studied most of the books on billfish, and have some theories."

Nobody minded. You never know when you're going to learn something useful. But it developed that Harvey's notion of a proper billfish bait was pretty far out. He selected a fat mullet from the icebox, and ran the leader through it. He placed the hook with finicky care. He did a neat job of sewing up the mullet's mouth. Everything orthodox so far, and well done for a first-timer. But then the guy reached into his pocket and brought out two narrow, six-inch ribbons, one white, the other red, and so help me, sewed them to the mullet's tail! One gathered that they were supposed to counterfeit blood and a trailing intestine, but Harvey didn't elucidate. He dropped the bizarre bait over the stern, paid out sixty feet of line, and settled back on the plank seat with his feet braced against a gas can, happy expectancy written all over his face.

"How many times I have imagined being here," he said, looking around at the cotton-candy clouds, the birds and the long hills of sunshot water. "And, oh boy, the fish I caught!"

But I'll bet that he never, in his gaudiest imaginings, came up with a fishing drama such as was in store for him. We cruised for two hours hunting fins. No fins. No nothing. I was thinking that we ought to change baits, and this time omit the ribbons, when Sharkbait stood up pointing at the wake. In a moment I saw them, two blue-black shadows sliding in behind the decorated mullet. They were sailfish. They planed upward and their purple, polka-dotted sails lifted. Side by side in the storm of sunlight, with the wake creaming about them, they were a sight to thrill a man to his marrowbones. If we'd had outriggers and two lines in the water, I believe that we would have scored a double strike. As it was, one of the fish took over.

It turned on power, and blasting ahead, spear-whacked the mullet. Sharkbait cut the motor. Harvey was slow, but he had studied those books, because he slacked off line without being prompted, and when the sailfish turned with the bait in its mouth he slammed the hook home, putting his weight behind the rod.

The fish jumped once when it felt the steel, and once again so close alongside that I could have thrown my hat past it. It was a good fish, around nine feet. For an instant it hung in the air above us, shaking its spear at the sky, trying to get rid of the hook, then it belly-whopped down full-length in a high sun-jeweled splash, and headed west. I think that all of us had forgotten about the second fish, but it was still in the act. After a bit, when the hooked fish, having completed its first run, boomed out of the top of a wave off yonder, its mate, companion, or whatever jumped with it. They came out three times faster than a countdown. This was something I had seen only once before, off Guaymas in the Gulf of California. Then as now it was both inexplicable and spectacular. Harvey was hollering like a Huichol buck on a peyote bender.

"Young man," he found time to inform Sharkbait in a husky voice, "I don't know whether or not I can lick this wonderful fish. But if I do, by golly, I'll have a $50 tip for you."

Sharkbait jerked around with his mouth open. I guess he was afraid that he hadn't heard correctly. But when he had convinced himself that he had, a beatific smile spread over his youthful pan. "Y-yes, sir. Thank you," he said. "You just keep cranking in line and we'll—uh—by golly, lick him or die trying."

But like the other time off Guaymas, the sailfish won. Sharkbait chased the fish, and Harvey had regained part of his line, when the two fish took to the air again. I do not know whether the second fish was striking the line with its spear or simply fell on it. I didn't have glasses and we weren't close enough to follow the details of the action with the unaided eye. Whichever was the case, the hook tore out, and I personally am convinced that the accompanying fish tore it out. It had been a grand show, but Harvey and Sharkbait looked like kids who had been disappointed at Christmas. Harvey put on another bait, complete with ribbons, and we trolled back toward port. I was waiting for Sharkbait to make a try at salvaging the promised tip. I had confidence in him. It wasn't misplaced.

"You know, Mr. Harvey," he said as we swung into the lagoon, "that ribboned bait of yours is a terrific killer. I have been trolling for billfish all my life, first with my father and then on my own, but I never before saw two sailfish fight over a bait. If I hadn't seen it with my own eyes, I wouldn't have believed it would happen."

Harvey had been silent, but now he beamed and said animatedly, "So that is what they were doing? Crazy about the bait, heh? Well, well," he chortled. "Then in a way it was my fault that I lost the fish."

When Harvey paid off at the hotel, he was still grinning jovially, and I couldn't help seeing that he added $50 to the amount he owed for the morning's bluewater adventure. Due to Sharkbait's mental agility, he'd just had the time of his life.

Sharkbait was scrupulously ethical, but the dream of owning a cruiser was always foremost in his mind, and he could figure out more fancy ways to make a dollar than a Syrian rug merchant with the rent due. He had to depend chiefly on tips, because with his poor equipment he could charge only a fraction of the $40-a-day rate standard elsewhere among skippers who had modern boats and fine gear. But he always, or nearly always, got the tips, and did so without sacrificing dignity. For example, there was the time we spent a week in July fishing with a young Texas oil scion named John. This was shortly after the estate of Jalisco announced that it was going to bulldoze the little thatch-and-adobe village of Navidad to make way for a fabulous resort town that would rival Acapulco.

John told us that he had come south to look the ground over, thinking that he might invest in one of the posh hotels planned for the area. Maybe so. But he spent most of his time fishing with us. We fished at sea for black marlin and sailfish, and ran up into Marabosco lagoon, poling through mangrove tunnels to reach hidden tidal lakes, where we enjoyed marvelous sport taking *pargo*, sea trout, snook and the silvery ichthyological dynamos locally called chilis. I regret that I have not been able to identify the chili. Possibly it is the fish listed in the books as the four-pounder. But whatever its proper name may be, it is a handsome critter, good to eat, and a fighter to curl an angler's hair.

"What's the best lure for those particular beauties?" John asked excitedly when we put into a rock-sided cove and he had his first look at chilis leaping and playing on the surface. "Oysters," Sharkbait said. "And the rocks here are covered with them."

With that, he grounded the boat and the two of us went ashore and began shucking oysters. I ate mine. After all, John wasn't my customer. The oysters were small and dark with a faint coppery flavor, a gourmet's delight, but troublesome to open. John, standing in the stern of the boat, baited up with an oyster, cast into deep water, and surprised himself by hooking a chili before he had reeled in ten feet of line. The fish performed a dazzling series of aerial acrobatics, jumping and twisting, somersaulting and greyhounding as if it weighed 400 pounds and was a tackle-smasher from away back. It got free. By this time Sharkbait was standing at John's elbow with another oyster on the halfshell. John looked past the kid, saw me in the act of swallowing one of the delicacies, hesitated briefly, then ate the oyster instead of putting it on his hook.

"Godfrey," he said, smacking his lips. "Never tasted a better oyster." He glanced at the jungle-green water. "Or fought a livelier fish."

The ensuing three quarters of an hour before the tide changed was fraught with curious action. Sharkbait shucked oysters as if his salvation depended on it, dashing back and forth between the rocks and the boat. John ate oysters and caught chilis, or fought chilis and lost them. When it was time to leave on the tide he had caught five fish, averaging three pounds or so, and was a happy man. Sharkbait was tuckered out. As for me, I was full of oysters. But on the way back to town I got to speculating about the episode. Certain aspects of it didn't quite add up.

At the village when we were alone on the beach tidying up the boat, I said, "If you knew we were going to fish for chilis today, why didn't you stop at the restaurant this morning and buy a quart of oysters for bait?"

Sharkbait grinned. "No drama is that. The way it is, I've got a grateful customer. I mean, how can he help being grateful after I practically worked myself into a heatstroke for him?"

Still, I figured the kid was going to draw a blank in the case of friend John. The Texan craved social activity along with fishing, and toward the end of his week with us was becoming noticeably restive, even irritable. He had fiesta fever, an acute yen for the haunts of neon. You get so you can diagnose it almost at a glance. The accepted remedy, of course, is an airplane ticket. But Sharkbait found a temporary substitute. We went out one day for sea turtles. It was Sharkbait's idea, and he forebore to explain why he thought today was a good day to hunt sea turtles. I didn't catch on at all. The whole plot was too clever for me. However, as sea turtle hunts go, we had a good one.

"The idea is to make a fast run at a basking turtle before it can submerge," Sharkbait said. He handed John an eight-foot steel-shafted harpoon with a line attached. "You throw this into him and hang on. It isn't easy." The kid's teeth gleamed in his saddle-brown face. "The last man I had out was pulled overboard and nearly took me with him."

We bucked tide rips around Cape Pedregal and turned into a jungle-fringed bight with a blaze of flowering trees above it in which macaws and parrots were holding a noisy debate about something or other. Ahead, 100 yards distant, loafing on the surface, was a turtle. It looked like a yellow-green boulder top except that it was rocking in the easy swells. John stood up in the bow, harpoon ready, and Sharkbait fed gas to the motor. The turtle must have been deaf or asleep, because we were within fifty feet of it, motor howling, the boat pounding over the waves, before it took alarm and headed for the bottom. Sharkbait chopped the throttle at the last instant, and John pitched the harpoon through a yard of water to hit the turtle almost dead center, the barbed point crashing through its heavy shell with an audible chug.

The boat was still coasting a fair clip, and John tried to snub the line around his hip, cowboy-fashion. It didn't work. Jerked over the bow seat, he landed in my lap and we both ended up on the floor planks amidst a couple of gas cans, some green coconuts for drinking purposes, and a supply of mullet and a sizable octopus that Sharkbait had brought along for bait in case we decided to fish. John had held onto the line, you had to give him credit, and when we had untangled ourselves we brought the turtle aboard. It weighed nearly 100 pounds, and judging from the barnacles on its carapace could have been 100 years old. We spent the rest of the day hunting for another turtle, but sighted none. It was late when we returned to the lagoon.

"That was fun," John said. "But what in hell does a man do for entertainment here after the sun goes down? If I sit on that hotel gallery another evening watching the waves, the pigs and the dogs I'll be a psycho case. No movie. Not a television set within 300 miles. You can't buy a magazine, and anyway they turn the lights off at eleven o'clock. He shuddered. "Tomorrow I'm heading home. I've had it."

"Tonight will be different," Sharkbait promised him. "We will have a fiesta on the beach. That is why I wanted a turtle."

The kid wasn't just talking. As he had promised, we had a fiesta, a dandy. The whole town turned out in Sunday clothes. We built a couple of driftwood fires under some palms and barbecued not only the turtle but also two coconut-fed pigs. There was a mariachi orchestra, a lithe little Spanish-Aztec dancer in a red bikini, and a group of singers who weren't professionals but could have been. Somebody brought fireworks, and an inspired soul ran along the beach and set fire to a mile-long windrow of sun-dried water hyacinth that had washed out of the lagoon during the last storm. Everybody embraced John and wished him health and a lifetime of happy days. In the midst of all this, to my inexpressible surprise, the church bells rang for five minutes. John found a spot under a palm and ate pig and turtle with the *muy sympática* dancer, declaring that, hang him for a liar if it wasn't true, this was the swellest party that had been thrown for him in his whole life.

Next morning, packed to leave, he hadn't ceased praising the village hospitality. "Look," he said to Sharkbait before the auto stage pulled out for Guadalajara, "after last night I think you're a genius, damn if I don't!" He handed him a fat envelope. "Here's something for you. And please buy the little dancer a present from me, will you?"

The stage left, horn blowing and everybody waving, and I sat down on some sacked coconuts and tried to figure it all out. I didn't get anywhere, so I appealed to Sharkbait. "Come on, give," I said. "I'm thick-headed maybe, but I know you didn't pay for that party. Or did you?"

"Nobody paid for it," Sharkbait said, busy counting the bills in the envelope. "You see, it was just a matter of timing. Yesterday was July 24, San Juan's day, which is a big holiday in Mexico because anyway a third of our people are named Juan or Juanita." He stuffed the bills into his pocket and carefully buttoned the flap. "Of course it was pure luck that our generous customer happened to be christened John."

Sharkbait actually was a genius. When it came to pleasing an angler to the point where the man would thrust cash upon him, I doubt that he had an equal south of the border. But not all of his stratagems succeeded. One day a swaggering, wisecracking mine operator named Pancho drove into town from the Cerro Vaca country, and announced that he had a special job of fishing to do. Sharkbait asked him what did he mean, special? Whereupon the guy regaled us with a hoary piece of Aztec superstition with white whiskers reaching down to here. Dead-pan, delivering it straight, Pancho said that a certain notorious skinflint had died owing him a considerable sum of money, so that naturally, according to the belief of the mountain people, the deceased was obliged to return during the anniversary week of his death in the form of an animal, bird or fish and allow himself to be taken in payment of the amount he owed. This was the week.

"*Hombres*, I'm really going to enjoy pulling the old miser out of the ocean as a fish," he said. "And when I see him I'll recognize him, don't worry. Where's your boat? Let's get going."

Some Pancho. In the big-game fishing business you meet some remarkable oddball types and usually manage to get along with them, but this comic came close to being impossible. Although he milked the Aztec gag dry the first hour of his three-day fishing trip, he wouldn't let go of it. He boated a nice sailfish, regarded it critically and shook his head. Nope. It wasn't the fish. Too lean and active. He took several fair roosterfish trolling a spoon over sandy bottom inshore, and rejected them for one reason or another, all of which were supposed to be funny. He killed an exceptionally large guachinango snapper and told us, uh-uh, because it was red, that while the departed debtor had many personal faults, being a Commie wasn't one of them. Haw, haw, haw. It was the most awful brand of sustained corn that ever banged my unwilling ears, and that is covering some territory.

"We could fake a motor breakdown," I suggested desperately the morning of the third day while Sharkbait and I were eating breakfast. "This can't go on. It's becoming cruel and inhumane in multiples of five."

"You can stand it another day," Sharkbait said. "Concentrate on the good trips we've had, or something. Because I have an idea that will maybe delight the man."

We picked up Pancho in the village cantina where he was telling some strangers about his unique project, no doubt causing them to wonder what sort of funny farm they had blundered into, and cruised out to Pirate's Rock near the harbor entrance. I had never fished here. I had never seen anybody fishing here. But Sharkbait eased in against the basalt upsweep, using the oars, and without consulting Pancho baited up with a fist-size chunk of sierra. Adding a weight, he slid the bait over the stern. Pancho, who apparently had bottom-fished before, let the bait sink into the indigo depths and began jigging.

Twenty minutes or so later something down there took hold. It was strong and heavy, but sluggish, no performer. The main thing, I told myself, was that it was alive. It would be good for another bum joke. The tentative grin on Pancho's face as he pumped in line revealed that he was hard at work on one that would definitely kill us. I wished I was ashore. I wished I had been lucky enough to come down this morning with pneumonia or at least galloping dysentery. But Sharkbait played along like a champion.

"I believe you've got him this time, sir," he declared so enthusiastically that it didn't sound phony even to me. "I think it's your fish at last."

Hardly had he finished speaking when a nightmare creature broke the surface, writhing, tying itself in knots, and striking at the leader with its snakelike head. It was a pea-green moray eel, some eight feet long and as thick through as my leg, snagged in the back. Pancho took one horrified look at the thing and moved hastily to the other side of the boat. I had a .45 in a shoulder holster, and I got it out. The moray looked as if it wanted to come aboard. Once on a shrimp trawler I had seen a similar moray take control of the deck until the mate blew it to kingdom come with a shotgun. I knew of fishermen who had died of infection caused by moray bites. Sharkbait was calm, but he had advantage. Because it was soon clear to me that he had expected that a moray would take Pancho's bait.

"Is that your fish?" the kid asked, reaching out with an oar. "Do you want a closer look?" Pancho, though badly shaken, managed to rally. "Absolutely that's him," he jittered. "To the very life. I knew he'd be the slipperiest, crookedest fish in the ocean." He drew a belt knife. "But I'm going to let him go so I'll have the pleasure—heh, heh—of catching him every year at this time if I want to."

He cut the line.

Back at the village Pancho paid for his boat time, deducting three hours because today we had come in early, and failing to include the cost of tackle he had lost and a vacuum jug he had dropped and broken, maintaining that he understood tackle loss would be absorbed by Sharkbait and that the jug almost certainly had been defective, probably when it left the factory, and was that his fault? Then he shook hands, said it had been a fine trip and thanks for everything, and he'd see us next year when it was again time to collect his bill. Ho, ho, ho, and what would life be without some laughs, eh, boys? He swaggered away and Sharkbait stared after him, eyes narrowed, but he said nothing. Finally he smiled and shrugged his shoulders.

Let's get back to Don Pedro and the unknown heavyweight fish we had lost under the Primavera cliffs. The storm continued all night, wind screeching and the thunder-drums booming without letup. It was the first time I had experienced thunder so violent that it jarred plaster off the ceiling. In the morning the storm had abated but there was a seaway that would have given an LST trouble. We stayed in port and Don Pedro held a series of conferences, very private, with the village elders. When the following morning broke calm and pretty we went back out to the cliffs and began deep-drifting another mackerel bait. I didn't think we had a prayer of success. True, I had known hook-torn fish to strike again in the same waters. But I knew of a whole lot more cases when they were so scared and suspicious that they'd flee at sight of a boat's shadow.

Today we were shot-full of luck. Our fish was dumb, hungry or arrogantly confident, for we had dragged the bait less than an hour, patrolling the foot of the cliffs, when he took it. There was no mistaking his weight and power. Besides, I slipped over the side with a skin-diver's mask and took a look down the line. There he was, old big stuff himself, opening and shutting his coal scuttle mouth, and now and then standing on his head to grind his nose into the sand. There were no rocks here, so he had to fight the tackle, and it was a losing fight, because it became plenty apparent that Don Pedro's 250 pounds were more muscle than fat. He had the back and arms of a weightlifter.

Forty minutes after it was hooked, the fish gave up and Don Pedro horsed it to the surface. It was, as we might have guessed, a huge jewfish, locally called *merou*, which in dialect means "chief." The species was scarce hereabouts but they had been taken, although few if any were as large as this one. We killed it with the harpoon and towed it to port. As there were no adequate scales in Navidad, we had to estimate its weight. We gave it 1,200 pounds. It wasn't a beautiful brute, and its fight had been more stubborn than dramatic, but no villager could claim to have taken a heavier fish. Don Pedro was so pleased and excited as a crowd gathered and he described his hassle with the jewfish and pointed out the wound made by the hook three days before that he shook and stammered like an old-time bridegroom.

For Sharkbait, bringing in the monster fish was an important professional triumph, but his truly great triumph came when Don Pedro laid a derrick beam of an arm across his shoulders, motioned imperiously for silence, and said, "As some of you know, I have bought beach land here on which a large hotel will be built. The hotel will need a sport fishing boat, the best. Today I will wire my agent in the United States to buy such a boat. My plan is to sign it over to a competent *capitán* and let him operate it on a longterm contract with the hotel, and pay for it out of the boat's earnings. The *capitán* I have selected is—this boy Sharkbait."

Thus the ever-pleasant but chrome tough and dedicated kid came out on top, and I submit that he earned the break. If he keeps pitching he'll probably own the hotel as well as the boat.

The Curse of the Chonchos

He was ancient and dirty, and his black medicine was The Curse of the Chonchos.

First let me mention about my dog Chica. She had been with me since that day at Guaymas five years ago when Tommy Jamison, Sport Fishing Director there, stealthily deposited a packing box on my porch. The box contained Chica and her several brothers and sisters. Since Chica was the runt of the litter, I fortunately was unable to give her away. She grew up in hunting camps and became, I will always contend, the smartest all-round gun dog in Mexico, equally competent on a duck hunt or in the jungle trailing a *tigre*. Small and black, silky coated, her ancestry was obscure, but she had it. She could think like a man. The Mexicans loved her. They regarded her as a person. So did I.

Now, about our fateful choncho hunting adventure. It began at the tiny thatched-hut village of La Cumbre, deep in the wildly canyoned Huichol Country. Policarpio and I brought the pack-train up to the village on a cold, misty afternoon. Policarpio was *mayordomo* of the outfit—a lean three-quarter Aztec type and very rough-barked. We pitched camp in a stand of oaks on the bank of a stream. Because it was customary, I then went in search of the local headman, to check in, sort of. His hut was at the foot of a cliff, smoke curling from the eaves, fronted by a refuse midden that looked as if it had been collecting here since before the Conquest. I knocked on the pine-shake door, and when a wheezing voice invited me to enter, pushed it open. Before I could step inside, however, Chica crowded hard against my legs, snarling. In a moment, when my eyes had adjusted to the dim, smoky interior, I saw why. The hair on the back of my neck started to lift.

It was quite a headman we had to deal with. Wrinkled and dirty, so ancient that you could have arrived at his age only by a carbon fourteen test, he sat crosslegged on a grass mat in the middle of the single small room. Manifestly, he was a *brujo*—witch doctor—of the snake clan, for tethered by a rawhide thong to a peg driven into the dirt floor in front of him was a big, a truly big, timber rattlesnake. The brute was coiled, but you could see that it was at least six feet long. Its body was as thick through as my forearm. I stood staring, ignoring the *brujo's* bland invitation to sit down. I knew from experience among the Huichols what was going to happen here in a few minutes. On the floor near the picketed snake was a pool of sunlight coming from a hole in the roof. When the moving spot of light covered the snake, the *brujo* would toss the reptile a live but hamstrung rat, baby opossum or some other beast small enough for it to swallow. A sacrifice to both the snake god and the sun.

Of course the *brujo* had known that I would visit him, and probably the grisly little ceremony was planned for my edification. But I didn't intend to be a witness. Snakes give me the shuddering creeps. So I got down to business fast. I told the *brujo* that we wanted to hunt in the area, and asked him about cats. He coughed, spat and allowed that the cat tribe was well represented, and that it would suit him just fine if we killed them all. Then I asked him about chonchos. I always ask about chonchos here. But since his people shot and trapped them for food, we would have to reimburse the village for each one we killed. I inquired, how much? Without batting an eye, he said 100 pesos per choncho. Which was outright banditry even for a Huichol *brujo*.

"I could buy a cow for 100 pesos," I protested. "Then why don't you buy a cow?" he said, and coughed some more.

Maybe he wanted to bargain, but I didn't wait to find out. The spot of sunlight had reached the rattlesnake. As the *brujo* finished speaking, he reached behind him and dragged a decorated string bag into view. There was something alive in the bag. I said, "Thanks, I'll give your generous proposition some thought. Meanwhile, have fun, chum." Chica and I left hastily. Behind us in the hut I thought I heard an animal scream.

But I had come for chonchos, and chonchos I would have. Actually the bird has a variety of names, depending on where you find him. His chief aliases are crested guan, ajol and chachalaca grande, while his solid Latin name is *Penelope purpurescans*. As a sporting bird he is tops, ranking with wild turkey. Naturally, in remote areas he is unsophisticated, but when he has been hunted he becomes as wily and full of tricks as any game bird on the continent. He seems to be most plentiful in the states of Oaxaca, Michoacan and Colima. Ornithologists believe that he may have been the domestic fowl of the ancient Aztecs, often mentioned by Spanish historians, but unfortunately never adequately described. It is a fact that he can easily be tamed. I have seen chonchos living contentedly in farmlots and even on the lawns of urban homes.

I have been informed by otherwise enlightened and hard-headed Mexicans that I didn't take the *brujo* seriously enough. Anyhow, several days later we killed tow chonchos, and a chain of troubles began. It was another mist-hung day. Mounted on two clever-footed mules. Policarpio and I rode up through the overcast to a sunlit ridge that was like an island in a fantastic pearl-colored sea. We were on a game trail, Chica was trotting ahead, when from above us came a *chee-oop chee-oop* sound. Policarpio said that it was a choncho. I thought it was a hen turkey. As either would be most welcome in camp, the cook being out of fresh meat, we got down and started a stalk. It turned out that Policarpio was correct but too conservative. Instead of one choncho, there was a whole flock of the birds.

Chica, working close, halted barely in time to warn us. Then there came the chonchos, eight or ten of them, twenty yards to one side and roaring straight down the slope. Their flight was so erratic as they banked and twisted among low, gnarled oaks that I couldn't get lined up. "Knock one down if you can," I said to Policarpio. He carried a long-barrel muzzleloader, about 16-gauge, and was good with it. The chonchos hedge-hopped past us, gaining speed with each yard, and then were over the cloud-sea covering the valley. Perfect targets. Going away targets, the kind I like. I cut loose with the 12-gauge and scored. At almost the same instant Policarpio fired. He did all right too. The birds fell into the sun-illumined mist, plummeting out of sight, and leaving no hole or ripple to mark their passage. It was an unearthly thing to see.

The mountainside at this point was nearly vertical, and farther down was planted to corn. We zigzagged after the chonchos, letting our mules find the way, and soon were below the cloud layer and at the edge of the cornfield. Some tough-looking Indian machete-men were cutting brush here. I asked if they had seen our chonchos fall. No, they hadn't. One pockmarked gent with a knife-scar across his cheek suggested that we only imagined we had killed two chonchos. No doubt the birds had flown away. At least, they hadn't fallen into this cornfield. I was watching Chica. She ranged above us to where the mist began, casting from side to side, and after a bit halted and looked back at me, wagging her tail. Policarpio and I went up to her. On the ground were some purple-black feathers and some spots of blood. Also the fresh prints of huarache-shod feet. A few minutes later Chica found where the other choncho had fallen, and been picked up. The Indians, standing in a group, were clearly enjoying the situation.

I thought, well shucks, I've outlived Ghengis Khan, Napoleon, Alexander the Great and other notable stalwarts, but if this is the place to end it, let's get going. I reached into my jacket pocket for a couple of buckshot loads I carry there. But Policarpio didn't hold with me.

"*Señor*, this not good," he said between his teeth. "It is the work of the *brujo*. I personally would like to fight. If I was alone I would fight. But I feel responsible for you. Therefore we had better go."

He was right. So we went, to the amusement of the Indians. It was the kind of thing that can lead to hyperacidity, but why get into an international fracas over a couple of chonchos? Much better to gulp down some pride. Only the trouble was, the *brujo* wasn't through with us. He still had an angle. When the morning of our departure came we had made up the packs, and I was checking them and the rigging. Into this bustle of activity hobbled the *brujo*, flanked by four of the hard case machete-men we had encountered at the mountainside cornfield. The *brujo* carried his painted and snake-carved staff of office. Planting it dramatically, he declared bronchially that since by our own admission we had killed two chonchos, we owed the village 200 pesos. He held out his hand. The money, please. For pure certified gall he rated all prizes, both foreign and domestic.

It was a mistake and I knew it, but I lost my temper. I told the venerable so-and-so to go home and feed his snake, because he and his bravos were out of their weight class here. If he thought he had a legitimate bill, he could send it to my agent in New York, *Señor* Edgar Allan Poe. Or he could paint it green and do you-know-what with it. But in the meantime please get out of the way because we had work to do.

The *brujo* regarded me with unblinking obsidian eyes. "You will pay," he said grimly. "Remember, every time you kill a choncho you will pay. For the rest of your life." With that, surrounded by the palace guard, he headed back toward his hut.

Six hours later and fifteen miles down the valley, we lost a mule. It was gentle, willing claybank that I had often ridden and for which I had developed considerable affection. I don't know what caused the animal's death. I'm no vet. It began limping, then lay down in the trail with its pack. Policarpio and the others, all of them mule-savvy, did what they could. But it wasn't good enough. The mule's leg swelled to twice its normal size, and something went wrong with the hapless beast's breathing. It perished miserably. This wasn't the first mule I had lost in Mexico. Probably it won't be the last. But I didn't like the circumstances. Too much coincidence. Policarpio, I guess, felt the same way.

"Do you believe that the Huichol snakeworshiper back there has any real power?" he asked after supper at the pine-knot fire as we sat smoking and listening to a couple of blue mockingbirds holding a contest. "I inquire because I am almost certain that our mule was snake-bitten."

"If you mean what I think you mean, the answer is no," I said. "The guy is a racketeer, cashing in on superstition. He isn't even a smart witch doctor. Just greedy and ornery." Such were my sentiments then.

My next experience with a choncho occurred during a visit to the delta country of the Rio San Pedro, where we operated out of a picture-postcard camp in a palm grove near a Cora Indian fishing village. It was midafternoon, hot and sticky, and we were sitting around in our shorts trying to cool off by drinking tepid coconut milk, a doomed project, when I became aware of a most unusual sound. Starting as a pulsebeat and growing in volume, it was a rhythmic choral booming, unlike anything I had ever heard except perhaps in some Igor Stravinsky recordings. I asked Policarpio what it is. He had already got to his feet and was listening intently. The sound came from downriver.

"It is a flock of chonchos," he said. "They always sing like that just before a big rainstorm."

"They're nuts. This isn't the season for rain," I said. "Can we borrow a boat from the Indians?"

Policarpio said, too eagerly, that he would bet anybody five pesos that it rained before nightfall, and that he would find out about a boat. He got us a canoe, a handsome but horribly cranky dugout carved from a white mahogany log. With Chica in the bow, we pushed off down the river. I took a critical look at the sky. There was a cloud bulging over the northern horizon, but it didn't look like a rain cloud. Nor did the air feel like rain. So I said okay, I would wager five pesos that the chonchos were lousy weather prophets. We rounded a bend into a long, still pool with yellow mudbars on one side and a steep rise of jungle on the other. I observed that there were crocodile tracks in the mud. I also saw something ahead of us in the pool that could have been floating driftwood, only it had eyes. It was a croc, a big one. I hoped that it would be around later. I like to shoot crocs, maybe because they scare me.

As things developed, I needn't have worried about this croc leaving. He stayed around, all right.

The chonchos, still making with rhythm, were hidden among the vine-roped trees. When he judged that we were within shooting range of them, Policarpio grounded the canoe and we got busy taking the jungle apart branch by branch. Fifteen minutes passed before we located one of the birds. It was in a wild-fig tree that overhung the green-brown water. Its bizarre feather crest was erect, and I could see its mottled breast bulge each time it gave its booming call. The bird was watching us, but I suppose that it was not afraid because it was accustomed to seeing Cora canoes on the river, and few of the Indians had firearms. As I said, there are trusting, unsophisticated chonchos as well as clever ones. I had to make this bird flush by banging a paddle against the gunwale. Even then it didn't want to leave the tree. It craned its neck a us, jittering on the branch, before taking off over the water.

Other chonchos were flushing but I didn't see them. I laid the barrel on my very own choncho and pulled, and he hit the water sixty feet out so hard that he bounced.

Before I could grab her, Chica went over the side after the bird. This was her worst fault and I had argued with her about it, no exaggeration, at least a hundred times, and got nowhere. She considered it was her prerogative to swim after a dead or crippled bird in the water. Maybe she thought she was a Chesapeake. I wouldn't know. But this time she was asking for bad trouble. I yelled at her, reaching for the .45 auto I carried in a shoulder holster. Policarpio yelled at her, and dug in with his paddle. By the time he got the dugout turned, Chica was halfway to the choncho. At his juncture, of course, Old Ugly the croc hove on the scene. To him it must have seemed a lovely setup, a chance to score a double with practically no effort. I saw the ripple first, then the long, green shape below the surface.

He was heading for Chica. I blasted three fast shots into the water within inches of his snout. The .45 slugs turned him, but he was stubborn or almighty hungry. This time he made for the choncho. Swimming about as fast as a croc can, he planed head and shoulders out of the water and grabbed the bird between his jaws with a gurgling crunch. I got in two more shots, and we were so close now that I couldn't miss. When he dived with the choncho, he left a spreading stain of blood in the water. Chica was swimming in a circle, confused by the shooting, trying to see what was going on. I hoisted her aboard by the scruff of her neck, and she at once twisted around to look for the choncho. There was no use bawling her out. Besides, I was too happy to have her safe aboard instead of in the maw of the croc.

Well, we started back to camp. Before we got there raindrops dimpled the river. The cloud moving in from the north was overhead now, and it no longer looked innocent. The shower became a downpour with a gusty wind behind it. Big, warm drops that splashed when they hit. Policarpio, poker-faced, plied his paddle without comment. I handed him five pesos. At camp, under our tarpaulin fly, with palm fronds curvetting wildly overhead, and a creek flowing where the cooking fire had been, we told the crew what had happened.

"The Huichol *brujo* was right," I said. "I killed a choncho, and I had to pay—five pesos." It must have been a bum joke, because nobody laughed.

"But it was a close thing for Chica," Policarpio said, taking her under his slicker. "One hopes no such danger will threaten her again."

Unhappily the history of hope is loaded with tragedies. On the next morning Chica pawed me awake in the gray quarter hour before dawn and I pretended to be sore. "Beat it, nuisance," I said. "Tell somebody else about your insomnia."

I covered my head with the blanket, but she pulled it off and rooted me expertly under the ear with her cold nose. So I abandoned sleep. Chica was facing the jungle across from camp, wagging her tail. It was her sign language for good news. I listened a moment, then sat up abruptly and felt for the 12-gauge beside me. Strange sounds were issuing from the dusky wall of greenery. A year ago I couldn't have begun to guess what kind of critter was making them. But now I knew. It was a choncho, that purple-black, bottle-breasted, almost-turkey-size prize upland game bird of western Mexico. Oh boy, how I wanted to kill one!

Partly it was because of the superb sport the birds provide. But mostly in this case it was to prove something. I believed that coincidence, my imagination and maybe a trace of native superstition had ganged up on me. I needed to find out.

While the choncho mewed, grunted, honked, chirped and made other *outré* noises, I arose and dressed. The rest of the camp was asleep. We were bivouacked at a spring in a gunsight pass on the western slope of the Sierra Madre, in the state of Colima. It was the 230th day of a tough and colorful hunt—a determined combing of these formidable peaks. With me at present were five helpers. We had a dozen assorted horses and mules, and a wondrously battered truck that I daily expected to collapse into a heap of its component parts. I tossed a pebble at Policarpio. He was stretched out near the ashes of the campfire, swathed in a red serape, with his head pillowed on his saddle. He opened his eyes, listened and surged erect.

"Hah," he said, "a choncho." He shook his pants and boots vigorously to dislodge any scorpions or centipedes that might have taken up residence during the night. "I have the feeling, *Señor*, that presently we will make a liar of a certain Huichol witch doctor, *cabrone* that he is."

I said the bloody blazes with the witch doctor and all his friends and associates; I just wanted to kill a choncho. I hoped that I sounded convincing. We waited for shooting light. The cook got up and started coffee. The other men were now awake. The sky changed from pearl to rose to copper, and then the sun topped the sierra, pouring a flood of glory down the shaggy slopes and chasing the deep shadow from under the jungle trees. The choncho was still calling, but intermittently. It had about finished its chore of welcoming the mountain dawn. Policarpio, Chica and I went after the bird. Possibly critics will hasten to inform me that dogs are not used in hunting chonchos, any more than they are used in hunting turkeys. So I will make reply in advance, as follows: Let the critics hunt chonchos their way, and I'll hunt 'em my way. Chica was special and she knew about chonchos. She was an asset. We needed her.

We eased through a perfumed tangle of temple-blossom vines to an open space. Some sixty yards distant, at the farther end of the opening, stood the dark-green, wide-spreading tower of a false-ebony tree. As nearly as I could tell, the choncho was in this tree or under it. Chica obviously shared my belief, although she was handicapped because there was no wind. She was sneaking along like a black panther, watching both the tree and thirty degrees of jungle floor. The choncho hadn't uttered a sound for a full minute. I hoped that it hadn't run. I hoped that it wouldn't flush with the tree between itself and us. I hoped a lot things. Suddenly Chica froze in her version of a classical point. She claimed that the choncho was on the ground. I moved up even with her and tried to spot the bird. No luck. I glanced around at Policarpio. He shrugged.

So I stepped ahead of Chica. Action occurred and it was the stuff of which nightmares are made. No more terrible thing ever happened in my hunting experience.

The choncho flushed fifty feet ahead with a brave blast of wings, clawing for altitude. It had been hiding behind a cluster of interwoven lianas. It was a dope for not running when it had the chance. I let go with the left barrel and feathers flew. Winged, the choncho sideslipped, hit a tree branch, and tumbled squawking and flopping to the ground. Chica was on it in a flash. She grabbed the crippled wing to prevent the bird from escaping, and backed toward me. The choncho, full of fight, pounded her with its good wing and raked her muzzle with its heavy, hooked beak. Chica had all she could handle—with finesse, that is—and Policarpio and I started toward her to end the matter. Then it happened. Less than ten seconds had elapsed since the choncho took to the air. A blink of time. But as I remember the episode, everything is in slow motion, each detail sharp, seen with great clarity.

There was no forewarning. Just Policarpio's yell, "*Ai* Chica—look out for the coral snake!" He sprinted ahead drawing his machete.

When I belatedly saw the snake both Policarpio and Chica were moving in and out of my line of fire. I couldn't shoot. I would have put shot into Chica and probably taken a leg off Policarpio. I suppose that the snake, two feet of brilliantly banded death, had been lying among fallen leaves waiting for the sun when the choncho crashed alongside it, or for all I know, onto it. At any rate, I saw Chica, with the choncho's neck between her jaws now, swerve toward the coiled snake, persuading me that she never was aware of its presence. I saw Policarpio sidestep Chica and lift his machete, the thirty-inch blade flashing in the sunlight. And I saw the coral snake, but couldn't tell whether it bit Chica or the choncho.

There was a split-second opportunity. The shotgun pointed itself, bucked, and the charge of No. 4s blew the snake into the ground and spun the machete out of Policarpio's hand. Chica was shaking the choncho, and likely broke its neck because it ceased struggling. She then let go of the bird and came toward me.

I said to Policarpio, "Did the snake hit her?"

He was holding his numbed right hand, watching Chica, his face an Aztec mask. "I do not know," he said. "But I pray to all the saints that it did not."

I saw Policarpio's lips moving. He was actually petitioning the saints. There was nothing else anybody could have done. Not one single thing. Chica took maybe a dozen steps, then looked up at me, a question in her dark intelligent eyes. An instant later she staggered, and went down on her side. I held her until it was over. It was bad but the cobra-type venom is fast and it was in a vein. A friend of five years, the greatest hunting dog I ever owned, gone in as many minutes.

"Do you know what I am going to do when this hunt is over?" Policarpio said savagely a couple of hours afterward as we were packing up to leave. "I am going back to La Cumbre with my four brothers and my one grown son, and shoot chonchos." He grinned like a wolf. "Perhaps the *brujo* will resent it. If he does, won't that be just too wonderful?"

Nobody could ever convince him, or the rest of the crew, that the *brujo* was simply a sick old charlatan who had tried to pick up a few easy pesos. As for myself, I have only this remark: I don't buy snakeworshiper magic, but I can't forget that I was trained in a hard, fast school to beware of coincidence.

The Mysterious *Onca*

Somewhere, says Russell Annabel,
this animal exists and I am going to bring it back. . . .
Not so, says Pete Brown. There is no such animal.
Which expert is right? Judge the facts for yourself.

It is not often that two authorities in this field get on the same trail in two widely different places—especially when they are hunting an animal that is not even known to exist. But when this does happen, you can be sure a good story is in the offing. Events have now reached the stage where enough facts are in to tell it.

The animal in question here is the *onca*. It is also sometimes spelled "onza." But when the Mexican natives talk about the small, deadly jungle cat they say "*onca*." That's what we'll call it.

You won't find the *onca* listed in natural history books because most scientists don't believe there is an undiscovered, unclassified new species of cat anywhere in the world, much less under their noses. The evidence *for* an *onca* is that in the desert country of the deep Southwest and in the heart of the Mexican jungle, the *onca* is a very real creature. A feared creature. A man-killer, as you will see.

The two men on the *onca's* trail are very much the kind of guys that like to see for themselves. One is *Sports Afield* Arms Editor Pete Brown, and the other is Russell Annabel, an ex-Alaska sourdough, now in Mexico. Pete got interested in the *onca* through his friend Curtis Prock, an Arizona jaguar and mountain lion specialist. If the tales were true and there was a strange, undiscovered breed of cat down in Mexico, Prock reasoned his dogs would run it. He and Pete did just that. They believe that they have discovered what the *onca* is. Annabel is at this writing still on the trail, still very much convinced the first *onca* has yet to be brought out of the bush.

Perhaps the best way to give you the background of what the *onca* is (or isn't) might be to tell how Annabel got interested in the yarn. The story of his *onca* hunt has been dogged by bitter disappointment and even violent, mysterious death. It all started when Rusty wrote us:

"Another story may be taking shape. Since 1932, when I first came down into these jungled parts, I have been endeavoring to kill an *onca*. So has every other *gringo* hunter with a fondness for hunting cats. To the best of my knowledge nobody has succeeded. The scarcity of the animal has given rise to all manner of bizarre yarns about it. Fran Dobie, for example, writes that he believes it to be a cross between a mountain lion and a tiger. Another well-known cat hunter, Lee Waddell, thinks that the *onca* is a barren female mountain lion, outcast from its kind.

"I never had any theories. I just wanted to see an *onca*, and kill it if possible. The closest I ever came to doing so was during a hunt in Nayarit, which I described in a *Sports Afield* story. But maybe the *onca* quest will pay off too. At any rate, my good professor of biology knows where there is an *onca* skin, and has sent for it. He says that the Indian who killed this *onca* probably could lead me to another. When I get time, and can afford it, I am going to run the lead down. Maybe it will prove to be another snipe hunt. But you can't win if you don't play.

"I really ought to keep quiet about it, but instead I'll yield to reckless impulse, turn up the kerosene lantern and record the episode for the home front, regardless of the probable damage to my professional reputation.

"We had dropped down to the isolated ranch of Carmen Sandoval to buy a couple of goats for use as bait animals. This ranch is in the heart of the *onca* country. It is on the north slope of Cerro Media Luna, the only area I know about in Mexico where almost every resident you meet has had personal dealings of one sort or another, mostly dramatic, with *oncas*. I mean, in these parts the *onca* is no mythical beast. Rather it is a highly respected, and by many feared, reality.

"*Vaqueros*, timber scouts, charcoal burners and other jungle folk keep telling me bigger and better yarns about the *onca*, which

I am dutifully collecting in my notebooks, and they have a common theme—the *onca* is a wily, dangerous killer of a cat, strictly no quarry for reckless amateurs or daydreaming slowpokes with a gun. I realize that much of this information has got to be watered down, divided by ten, and then taken only with a sizable grain of salt. But, still, the boys have lived here all their lives, and they do sound convincing. At any rate, largely through my eagerness to make a kill, I have developed an *onca* twitch. I keep looking over my shoulder, and hear things in the night. Which probably, on the basis of experience, will turn out to be a rewarding state of mind."

Time after time Rusty or one of his men had an *onca* within reach only to have it slip from their grasp. An Indian killed one over a bait staked out in the jungle. The Indian disappeared with the carcass. Rusty and his No. 1 assistant, a Mexican named Policarpio, were furious, blamed themselves for talking up the *onca* too much to the natives, to the point where the primitive back-country people considered them medicine to ward off evil spirits. Reports reached them that two *oncas* killed and ate a man near the town of Pueblo Juarez. The hunters moved to this area, set up camp, and staked out baits. Then tragedy struck. One of Rusty's men was found dead at the bottom of a cliff. He had been watching a dead mule killed as bait for an *onca*. His rifle had been fired once. The cuts and scratches on his body indicated he had been mauled by a cat. But there was no cat to be found. Again, no *onca*.

Annabel expanded his operation, determined not to let up on the search. He wrote:

"Well, if we win this campaign for an *onca* I will unhesitatingly stand up in public and declare that we deserved to. And I believe that we are going to win.

"We have covered the entire wild sierra country of the state in which the *onca* is known to exist. We have around twenty experienced hunters out, most of them full time. As a necessary stimulant, I have offered a reward of 1,000 pesos for the skin and all the bones of an *onca*. In this country that is a lot of money. I would hate to speculate as to what some of our mountaineer recruits actually would do for the sum. Of course, I wanted to kill the *Sports Afield onca* myself. But I was forced to the decision that the main thing was to get hold of an *onca*, and write the story of the hunt.

"It became too apparent after the first month of the hunt that a man could spend his whole life in these awful upended boondocks trying to kill an *onca*, and if his luck was bad, never lay eyes on one.

"But given a little luck. . . . The other day the president of the State Engineers' Society, driving from Armeria along a black road into the Sierra, with four other engineers in the car, saw an *onca* bound across the road and halt in the shadow of a cliff 100 feet distant. It was an easy shot, and all present affirm that the animal was a veritable *onca*. It had a gray pelt and heavy shoulders with oddly skinny hindquarters. It was larger than most pumas. The long tail was characterized by what Sierra hunters call the *mota*, a tassel that usually is dark red, but sometimes white. But there wasn't a gun in the car!

"After the good president had called to tell us about the incident, my *majordomo*, Policarpio, who has been in the saddle steadily since New Year's combing some of the most horribly rugged areas I ever saw, without seeing even a flash of *onca* hair, got up stiffly and said to excuse him, please, he was going to step outside a moment and maybe be sick.

"Almost as bad, two weeks ago the little state development magazine *Colima* came out with an account of an *onca* kill at a place called Temisquintli. The kill was made by an itinerant mountaineer shooting a lead slug in a .50 caliber muzzleloading shotgun. We had spent four hard days in the Temisquintli area lining up hunters. But the successful guy wasn't one of ours. I have his name, but nobody knows where he is or can even suggest likely spots to look for him. The mountain men here wander like timber wolves, and they don't sign registry books.

"Thus, one *onca* has been sighted and two killed by others during our hunt. I mentioned the first kill in a letter—an Indian shot the cat off one of Carmen Sandoval's baits. But I don't believe that any more kill-and-disappear episodes will occur. We have covered too much territory, and have too assiduously spread the news of our reward offer. I feel certain that the next man who kills an *onca* will come in with skin and skeleton. He'll have heard the word, and nobody in these parts is about to miss out on collecting 1,000 pesos.

"I feel that we have proved that the *onca* is not a myth, and we know where he lives. The campaign we have got under way will increase as word that a reward is offered seeps into the odd corners and crannies of the Sierra. Like a battle, the campaign couldn't be stopped now even if we wanted to stop it. A dozen years from now, you may be sure, Colima mountaineers, with the reward in mind, will be praying for a chance to kill an *onca*. Somebody is bound to get lucky, and I have taken the precaution to make it clear to state authorities that I will pay only for the first *onca* delivered.

"In the meantime I'll expect each day that some shaggy hunter will come up with an *onca* and get his name in the Americano magazine *Esports Uh-Feel*, which is the best any of my boys can do with the magazine's name."

Pete Brown considers that his friend Curtis Prock is that hunter. Prock brought out of the hills near Tepic in the Mexican state of Nayarit two kittens which were positively identified by all the natives who saw them as *oncas*. Brought back to Phoenix, Arizona, home port for both men, the kittens were immediately identified by a zoo curator as jaguarundi. Now the jaguarundi is also a little-known, seldom-seen cat, but its scientific identity has long been established. It isn't new. Is the *onca* another name for jaguarundi? But let Pete tell the story in his own words:

"For several years I've been harboring an ever-growing desire to make the acquaintance of an *onca*. I've read about them in stories, and while on hunting trips into Mexico I've listened to fantastic tales of the ferocious *onca* from Mexicans themselves.

"On June 17, 1958, I attended a program of the 38th Annual Meeting of the American Society of Mammalogists held at the University of Arizona in Tucson. Leading mammalogists from all over the country were in attendance. Robert E. Marshall made a twenty-minute report on "The *onca*—a little-known form of large feline carnivore from western Mexico." Of course most mammalogists are very, very skeptical of such a subject—they can't afford to be otherwise.

"Still, reports and stories of the *onca* have persisted and at least one man I know in Arizona has insisted that it is a yet unclassified species of cat. He has spent months on end in Mexico attempting to capture one—dead or alive. He badly needed an *onca* body, and it would take at least one body to prove his point. The fact remained that no one had ever delivered one of these strange and elusive cats as evidence for the mammalogists. At least none which were identified as an *onca*. There has been a missing link.

"I think I've finally met two live, honest-to-goodness *oncas*. If true, the great *onca* mystery is about to be exploded. In order to supply the missing link, it was, of course, necessary to get one of the cats in question. Once the evidence is captured it is then necessary to determine that it is what has been referred to as the *onca*. It wouldn't be fair to capture just any old cat that happened along and declare it to be the *onca*. If this could be done I have a big old mixed-up tomcat which might give the mammalogists cause to ponder.

"About one year ago it looked as if we might have a good clue to an *onca* when Curtis Prock returned from a Mexican hunting trip and reported that his hounds had run two very strange-looking mountain lions. He caught a glimpse of them and that was all. He said they were about the size of a small female mountain lion, long neck, small head, almost black along the ridge of the back, and exceedingly fast. His description seemed to fit what I had heard about the *onca* in Mexico, and I so informed Curtis. He thought he could go back and get one of these cats and was all for doing it—and so was I. We planned to make the attempt together, but I was delayed on another trip and couldn't go.

"Curtis hit the jackpot. He took a customer on a jaguar hunt, collected the jaguar and headed for the area where he had seen the unusual cats the year before. The dogs struck a trail almost immediately and after a short chase treed the cat—or as it turned out, cats—about a mile from a small Mexican farm. As the men came up, the cat jumped clear of the tree and escaped, but it left behind two kittens. With Curtis, at the time the big cat was treed, was a Mexican who had lived in the area for years and claimed to be familiar with the *onca*. He assured Prock that the treed cat was without question an *onca*.

"Curtis gathered up the two kittens, a male and female, and brought them to Phoenix. He figured they were about six weeks old. For several weeks now we have been observing the kittens at play and at feeding time. At play they carry on like most kittens, but when there is any suggestion of food in the offing, their ears go back, there is a low growl in their throats, and all the play goes out of them. They are fed in well-separated pans and at the same time. At feeding time they tangle at the least provocation. It looks and sounds as if they are going to kill each other for sure. The first day I saw them being fed, Prock set the pans down on the concrete porch. Only one of the kittens, about twenty feet away, saw the pans as they were placed on the floor. This alert kitten covered the distance to the pan in a split second. He lit with all four feet in the pan. The pan picked up his momentum and carried him for a foot or so along the floor. Before the pan skidded to a stop the little monster was trying to claw the milk to death. As the pan came to a stop he was upon his hind legs and ripping the air with extended claws. At the same time he was growling, snarling and biting. All this fuss and there was nothing near him to contest his rights to the milk. As long as there is any food present they never cease this display of vile temper. Even as young kittens the speed with which they act is almost unbelievable.

"I called Mrs. Prock up one day to see how the little varmints were doing. She said they were the healthiest young cats she had seen. 'But,' she commented, 'I just don't know whether I wasn't to keep them here. They fight something terrible—they're going to kill each other—I'm half-scared of them.' This reference to two kittens about half the size of a house cat surprised me. I've seen Mrs. Prock handle a half-grown mountain lion the Procks were raising with little concern as it carried on in a manner that terrified me.

"It just so happened that a few days after Prock arrived in Phoenix with the kittens Dr. Ivo Poglayen, who is with the Rio Grande Zoo in Albuquerque, New Mexico, was on his way back from a trip to old Mexico and stopped in Phoenix to see the Procks. He immediately identified the kittens as jaguarundi. Dr. Poglayen has spent a lot of time in Mexico and he assures me that what the Mexicans call the *onca* is a jaguarundi. A recognized authority on Mexican wildlife goes a step farther. He is Dr. Bernardo Villa, mammalogist with the Institute of Biology at the University of Mexico. His job, naturally, takes him into the Mexican hinterlands and calls for exacting study of all things having to do with animals. Dr. Villa reported to me that there are several known animals in Mexico that in specific regions are called *oncas*. In one area he is familiar with, mountain lions are called *onca* by the local folks. Apparently, in other areas, jaguarundi are.

"As you will see from the pictures, Prock's kittens, in keeping with the descriptions of jaguarundi, have an otterlike head and are unspotted. There are two distinct color phases of jaguarundi; a grizzled gray (pepper and salt with black) and a red phase (rusty red sprinkled with black). These are dark with the salt-and-pepper effect, so I assume they will grow up as grays. I am told that the jaguarundi when full grown averages about forty-two inches in length. However, there's not what you would call an abundance of data available. Jaguarundi, being fast and extremely sensitive, are seldom seen and are considered rather rare in captivity. They are found in many parts of South America, throughout Central America, Mexico, and as far north as southeastern Texas.

"We hope these kittens continue to live a healthy life so we can watch them develop. At this stage of the game they certainly show every promise of living—they're too mean to die. I have no doubt but that they will grow up to be jaguarundi and there seems little doubt that they are the same animal referred to as an *onca* in Mexico."

So there you have it. One man convinced; another still on the trail. Has Pete come up with the final answer: That "*onca*" is a jungle name for several kinds of cats? Certainly most scientists, as Pete points out, who are trained to be skeptical until overwhelmed with evidence, would agree with Pete.

Yet the possibility must have occurred to Annabel. With his intimate knowledge of the jungle cats and his wide store of woods lore, he would certainly have spotted it if the countless people he has talked with were describing known cats or cougars, jaguars—or jaguarundis. He, in the jungle, on the trail, remains convinced.

We're inclined to wait and see what he comes up with.

The Shootingest Characters

I will never, if I live to be as old as the Great Wall of China, forget a single moment of this fabulous hunt.

"Pal, this is a starvation camp," Lucky Hal said to me in the icy gray tropical dawn. "We are down to the ultimate crusts. So please kill us a nice fat deer, hey? Science will bless you for it."

Four toilsome hours later I was sitting on a rock beside my bewhiskered hound Snowser, with snow ghost-dancing out of the south, smoking a cigarette and waiting for a buck in the lava breaks below me to make the next move. I had heard the buck snort. He was there, all right. It occurred to me as I waited that probably nobody had ever made a stranger deer hunt. Only a few miles distant were lush jungles, hot and humid, festooned with exotic blossoms and rich in fauna that would never know cold. Yet here I was, snow piling up on my hat, as cold as I ever was mushing the winter trails of Alaska. Geographically, I was at the 10,000-foot level on Colima Volcano, western Mexico, whence I had journeyed with a museum party headed by Lucky Hal, an amiable giant who lives like a timber wolf and hunts as tirelessly. Down the hill the top of a skinny pine snag began to gyrate unaccountably. I stubbed out the cigarette, and Snowser and I eased around the slope to a better vantage point.

Under the snag, polishing his antlers, was a white-tailed buck. While I watched, he bounded back, shook his head threateningly, and slammed full-tilt into the snag. He snorted and pranced. He glared at imaginary enemies. He was just plumb loaded with notions this snowy noon. I moved toward him with a boulder for cover, and when I next took a look he was close enough for a shot. So I cut down on him with the muzzleloader, holding on his head, and he ran 100 yards and died in a thicket, his jugular torn by buckshot.

There are many ingenious ways to carry a deer without a packboard, all of them bad. When I reached camp after two hours of battling outrageous combinations of brush and lava slides, the wind now howling like lost souls, I was bloody, tallow-smeared, bone-tired, and soaked to the skin by snow that had melted between the carcass and my back. Lucky Hal and his Mexican assistants had been out setting traps. They hadn't eaten since breakfast because there was nothing to eat, and they eyed the deer with hungry anticipation.

"Turning out to be a swell hunt, hey?" Lucky Hal said jovially.

"Put it this way," I said. "I will never, if I live to be as old as the Great Wall of China, forget a single moment of it."

Here I'd better explain how it started. Four days ago I was on the sunny seaward gallery of the Hotel Colima, in Cuyutlan, enjoying the surf and having a soft drink with Panchita, the pretty new waitress, when Lucky Hal clattered up in a prairie-schooner-type truck with three hard-bitten Mexican helpers armed like Balkan guerrillas and a list of specimens for which, he said, his museum was panting. Panchita stared at him. Lucky Hal stands six feet, four inches, carries a hogleg .45 stuck in the waistband of his jeans, wears a huge black Stetson at least as battered as the one Gabby Hayes made famous, and always needs a shave. Giving us his best personality smile, he said that he wanted me to spend a few days collecting with him. This was partly, he admitted, because there was a giant candingo on his list, and offhand he didn't know where in Mexico to start looking for a candingo or tayra, a member of the weasel tribe.

The fact was, I didn't either. The candingo, averaging ten pounds—imagine the demoniac little weasel of the States with this weight—is a legendary beast, probably the fastest and most bloodthirsty killer for its size on the continent, as *paisano* poultry farmers will ruefully testify. Back-country natives have a superstitious fear of the animal, and many would not willingly occupy the same square mile with one. My experience had been that the candingo was where you found him, in a treetop, in a cave, on a stream-bank, under a corncrib. But at the word "candingo" Panchita opened her mouth to say something, then blushed and stayed silent. I had salvaged Panchita and Snowser from the hurricane that had scrambled Manzanillo some months before, and while she was making a success of her job here, she had not yet got over being shy with strangers. Manifestly she knew something interesting about candingoes, and I made a mental note to find out what it was.

"First we'll drive to a beach I know about," Lucky Hal said, "and shoot some yellow-shouldered bats. More fun than trapshooting, and twice as difficult." I said okay, he had a recruit. Within fifteen minutes I had hoisted Snowser and my gear into the truck and we were heading north on the first phase of what was to be, I'll swear, the most remarkable hunting adventure of my life. Lucky Hal hadn't been kidding when he said that shooting yellow-shouldered bats was difficult. At twilight we parked on a palm-fringed beach near Cerro Monos where, according to the Indians, the Emperor of China used to land from his golden-prow sailing ship to trade with the Aztec King of Colima, and got busy burning powder for science. The bats, dozens of them, dived, circled and zoomed erratically between us and the crashing Pacific surf, more like wind-blown leaves than flying animals. It was impossible to swing with them. The trick seemed to be to guess where they were going to be next, and shoot there.

I missed five shots before I brought one down. It was a tiny creature, less than three inches long, with bright epaulets and a face like a bulldog. Lucky Hal and the Mexicans were strung out along the beach, shooting steadily. When full darkness came we had busted a heap of caps and killed only six bats. But good old Hal said that we had done all right, and museum patrons and zoology students would remember us in their orisons. I figured that we would now make camp. I had a lot to learn about this outfit.

"We'll take a *pasear* toward Jalipa," Lucky Hal said as we traced our steps to the truck. "We might pick up something good there. I feel real lucky tonight."

I knew the road and it was terrible with stretches that, as the saying goes, would spook a goat and bog a snipe. But there we were, bouncing and rattling along in the starlit night, heavy jungle on both sides, the sierra looming black above us. When eyes flashed green in the headlights, eager-beaver Hal slammed on the brakes. Everybody hit the ground and, Snowser ahead, ran toward the spot where the eyes had disappeared. The Colima jungles after dark are not hospitable. There are hostile plants, animals, bugs and reptiles lurking for the unwary. But with what amounted to a mass disregard for consequences, we switched on our headlamps and plowed into the greenery. Snowser presently treed the animal, and one of the Mexicans shouted that it was an opossum. Lucky Hal shouted back that we didn't want it. Five miles and a hundred chuckholes later, in a ravine where a streamlet spilled across the road and tremendous tree-canopies blanked the sky, a dark underslung animal loped into the lights and we made another panic stop. I had candingoes on my mind, and for an instant had the wild conviction that the beast was a candingo. But it paused at the roadside, staring at us, and as the headlights shone full on it I saw that it was a jaguarundi.

Not rare but hard to come up with, the jaguarundi is a cat built sort of like a slimmed-down dachshund. This one, one of the red-brown ones, didn't know it, but it was destined to become an exhibit. A jaguarundi was included on Lucky Hal's want-list. Snowser leading the way, we again broke into the dragon-green jungle. I inadvertently brushed against a *mala mujer*, a wicked variety of tall stinging nettle, and was berating myself and nursing a burning hand, when Snowser yoop-yooped that he had treed something. The tree was a vast false-ebony with seed pods a foot long and limbs as thick through as a man's body. As Lucky Hal and I walked around it, a variety of birds sounded off in protest, and a big green iguana ran noisily across the branches trying to keep out of the lights. There was a rattle of claws. Bark fell. Snowser reared up with his front paws against the tree and bellowed an invitation to battle. Then we spotted the jaguarundi thirty feet up on a limb. Hustling Hal gave the handsome little cat a blast from his 12-gauge, and the animal thudded to the ground. Uttering sounds of delight, he picked the kill up.

"Wonderful. Wonderful," he declared. "This trip we are hotter than a country boy's pistol. My curator will be delighted. He will mention us in dispatches."

Turning back toward the coast as a rib of moon topped the sierra, we saw a white-tailed doe and a coati. Then Lucky Hal braked hard as a forest rat scuttled across the road. Forest rats were on his list. While the Mexicans set a battery of traps, some baited with scent, others with peanut butter, Lucky Hal and I walked ahead. A snake slithered into the road and Lucky Hal sprinted forward for a look at it. The snake was a heavy, powerful six-foot black-and-yellow alicante, venomous and aggressive. It towered, hissing, wanting to fight. I held Snowser, whose whiskers were bristling with defiance, and Lucky Hal shot the snake and kicked it into the ditch. We patrolled the road for better than an hour without seeing anything else. Then, back at the truck, the Mexicans halloed. We returned, and they had a white-browed, tree-climbing xenomy rat that had fallen for a peanut-butter bait. Lucky Hal said that it was rare. From the way he handled it, you'd have thought that it was a platinum mink. Continuing, we drove through banana and papaya plantations to a beach south of Magdalena and halted under a moon-shadowed dune. I broke out my sleeping bag and mosquito net, and as it was now two o'clock, expected that Lucky Hal and the Mexicans would do likewise. Instead, they departed afoot back up the road with a sack of traps. Lucky Hal called over his shoulder that later they might scout the beach for turtle eggs. The moon was right for sow turtles to come in from the sea, he added. Wondering if these men ever slept, I searched the truck for a bedtime snack, found only a stalk of tired bananas, ate half-a-dozen and turned in. I was bedded down on gravel but it felt like an innerspring mattress. I didn't however, get to enjoy it long. Off on the edge of the night a shotgun boomed, waking me, and before I could resume slumber along came Lucky Hal and the Mexicans with a specimen bag half full of turtle eggs. Laughing, Lucky Hal said that a coyote had found the eggs first and was digging them up and eating them. He had missed the coyote, trying for it at too great a range, but had harvested fifty unbroken eggs.

"Roll out and regale yourself with a beachcomber cocktail," he said. "Just the thing to give a man vitality and stuff."

I rolled out. It looked as if sleep was going to be impossible anyhow. The beachcomber cocktails consisted of raw turtle eggs in chili sauce from a bottle adorned with a representation of Satan blowing flames, served in a tin cup. Good. I downed two before getting back into the sack. Lucky Hal and the Mexicans were still gulping turtle eggs and chatting spiritedly when I finally conked out. When I woke with the copper-rose sunrise in my eyes and meadowlarks singing over the dunes, the crew was setting up folding tables end-to-end and rigging a fly over them. This was their laboratory. I made coffee, and with it consumed more bananas and turtle eggs, while they weighed, measured, logged, skinned, tagged, dusted with arsenic and stuffed with cotton the night's take of small animals—bats, mice and gophers—and tacked the jaguarundi pelt onto a board. When the chore was finished, Lucky Hal remarked that the larder was mighty low and we would have to replenish it. Anybody would have assumed that he meant we would drive to a town and do some shopping. But not on your old mezzotint. It developed that these jungle wizards could give the king of the gypsies lessons in foraging.

We headed east on the state highway, drove an hour and turned into a dirt road that led up the Armeria river valley through dense vine-hung jungle, to a flat squeezed between the river and a vista of cornfields and coconut groves. Here we parked the truck, and the Mexicans left with their shotguns. Lucky Hal and I strung up a spinning rod and went down to the river. There were fish in the pools, but they wouldn't take any lure we had. They looked like carp and maybe were. On the way back to the truck I asked Lucky Hal how he had gotten his start as a collector. Grinning, he said that when he graduated from high school his father told him it was time that he chose his life's work, and he answered that he wanted to spend his life hunting and fishing. His father said that this was a praiseworthy ambition, indeed, but unfortunately he wasn't a wealthy man and couldn't support him in it.

But there was an angle, his father said. Study zoology, become a collector, and he'd actually get paid for hunting and fishing. So Lucky Hal went back to school. Since taking his degree, he has worked exclusively in the field, one of the band of professional collectors behind the natural history exhibits enjoyed by millions in the nation's museums. He is at present sponsored by a university, his museum and the Mexican government. The information that he and his colleagues gather, regarding game populations and their distribution and strength, has proved of inestimable value to wildlife management. In my opinion, these collectors are today the world's most expert hunters and maybe the most competent woodsmen. For a smart lad with a taste for useful adventure in wilderness gamelands, it would be hard to name a finer occupation.

Shotguns had banged intermittently off yonder, and after an hour or so the Mexicans came back burdened with loot. They had an iguana, an armadillo, a blue rock dove, three fat yellow-head parrots, six coconuts, some green corn, some tomatoes, a hatful of chili peppers, a squash, and a giant tropics toad. I said that I had an unparticular stomach and would hold still for everything but the toad. At it I balked. Lucky Hal said to take it easy, the toad was for the museum. The plantation produce, the Mexicans said, had been donated by a foreman who wanted the outfit to return and deal with a gang of coatis that was nightly raiding the fields. They also reported they had asked the foreman, an old-timer, if he knew where a candingo might be found, and he replied that he not only didn't know, but didn't want to know. When the plunder had been stowed, we drove into the sierra beyond Tecoman, a distance of thirty miles, and parked under the shaggy, cliff-hung slope of Cowhead Mountain. Lucky Hal scanned the mountain with his glasses.

"Don Vincente the Bandit's cave is up there somewhere," he said. "Supposed to be cannibal bats in it with a two-foot wing-spread. As soon as we get some grub started, we'll investigate."

During the drive from the river the Mexicans had dressed out the assorted creatures they had killed, except the toad. They now built a fire and one of them, who apparently doubled as cook, cut up the meat and put it into a stew pot, added squash, corn, tomatoes and chili peppers, then more chili peppers, sloshed in some water from a canteen, included salt as an obvious afterthought, and set the kettle on rocks over the fire. This accomplished, we began climbing. The day was hotter than $10 worth of tabasco. It was so hot that Snowser's whiskers drooped. Partway up the 1,500-foot pitch I saw what looked like fresh cat sign, scats with fur and feathers in them. But there were no tracks by which I might have identified the animal. We climbed over a cactus-studded rim, and there was the cave mouth, low and sinister-looking. One of the Mexicans said that the cave contained the hidden treasure of Don Vincente who, after preying for years on merchants traveling the Camino Real, had been ambushed with his gang by troops and killed. I said that since my finances were currently low, I wouldn't at all mind stumbling over a cache of ingots, pieces-of-eight, or whatever.

"I'll settle for a cannibal bat," Lucky Hal said.

We put on our headlamps and Lucky Hal took a bat net from his pack, an expensive imported Japanese silk "mist" net, fine as gossamer, and nailed it across the cave's entrance. The plan of operation, he said, was to go inside as far as we could and chase bats into the net. If there were cannibal bats among them, he said, plenty of action would result, and probably he would have to buy a new net, as it was practically a cinch that this one would be ruined in the fracas. As a prophet Lucky Hal was only fair. We were heading into action of a gaudy sort, but not entirely the kind he expected.

Fifty feet inside, the entrance widened into a large stalactite-crowded chamber with tunnel-like branches leading from it. We separated here, each taking a branch. The one I drew was narrow and crooked, encrusted with lime deposits that glittered like polished agate. Bats flew past. Snowser growled worriedly. The bewhiskered hound didn't like the place, and that made two of us. Caves never were my dish. I get lonesome for the sky. I rounded a bend and saw, thirty yards ahead, a heap of rubble that reached halfway to the roof. Something moved among the rocks. Eyes gleamed. At first I didn't see the animal clearly, but its shadow on the seamed wall, exaggerated and distorted, could have been painted there by an Altamira cave artist with a hangover. I cuffed Snowser behind me and adjusted my light. The probing beam fell squarely on—a candingo. Red-gold and yellow, otter-size, this giant of the weasels was beautiful. He stood on his hind legs, weaving as he faced the blinding light. I had the impression that he was unafraid.

I snicked back the hammer of the muzzleloader, grateful that the gun was charged with birdshot because to have damaged such a pelt would have been a crime. Aztec hunters tell you that the candingo possesses the evil eye, and can be killed only by three persons standing in a row. The middle guy does the shooting while the outside two absorb the beast's baleful gaze. Maybe this candingo was trying to put the whammy on Snowser and me, but if so, powder and shot were more potent. I fired, and everything happened. In the confined space the report was cannon-loud. Rocks fell. Dust and choking powder smoke filled the passage. Bats whipped out of the murk like misguided missiles. Snowser lunged ahead, yelling his war cry. More rocks fell. Somewhere, faintly, I heard Lucky Hal shout a query. Then, so help me, two candingoes streaked past so close that, if I had been expecting them, I could have laid out at least one with my ramrod. I was reloading as rapidly as I could, guessing at the charge, when Lucky Hal, the museum's white hope, galloped into the passage. I told him what had happened, and he at once crawled in under the bank of smoke.

"The luck gets better and better," he gloated, wheezing, when he came back into view with the candingo. "My curator will be overjoyed. He may even stop dividing my expense accounts by two. Thanks, pal."

I told him that, shucks, it was nothing that any red-blooded, clean-living American boy couldn't have done, and he was welcome. We decided that the other candingoes had made a clean, if temporary, getaway, and went out for a look at the bat net. It was a mess and there were no bats in it. Something, probably a cannibal bat, or several of them, had torn the middle out of it, and the standard issue bats had made use of the providential exit.

When we got back to the truck, the stew was ready. It was good, and interesting because you were kept busy trying to identify the meat you were eating. The meal finished, Hustling Hal said he thought we had better go up onto Colima Volcano while his luck was running high and try for a stygian owl, on account of the bird was on his list. It would be, I knew, an all-night drive, but that didn't seem to matter.

We piled into the truck and took off. The highway as far as Ciudad Guzman was good and we made fast time, but from there on we had a dirt road and the truck crawled along, lurching and jolting. At four in the morning the grade ended smack against a pine tree, and Lucky Hal informed us unnecessarily that this was it, our home away from home. Snow glimmered on the volcano's crest. It was cold enough to freeze the ears off a yeti. I found my sleeping bag and spread it while the Mexicans gathered pine-knot fuel in a tarpaulin. I could have used some coffee, but I needed sleep more. So I sacked down.

"Of a truth," I heard one of the Mexicans say between chattering teeth, "it is a very crude climate up here. We may all freeze."

Lucky Hal has the constitution of Wotan, but he was shivering visibly. A shotgun blast woke me in the dawn's early night. I ignored it, and went back to sleep. The shotgun boomed again, and there was the sound of hammering. I sat up and rubbed my eyes open. Durable Hal was nailing the candingo pelt onto a board, whistling in a seedy monotone as he worked. On a rock beside the fire a kettle of coffee steamed. The good smell of pitch smoke filled the air. I dressed, and poured myself some coffee. While I was drinking it, a Mexican came in with two red-legged, partridge-size *gallinas del monte*—mountain chickens—which accounted for the shots. Lucky Hal said that the skins would go to the museum, but we could eat the meat. This reminded him, he added, that we were again low on grub. So would I please fare forth after breakfast and kill a deer? The other two Mexicans came in from setting traps, and by the time we had eaten the remainder of the stew, the last of the bananas, and what was left of the squash, snow was sifting through the pines.

"A monkey eagle came over a while ago," Lucky Hal said, gnawing hopefully at a fire-blackened piece of rind from which he had already eaten the roast squash. "Collected in these parts, he'd be a prize. I am going to scour the area."

I wished him well, and left to kill a deer. I've already told you how, what with one thing and another, I spent most of the day doing it. When the snow-filled dusk was upon us, and we had dined sumptuously on broiled liver and some aged tortillas that previously had been overlooked under a pile of gear, my incredible friends ran their traps. They returned around eight o'clock (using their headlamps) with a miscellany of rats and mice and a bushytail gray squirrel that, Lucky Hal said, wasn't rare but was needed to complete a group. He said that during the day nobody had caught another glimpse of the monkey eagle.

I turned in with no further delay. I was getting smart. The thing to do when you were with these people was to sleep whenever and wherever you could. That night I got a break. I logged a solid three hours before Lucky Hal shook me awake. "Listen," he said dramatically. I listened. Away up toward the volcano's summit a dog barked. At any rate, it sounded like a dog. "*Yow yow yow.*" I asked Lucky Hal if lonesome hounds were on his list too.

"Hah! That thing you just heard," he informed me, "is a stygian owl. Very rare. Come on, get dressed. You can help me collect him." "Gee thanks," I said. "I'll never forget this."

I was about to add that he knew what he could do with the stygian owl, but thought better of it. After all, it wasn't given to every man to help collect a barking owl, very rare, on the top of a volcano at midnight in the teeth of a tropical snowstorm. I dressed, persuaded Snowser to come out from under the truck, and we left. Happily, the owl was a vocal bird, and after only an hour and a half spent blundering about in the snowy brush, we homed-in on the sounds he was broadcasting, and discovered him sitting in lonely grandeur in the top of an evergreen oak. The headlamps revealed him to be a medium-size owl, black and gray, with no horns. Lucky Hal had tripped in the brush and was slapping the barrels of his 12-gauge, growling profanely. I asked him what was wrong, and he wailed, "Shoot the owl, dammit. I can't—snow in my gun barrels." So I laid the muzzleloader on the bird and let go with a charge of No. 4s.

Flame seemed to lance halfway to the tree, and I had to sidestep to see around the wind-blown drift of smoke. The owl squalled, clung upside down, fell onto a snow-matted branch, then pitched to the ground and looped away into the thickets. Snowser, half frozen but eager, icicles on his whiskers, tore after the wounded bird. He caught it after a fifty-yard chase and held it down with his forepaws until we arrived, getting his nose and ears bloodied by the bird's beak. Lucky Hal killed the owl, and after admiring it, smoothed its feathers tenderly and placed it in his specimen bag. He then borrowed my ramrod to poke the snow out of the 12-gauge.

"My curator will embrace me," he asserted. "He will award me the Class C citation. That's the one on white paper." I told him that some day no doubt he would be a curator himself, and maybe wear a homburg and carry a cane, but meanwhile let us get the heck back to camp and alongside some fire. We headed down through the timber, and when we reached camp the snowstorm had become a blizzard. Lucky Hal said reluctantly that he guessed we had better pull the traps and get out of here while we could. This was jake with me. The Mexicans got up and he disappeared with them into the forest, to return more than an hour later with the traps and various gophers and mice. Boarding the truck, we ground toward the flatlands. I went to sleep. Some time later, after the sun had risen, I was jerked awake when the truck halted abruptly. Before I had time to ask Lucky Hal what was going on, he grabbed his shotgun, leaped out, and ran in among the close-packed pines. Snowser and the Mexicans followed. I stayed where I was. A shot crashed, and after a bit Lucky Hal returned carrying what appeared to be a large undistinguished-looking hawk. His bearded, bony face was split in a wide grin.

"Can you beat it?" he said. "He was sitting right there in a snag waiting for us. A monkey eagle. They may be common as crows elsewhere, but boy, this is the first one from these parts."

"Take me to Cuyutlan," I mumbled. "I desire to hold conversation with Panchita."

We dropped down past Old Man mountain and soon were in the lowlands, sunny jungle all around us. Lucky Hal stopped at a plantation and traded part of the deer carcass for at least 200 oranges, a stalk of bananas, some cucumbers and a five-pound brick of goat cheese. We went on, peeling oranges. An armadillo started across the road, and Lucky Hal braked automatically, then changed his mind and fed the engine gas. He was fond of armadillo meat, he said, but had been wary of it ever since a family of Mexicans over in Michoacan, friends of his, died after a repast of armadillo stew. It seemed that armadillos ate coral snakes, and sometimes in the digestive process the snakes' cobra-type venom got out of hand. I said thanks for the information. As of this moment armadillos were crossed off my diet. We pulled into

Cuyutlan toward midafternoon, and it seemed to me that I had been gone a month. While Lucky Hal and the Mexicans set up their laboratory to prepare the specimens they had taken, I told Panchita about killing the candingo in the cave and asked her what she had been about to tell us about candingoes four days ago when shyness stopped her.

Panchita said, well, it probably was just a silly old story, but all the country people believed that candingoes had the evil eye and used it to guard treasure. It was almost impossible to kill a candingo, she said, but when one was killed, the spot where it died was the place to dig for buried gold and jewels. She would have told us this the other day, she said, but Lucky Hal awed her. I said to think nothing of it, he awed me too. But I decided that some day, just for the sport of it, of course, I would go back to Don Vincente's cave with a pick and shovel and find out what was under that rubble heap. When Lucky Hal and the Mexicans had finished with their specimens and eaten dinner, Lucky said that they had to leave.

"We're going to Jug Mountain in Jalisco to try for singing quail," he said. "Then maybe we'll work the volcano again. While the luck still runs good."

I watched them drive off.

The Craziest Cat Hunt

I don't require—I don't even want—an audience when I hunt. But the night I was after the cat there was music and people and confusion such as I have never known.

"*Amigo, amigo*, guard yourself," Don Basilio bellowed. "There is a cat right in front of you—on the same limb!" He had to bellow to make himself heard above the syncopated uproar taking place down there in the tropical darkness where he stood. "I just saw its eyes," he informed me with added decibels as the music swelled in a fancy crescendo.

He wasn't telling me anything. I had the cat squarely in the beam of my headlamp, but at the moment didn't know what, if anything, I was going to do about it. I was in trouble, and had the unhappy conviction that the trouble was going to get a whole lot worse before it got better. Which it definitely did.

I want you, please, to visualize the scene. If it seems fantastic, don't blame me. I was just the hardworking, long-suffering guy in the middle. But I admit that I asked for what was about to occur, and that I had known better. I was so sleepy that I would have traded an interest in Fort Knox for a night's slumber and I was forty feet up in the windy top of a vast false-ebony tree, perched precariously on a swaying limb. My muzzleloader was clutched in one hand, while ten feet distant crouched a rare and beautiful margay. The little cat was on the feathery outer tip of our common branch, ears flattened, snarling demonically, eyes as full of green fire as Peruvian emeralds. Its hair stood on end, its back was humped like a Halloween cat's, and its tail twitched threateningly.

This was the fifth night of Holy Week, and the tree I occupied was in the poultry yard of Don Basilio's Four Winds cattle-and-coconut *rancho* in the state of Colima. A family of margays had been systematically raiding Don Basilio's flocks of guinea hens, chickens, ducks, pigeons and turkeys, and I had been invited here to deal with the jungle assassins if I could. But I never expected anything like this. Below in the firefly-starred darkness a six-man mariachi orchestra was banging itself silly playing Pancho Villa's marching song, my outsize bewhiskered hound Snowser was trying to climb the tree to assist me, yelling his head off in frustration, and squads of sports-minded guests, loaded with fiesta punch, were arriving from the ranch house to witness, they obviously hoped, the death of a family of margays. I told myself desperately that likely they would be treated to a more dramatic spectacle than they expected.

"Answer me something!" Don Basilio hollered. "What is wrong up there? Why don't you shoot the murdering cat?"

Nothing would have pleased me more than to oblige him. But I was grievously handicapped. In the first place, I was spooky about the wildlife in the tree. Covering close to a quarter acre, it was an arboreal campground inhabited by snakes, iguanas, lesser lizards, hostile bugs, vampire bats, rabies-carrying forest rats and squirrels, and at least three margay cats. In addition to this fauna, around 100 head of domestic poultry roosted in the tree. Clambering about up here at night was a chore to give Tarzan goose pimples. In the second place, I was in no position to shoot. The limb swayed wildly in the wind, and there was nothing against which I could brace my feet or back. I know beyond doubt that the heavy recoil of the muzzleloader would belt me backward off the limb and I would collide with the ground at a high rate of speed, probably breaking more bones than the Colima medics could repair in six months.

Thus the margay and I faced each other in the festive, music-filled night. I will always believe that the diminutive killer was fixing to jump at me. The size of a small house cat, it was tawny gray with dark brown spots arranged in stripes running lengthwise of its body, and with a long ringed tail. It looked ornery enough to give you a bad time indeed if it got at your face and eyes. I didn't want to take the light off the margay to look, but I had the feeling that there was a limb close above me. If there was one and I could get hold of it with my left hand, I could maybe point the muzzleloader pistol-fashion with my right and blast the hard-boiled pygmy *tigre* to kingdom come. It was the only out I had. So I raised the gun experimentally, and balancing myself like a man on a busy broncho, reached for the limb that I hoped was there. Hallelujah! Everything happened. The limb was there, all right, and I got a good grip on it—but to my horror found that I was also gripping something cold, scaly and squirmingly alive. It was a snake, species unknown, but apparently sizable. The outraged reptile hissed like a broken steam pipe and struck down at the headlamp, providentially missing me. At the same instant the muzzleloader blasted. I didn't shoot intentionally—it was sheer reflex. But I jerked my hand away from the limb, and now, off balance, I didn't have a prayer. The gun's recoil toppled me, and as in one of those falling nightmares that psychiatrists love to theorize about, there I went, crashing through leafy canopies, bouncing off thick, unyielding limbs, trying to catch hold of something to stay the fall but with no luck. The ultimate triumphant bit of intelligence in my head before I landed noisily on a marimba and broke through it to the ground was that, with the shot, I had heard a cat scream.

Here I've got to explain how this cat hunt, the weirdest yet, began. I was eating breakfast in the open-sided restaurant of the Hotel Fenix in Cuyutlan, a normally drowsy resort village down on the coast, and had decided to take to the hills because now, during the Easter season, the town had swelled to ten times its usual population and the carnival pace was too fast for me. I couldn't get any sleep. Mariachi bands, marimba bands, wandering troubadours and combinations thereof, played night and day, in the hotel lobby and in the corridors, on the sidewalks, on the beach, wherever they could find standing room and listeners. How the Mexicans themselves slept, I will never know.

Me, I couldn't keep my eyes open. Twice during breakfast I had dozed off and only crack-of-doom trumpet blasts had kept me from pillowing my head in the scrambled eggs.

I was signing the check when a pickup truck made a burned-rubber stop alongside the restaurant. In it were Don Basilio and his husky, pretty, green-eyed daughter Trinidad.

Don Basilio, a bull-shouldered alp of a man slid from behind the wheel and with hand extended, boomed, "We want you to come to the ranch with us to spend the rest of Holy Week."

I said, "Well, thanks," and after thinking it over, added, "But tell me one thing. Is it peaceful at your ranch? Could a man get some sleep? Or would he need ear plugs and Nembutal?" "Of course it is peaceful at Four Winds," he said, sounding indignant. "It is the most peaceful ranch in the state. I would personally," he said, "break anybody's head who disturbed the peace there." Said Trinidad quickly, "It is a social invitation, you understand. But we hope that you will bring your gun and your dog. There is a certain matter. . . ."

They then told me about the margays. Three had been seen, an adult female and two nearly grown cubs, and the animals were making almost nightly raids on the poultry yard. Traps had proved useless, there were no trained cat dogs on the ranch, and none of the *vaqueros* had been able to get a shot at the nocturnal marauders.

"I keep racing pigeons in a loft built for them in the poultry yard," Don Basilio said. "One of the birds was, I think, maybe the fastest in the world. I had an interesting bet made with my neighbor Fernando Gonzalez about this. I use the past tense," he said brokenly, "because my wonderful racer, Paloma Azul, is dead. The margays climbed into the loft and killed him. Please get your gun and your dog and come with us. We need you."

This was flattering. It made me feel like a traditional White Hunter. But they knew that I had killed a piratical and particularly elusive margay for Don Dionicio on his Golden Skull Ranch over in Nayarit, so their request was sincere. I did some more thinking, and it added up okay. I needed sleep like a wounded man needs plasma. Moreover, I knew some museum directors who were panting for margay specimens. It was too good an opportunity to pass up.

"Okay, it's a deal," I said, "since you guarantee that Four Winds is loaded with peace and tranquility, and a man can actually sleep of nights."

I should have known better, and no doubt you have already guessed what fate did to me. We drove two hours through sunny, flower-festooned jungle, then came in sight of ranch headquarters—pastel walls, red tile roofs, and brilliant splashes of bougainvillea. And anyhow twenty parked cars and a horde of people loafing or milling about on the main ranch house gallery and in the tree-shaded yard. Even at the distance of a quarter of a mile I could hear the music. Two bands were playing, different pieces, of course, and the uninhibited Mexican trumpets were something to lift a man's sombrero right off his head.

"See, I told you," Don Basilio said pridefully as we drove into the din. "Here everything is peaceful and tranquil. Here you can be contented, with beautiful music to soothe you, so that you can concentrate on the problem of killing those three margays."

Trinidad sighed blissfully, and said, "And tonight there will be dancing under a pretty yellow moon. They will probably dance and sing until the roosters crow in the morning."

I said, "Oh, boy, how wonderful. But meanwhile, please lend me a horse. I want to cruise around with Snowser. Get acquainted with the country. We might even pick up something, *quién sabe*?"

My mendacious intention was to sneak off into the boondocks and spend the rest of the day sleeping under a tree. But no soap. Fiesta and the benevolent intentions of my host snared me around the windpipe again.

"You are truly an eager hunter of cats," Don Basilio said fondly, putting his hands on my shoulders, "to leave this music and all the guests and begin your hunt so soon. It is a trait I appreciate from my heart," he said, banging his chest. "But I must send a *vaquero* with you to show you the fence gaps, the stream crossings, and the paths through the thorn jungles." He paused, brow furrowed in thought, lips pursed. "But what *vaquero*? You understand, *amigo*, that during the *Semana Santa*—Holy Week—our people celebrate. I fear that. . . ."

"Papa," said Trinidad. "I could show him. I will be happy to because, as you know, I loved the great Paloma Azul almost as much as you. Really, I won't mind at all. Besides, we will be back in time for the moon and the dancing."

I protested that it was too great a sacrifice for her to make, got nowhere, and presently found myself stowing my gear in a room directly over the gallery where, as Don Basilio assured me, I could hear the music better. Then, carrying the muzzleloader and a .30-30, and with Snowser shambling behind, I followed Trinidad to the corral where two fiesta-happy ranch hands were making a project of saddling a pair of saddle horses, a buckskin and a bay, both good-looking quarter-horse types. I was practically walking in my sleep. I tripped over shadows. If somebody had asked me quickly what my name was, I probably couldn't have told him.

Anyhow, I mounted the buckskin and Trinidad and I took off to tour the surrounding terrain. It was hot, so hot that the blue wall of the sierra shimmered in the heat waves and kept breaking apart into improbable mirage shapes. I was beginning to be afraid that I would go to sleep and disgrace myself by falling on my head, when we topped a rise above a jungle-rimmed watermelon field, and Trinidad reached out quickly and touched my arm.

"Javelinas," she whispered. "They are eating the watermelons of my Papa. If they have eaten the special watermelon, it will be almost as great a loss to him as the death of the marvelous Paloma Azul. Because he had made a bet with our neighbor Fernando Gonzalez that this year he would grow the largest watermelon ever seen in this valley."

I still hadn't spotted anything. But after a moment I got my eyes focussed, and made out a band of maybe fifteen javelinas over yonder at the jungle's edge about 450 yards distant. I put my glasses on the animals and saw that they were mixed sows, young boars and piglets, bossed by a big, old high-humped *manadero* boar. They were rooting the plump, ripe watermelons about in a kind of frenzy, each adult pig trying greedily to feed on two or three melons at the same time, the red pulp slobbering out of their chomping jaws, while the piglets scavenged what they could get.

"We must stop them," cried Trinidad. "I only pray that they have not already eaten the special watermelon of my Papa."

With that, she hung her spurs in the bay's ribs and went down the steep, brushy slope like a Valkyrie with urgent orders from Wotan. My buckskin followed and I woke up sufficiently to stay in the saddle. The javelinas saw us coming, and fled into the jungle. Then we were among the watermelons, and presently Trinidad hauled back expertly on her Spanish spade bit and sat the bay on his haunches.

Here I beheld a sight that may interest agriculturists. Lying on the sunbanked sandy loam, fat and reddish green, was the grandfather of all watermelons. There was an apparent reason for its extraordinary size—a growth-encouraging stratagem that I had never seen before, or even heard of. Lashed to a stick driven into the ground beside the melon was a bottle of sun-curdled milk. From the bottle ran a rubber tube which ended in a goose quill stuck into the thick vine of the melon. The melon was being fed milk much as a hospital patient is given a transfusion. The javelinas hadn't touched it.

"The pigs will return," said Trinidad anxiously. "We will have to take a stand on the hill over there"—she gestured to a rise of land—"and kill the *mandero* boar. Then the others will stay away from here and the special melon of my Papa will be safe."

We found a likely spot, tied the horses, and sat down in the shadow of a rock to wait. I at once went to sleep, but not for long. Trinidad touched my shoulder and whispered, "The pigs have returned." I got my eyes open, located the pigs which had come back to their identical feeding spot, and picked up the .30-30. My first shot hit a rock under the boar's belly, causing him to buck like a broncho. The second—heaven help me, I thought—hit the special watermelon that lay two feet ahead of the boar's snout. Anybody who has never seen a softnose blast into a ripe watermelon has missed something. The melon exploded, which ended Don Basilio's wager with his neighbor Fernando Gonzalez. I levered another shell into the chamber, and as the pigs streaked for the jungle, stretched the *manadero* stone cold dead with a shot through the spine. We rode down to the kill. Trinidad sadly inspected the ruined special watermelon.

"I think we had better make it appear that the javelinas were eating it," she said soberly. "To maintain good relations during this holy season." She found a jagged chunk of obsidian and made tooth marks on what was left of the melon. "I feel sad about this," she said, "because it is the first time I have ever deceived my Papa."

The buckskin was blood-shy, and I had to ear him down while the husky Trinidad picked up the forty-pound boar carcass with one hand and lashed it behind the saddle. I said, "You'll make some hunter a good wife." She replied firmly but with her green eyes downcast, "I will if he proves that he can kill margay cats." Whereupon I took a grip on the cheek of the dancing, snorting buckskin's bridle, stuck my thumb in his eye to give him something else to think about, and swarmed aboard.

Meanwhile, back at the ranch, as announcers say, things had been added. New guests had arrived from Guadalajara, bringing another mariachi band and a pseudo-calypso singer who made up bright little songs about whatever caught his fancy, and patently was a great favorite. I said to Trinidad as we delivered the *manadero* carcass to the cook, "Now it is really going to be peaceful here. Heavenly, but good."

She said happily, "*Si*, but only wait until the moon comes up." I replied, "But unfortunately I have a date with some margays. Therefore, with your permission, I will repair to the poultry yard as soon as I get something to eat, and there await the arrival of the cats, if they show up."

At dusk I sat down in a fence corner, Snowser beside me, with the pigeon loft above and the enormous false-ebony tree overshadowing everything, and hearkened discouragedly to the blare of music 300 yards distant. After a bit the moon rose, and the celebrants at the ranch house began firing rockets into the air, which burst as beautifully as a flak barrage I had once seen over Okinawa. Filled with a sense of mission, I honestly tried to stay awake, but it was a losing battle. After an hour or so, despite everything, I went to sleep. Snowser woke me. The gaunt, oversize bewhiskered hound was leaning against my shoulder, obviously scared. I thought, holy cow, if he was scared and wanted protection, there must be at least a *tigre* in the poultry yard. But coming full awake, I reminded myself that he was a promising *tigre* dog, and if anything, was too brave against the spotted dog-killing jungle cats. Which left me barren of ideas.

I was beginning to get spooky myself. Nothing moved in the moon-patched yard. But Snowser kept crowding against me, shaking like an electric mixer. There was a swell of music from the ranch house, a rocket burst above us, and I thought I saw movement in a pool of velvet shadow five feet to my left. Acting on sheer defensive instinct, I thumbed the switch of my headlamp and clicked back the hammer of the muzzleloader, ready for anything—I thought.

Holy *frijole*, caught in the slicing white beam of the lamp was a sight that would have daunted Davy Crockett, Dan'l Boone and maybe even Ben Lilly. Because there in the glare of light, business end turned toward me, tail upraised, was a glandular freak of a Mexican skunk. He had me zeroed-in, but I had him, too. Apparently we both fired at the same instant. The charge of No. 4s blasted the skunk ten feet against a vanilla bush, where he lay lifeless, a smashed lump of fur, flesh and bones. But he had hit both me and Snowser. I fled. I beat it out of the poultry yard, retching, eyes smarting, wishing that the animal had been a *tigre*. How I was going to extricate myself from this ghastly situation without loss of all professional dignity was a problem I couldn't begin to solve.

One break was that the incidental banging of the rockets seemed to have prevented anybody from having heard the shot. I mean, the orchestras were still playing. No investigating parties were converging on me. My hastily formed plan of action was to sneak into the back door of the ranch house to my room, throw my horribly redolent clothes out the window, shower, rub myself down with some wildly perfumed Mexican shaving lotion I had bought because no tamer brand was available, and then put on some other clothes and come down and somehow clean up Snowser. I had read in *Sports Afield* that shampooing a dog with tomato pulp would rid him of skunk stink. So, with Snowser whimpering on the steps, no doubt thinking that I was betraying him in this dire emergency, I eased through the back door, took of my boots, and tiptoed toward the stairway. It was certain that the skunk-stench would fill the house, but I hoped to reach my room before anybody began searching for the source of it.

However, as I was passing the arched entrance to the cavernous kitchen, a contralto voice froze me in my tracks.

"*Válgame Dios*, is that you smelling like that?" Trinidad asked. She had it all figured out at the first glance and the first smell. "I thought I heard that muzzleloading gun boom," she said, wrinkling her nose and laughing at the same time. "Come along upstairs with me." Five minutes later I was in a bubble bath, the first one of my life, the perfumed bubbles heaped up like an Alaskan snowdrift. Later, Trinidad brought me clean clothes, and then we went down to the backyard and scrubbed Snowser with ripe tomatoes and sluiced him down with anyhow fifty gallons of water. As we were completing this chore, Don Basilio arrived. Holding his nose, he rumbled that he had realized that an emergency had occurred.

"But anyhow," he chuckled, "the wind is blowing toward the house of my esteemed neighbor Fernando Gonzalez. By this time he is searching under chairs and tables for the skunk." I said, with as much dignity as I could muster, "Excuse me, please, I am going back to the poultry yard. Because I will bet that the skunk odor will bring the margays in. They will conclude that a skunk is competing with them for the ranch poultry franchise." Said Trinidad, sniffing at her hands, "I will go with you. For I doubt that I am now socially acceptable."

I said, "No. Stay here. Your Papa needs you to keep the music, the dancing and the singing going. And the moon is up. Snowser and I didn't come here to celebrate. We came to avenge the great Paloma Azul. Remember?"

The bewhiskered hound and I departed, over ardent objections, and again took up a stand in the poultry yard. A moderately hard wind was blowing off the sierra and it brought the mariachi music almost alongside me. I dozed, jerked awake, thought bitter thoughts, and then, holy Jehoshaphat, Snowser was on his feet growling, and some alert hens in the false-ebony tree were cackling hysterically. Hoping it wasn't another skunk, I cuffed Snowser down, switched on my headlamp, and swept the yard. Nothing. But Snowser kept telling me that we had a visitor, or visitors. I got up stiffly and started to walk around the tree. I had taken maybe a dozen steps when I caught the gleam of eyes fifteen feet up. I fired without seeing the gun barrel, and a cat yelled and thudded to the ground, and then Snowswer was shaking it. It was a margay. In the beam of the light I saw two other margays disappearing up the tree.

As I was circling the tree trying to pick up the animals, I heard the sound of running footsteps. It was Trinidad. I told her what happened, and we walked around the tree trying to spot the cats. Then here came Don Dionicio followed by sundry friends and a marimba orchestra.

Trinidad said that she would climb the tree and chase the cats down for me to shoot. I heard myself say that if anybody climbed the tree, I would. Maybe it was because I wanted to get away from the marimbas. I don't know. Anyhow, I started climbing, and had nearly reached the top of the tree, balancing myself on a windy limb, when I saw the cat's eyes.

Well, I've told you what happened. I reached for a branch and there was a snake on it. The muzzleloader kicked me backward, and I fell. A multitude of assorted poultry flew. At some point during the fall I was intimately associated with a turkey, but we parted company and the law of gravity brought me to the ground so forcibly that I felt myself bounce. Snowser was raging. Don Basilio was shouting that the great Paloma Azul had been avenged. Trinidad had a powerful hand under my shoulders and was asking me if I was killed and I told her no, I didn't think so. It developed that in my fall I had dislodged a margay cub that had fallen practically into Snowser's jaws and he had shaken it silly but hadn't injured it too much. Don Dionicio had swathed it, struggling and yelling, in his shirt, and was now holding it helpless in the fold of his weightlifter arms. I lurched up, and said to Trinidad, "I still think you would make some hunter a good wife." She giggled, a strange sound for her, and said, "But who would marry a hunter in bad debt—one that fell through an expensive marimba, breaking it to splinters?"

I said, "Did I smash a marimba? Oh, happy day."

We returned to the ranch house, and I asked Don Basilio if he would lend me a horse, a sarape and a machete. I had important business in other parts, I said, but I would return. He said he was against it, but he would. When the horse and the gear arrived, I took off, with Trinidad waving good-bye with a flashlight. I was looking for a place to sleep. I had my eye on a dark mountainside.

I guess that does it. See you someday in Mexico during Holy Week.

Ladies . . . with Guns

I can only say that I have never guided a huntress who did not turn out to be a character. In fact, one word describes them all . . . unpredictable.

"Great balls o'fire! Take cover for your life!" Old Frank hollered at me when the .30-06 crashed and the grizzly rolled. "That redhead cheechako woman has ruint us."

For a while it looked as if she had. The bald-face grizzly she had shot when nobody was looking—a big one—had let out a couple of airhorn bawls, sagged briefly against the mountainside, and then, holy suffering, had come pinwheeling, bouncing and free-falling down the steep 400-yard slope directly at our stalled packtrain. The consequences were bound to be dramatic. This was in Louis Creek Pass, under the tremendous silver peaks of the Alaska range, in June. Old Frank and I were the hardworking guides of the party, and Mr. and Mrs. Boatright were our clients. Below the trail we were on gleamed six-foot snowdrifts. Above it, where the timber petered out and the sun had got a chance, the slope was bare, showing the pretty green of new grass, bluebells and Indian celery. I suppose that the grizzly had been behind a rock feeding. At any rate, Old Frank and I hadn't seen it. We were busy with a spruce snag that a winter wind had blown across the trail.

I had chopped through the windfall, and Old Frank had just tied onto it with his *reata* to drag it out of the way, when the trouble exploded. Every Alaska packhorse, no matter how dumb in other respects, knows that it is the height of prudence to get out of the path of an oncoming grizzly. Our ten knotheads couldn't flee up the trail on account of the windfall. So they whirled, squealing in terror, banging their packs together and slammed in wild, disorderly retreat back the way we had come. They just wanted to get gone from here. Mrs. Boatright, a plump, seemingly placid tenderfoot matron with bright sorrel hair, who I figured in my innocence had come along on the hunt chiefly to keep her woodsy husband company and see that he didn't get his feet wet, had dismounted to shoot. She was now crowded close in against the bank, the only safe place hereabouts.

Mr. Boatright had also got down, to take photographs, but was trapped on the outside of the trail. I saw the poor joker flap his arms desperately at the thundering tide of horses, then leap off the trail into space like a giant mackinawed bullfrog with a ten-gallon hat. The spring snow was so soft that he apparently splashed right through it to the ground.

Old Frank didn't do any better. As he turned in the saddle to stare popeyed at the tumbling grizzly, his snorty blue roan mount, unwilling to be left behind by its mates, bogged its head and came unstuck. Old Frank could ride. He was a bronc-twister from away back. In the First National Bank of Butte, Montana, there used to hang, and maybe still does, an oil painting of him sitting tight and purty on the famous rodeo outlaw Midnight. But this wasn't his day. The weight of the windfall jerked his horse off balance, and pawing at the sky, the animal fell off the edge of the trail with him. True to the rough-string riders' dictum that when you gotta go, go clean, Old Frank parted company with the roan in midair, to land headfirst, arms and legs all sprangled out, in a drift. These *outré* bits of action registered on me, like flickering scenes from a haywire movie projector, while the grizzly was covering, at varying rates of speed, some four-fifths of the distance to us.

Maybe the bear was dead, but then again maybe it wasn't. Anyhow, with my dorsal vertebrae congealing, I started running toward the placid Mrs. Boatright. I could still see her dynamically red head against the winter-killed grass of the bank, so the horses hadn't trampled her under, and she was still in there pitching because *ka-wham!* there went the .30-06 again. Ahead of me the grizzly soared over the trail, struck a spruce heavily, and spun into the tops of some snow-buried alder brush. The animal looked plenty dead but I kept going. I didn't have my rifle. My horse had made off with it. When I reached Mrs. Boatright she was chambering a fresh shell and wearing a ferocious Calamity Jane scowl as she peered over the trail trying to locate the brush-hidden grizzly in order to give it another round. Getting behind her, I said that I had just had a closeup look at the bear, and in my opinion the animal was no longer of this world. At this she visibly relaxed, and I seized the opportunity to reach over her shoulder and thumb the safety latch of the rifle. Then, a shaken man, wishing I had an aspirin, I started to speak my piece. "Madam, you have shortened my life," I said accusingly. "Why in the. . . ."

But she didn't hear me. She was gazing down the trail at the rumps of the departing horses. Her placid expression was back. "Where," she asked, "is everybody going?"

The above is just an example. I have in my time shepherded a slew of huntresses, young and old, native and foreign, pretty and prettier, and for a long while, as the saying goes, they had me fighting my hat. But no more. Boy, I have at last got smart to them. My bitterly won secret, for the benefit of hardworking guides and woodsy husbands who may be having trouble, is as follows: Each morning when I get up and pull on my boots, I repeat firmly to myself, "I absolutely will not be surprised at anything that happens today." I'd better add that nothing herein is to be construed that I am against huntresses. The truth is, I am all for them. It's just that they have, jumping Jehoshaphat, subjected me to experiences from which I never expect to recover completely.

Take another example. There was the hunt I made with the icy princess. I did not, I hasten to state, supply the name. It was given to the lady by the bemused hotel staff at Barra de Navidad, Jalisco, where she hired me to take her *tigre* hunting. She was a structurally remarkable blonde with a Conover walk and eyes like sunlight on Yucatan jade, about eight in the hardness scale, and was traveling in Mexico alone. If you are wondering why she wanted to kill a *tigre*, I can only reply that so was I. Anyway, I found myself occupying a *tigre* stand with her, for the third night in a row, on the top of an Aztec pyramid temple in the jungle above the muddy Rio Armeria. It was close to midnight, black as a wolf's throat, and thunder was cannonading over the sierra. The temple was maybe forty feet high, with grass and San Juan brush growing on its steps, and one side was in rubble where somebody had dug for treasure. The temple was the only elevated spot around there. I hoped that it would give us an advantage if a *tigre* showed up.

Out front, between us and the solid-black jungle, on what had been a paved ceremonial plaza, we had a white kid goat tied to a trimmed sapling. The kid was unhappy. It kept pacing back and forth to the end of its tether, fighting the rope and bleating. I was sorry for the little cuss. But without using a live bait, I didn't know how to get the icy princess a shot at a *tigre*. My dogs were on another hunt. Waiting at a dead bait would take too long, and as for trying to call a *tigre* in with a dried-gourd-and-resined-string *pujadera*, I never was any good with one of the things. So I had bought the goat. First, however, I consulted the icy princess. I explained that some folks, especially women, objected to the use of live animals as bait. The bleating of a scared kid in the jungle gloom could become pretty sympathy-provoking. The icy princess gave me an amused look that established me where I belonged, several cultural horizons distant.

"By all means, buy the goat," she said, sounding like Tallulah. "I'll try to control my womanly feelings for the beastie."

Time dragged its feet. Thunder continued to bang. Nations of tree frogs trilled for rain. The luminous dial of my watch showed that three hours had passed when, off to our left, a section of the frog chorus suddenly became quiet. I reached out and touched the icy princess. I wanted to be sure that she was awake. She was. Another quarter of an hour went by, and the lady leaned over and said that she would give 100 pesos if she could smoke a cigarette. I opened my mouth to tell her that I was chewing pipe tobacco and she could have some, but the words got lost. Because just then, somewhere close, a *tigre* coughed. I submit that no more threatening sound is likely to be heard between Tiajuana and Quintana Roo, traveling either way, than a *tigre's* hoarse rattling cough at night in the jungle when you may well be the object of the cat's intentions. I waited, straining my eyes and ears, resisting the temptation to switch on the spotlight. It is something, believe me, that you never get used to.

"This is the creeps," whispered the icy princess, still sounding like Tallulah.

"Lady, I concur," I whispered back.

The kid, bleating frantically, was now really struggling to break loose. It didn't need a blueprint. It knew what was coming. I wondered if the icy princess regretted our use of the animal, but I realized she was the ineffable, chain-mailed-type of huntress who might have been seen powdering her nose in the midst of the Deerfield Massacre. Suddenly there was a scuffing sound and the kid's bleating ceased. Hoping I had timed it right, I told the icy princess to get ready. I switched on my lamp at the same instant.

There stood the *tigre*, pinned in the light sixty feet distant, a wonderfully beautiful brute, spots showing boldly, tail twitching, eyes shining green as Inca emeralds. He hadn't killed the kid but was half-crouched to pounce on it. Swinging his head toward us, he raised one paw as if to ward off the light. The kid was down, tangled in its tether and kicking the stones, the sound I had heard. *Baloom!* The icy princess blasted with my buckshot-loaded 12-gauge. She scored. With the Deadwood on him at this range she couldn't have missed. The *tigre* screamed, reared high and fell backward, then recovered himself and made a stumbling rush to cover behind some fallen blocks of carved stone. In a case like this the only sane thing to do was wait—even if we had to wait until morning. But before I could stop her, sweet Quetzalcoatl, the icy princess went flying down the temple steps and out.

Horrified, I sprinted after her. No doubt the *tigre* was even more surprised and shocked than I. Anyhow, he broke from behind the pile of stones and headed for the jungle, hard hit and running slaunchwise. He hadn't covered twenty feet when the icy princess shellacked him with the second barrel.

This time, having taken most of the buckshot charge in his head, the big spotted cat went down like a sack of tortilla meal, and stayed down. When my hair had settled tentatively into place and I could trust my voice, I remarked to the icy princess that her *tigre*-killing technique was kind of breezy. Was she tired of living, or what? She knelt beside the kid.

"Help me find out if the poor darling is hurt," she said in that smoky cafe-society voice. "I'm going to take it home with me. I sat there all night thinking that if the *tigre* killed it, I would never forgive myself."

Things like that, if he isn't careful, will leave a hardworking guide walking around in a vacuum warbling "Good King Wenceslaus." But whenever I hear a clinical discussion of huntresses and their adventures in the wilds, I think about a slender, steady-eyed girl, name of Dorothy, with dark hair that shone like sewing silk. Her woodsy husband Bill brought her north from Chicago for a white sheep hunt, her first one. Before we left Anchorage I took the two of them out to the rifle range. Bill proved to be a good shot, but Dorothy was better than good.

"She's a killer," I said to Bill, meaning it. "I'll bet a box of cigars that she drops her ram the first shot."

I liked her. I hoped she would take the moss-horned grandpappy of all white sheep. But I lost my bet with Bill. Two mornings later, in a canyon that banged up against a hanging glacier, we sighted five rams. Half a mile distant, they were on a shale pitch above a cliff-walled lakelet. One had a grand head. Although it is always an agonizing guess until you read the tape, I decided after looking the head over with 12X glasses that it could be the best I had seen in years. Bill, using a spotting scope, was grinning happily. The old-timer who discovered that Nome beach had a gold foundation couldn't have looked more delighted. Then he remembered something. He and Dorothy, he said, would have to toss a coin to see who got the shot. Fishing a quarter out of his pocket, he spun it into the air.

Dorothy said, "Heads," and it came down heads. She quickly said, "Best two out of three." But Bill vetoed that. With no envy in his voice, he said that she had won and it was her shot.

By dint of a tough stalk over razor-edge shale, we reached a point 350 yards from the sheep. Dorothy appeared to have taken the stalk like a veteran. Her breathing was even and she looked calm. Exercising a hardworking guide's privilege, I felt her hand. Its palm was dry. So I checked the scope, and already feeling as victorious as Hillary and Tenzing on top of that big hill, told her to cut loose when she was ready. What happened was terrible. I mean, it strained my credulity quotient even while watching it. Dorothy of the sewing-silk hair, the supposed killer, flubbed the show. *Blowie!* barked the .270 and, holy cow, rock dust spurted ten feet above the ram. She worked the action and shot high again as the sheep fled in headlong panic. Bill was pleading with her to lower her aim, but she paid no attention. The rifle kept hammering and the slugs kept going high. Finally the magazine was empty and she stood up.

"Kill him, please," she said to Bill. "I can't."

Bill missed the running ram twice but hit him on the third try, and the sheep rolled down over a cliff, landing with a spectacular splash in the lakelet. Everything considered, it was a neat bit of shooting. Dorothy apologized for her performance. She said she had heard about buck fever all her life, and now she knew what it was like. To cheer her up, Bill and I told some Bronze Age jokes about the malady, and assured her that it was something that could happen to anybody and was nothing to be ashamed of. We went over and salvaged the trophy and it was as good as we had expected, large enough perhaps to win mention in the book of records—forty by fifteen and one-half inches. Dorothy took her ram, a smaller one, three days later. She killed it with one shot at 600 yards. It was mystifying. It baffled me. I kept thinking about the two conflicting episodes, and got nowhere.

Four months later the surprise payoff smacked me. I was on a winterbound trapline over in the Talkeetnas, peeling marten, when an Indian snowshoed in with some Christmas mail. There was a package from Dorothy. It contained two boxes of cigars and a note. The note read, "You understand how much killing the big ram meant to him." I got it. The implication was clear. She had made Bill a present of the sheep by deliberately missing it. As the Indian and I fired up a couple of the cigars, I saluted Dorothy the killer . . . another surprising huntress.

Perhaps the greatest fault I find with huntresses is their confounded insistence on keeping things superneat in camp. They will not understand that in a hunting bivouac a guy is entitled to a certain amount of robust, picturesque untidiness such as whiskers, socks drying over the stove or grill, eating with his galluses dangling, and leaving his hair uncombed. This is man's escape from domestic spit-and-polish. He has been enjoying it a long, long time. It is good for his soul. But you can't convince the ladies. My helpmate Dell provided a classic case in point. Although city reared, she had become outwardly a professional huntress after three years in the north with me. She had worked on the trapline, helped roll cabin logs, taken a hand at butchering game and toting the meat, and lived in siwash camps a hard week's travel from civilization. I believed that she was the exception, the huntress that proved the rule, until she hauled off typically one October night and lambasted me with a twenty-ton surprise.

We were hosts to a party of moose hunters at our backwoods cabin, and that night after supper I told the group about a slapstick experience I'd had there last fall with a black bear while Dell was in the States.

This bear, I related, was a grub thief, a determined so-and-so, and crafty. I had a shoulder of moose hanging from one of the porch rafters, and for a week he had been doing his damnedest to steal it from me. Hardly a night passed that my Briard bitch, Punkins, who slept inside the cabin, did not sound the alarm. But I had never yet been able to surge out of bed, grab my rifle and open the door in time for a shot. Of course, I could have hung the meat in the cache where it would have been safe, but it was so much more convenient there on the porch. When I wanted a steak, all I had to do was step outside and slab one off—the ultimate in sourdough efficiency. Besides, I had a plot. The meat was bait. If the larcenous bear kept fooling around, sooner or later I would hang his carcass on the porch too. This was a prime blueberry year—tons of the big sweet berries on the nearby ridges—and if there was anything I liked better after the weather turned cold than a juicy roast of fat blueberry-fed black bear, I said, I couldn't think at the moment what it was.

To better my chances, I oiled the door latch and hinges, and piled empty five-gallon kerosene cans under the meat. The idea was that the bear would make a racket but I wouldn't. For two nights following this the animal didn't return. But on the third morning came gaudy action. I arose early, put the coffee pot on, and washed in the tin washbasin, using Dell's carnation-scented foofaraw soap. I got some of the soap in my eyes, and was cussing the stuff as I blindly fumbled the door open to throw the water out. Everything happened at once. I threw the water, and great day in the morning, there was a terrific clatter of cans, a bear bawled practically in my face and kept bawling, Punkins shot past me yelling her head off, and the woodpile toppled onto a couple of washtubs with an earthquake din that should have registered on seismographs in Seattle. Wanting no part of such a fracas in my condition, I leaped back into the cabin and slammed the door. As I reconstructed things later, the bear had been reaching for the meat when I hit him in the muzzle with the soapy water. Whereupon, as blind as I, he earnestly set about tearing the porch down in his efforts to escape.

Anyhow, he made his getaway. When I could see again, Punkins was clamoring two ridges distant. Thus by a fell wrench of fate I lost the blueberry-fed bear I had planned to eat when the weather got cold. But since this was my yarn and I was spinning it with a hardworking guide's strategy, I told our guests that I killed the animal ten days later in a meadow up the creek. When, as I had hoped, one of the more alert hunters asked skeptically how I knew it was the same bear, I replied that, boy, he surely was unacquainted with the lasting quality of the carnation scent in Dell's brand of foofaraw soap. Personally, I thought it was a fair-to-middling bedtime story. But as I finished I caught a wounded-panther flash from Dell's eyes and knew that, somewhere along the line, I had pulled a boner and was in trouble. Sure enough, as soon as we were alone she opened up on me, this wilderness-schooled presumable professional huntress, point blank.

"Letting people know that you hung meat on the porch like a brush Indian," she raged, "and threw dirty wash water out the front door. I never was so humiliated!"

It is a fact that I have never guided a huntress who did not turn out to be a character—but a pleasant one, eminently swell to work for. A truly memorable lady in this respect, one who belted me bowlegged with an act and a sentence, was a visiting Wisconsin poetess whom I encountered at Carmen Sandoval's ranch in the sierra above Pueblo Juarez, Colima, where she was spending her vacation. Trail-grimed and weary, shaggy as a Transylvanian sheep dog, I had come out of the river jungles with my cat hunting crew to loaf a few days amidst unaccustomed luxuries such as a spring bed, a shower bath and meals served on a table. I was looking forward to this rest before taking off again on another cat quest. But my friend Carmen, a tricky gent when work was involved, hustled me out onto the gallery before I'd even had time to shed by spurs and gun and change into a clean shirt, almost as if he feared I would get away. He introduced us. Dreamy was the descriptive word for the poetess. A tiny brownette in jodhpurs, boots and a buckskin shirt sporting a lunatic fringe, with eyes the color of woodsmoke, she was curled up on a sofa with a coke in one hand and a book of Dylan Thomas verse in the other. Despite the shirt, she didn't look any more like a huntress than I looked like Abou ben Adhem. But incredibly she was.

"It is so wonderful here," she said in a dreamy little-girl voice after acknowledging the introduction. "The savage jungle, and the strange birds and animals. But driving up the mountain," she said, "we saw a deer and it reminded me of shooting trips in Wisconsin. I have been trying ever since to persuade Mr. Sandoval to take me deer hunting."

Beaming mendaciously, Carmen said that it was true, and nothing would have pleased him more, but unfortunately he had been busy. Now that I had arrived, he said, everything was solved. Of course, deer weren't numerous in the vicinity, he admitted, and the few present did seem to inhabit the more thickly jungled parts, but still he had no doubt that in four or five days, weather permitting, we would find and kill a fine buck. Naturally it would be more entertaining for the young lady to hunt with a fellow American, no? He had me. I was licked. So I mumbled sure, count on me, I'd be delighted, and there went my time for loafing amidst luxuries. But the way things developed, I wouldn't have missed this surprising hunt for anything at all.

Five long days later, in the blaze of a strawberry-and-copper sunrise, the dreamy poetess and I took a stand above a water hole at the foot of a huisache-clumped jungle wash. We had now put in a good thirty hours of hunting without seeing so much as the flash of a deer's tail. But if the lady was discouraged, she didn't show it. She sat cross-legged on a serape, my .30-30 beside her, gazing starry-eyed at the sunrise colors, and watching tórtola doves and some noisy green jays with yellow tail feathers pitch in over the liana-hung trees to water. She was the breathing portrait of a contented but misplaced person and I figured she was most likely composing a poem to the jungle morning. If by some strange chance a deer did wander by, I thought, it was even money she would declare rapturously that it resembled Bambi, and refuse to shoot. Bankers, necktie salesmen, grocery clerks and other intelligent fauna were still in bed asleep, and here I was.

On this pessimistic note, things picked up. Across the wash a flight of violet-headed parrots burst like splitting atoms out of the glossy tower of an ahuehuete tree, shrieking wildly. When they circled back I knew that they had something, an animal or a man, spotted. I told the dreamy poetess that maybe something was going to happen, and it would be a good idea to be ready. She twinkled her woodsmoke eyes at me and patted the breech of the .30-30. So I supposed that she was ready, or thought she was. Ten minutes passed. Then, out of the creme-de-menthe shadows behind a theatrical screen of moonflower vines, stalked two whitetail bucks. They were some thirty feet apart, all rucked up and glaring at each other, very autumn-happy. As there wasn't much choice between the trophy-average racks they carried, I advised the dreamy poetess to take the nearest buck. She started to raise the .30-30, then lowered it.

A jungle drama was beginning, a honey. With no preliminary sparring, the bucks had bounded together, fighting. By any standards, it was some battle. Grunting, antlers clashing, hoofs pounding the sand, the two feinted and lunged, gouged and battered their way across the wash to the water hole. I was at last, stone the crows, getting a kick out of the hunt. I hoped the dreamy poetess wasn't too appalled by the violence and would delay shooting. To have stopped the fight now with a bullet would have been a shame. I didn't know it, but I needn't have worried.

At the water hole one of the bucks lost his footing in the mud and was wrestled to his side. Before he could get up the other, a dirty fighter if one ever lived, bounced about six feet into the air and came down on him, sharp hoofs bunched. Uttering an explosive *whoosh*, the downed buck rolled completely over, and was lurching to his feet when the rough-and-tumble expert antler-raked him in the belly and jumped on him again. Boy, I never saw anything like it. The buck taking the beating was on his knees, but he succeeded in hurling himself forward with his hind feet, into the water. As he came up splashing, his bravo antagonist made another fancy jump at him, higher than the others. It ended in death. *Blam!* the .30-30 whipcracked, and the leaping buck twisted in the air, shot through the heart, to come down crosswise and kicking on top of the buck in the water.

The dreamy poetess hadn't bothered to stand up. It was one of those beautifully casual shots that most hardworking guides, and woodsy husbands too, wish they could make. It occurred to me, in a dazed way, that back home in Wisconsin the lady might be renowned as a poetess, but certainly she must also be known as a deerslayer of awesome ability. When the miraculously rescued buck had sorted himself out of the mixup and beat it back into the Paul Gauguin greenery, where undoubtedly a doe was waiting, I turned to the dreamy poetess and respectfully lit a cigarette for her.

"Did you finally shoot him," I asked, "because he was jumping on his poor downed opponent?"

She thought it over a moment, real serious, while the javelin flight of violet-headed parrots screeched above the dead buck and jungle voices for a mile around were inquiring what had happened. Then, wouldn't it cock your pistol, she walloped me for the second time this morning. "When is it possible except when he is down," she counter-questioned in her dreamy little-girl voice, "to jump on a poor opponent?"

I guess that does it. See you on a big-game hunt with your huntress.

Chubasco

No Aztec in modern times ever experienced such a storm as the one that bellowed out of the southwest for six hours that night, faded, only to strike again with new fury.

"Listen. Hear them? Geese in the sky," said the man with the bloody bandage around his head where he had been hit by a flying plank that blew out of the eldritch darkness. "How I'd like to be on the flats at daybreak with a shotgun. Boy, oh boy," he breathed raptly.

They sounded like snow geese, a sizable flock, and they were circling in the black sky just above the ridges, hunting a haven. They didn't have much time, for these geese were over Manzanillo, Colima, at 6:15 on the fateful morning of 27 October 1959. The hill-girt seaport city of 20,000 souls was at the moment in the eye of one of history's most savage hurricanes. It was the dreaded *chubasco* wind of the Aztecs—the dark destroyer—but no Aztec in recorded times ever experienced such a *chubasco* as the one that had bellowed out of the southwest for six hours, then faded, and was now about to strike again with added fury. In the uncanny calm of the eye, rain pounded down on the wreckage-strewn street. There were no lights. The battered city lay in gloom and stunned silence except for the sounds of the rain, the unending, hammering tropical rain, and the wild calling of the desperate geese.

"A lot of guys prefer cacklers and blues," said the man with the bandaged head. "But I dunno, I always like the snows. Their style suits me just fine."

I said it was a matter of taste but he had a point. Geese had brought me here. Yesterday I had been at Cuyutlan, a sleepy resort pueblo on the coast forty miles south. I was eating breakfast in the engagingly beat-up Hotel Colima with Salvador, the manager, and his husky mother, Maria Luisa, when geese began clamoring over the dunes. Flight after flight of snows and white-fronted geese were heading for the lagoon two miles distant, and with them, as if flying convoy duty, were squadrons of lesser waterfowl: pintails, teal and shovelers. We gave up trying to eat and went outside to gawk at the phenomenon. The mixed flight kept streaming past, and now here came what looked like the whole pelican population of the coast. I had lived at the hotel off and on for two years, but had never seen anything to equal this. Salvador had been here all his life, and he said that he had never even heard of anything like it.

"A terrible *chubasco* hurricane is coming," said Maria Luisa. "The ducks and geese know it and are seeking shelter."

All of us had heard the newscast. A hurricane had passed by Acapulco and moved slowly up the coast, but had veered off northwest and would die somewhere at sea. Salvador told Maria Luisa fondly that she was dreaming. Obstinately she said no, she wasn't. So he said all right, since she was a greater expert than the meteorologists, how did she know that a *chubasco* threatened? "Because I couldn't do a thing with my hair this morning," she replied. "And now the sky is full of frightened ducks and geese."

Salvador and I didn't argue. We had sport on our minds. Thirty minutes later we unloaded from his pickup on the bank of the opal-blue lagoon, and entered upon what could have been the waterfowl-shooting experience of our lives. I was using my muzzle-loader and it handicapped me somewhat because it took so long to reload.

But I did all right. A goose came tearing over and I swung on it and pulled, and kept swinging for the interminable instant until the charge fired, and the goose, a speckled belly, somersaulted down so close past Salvador's head that he flinched and missed a shot. We didn't need a blind. We were under the dunes, and the birds were winging in so low to the water that they were in range before they saw us. Salvador banged away methodically with his 12-gauge double, and I patiently loaded, fired and reloaded. Both ducks and geese were now towering. Plenty of them knew that we were here, but they didn't want to leave. Innocent new arrivals continued to top the dunes, and we had killed six geese between us when—the worst thing that could have happened—I ran out of caps.

As there were no caps available in Cuyutlan, I told Salvador that I would have to go to Manzanillo on the auto stage and buy a box. I would be back in plenty of time, I promised, for some afternoon duck shooting. Salvador, a thoughtful twenty-three-year-old, advised me to take my gun. There just might be, he said, even more birds on the lagoon behind Manzanillo than there were here. That was how I happened to have the muzzleloader with me when I arrived in the seaport city. It had begun to rain, a real drencher, by the time I checked the gun with Pidi, the bartender at the Hotel Foreign Club, and headed across the pretty shade-tree-dotted plaza to buy caps. When I had made the purchase I telephoned the stage station to find out when the next stage left, and was told that owing to a washout there would be no further service south today. Stuck, I bought a copy of *Sports Afield* and returned to the Foreign Club to read it. The rainstorm had now become an authentic cloudburst. It soon grew so dark that Pidi turned on the lights at his end of the big open-sided hotel cafe.

Nobody had any warning. The harbor was full of ships and small boats. Despite the rain, shops were doing a brisk business. Evening came, and in the residence section, most of which clung to the steep sides of the circling rocky hills, lights twinkled homily. I loafed and read.

Then at 11:45 P.M. the mighty *chubasco* blasted in.

First came a series of gusts that whirled sheets of rain through the tossing plaza trees. Then with a sound like the howling of a thousand wolves the full weight of the hurricane hit. As Pidi and I watched from the shelter of a pillar, sheet iron, planks, tar-paper, signs, coconuts, the top of a tree and a baby carriage blew across the square. Sparks showered and arced as power lines fell, and the lights went off all over town. A man caromed in out of the mauling wind and shouted that a palm on the other side of the square had fallen and perhaps killed his brother. He wanted to use the telephone to call an ambulance. But the telephone had ceased functioning. Now another ominous sound was becoming audible, the crashing of monstrous waves breaking over the seawall half a block distant. Realizing that a first-magnitude disaster was upon us, I got a pad of paper at the hotel desk and began making notes. I believe that they were the only eyewitness notes taken by a writer.

While buildings toppled and the crazy doomsday yelling of the wind increased in pitch, I maneuvered over to the municipal palace, wading through knee-deep water, trying not to think about blowing glass and sheet iron, and tacked diagonally to the Hotel Madrid which stands a few yards from Red Cross headquarters. I got there as the penthouse blew off the hotel roof and the pieces whipped into the street I had just vacated—proving that the age of miracles had not yet passed. A waterfall was pouring down the stairs into the patio. The manager, her two children and several guests were crowded into a small room off the entrance, and a guest dragged me in. Somebody was praying. Houses on the hill directly above were disintegrating and the parts were landing on the hotel or cannonading against its walls. It sounded like one of the busier days on Okinawa. I waded out and stood in the doorway. An urgent citizen with a flashlight clawed his way in and said that a woman had been killed down the street, almost decapitated by a piece of sheet iron. He added that he wished he had a drink.

I stayed at the hotel until shortly after six o'clock, when the eye passed over. Part of the time my unknown friend with the bandaged head, who wanted to talk about geese, stood vigil with me.

"Do you think they made it down to a safe place?" he asked earnestly as I was leaving. "The snows, I mean."

I said I hoped they had, and that he would meet them some fine morning on the flats. Feeling used up around the edges, I went back through the water-filled streets in the black eerie calm to the Foreign Club. I was trying to get some coffee from a shaking cook when the warlock wind began thundering again, this time from the unprotected west. Debris that had blown to one end of town now began blowing back. In my time I have witnessed China Sea typhoons, Aleutian williwaws, and other Mexican hurricanes, but this brute of a wind topped them all. A young American lad known as Big Mike joined me behind a pillar and said that his new car, a $6,000 sports roadster, had been blown over the seawall.

By eight o'clock there was enough light to see the hills. Where picturesque pastel homes had stood there was now tangled wreckage. A block of waterfront warehouses was in rubble. The freighter *Santo Thomas* had broken up against the stone jetty, and was on her side. A Mexican destroyer was aground. Three others, moored near the hotel, looked as if they had been under shellfire. Across the bay the freighter *Sinaloa* was on a reef, and I was to learn that three American women had drowned, trapped in their stateroom. A statue of Miguel Hidalgo, father of Mexican independence, stood among ruined plaza trees with hands turned palms out in the attitude of a righteous man demanding an explanation.

"The American Navy will soon arrive," said the nervous cook, who had at last got some coffee made. "It always brings aid."

Cornering across the square, a gigantic sea bulled over the cement wall and knocked down a softdrink warehouse, and the commingled contents of thousands of smashed bottles foamed into the torrent of seawater. Six half-naked seamen from the *Santo Thomas*, covered from head to foot with black oil, struggled up the street, making for the Red Cross. Other refugees were appearing. A blind man with a terrified pet coati on his shoulder came out of a smashed doorway, and blown by the braying *chubasco*, vanished around a corner. A woman leading a girl of perhaps eight tried to cross the plaza as a heavy limb was torn from a tree; she escaped injury herself when the limb struck the child and killed her. Out front an unidentified flying object struck a metal-cored cement lamppost and bent it double. Trucks were now creeping through the streets with casualties. A driver I knew shouted that the suburb of Salagula had been destroyed by a ten-foot wall of water. I finished gulping my coffee, and battled my way toward the Red Cross station. A woman clad in a slip and bathrobe, carrying a Pekingese dog, spun into me at the corner and I attempted to steady her, but the dog, a tough character, bit me and I went on.

From a sheltering alley mouth Sgt. Clyde Boatright (Ret.) an old fishing pal, bawled in a parade ground voice, "Hallelujah! Whaddya say, boy?" I gave him the stock reply, "Save your money. It's going to be a long, hard winter." A hundred or more soaked, tragedy-dazed people were huddled in the Red Cross station. Workers were chopping up a steer carcass with an ax and passing out the still-warm meat. A truck pulled in with bodies. Feet stuck out from under a rain-sluiced tarpaulin. *Medicos* worked under emergency lights fed by a hastily rigged gasoline-driven generator. Hollering above the incredible wind, a weary police lieutenant told me that radio operators had been unable to raise nearby towns. Thus their fate was unknown. The death list here, he said, had reached 200. Last night the wind, he informed me, had registered 150 mph on the weather station anemometer, the instrument's maximum. He handed me a packet of white pills, the label of which was in English, and asked me what they were. I told him they were sulphur pills, and he said disgustedly that, *Chihuahua*, what he wanted was aspirin.

I climbed the stairs to the second floor of the building and found Brigadier General Enrique Melendez Martinez, military commander of the area, and asked him if he had any information regarding Cuyutlan.

The general shook his head. Telephone and telegraph wires were down, he said. Railroad bridges were out. The highway was blocked by fallen trees and probably its bridges were out too. I told him that if I could find a horse I was going to make the ride to Cuyutlan. My friends were there. In the event the town was hard hit, they would need help. The general wished me luck, sounding as if he figured luck was going to be a large requisite. It was now nine o'clock and I thought that the awesome wind was abating. Returning to the Foreign Club, with two big wharf rats scuttling ahead of me, I asked Pidi to find me a saddled horse, a machete and a serape. He said he would try. In fact, to count on him.

I wanted some cigarettes and there were none at the hotel desk, so I took a long chance and crossed the open plaza to the Paris billiard hall to buy some. The roof of the place had fallen in, the juke box had been crushed, and timbers and broken tiles lay high-piled on the billiard tables, but the slicker-clad owner, believe it or not, was behind the counter. He sold me a carton of cigarettes and meticulously made change.

As I was toiling back across the plaza something—I'll never know what—hit me in the mouth and knocked out a long-cherished pivot tooth. At the Foreign Club a hollow-eyed man with a broken arm in a sling asked me if it was true that the entire west coast of Mexico was a disaster area. I told him he would have to inquire of somebody else. At eleven o'clock the Biblical deluge of a rain ceased and the killer wind died. Overhead a sullen glow showed through cloud wracks. Big Mike, the lad whose car had blown away, came downstairs and said, "Otherwise how are things?" I asked him if I could borrow his radio, knowing that he had a good battery-powered portable transistor set. During the ride to Cuyutlan I wanted to know what was going on. Big Mike said sure, I could take the radio, but there was nothing on the air except static. I then bought part of a cooked ham, a loaf of bread, a pound of cheese, and some coffee and sugar, and borrowed a tin kettle from the cook. I stowed these items in a flour sack also obtained from the kitchen, and reclaimed the muzzleloader. Half-an-hour later Pidi told me that a *paisano* had arrived with my horse and equipment.

The animal proved to be a chunky sorrel, always my favorite color of horse, and the *paisano* said that his name was Valiant, which I hoped he would turn out to be. I tied my assortment of gear to the turret-bowed Mexican saddle, said so long and good luck to Pidi, Big Mike and the *paisano*, and stepped aboard.

At the *chubasco*-torn outskirts of town a big, rangy, bewhiskered silver-gray dog fell in with me. Perhaps he knew the horse, or maybe he just wanted to get gone from here. When it became evident that he was a recruit, I named him Snowser. An hour later I came to a river where yesterday there had been a dry wash. The concrete bridge had fallen in. I rode upstream through wind-stripped jungle where purple-and-yellow tree-climbing land crabs swarmed, found a ford, and with the radio in my arms and Snowser swimming after me, made a perilous crossing amidst heavy drift that included the thatch roof of a house. A broken-winged pelican flopped ahead of me and some wild Muscovy ducks, goose-size, flew out of an inundated thicket. Valiant had done well in the river. It told myself that probably he was one of the good ones.

Angling back on a long slant toward the highway, I wove a difficult way through a blown-down coconut plantation, got into flood water where buzzards sat on a spine of black lava rock waiting for a chance to get at two drowned cows, and had to return to higher ground. I reached down and switched on the radio, and got a Texas station broadcasting news. Sandwiched between political stories was the information that a hurricane had struck the Pacific coast of Mexico and twenty persons had been killed. I turned it off. On a hillside, as the sun was westering in an innocently clear sky, I rounded some fallen primavera trees into a group of whitetail. There were five of them, three antlered bucks and two does. *Chubasco*-shocked to a point beyond fear, they stood staring dully as I rode past 200 feet distant. Hardly had I left the deer behind when, in a hollow near a flattened cornfield, I sighted a thread of woodsmoke and then two thatched huts, one with a side blown out, the other on the ground with a thick kapok tree across it.

A shirtless man, wild-eyed and slobbering, came running toward me from an open fire in the dooryard. "The wind, *señor!*" he screeched, pointing seaward. "The fearful avenging wind of *Dios*. Prepare yourself, for it comes again." I reined in, but he kept going. When he had disappeared into the jungle, I headed Valiant over to the standing hut. Out of it walked a *mestiza* girl. Maybe eighteen, she was square-shouldered and slender, had crow-wing hair and luminous dark eyes, and perhaps was pretty but you couldn't tell because her face was swollen from weeping. She carried a serape, a bulging woven string bag, and a framed color print of the Virgin of Guadalupe Hidalgo. I asked her if there was anything I could do here, and she said no. Last night the falling tree had crushed and killed her aunt, but she and her uncle had already buried the woman. Her uncle had later begun talking wildly and it was clear that he had lost his reason. He was the man who had screamed to me about the wind and fled into the jungle. The girl said that she wanted to go to Guadalajara and find work, but the first necessity was to get away from here. She went around behind the hut, to return with a saddled mule. She then said that her name was Panchita, and if I didn't mind, she would ride with me. I said to mount up and let's get going.

But the dirt road leading to the highway was impossible on account of jackstraw-piled fallen trees, so I had to turn back once more to higher jungled ground. Partway up the narrow basin we were in, at the rim of a *chubasco*-blasted banana planting, we sighted five deer, presumably the same ones I had seen earlier. I dismounted and slid the muzzleloader out of its boot. It was now manifest that the ride to Cuyutlan through the world's-end litter of smashed jungle was going to be plenty rough and grub I had brought wouldn't last. As the gun was loaded with No. 4 shot, I spilled half-a-dozen buckshot on top of the charge and rammed down a light wad. The deer let me approach within 100 feet before they took off. Hoping the gun would hold together, I laid the sights on the nearest buck and fired. The recoil kicked me two steps backward and numbed my shoulder, but the buck, after a staggering run into the banana field, fell dead.

I started to work on the carcass with my pocketknife — and was cussing its inadequacy when Panchita joined me with a keen-bladed Sayula butcher knife she had taken from among her possessions in the string bag. You could see as she worked that this wasn't the first deer she had helped dress out. I tied the buck behind my saddle and we found the grade of the ancient cobble-stoned Spanish *camino real* and climbed into the unfamiliar leafless jungle; past a dead pinto horse with a splintered tree across its back; past a large square of boat canvas that had blown from heaven knew where and now hung in a treetop like a flag of surrender; past a crippled white-tailed deer with button antlers, that hobbled away painfully without looking back, to a meadow on a hillcrest. Here a family of four, a man, a woman and two children, were camped. The man was lying on a serape, and his face was the color of pipe clay. They were sierra people, charcoal burners, the woman told us, and had been on their way to visit a married son in the lowlands and help him harvest his corn, when trouble overwhelmed them. First the shattering *chubasco* and the cloudburst, and then, this morning, the man had been stung by a yellow scorpion.

With vivid pantomime, she showed us how he had been reaching for a piece of wood to put on the fire, how the scorpion had struck his hand and clung, and how he had pulled it loose with his teeth and spat it into the coals. Now he was very ill and there was no food for the children. There was no medical aid or advice I could give, but we had the deer which I gave to them withholding only the liver. The woman's voice and her expression as she thanked us indicated that she regarded the meat as a reprieve from a tough sentence indeed, which maybe it was. We went on.

While the sun dropped in a brilliant smear of copper and rose, and echelons of yellow-headed parrots, strangely silent, streaked overhead to some secret roosting spot, we rode down to a flat shining with the flood water of another cloudburst-born river. As I was looking for a campsite near the water, somewhere close upstream a burro brayed as if in convulsions, and I thought I heard somebody shout. Turning the tired sorrel in that direction, I presently saw a boy on a white burro coming toward us through the twilight shadows. He was a skinny, shock-headed Indian youngster of about ten, in a tattered blue shirt and watersoaked jeans, barefoot. Still fifty feet distant, he began telling us in half-hysterical, machine-gun Spanish who he was and what his troubles were. His name was Raul and he had lost his father, his mother and a younger brother last night when the flash flood roared out of the sierra and took their hut. He couldn't remember, he said, how he had been saved. For a while he and his mother had clung to a floating tree that had ripped through the hut, and then his mother was no longer with him. He guessed that he must have swum ashore, although he couldn't recall having done so. This morning he had found the family burro on the bank, and since then had ridden up and down the valley shouting for his parents.

"Take me with you," he cried. "Don't' leave me here to be killed by the wind and the water."

Panchita stepped off the buckskin mule and ran to the boy. Lifting him down, she talked to him while I unsaddled. I decided that she was probably one of the good ones too. Pidi's *paisano* friend had included a *reata* as an accessory to the saddle, so I was able to picket Valiant on some fair grass. The mule and the burro I hobbled with rawhide thongs taken from the muzzleloader's boot. I cut some deadwood and got a big, bright fire going. Panchita, as if she had been doing it all her life, as maybe she had, broiled liver on a tilted flat rock, sliced bread and cheese, and made coffee. As we started to eat, I heard a swift rustling on the leaves behind me, and turned to see a green centipede nearly a foot long come into the firelight. I made a grab for the machete, but Panchita got it first, slashed the centipede in half, and scooped the writhing parts into the fire.

Some twenty minutes later Valiant snorted and pounded toward us to the end of his tether. I went to him with the muzzleloader. Snowser, all bristled up and walking stiff-legged, accompanied me. The sorrel was looking upstream, trembling. I caught the green glow of an animal's eyes reflecting the firelight, but too briefly to shoot or to make a stab at identifying the beast. Judging from the horse's actions, it was something big, possibly a *tigre* or a puma. Snowser wanted to pursue it, but I held him back. I told myself that most likely the bewhiskered dog was also one of the good ones. It occurred to me that much of the sierra's wildlife, fleeing from the *chubasco*, had sought shelter in the lowland jungles, and that the surviving wildlife of this valley had joined the newcomers in prowling the water's edge. Before morning I was sure of it.

After finishing our meal, I gave Raul my serape, and stretched out on the foot-deep leaves, using the saddle blankets as a cover. I was beat to a frazzle. It had been an eventful twenty hours since the unheralded *chubasco* banged against the land from nowhere at all. With Snowser curled beside me, and Panchita and Raul across the fire, I burrowed down into solid sleep. Toward one o'clock the dog woke me, whuffing. I reached automatically for the muzzleloader, and sat up. There was a big spread of blue-white stars and the sierra was hunched tall and black against them. Snowser seemed to be worried about something down by the water. Throwing a handful of twigs on the coals for light, I pulled on my boots and went to investigate. A dead tree with limbs that reached over the bank had grounded in the brush. I was about to step under one of the limbs when the feebly burning twigs on the coals flared up brightly. At the same instant Snowser, snarling, crowded against my legs. Movement above me caught my eye.

Coiled around the limb, holy mackerel, its weaving head practically in my face, was an enormous snake. In the flickering firelight its eyes shone like jewels. The body of the snake was as thick through as my leg. The reptile hissed—a loud gargling sound. I jumped back, stumbling, and before I could shoot, the huge snake let go of the limb and thudded to the ground. I blasted a charge of buckshot into it. The snake in its death throes flailed the brush and the water like a lashing steel cable. Panchita appeared beside me with the machete. Her lips were drawn back from her teeth and her eyes were narrowed in such a fighting mask as I had seen carved on the stones of Indian temples. By the time I had the gun reloaded, the snake was dead. It was a nine-foot boa. Since it is the firm belief of Mexican hunters that boas travel in pairs, I pushed the twitching coils of this one into the water, hoping that its mate, if it had one, would follow. In a way, I was sorry I had shot the snake because boas are pretty harmless. Anyhow, everything back to abnormal, I lay down again, but didn't sleep well the rest of the night. An opossum, two armadillos and a rabbit wandered past, and with a great flapping of wings an owl killed something that died hard and noisily.

When the first mother-of-pearl flush lighted the east, and the birds raucously greeted the new day, we breakfasted on ham, cheese and coffee, and rode upstream looking for a ford. We found one after plodding through interminable blowdown, only to discover after crossing that a newly formed slough and a belt of uprooted wild oil-palms barred us from returning to the old *camino real*. At nine o'clock I switched on the radio and got a newscast from Guadalajara: *". . . situation at Manzanillo continues uncertain. No communications. The governor will fly to the area by helicopter today. . . ."*

A little later the first plane came over, a single-engine job. The pilot, I thought, must have studied flying in a jujitsu school. Anyway, he was a genius at bending the plane through canyons and around mountainsides. We topped a long rise and halted to let the animals blow. On the slope below us a covey of black-throated Montezuma quail was picking gravel. We could have used half-a-dozen for a meal, but my chances of killing that many with the muzzleloader were mighty slim.

Then Snowser whuffed, the quail whirred away among the bare trees, and Raul pulled excitedly at my sleeve, pointing. The skinny boy and the bewhiskered dog made a good team. Far ahead of me, they had spotted a band of javelinas. There were ten or a dozen of them. Eighty yards distant, single file, they were coming obliquely up the pitch toward us. When they were close enough, I chose a young boar and killed it. Panchita insisted on dressing it out. In her hard jungle code I suppose it was a woman's job. She brushed back a crow-wing lock with her forearm, and smiling for the first time, saying, "Do you like that smoke-spouting gun as well as the other kind?"

I answered: "Of course. It's the most. I couldn't get along without it."

She said: "Well, yesterday it saved some helpless ones from hunger. So I like it too." Then she looked stricken as though she

had said something she shouldn't have. With the meat behind my saddle, we switchbacked into another valley as the shadows shortened and it began to get hot. A strange migration of large yellow butterflies drifted westward off the sierra.

Traveling with the butterflies, we came to wind-destroyed cornfields and a cluster of badly damaged huts. A man repairing a roof saw us, and shouted. When people gathered I asked them if anybody had any word of Cuyutlan. Nobody had. A white-headed elder with a sonorous vice and a roman beak of a nose said that the villagers faced destitution because their crops were gone, but rejoiced because nobody here had been killed. He kept referring to Panchita as my *señora*, which embarrassed me and amused Panchita. As they were out of meat, I gave them most of our javelina. The elder took off his sombrero, made the sign of the cross, and said, "I pray that Cuyutlan has been spared."

The yellow butterflies still with us, we rode on. In the next hollow an autumn-fat raccoon peered at us from a lodged tree above a guava thicket, but I wasn't interested, nor was Snowser after I told him to come on, we could do better.

At lunchtime we stopped at a deserted farmstead and foraged green corn, bananas and tomatoes, competing for the latter with anyhow a thousand hungry white-winged doves. We then dined on broiled javelina chops and corn which had been roasted over a coconut-husk fire. Young Raul was beginning to enjoy things. With Indian resilience, he had already largely recovered from his nightmare experience. He asked me if I did much traveling and hunting, and I said yes. Whereupon he dealt himself in. The life, he declared, was going to suit him exactly. Panchita of the crow-wing hair told him sharply that he talked too much. Still surrounded by yellow butterflies, we busted through a hurrah's nest of blowdown to the two-lane blacktop highway, and after a bit came to the crossroads four miles from Cuyutlan. Off yonder toward the tranquil, sweetly blue horizon we saw a helicopter buzzing north, and assumed that it carried the Governor. When the glitter of the lagoon showed ahead, I dismounted and approached the brush-grown bank afoot. We had only enough meat for another meal, and there was no telling what conditions were in Cuyutlan.

Some egrets, white herons and cormorants occupied a mud shoal midway across a narrow neck of water, and a raft of coots was paddling about. But there was no sign of the countless ducks and geese that had been here two mornings ago. I was about to leave when, in against the bank, I saw a moving dark object through the screening brush. It was a lone white-fronted goose. I stepped into view. The goose got up, beating the water, and when it was over land I killed it. Raul and Snowser retrieved the bird. We went on, crowding the animals, and soon heard surf echoing from the dunes. The red roofs of Cuyutlan came into sight, and they looked undamaged. Then we turned up the grassy lane to the hotel. It was standing but had taken a hammering. I could see that waves had pounded through the front door and out the back. Mattresses, bedding, garments and pieces of furniture were drying in the street.

Salvador saw us, and sang out happily, "Did you remember to buy the caps?"

I turned Panchita and Raul over to Maria Luisa. They both said they wanted to stay, and in the circumstances there were certainly enough chores here so that they could earn their keep and more. As for the bewhiskered Snowser, he flopped contentedly on the gallery, already at home. Fate had been kind to Cuyutlan. Only the edge of the juggernaut *chubasco* had swiped the town. But the news from other parts was grim. I turned on the radio and picked up bulletins from Los Angeles: *". . . probably the most vicious hurricane ever to strike a North American shore . . . 700 believed dead in Manzanillo . . . nearby Minatitlan buried under a mile-wide sea of mud, with 600 dead . . . Parota wiped out . . . no information regarding Cuyutlan . . . medical supplies being rushed . . . Bulldozing graves . . . first damage estimates, $280 million . . ."*

I went down the corridor for a look at my room. Surf had broken the window shutters and a couple of tons of sand had washed in and apparently churned about cement-mixer fashion for hours. Nothing was worth salvaging. Thus, holy suffering, my remaining tangible assets were the muzzleloader and the clothes I stood in.

But I felt lucky. Boy, I felt really lucky.

When the Fish Went Nuts

When the solstice storms strike they are bad—but fishing is wonderful. In fact, you never know what you'll catch next.

"*Un milagro*—a miracle," Tomás hollered above the Wagnerian uproar of wind, thunder and surf when the huge, mysterious fish struck in a way, and in a place, such as we had never known a big-game fish to strike. "But then this is the time," he added complacently, "when our fish go crazy—as I told you yesterday."

"The fishermen go loco too," I said. "Otherwise we wouldn't be out here."

We were in a madly pitching flat-bottomed skiff powered by a stuttering outboard motor, with towering sea-dunes ahead and mangrove jungles behind, near the southern end of storied Laguna Caimanes, in the tiny state of Colima. Five minutes ago we had sighted a fin that didn't belong in a place like this. I was casting a plug for *robalo*—snook to Atlantic Coast fishermen—when the fin knifed the surface 200 feet distant, heading in our direction and coming fast. Blue-gray and peaked, it wasn't the dorsal of either a shark or billfish, or of any other fish that I could think of at the moment. Beneath the fin I could see the shadowlike form of the fish, and it was big. I mean, it was fabulously big. The thing approached within a few yards of the plug, then turned in a swirl of water and disappeared.

"Whatever that monster is," I said as I desperately reeled in the suddenly inadequate *robalo* gear, "it came out of the ocean. Nothing in its weight class ever lived in fresh water."

"And I personally never saw a fin like that in salt water," said Tomás. "Not in my whole life, and I was born on a fishing boat."

We had brought along 3/6 gear for reasons that will become apparent. Working as fast as I could, I bent a silvery half-pound sea trout on the Norwegian hook, and Tomás yanked the venerable motor to life. We trolled across the 500-yard-wide lagoon three times. Nothing happened. So Tomás took us in a wide arc that brought us into the *creme de menthe* shadows of the mangroves. Here the big fish, or one of its brethren, struck. With the westerly sunglow in my eyes, it looked as if a gleaming bronze cutlass had thrust above the tumbled water to slash at the lure. There was a jolt, and line paid out. I hit the fish as hard as I could with the Tyee Club gear and it ran, but did not jump. It was powerful, fast and heavy. It didn't feel like any fish I knew. I wished I could get a good look at it. I wished I had heavier tackle. I wished a lot of things.

"If we ever boat this beast," I said, watching line dissolve off the reel, "we'll have to wire Francesca la Monte at the American Museum of Natural History to find out what it is."

Thunder continued to cannonade. The wind was increasing. The fish ran toward the opposite shore and Tomás tried to chase it, fiddling with the motor's carbureter as he did so. A bucket of water came over the bow and landed in my lap. I said to myself: "You wanted an adventure, son. So you've got one. Have fun."

Here I must explain how this extraordinary fishing trip came about. It was the morning of July 3, and I was eating breakfast in the sunny open-sided restaurant of the Hotel Fénix in Cuyutlan, a resort down on the coast, sharing a table with Tomás Ramírez. We had worked through the first pot of coffee when an Indian fisherman clad in salt-streaked shorts and a string of blue amulet beads came in from the street half-dragging the biggest *robalo* I had ever seen. While I gaped at the magnificent fish, Tomás' brother Dámaso bought it from the Indian for ten pesos, then whacked it into four chunks with a machete and stowed it into the icebox. He tossed the head and tail to a couple of ribby dogs, who at once disappeared with their bounty. As sons of the hotel owner, Tomás and Dámaso bought fish daily for the hotel kitchen, and manifestly didn't think that there was anything unusual about the incredible *robalo*. As nearly as I could figure out later, it would have measured better than thirty-inches—big enough to cause any angler to run a temperature.

"Ask him where he caught it," I said urgently as the Indian started out the door counting his money. "Don't let him get away."

"But we know where he caught it," Tomás said. "He caught it at La Boquilla, the new mouth of Laguna Caimanes. It will be very good for dinner tonight," he said. "Come and see how fat, firm and fresh it is."

Louise
Lopina ©86

I said I would take his word for the *robalo's* culinary possibilities, but to tell me, for gosh sakes, about the new lagoon mouth, where it was located, how to get there, and why it was new. Thus I first heard about La Boquilla. It seemed that the mighty hurricane of October 27, last year, which wrecked the port city of Manzanillo and a dozen or so villages, had driven crashing seas through the coastal barrier dunes to form an opening into Laguna Caimanes. Fishermen had recently discovered the new mouth, and were taking rare harvests of fish there—*robalo*, pargo (snapper), sea trout, guachinango (red snapper), ladyfish and other notable species. Whereupon I replied that I would like to go there at once. Today. Lagoon mouths on this coast offer an exciting, suspense-filled brand of fishing that you can't find anywhere else. And a new mouth was a fishing spot to explore without delay.

"The weather will probably be terrible," Tomás said. "The solstice storms are overdue, and when they come they are bad. But," he flashed a toothy smile, "the fishing will be wonderful. Our fish celebrate the solstice weather, but don't ask me why."

I replied that weather was a gamble that fishermen took at all times and wherever, even in the old farm pond. So let us, please, get started for La Boquilla. Tomás shrugged, and said that he would be ready in twenty minutes. Dámaso looked at the sky, which was a beautiful hot Aztec-blue streaked with mare's tail clouds, and allowed that he had important business today but would join us tomorrow, *Dios quiere*—God willing. Dámaso is a cautious soul, a guy who never, I'll bet, drew to an inside straight or went on a blind date. Which is commendable up to a point, but you miss a lot of fun being that way. Tomás and I loaded my bewhiskered hound Snowser and our gear into the battered hotel truck and drove to the lagoon, where we transferred into the aforementioned skiff. The lagoon winds, branches and turns back on itself for forty miles through tangled jungle, and used to be the haunt of pirates, smugglers, crocodile hunters and assorted colorful gentry. Today it is a kind of unofficial wildlife refuge. For adventurous souls desiring a different kind of vacation, I recommend it.

We clattered through the shimmering, blue-hazed midday, past the ruined huts of crocodile hunters who had made more money than they could spend while their saurian prey lasted, past green fairyland islets, past dark mangrove-roofed tunnels that led nobody knew where, past great colonies of egrets, ibis, cranes and roseate spoonbills huddled on mud bars. In the afternoon we came to La

Boquilla, a channel that cut through dunes to the grand open blaze of the Pacific. The tide was running like a steep-pitched river. Fish were rising. You could see the platinum shine of them in the shoulders of the easy swells. Without taking time to unload the skiff and make camp, we began casting. We were both using light old-fashioned, saber-steel rods, linen lines and bass plugs, a combination that I personally will always like because I grew up with it.

A fish hit and I missed the strike but got a look at the fish. It was a corbina, or spotted weakfish, or sea trout, or whatever the species is called where you fish. Tomás brought one in and killed it for supper. I hooked two and lost them. None was big. Around two pounds. Then I tied into a good one, a ten-pounder that proved to be an orange-mouthed sow, and I hassled it in and killed it. In some parts the sea trout is rated low as a gamefish. But here on this coast they are popular, and on light tackle will keep a man plenty busy. I am all for them. I am an aficionado. I don't see how anybody who ever fought down a lively Colima sea trout and ate steaks from it broiled over hardwood coals on a jungle beach could be otherwise. We kept casting and the sea trout kept hitting. Probably we were drifting with a school of them. It was wonderful. After a couple of hours I had a charley horse in my right shoulder, and had lost track of the fish we had brought in and released.

Tomás said, "*Ay Dios*," and at the same instant thunder boomed and rain slashed across my face. "Here comes the first solstice storm," he said.

We headed for a strip of sandy beach under the looping, vine-patched dunes. A wind blew out of the south as suddenly as the rain had started, and blue-white lightning forked down and broke the top out of an age-old ahuehuete tree that maybe in past times had been worshipped by the Tarascan Indians who first lived here and practiced tree-worship among other curious pagan rites. Tomás steered straight and true for the beach—too straight and true, for there were rocks and submerged snags in the shallows. We hit something, and the propeller pin sheered. The skiff broached. Snowser, a dog acquainted with emergencies, jumped overboard without hesitation and swam for the shore. Tomás, full of responsibility, also went over the side and, up to his navel in water, got the skiff straightened out and horsed it ashore. The boat wasn't really swamped, he pointed out. But it was one-third full of water and our gear was floating.

I disembarked from the pounding boat and accepted Snowser's congratulations that I was safe ashore. We didn't have a tent or tarpaulin. Instead we had a twenty-by twenty-foot sheet of transparent plastic material. It appeared to be waterproof. Tomás, clearly embarrassed on account of having nearly wrecked the skiff, said that he would put up camp and I should go ahead and fish. He didn't have to twist my arm. I walked along the beach in the hammering rain to where the mangroves began, and pitched a plug in against the snake-tangle of roots. With the wind behind me, casting was no problem. I had the feeling that I could have put the plug out there 500 yards if I'd had that much line. The lure landed on a wave crest and I started it in. Something flashed at it but veered off. I tried half-a-dozen more times at the same spot. No luck. Then, making a final attempt, I got a solid strike and set the hook. The fish jumped, and kept jumping. It was a chile. Around three pounds.

I do not know the correct name for the chile. I can't find him in the books. But he is a fine fish, fun to catch and good to eat. He operates sort of like a fresh-run silver salmon, and looks like one when he is in the air, which is most of the time if he has a hook in his face. This one was doing his prettiest when I saw another fish behind him. Then a tall, limp, painted dorsal broke the surface. The fin could have belonged to only one fish on earth, the fantastic and aggressive roosterfish. My chile jumped over a rock and the roosterfish jumped, or rather skidded, after him. For a moment all was action and confusion, then my line fouled on the rock and the hook cut out. I reeled in, licked but happy. Rain was now coming down in a battering torrent and thunder was banging in continuous salvos. The wind was driving sand and gravel against my legs. I turned to see how Tomás was making out. As I did so, Snowser crowded against me the way he does when something unwonted is about to take place and he wants to be sure that I am alert to the occasion.

Tomás had lost control of the new-fangled plastic shelter. The wind had got under it, ripped it free of the pegs he had driven into the sand, and here it came. I didn't have to try to catch it. It caught me. Swathed in the thing, Snowser and I went down hanging onto each other, and were trying to extricate ourselves when Tomás came to the rescue. Between the two of us we got the shelter pitched and anchored with rocks. We then built a fire, made coffee and broiled corbina steaks. The storm howled like a thousand wolves, and surf beating against the other side of the dunes shook the earth. Suddenly it was dark. We got into our blankets, and I told myself that this was swell—elemental drama, a night filled with nature's oldest and most inspiring music, and a lagoon full of waiting fish. Egotistically, I told myself that any angler

louise lopina

could get a kick out of a soft summer night with stars, lapping wavelets and a jungle breeze loaded with exotic flower fragrances, but that to enjoy a violent night like this one you had to be a special hairy-backed kind of fisherman.

At which point, half asleep, I received one of the shocks of my life.

Snowser, curled beside me, bounded to his feet snarling like a buzz saw in an oak knot. Tomás yelled, "*Dios*, protect us," and for the first time in our acquaintance sounded scared. I sat up, clawing for my .45. I don't know what I expected, but certainly it was nothing like what I beheld. Straight toward us down the black beach, against the wind, was rolling a ball of blue-green fire. It was perhaps three feet in diameter and was coming right along. "It is *El Diablo*," Tomás said. I thumbed the safety latch of the Colt, and as I leveled the gun defensively, the uncanny globe of radiance soared twenty feet up to perch on the threshing frond of a wild palm. Then, so help me, it dropped down and came to rest on the tip of the casting rod I had left standing against a boulder. Ectoplasm, the burning bush, the Apocalyptic vision and other *outré* explanations had been chasing themselves through my head, but now I knew what the phenomenon was—St. Elmo's fire, and harmless. I had seen it in various colors on the wings of airplanes, even on the propeller tips.

The ball of fire winked out, and I tried for five minutes to explain in Spanish to Tomás what it was before I realized that I didn't know myself exactly what it was, and gave up.

"It is a sign that fishing will be good tomorrow," I said.

Tomás snorted. "I have decided that it was some of your American Fourth of July fireworks. Clever people you Yankees. Many scientific secrets."

Dawn broke clear and innocent over the sierra, and we went out early, skipping breakfast, to find out what the solstice would offer today. I still had *robalo* on my mind, and presently we found some *robalo*. They were rising in the mouth of a narrow, obsidian-dark inlet into the mangroves that the backlight of sunrise had just begun to touch. They were making a considerable disturbance on the surface and sounded like pigs eating out of a trough. You didn't have to be a *robalo* expert to see what we were going to be up against. There were mangroves within twenty feet, and of all fish, excepting only the pargo, the *robalo* is the champion at tangling lines and causing the loss of leader and plugs in the roots and hanging branches of mangroves.

We started casting. We got strikes and lost fish and gear. I also lost my temper, and Tomás thought it was funny. I hooked a *robalo* that looked like a record fish to me, and it ran under the boat and into the mangroves on the other side. I resorted to craftiness and gave him slack, thinking that he might return to open water. Instead, he went deeper into the horrible tangle of roots and wove a pattern with the line. I finally had to cut him loose. A caiman splashed. I spotted *tigre* tracks on the bank. We backed the skiff out of the inlet and tried to coax the *robalo* to us. After a fashion, this worked. We boated three. One that I took was a pretty fair fish, but nothing to compare with the one the Indian commercial fisherman had sold at the hotel. The tide was running in now, and you could see schools of bait fish everywhere. I thought I saw a swift shadow in the water that looked too big to be true, and told Tomás about it. He lifted his shoulders in the eloquent Mexican shrug.

"During the solstice every kind of fish comes into the lagoon mouths," he said.

I believed him because I had already seen a roosterfish, a species which normally wouldn't be caught dead in any kind of lagoon or estuary. But I said, "Why?"

"Because with the new season the ocean waves change direction," he said. "They churn up new parts of the ocean bottom, making more food for small fish. The small fish come in to feed, and the big fish come in to feed on the small fish. So the small fish flee into the lagoons. The killer fish pursue them."

It sounded reasonable, and anyhow, hang the reason, the fish were here. We abandoned the *robalo* to their fate and went out into the lagoon. I boated a guachinango, one of the species of red snapper and an eating fish, when prepared Colima-style with chilies and chopped olives, to put a gourmet society into ecstasy. It took a No. 4 silver spoon and weighed eight pounds. I hooked a shark, species unknown, and lost it along with fifty yards of line. I caught some nice pargo that were so stuffed with infant bait fish of some kind that they couldn't fight worth a lick. I caught three corbina. Tomás meanwhile was doing all right for himself. If you could call this freshwater fishing, and technically it was, I don't know where you could beat it. We could have loaded the boat. Tomás reeled in his line, rolled a cornshuck cigarette, and relaxed. Tomás is a blasé fisherman. He had seen everything. Or at the moment thought that he had.

Because this was when we sighted the fin of the great unknown fish.

I've already told you about hooking the giant, and that by now thunder was talking again and a wind was tuning up. The waves were a strange green-gold because of silt coming out of mountain streams and breaking in on the tide. In the stormlight, with the fish running, with Tomás endeavoring to chase it and the balky motor fighting him at every asthmatic revolution, with the Tyee Club tackle seeming too light for this chore, it was a scene, a situation, that should have had "For Poet-Fishermen Only," on the marquee. However, we were not poet-fishermen. Our most earnest desire, and the heck with esthetics, was to bring this nameless brute in and find out what kind of fish he was. I can speak for Tomás because that was what he was saying to himself, in effect, while he worked on the now dead motor. The fish ran and went to the bottom, turned in blazing circles and shied away from the boat and the mangroves, and all the while kept trying to work back through the channel to the ocean. But the 3/6 tackle is formidable, as the ghost of many a Campbell River Club tyee salmon would ruefully testify, and the motor was running again, though without much strength.

"We've got him," Tomás said. "If only we don't swamp. If only this motor will last a few more minutes. If only the hook stays in. But," he added, "I wouldn't have believed it could be done with that cobweb gear you are using."

We came alongside the now feebly struggling fish. A bronze cutlass lifted from the water and slashed at the boat, hitting with a blow that made the skiff shudder. This was a sawfish. Not the largest I had seen, but not the smallest by a long shot. Four hundred pounds, at a guess. I had never heard of one taking a trolled bait. I had never had any idea that they were so fast. I didn't want to kill him, but I didn't want him to sink the skiff or chop my arm off either. So I shot him with the .45.

The motor was finished. It wouldn't start again. We chopped the sword out of the sawfish as a trophy, and rowed for the shore. Snowser was seasick. I was thinking about the long walk back along the ocean beach to Cuyutlan in the rain, when we heard the drone of an outboard motor. Tomás listened, and grinned.

"A lucky day," he said. "We have transportation. It is my cautious brother Dámaso, come to join us because he thought the storm was finished."

I said, "Viva Mexico."

Tomás said, "Happy Fourth of July."

Storm Ducks with Crocs

"Don't shoot!" I shouted to the red-headed twins as the flight of teal came barreling down the gray Nayarit stormwind, heading for the broad, eddying pool of the shrunken Río San Pedro out front. "This is a ghastly place. It's strictly trouble. Bad. We'll have a tragedy you'll never forget."

They didn't hear me. Maybe they didn't want to hear me. Maybe the *chubasco* wind swallowed my words. I'd like to be charitable about it. They both worked their guns, and they were good duck shots. The reports of the 12-gauge scatterguns sounded flat in the wind, like planks clattering together half a block distant, and two teal spun down crazily to splash into the jade-green upper end of the pool, where the silver spillway of the river came in. Perhaps I was to blame, at least in part, for what happened thereafter. Every hunter is fascinated by expert shooting, or should be. For the critical few seconds of this matter, I had watched the gunners and their targets. The borrowed Labrador retriever we had with us, an honest, innocent dog, streaked past me and plunged into the water. I had intended to hold him back and abandon the ducks.

He was swimming strongly through the wind-rippled eddy toward the ducks when I saw the dark underwater shapes converging torpedo-like on him. I knew what was going to happen, but there was nothing I could do. So I got emotional. Out of character. I said to the twin redheads, football players, college boxers, loaded with money and political authority, "Damn you, I asked you not to shoot. If that dog doesn't come back safe to land, I am personally and vindictively, at my age, going to do what your father should have done to you when you were brats. I mean, I am going to beat the living bejeepers out of you individually or collectively, or perish trying"

I wish to say, I'd had a large plenty of these two jokers. You couldn't help liking them, but there was a limit. When I was serving my apprenticeship as a guide in Alaska, a guide was a sort of combination woodsman, butler and diplomat. Your hunters could do no wrong. For cheechakos (first-time hunters) you performed almost every task from helping them blow their noses to getting them to the latrine and back on dark nights. You had a stock of alibis for their bad shots. If one of them took a substandard trophy—and boy, it always seemed to me that they never shot the animal you pointed out, if there was a choice—you allowed enthusiastically that although the trophy might be small, it was the most beautiful you had seen in years. The idea was to send them home happy. A good idea, and a sterling apprenticeship. But times change. In the first place, I hadn't wanted to be on this hunt. In the second place, if I had known what I was going up against, I never would have taken on the responsibility.

I watched the black Labrador, whose name was Pedro, and I would have bet that he didn't have three minutes to live.

The way this began, I was sitting at a sidewalk table at the hotel Fénix, in Cuyutlan, watching the pelicans dive into the surf at the end of the street, watching the girls go past to the beach with Mother Hubbards over their swimsuits. I was listening to a guy on the radio who was issuing a storm warning; enjoying the day, feeling no pain, when a youngster arrived panting. (He was panting a little too much; what he was pitching for was a tip.) He handed me a slip of paper from the telephone office which stated that I had a telephone call from Nayarit, far to the north. I at last received the call, via Mexico City, through a dozen operators, after sitting on a wooden bench outside the telephone office for two hours in the broiling afternoon sun. It was from Don Dionicio, owner of the Golden Skull Ranch, a cattle-raising, cockfighting, poker-playing, skeet-shooting, 250-pound, longtime friend of mine.

"Come here at once!" he bellowed over the static-loaded line. "I need you. I am in trouble."

I said, "What kind of trouble?"

"You wouldn't believe me if I told you," he shouted. "Just come here. Start today, please." Without giving me opportunity to agree or argue, he hung up. Or some operator cut the line.

Well, you do such things for friends. It's old-fashioned. It's Quixote-ish. But if you're an old-timer, it's the way you operate.

You just pack your warbag and go, prepared for anything from a christening to a feud. Nobody met me when I got off the single-engine feeder-line plane at Tepic. I found a taxi but the driver didn't want to take me to Golden Skull because most of the road was private and he was afraid of Don Dionicio's *vaqueros*. I persuaded him that he should be more afraid of them if he refused to drive me, and we took off. Streaming across the lane of gray sky above the jungle-rimmed road were wedges, groups, mobs of waterfowl. I identified mallards, teal, widgeons, bluebills and white-fronted geese. They were all headed in the direction we were going, flying low, flying fast. As Tex Cobb in Alaska used to say, I would have given my left ear and half the trimmings to have gotten out of this taxi with my scattergun. But, holy Moses, I was on a *mission!* My friend Don Dionicio was in mysterious trouble. I claim, and could make a good dramatic statement to the effect, that the now vanished generation of rough-and-ready woodsmen who brought me up were the outstanding romanticists this continent has seen or will see.

"There is Golden Skull," said the taxi driver, looking as if he wanted to climb into my lap for protection.

It was indeed. Pastel buildings with red tile roofs, clustered among beautiful spreading flattop shade trees. Above everything, the turquoise blue loom of the great Sierra Nayarit. And beyond through weaving jungle, emerald flashes of the San Pedro Lagoon. Leather-armored *vaqueros* were loping their ponies toward us. I had been watching the skeins of waterfowl heading for the lagoon, my face practically pressed to the windshield of the taxi. I told myself that if this was going to be a hunt, if that was what Don Dionicio had in mind, it would be a honey. You didn't have to be a meteorologist to know that a big storm was coming. The ducks knew it. They were going to shelter under the tangled mangrove walls of the lagoon, raft gathered with raft, species intermingled, all of them bursting-fat with rice they had looted from fields in Sonora and Sinaloa. It was a shotgunman's dream. My spooky driver braked the taxi down and I got out and waved to the *vaqueros*, and then I saw something that I had never expected to see.

Carmen, on the wide-tiled veranda of the main ranch house, was doing a jitterbug dance with a red-headed character, obviously American, while another identical red-headed character clapped his hands in time with the hi-fi music and shouted, "Onward! Onward!" Carmen is Don Dionicio's daughter. Carmen is very special. I think that she is now twenty years old. I have known her since she was a child. She can top off an ornery bronc without getting her hair-do disarranged. She can throw a butterfly loop at thirty feet with a rawhide *reata*, catching both front feet and the head of a running horse or critter. She can shoot fairly well. She can also dance the native solo dances, and make them look good. Carmen is beautiful, assembled like a Swiss watch. But jitterbugging! I got out of the car, motioned the *vaqueros* aside, and headed across the compound toward the veranda.

The redhead clapping his hands hollered, "Hey, look who comes —a countryman."

I said, "What the hell goes on here?"

"Our duck guide. Right?" They shouted in chorus. They must, I thought, have trained as cheerleaders. The chap who had been dancing said, still holding onto Carmen's hand, "When do we go? We have been waiting and waiting." Sore as a bear with an impacted tooth, I ignored them all. I beckoned to Pablo, the stiff-backed, iron-faced ramrod of the *vaqueros*, gave him some money, asked him to pay the taxi driver, and said, "Where is Don Dionicio? Why is he not here? What is happening on this ranch?"

Behind me Carmen said, "He is ill. He sent for you to take charge of some business. He cannot see anybody now. The doctor is with him." It didn't sound that rough in Spanish. English is an abrupt take-it-or-leave-it language, whereas the romance languages leave a loophole, an out, in every phrase.

I said to the two redheads, "Okay. It sounds as if I'm your guide. Get your equipment together. The ducks are flying—and not to jitterbug music. Apparently I've come halfway across Mexico, which is a large country, to help you shoot some ducks. *Andale!* Let's get going." Still not looking at Carmen, I said to Pablo, the ramrod, "I'll need the Jeep, and a retriever dog if there's one on the ranch." Then I went into the house and up the Spanish colonial winding stairs to Don Dionicio's rooms. There was a skinny, important-looking medic wearing a black silk suit, who put a forefinger to his lips and said, dramatically, "Shush." And there was Don Dionicio on his bed, which somebody once described as being approximately the size of the state of Chihuahua, with his right foot and half his leg heavily bandaged and resting on pillows. The thoughts crossed my mind that perhaps he had been shot in a country feud, or tossed by a bad horse, or clawed by a *tigre*—things that can always happen to a *ranchero* in this wild country.

"It's gout," he said in explanation. "I always thought gout was a comic-strip joke. It isn't. I hope you never suffer from it." He took a deep breath and passed a hand over his big face. "Those gentlemen downstairs," he said, "the ones with red hair, are the sons of a man with whom I must do important business. They claim they want to hunt ducks. Please take care of the matter." He pointed a finger at me. "Please take care of everything. You understand?"

The medic had me by the elbow, urging me toward the door. I said over my shoulder, thinking of Carmen's jitterbug performance downstairs, "I read you loud and clear. Rest easy. This is going to be a pleasure."

Pablo had the Jeep ready and the aforementioned dog was tied in it. The twin redheads arrived, dressed like Abercrombie and Fitch models. Carmen had disappeared. We took off, bouncing down a dirt road toward the river. Ducks were whipping overhead. The redhead next to me reached over and turned off the ignition, then stepped out before the Jeep came to a halt, and began firing. His brother leaped out the other side of the Jeep and opened up. I don't know how other folks feel about it, but when I am driving a vehicle, I don't want anybody fooling with the controls. So I sat there smoldering. But these extroverted kids could shoot. They carried automatics, and down here nobody I know ever heard of a magazine plug, so they practically filled the air with No. 4 shot. The ducks were shovelers. I have always liked shovelers. Many hunters don't, but I do. They suit me just fine.

Three shovelers plummeted into the jungle. The redheads came back to the Jeep, reloading. I still didn't even know their names. I didn't know the dog's name. I never in my life, anywhere, started a hunt in worse circumstances. "Well, that was nice," said one redhead. "Send the dog after the ducks, hey?"

"He's a stranger here," I said. "I haven't yet become acquainted with him. Meanwhile, you know where the ducks fell. Go get them. You're both active and healthy—up to now, anyhow."

Without argument, they went after the ducks, found them, and brought them back while I consoled the Labrador, who wanted to work.

Nobody said anything more and we drove on to the riverbank. The river was down. Although it is one of the biggest—maybe the biggest—in Mexico, dry weather, *un año seco*, had shrunk it to a creek and a waste of gravel bars. The coming *chubasco* was tuning up good, and I wanted to be on the other side, where there were some ponds, and we would be upwind from the river. We waded a riffle, knee-deep. We were midway across when a dark object that could have been a drift log came sliding down toward us. Only it wasn't a drift log. It was a crocodile—a caiman if you are particular about terminology—maybe eight feet long. The Labrador was having difficulty. He couldn't keep his feet on the bottom, and a slant of current was taking him away from us, into the path of the croc.

I got out my .45 from its shoulder holster under my shirt. The croc was about fifty feet distant. I knew as well as I knew anything, that if it and the dog came together, the croc would bite a chunk out of the dog as it went past, perhaps take the dog with it to wherever it was going. I'm not as good with a handgun as I used to be. Sometimes I suspect nobody is. But I emptied the clip at the croc's eyes—he couldn't hide, the water was too shallow—and I think I hit them both. Anyhow, he went past us, doing flipflops and other acrobatics and I managed to grab the Labrador by the neck and tow him to water where he could get his feet on the bottom.

One redhead said to the other, "Did you see what I just saw?"

"I think so," said the second redhead. "Gets interesting, doesn't it? Gives one to think."

We floundered ashore and went through the windy low jungle to the first pond, and it looked like a place at Stuttgart, only there were more ducks, and more different kinds of ducks. There were ducks on the water, and ducks coming in, some that were old friends, and other kinds that I had never seen before. Trees and snags stood in the water. The ducks wound among them as they came down from the storm sky, twisting and turning, flaring to kill speed, trying to find room to land. They wanted shelter. They didn't need a weather prophet or a barometer, they knew it was time to get down or be blown back north to wherever they had started from. The twin redheads shot their guns hot, knocking off a lot of tree limbs and killing a few ducks. The Labrador brought the ducks in. He was happy to be working and I liked him.

By now the pond was thoroughly shot up and the ducks were leaving, beating downriver, across the wind. There was one more pond over here, small but good, and we made a stalk to its edge, keeping the eager Labrador behind. Parting a screen of windy rushes, we beheld a curious sight. There were so many sanctuary-seeking ducks here that they hadn't found room on the water, with the result that a horde of them were huddled on a tilt of smooth, cattle-grazed grassland that went up fifty yards to the jungle. I had seen this before when ducks were migrating ahead of a storm, but never on such a scale. If there was any way to prove it, I'd bet there were 2,000 birds over there on the grass, mixed species, all of them nervous because they felt vulnerable to predators when not on the water—and every doggoned one of them within shotgun range, which is to say about forty yards distant. As for the birds on the water, many of them were too close. They were paddling, riding the wavelets, swiveling their necks, manifestly wishing the heck that they were somewhere else but not caring to move.

I stepped aside and said to the twins, "Harvest some ducks. You'd never get a better chance, even if the neighbors let you grow up."

The ducks across the pond, on the grass, were mostly shovelers, and I had hoped the twins would kill some of them, because the cook back at the ranch liked shovelers too, and could prepare them like New York chefs wish they could. But the redheads didn't have a chance. The ducks on the water got up first, blanking our view of the others. These ducks were mostly teal and widgeons. You didn't have to be able to shoot. There was a solid wall of ducks beating off the water, scared and desperate, with that other mob of ducks beyond them. You couldn't see daylight through them.

The twins emptied their guns, and when everything had quieted, there were six dead ducks on the water and two cripples. I must explain at this point that if you are hunting on the property of a powerful *ranchero*, and use reasonably good judgment, there is no daily limit; so the red-headed kids hadn't fractured any limit law. To make myself clear, you could kill one duck on this ranch if Don Dionicio didn't know you, or didn't like you, and you'd find yourself in the bucket pronto, whereas with his permission, and if he had use for the birds at the ranch, you could kill plenty and receive his congratulations. The Labrador brought in the dead ducks and hunted down the cripples. I talked to him a while and told him how good he was. Mostly, I like dogs better than people, and this black, broad-chested, heavy-shouldered brute with his alert eyes and his mouthful of gleaming white teeth was, I knew, a very good dog indeed. I made a note to find out who owned him and whether or not a deal could be made to transfer his ownership to me.

A wild gust of wind hit me, and I looked back to see all the fiercely green jungle, clear to the top of the sierra, bending and tossing. It was the first real blast of the *chubasco*.

"Why didn't you shoot, Dan'l?" asked one of the twins, tapping the stock of my muzzleloader. "There were plenty of ducks to go around. Besides, we'd sort of like to see you cut loose with that thing."

I thought, okay, brats. Just wait. Presently a duck came over, a lone teal. It was high, and with the wind behind it, was probably logging about 100 feet a second. I was an idiot. I tried for him. I led the bird about ten feet, and fired. I mean, I pulled. The hammer made its long swing, the cap broke, the charge fired and the gun bucked, and as usual the whole process seemed to take five minutes. The teal kept right on going. Our Labrador gave me a sorrowful look, ears drooping. I carry a muzzleloader because I like the gun, and maybe partly because nobody else does. With luck I would have dropped the teal. But luck was sour.

"Sure makes a lot of smoke," one of the redheads remarked. "Sorry you didn't score." He sounded as if he meant it, and boy, my ears were tuned in on him. All I needed right now was some sarcasm.

"We will now," I said, "wend our way to the ranch house, on account of by the time we reach there this wind would blow the ears off a brass monkey."

The *chubasco* literally blew us through the big front door of the ranch house. It howled and screeched, shaking the tile roof, rattling gravel against the windows. It made this lamplit, comfortable shelter very welcome. I went upstairs and reported to Don Dionicio, whose gout and temper had not improved. "If this wasn't such an important business matter I am engaged in," he growled, "and if it wasn't a fact that I always need more money than I have in the bank, I would call the whole thing off. But as it is. . ." he shrugged his massive shoulders, and winced as a pang ran through his leg. "Do the best you can to keep things under control."

It was apparently up to me to decide what he meant by 'things.' This I had already decided, but plenty. I went back downstairs and we ate dinner. Then the redheads began playing records on the hi-fi set again, and holy suffering, this time they recruited Juanita, one of the maids, to act as a dance partner along with Carmen. I tell you, such things simply cannot be done in the home of an aristocratic Mexican, especially out in the back country. I sat over in a corner and listened to the *chubasco.* I hoped nobody was going to be killed. I wondered if Carmen had lost her mind. I told myself that it was a lucky thing that Don Dionicio couldn't make it downstairs.

Finally it was late, and Carmen and Juanita excused themselves. I beat it to my room and slept while the storm roared. By morning the wind dropped down the Beaufort scale to a mere twenty-mile breeze. I informed the redheads that we would go out again for ducks—unless they planned to spend the day dancing or in other social exercises.

We hunted down the bars of the skinny river, and in the potholes there were ducks, mostly shovelers—I had never on one hunt seen so many shovelers—and the twins killed several. None of us talked much. Heavy gusts boosted us along. Then we came to the big pool I told you about at the beginning. The red-headed whiz-kids shot a couple of teal after I had asked them not to shoot, and the Labrador went in after it. I hadn't had time to explain. It shouldn't be necessary for a guide to explain or draw pictures. It adds up to this: If you go out with a guide, trust him. If you don't trust him, get another guide whom you do trust, or go out on your lonesome. Simple. These kids had come hunting with me as their guide, and when the emergency occurred and I told them not to shoot, they brought those teal down out of the sky and the birds fell smack in the middle of the pool, and the good honest Labrador plunged in after them.

I tell you, I was at this moment quite probably the most angry, despairing person south of the border. But what happened taught me a valuable lesson concerning the new generation inhabiting this hemisphere. My personal conviction still is that these kids are somewhat nuts. But you've got to respect them. I would like to know them better.

This river pool, the largest in a dozen miles, had become the refuge of the crocodile population of the area, and naturally all of the brutes had to be hungry. The croc I had shot on the riffle probably was heading for this spot, for deep water. The place would have been a hide-hunter's bonanza. Without wishing to sound like an expert, I had seen the situation at a glance. Now there was the Labrador, the good retriever, swimming dutifully to destruction. There were swirls on the water, ugly-toothed jaws clapped, and the two teal disappeared. I had the .45 automatic out. Croc shapes were converging on the Labrador. I began blasting slugs ahead of them. I yelled at the dog, but tell me whoever called a good retriever out of the water.

Then the most terrible thing happened. I didn't have time to prevent it. I was busy watching the dog. The twins shucked their coats and boots and dived in to the dog's rescue—you could sit down and figure for a month, and not come up with a ghastlier situation. I have no idea what these locos thought they were going to accomplish. Fight hungry crocodiles with their bare hands? Immolate themselves on the altar of error? Hell, I didn't know. I had three clips of shells. I just stood there and kept shooting at shadows.

And then there came the whiz-kids back to shore, herding the Labrador. They climbed the bank and I leaned against a snag. My knees were shaking. I said in a voice I didn't recognize, "Were you guys dropped on your heads when you were babes? Have you been under psychiatric treatment lately?"

One of them said, "Let's go home, Dan'l. It's been a large day." The water was boiling with crocs. The Labrador had to be held by the back of his neck. He still had the teal on his mind.

At the ranch house, after the twins had changed into dry clothes and we had gulped some needed fortified black coffee, one twin said to me, "Dan'l, how long since you'd been on a house party with high school or college brats?" I said, "I don't remember. A long time, I guess. What difference does it make?" The other redhead said, "Because customs change. You need to get around more, Dan'l. You really do."

I tried to get sore at them but it didn't work. I said, "Go ahead, start the hi-fi again. Have fun. I'm going upstairs and converse with Don Dionicio." And I aimed a finger at Carmen and said, "Behave yourself, or I will give you the spanking of your life, where it'll do the most good."

Carmen smiled sweetly and said, "Why not now?"

Well, it took me a long time to learn, but as a lot of harassed guys in similar circumstances will testify, you can't win.

The *Tigre* of Santa Rita

"Get out of bed, lazy one!" shouted the plump wife of Pancho González in the middle of the night, pushing him with both hands. "Something is killing the pigs—the meat of our children. *Andale!* Hurry! Oh, why did I ever marry such a lazy man?"

She wasn't quite right. Nothing was killing the three spotted pigs in the palm-log pen a few yards from the house. But something had arrived with that dire intention, and the pigs knew it. They had the wind in their favor. They were Mexican pigs with experience. They knew what was coming, all right. Death. A shadow within shadows in the star-dappled night, it came on, silent, and the pigs rioted as only frightened pigs can riot. Because the animal closing in from the mountain jungle was, with one exception, the most dangerous beast of prey on the continent—a jaguar, a *tigre*, *el Señor de la Selva*.

This was in the tiny village of Santa Rita, in the tiny state of Colima, huddled under the towering green-jungled Sierra Madre, a village of thatched huts with intricately woven mud-wattled walls and palm-rib fences, a village based on the corn economy of Mexico, its men accustomed from childhood to hacking back the encroaching jungle with machetes to preserve their fields; their lusty, vital women accustomed almost from birth to the fierce guardianship of the food supplies on which the existence of their families depends. Meat is a luxury. Usually it is pork. Therefore one treasures one's pigs.

"Get out of bed, lazy one!" the wife of Pancho shouted, now placing both feet in the middle of his back and pushing, so that he was propelled to the floor. "Can you not hear? The meat of our children is in peril."

Pancho, maybe more afraid of his wife than he was of what unknown threat was at the pigpen, picked up his machete and stumbled outside. He was not fully awake. There wasn't much light coming from the sky, but he could see that something bad was occurring. And he could hear it. Nothing in the world can produce more anguished and distance-carrying screams than Mexican pigs faced with imminent destruction. The entire mountainside echoed. Pancho, barefoot and clad only in faded, tattered blue shorts, jumped the palm-log fence and waded into the center of the disturbance. Shadows were milling all about him in the calf-deep mud. But directly ahead something was endeavoring to climb the fence with a captured 200-pound pig.

Pancho closed in, coming awake fast, frightened pigs banging against him, slipping in the mud, and swung the machete.

This heavy, broad-bladed, horn-hafted weapon is thirty-six inches long and is as dangerous as any cutlass a pirate ever used on the seven seas. Pancho set his feet and struck with all the trained force of his arm and back muscles. He felt the three-pound blade bite through flesh and bone, and knew that he had killed. But there were complications. While a shadow lay struggling in death at his feet, another had jumped the fence and vanished into the mountain jungle, and Pancho had the horrible feeling that the latter wasn't a pig. A pig didn't float over a fence that way. A pig wouldn't have fled into the jungle. Pancho was endeavoring to arrive at the solution to this enigma when his wife came along with a gasoline lantern.

She shone the light on the dead animal and on the tracks in the mud, and shouted as only an indignant Mexican housewife can, "Tonto, you have killed our best boar pig, and have let the *tigre* of Santa Rita escape. My mother was right—you are a burrohead."

"There was no light," Pancho said defensively. "And your mother is a female dragon."

"Anybody who can't tell a boar hog from the *tigre* of Santa Rita is, *en verdad*, a burrohead, and do not insult my mother again or I will break this light over your head of a burro." She hauled off with the lantern, but then, with a swift change of latin temperament, waded through the mud and flung her arms about him.

"But thank *Dios* you are alive," she wept. "He might have killed you. Then where would I and your children be? After all, what is a pig? I would rather have you alive, my Pancho."

Here I must explain about this *tigre*. The species is not ordinarily aggressive. Like the timber wolves of Alaska, which used to be man-killers but now are not, the *tigres* have learned about the weapons of modern man and are most cautious. Crowd a wounded one, or female with cubs, and you may get a fight. But except in rare cases they desire to live in peace with the human race. The *tigre* of Santa Rita, however, had a foul reputation. According to the *paisanos*, it had killed and eaten at least three men and a multitude of stock animals. The Indian priests in the vicinity had a litany which they recited on appropriate occasions: "From devils and evil and the *tigre* of Santa Rita, may heaven protect us." I personally was about as skeptical about the beast as a professional hunter could be. I mean, I had my fingers crossed. I had heard the wind blow before.

I was sitting in the sunny open-face restaurant of the Hotel Fénix in Cuyutlan eating some rose-color papaya for breakfast, watching the brown pelicans dive for mullet in the surf fifty yards distant, watching the village pigs hopefully chasing crabs on the beach, when Doña Rosario, the hotel owner, strode in and leaned on the table with fire in her fine Spanish eyes. "You aren't doing anything," she declared. "You haven't done anything for a week but eat and sleep. Your mule is getting fat. Your dogs are so stuffed that I doubt they could run a mile. You have gotten lazier than my sons, and that is not possible, *Dios* is my witness."

I swallowed a chunk of papaya and said, "Okay, what is it that you want?"

She said, "I want you to go at once and kill the *tigre* of Santa Rita. You heard what happened at the little ranch of the Gonzàlez family. They are relatives. They lost a boar pig and Pancho could have been killed, the burrohead."

I said, "Look, I don't think the Santa Rita *tigre* exists. I've been hearing about the cat for ten years, and I believe it isn't one but a number of *tigres*. A cow is killed, a man gets mauled, and the blame falls on the mythical *tigre* of Santa Rita. You want me to kill all the *tigres* in this part of the state? Take it easy. This is a beautiful morning. Why spoil it?"

Doña Rosario, who is a kind of Tugboat Annie, only pretty, flashed her teeth in a bright, wicked smile. "Go kill the *tigre* of Santa Rita," she cooed, "or I am going to take a vacation, and everybody here stops eating. You understand?"

I understood, all right. I have been in this sort of business practically all my life. I understood that, to avert a commissary crisis, I was going to have to kill a *tigre*, any confounded *tigre*, and pass it off on the populace as the *tigre* of Santa Rita.

So I went for Pony, my black saddle mule, who really was getting grass-bellied, my four cat dogs, who also didn't look exactly in fighting shape, my veteran *secundo* Policarpio, who had attended a country fiesta and wore an unaccustomed pallor. I also recruited Tomás, the tall heavy-shouldered son of Doña Rosario, and set forth with five packhorses for the ranch of the González family. I thought that to further my plot it would be best to start from here. Besides, the rumor was that Pancho was a tracker, and I needed a tracker. It had rained since the pigpen fiasco, and my dogs couldn't possibly have picked up a scent. As it turned out, Pancho was anything but a tracker. I am not good at following soft-footed game. I never was. But I would bet that Pancho González couldn't track an elephant with bleeding piles through ten feet of soft snow.

"I will know the track of the *tigre* murderer when I see it," Pancho declared. "He has paws this big." He made a platter-size circle with his hands.

We spent the night at the ranch, camped in a mango orchard, and took off in the morning for what, I will always assert, was the doggondest *tigre* hunt I ever made, and I hope I never have to make another like it. With the first warmth of the sun a vast flight of dragonfly-like insects appeared, an apparently endless cloud of them, heading north. A bad sign. Then gangs of lilac-headed parrots streaked over the treetops, bound in the same direction and making no noise. A worse sign. I said to Pancho, "You live here. What's going to happen?" Pancho swiveled in the saddle to judiciously inspect the entire horizon circle, and presently allowed that it was possible, just possible, that some rain might fall. What a meteorologist the world lost in our Pancho. The bugs and parrots kept passing overhead, and I set our course with them. Something dire in the way of weather was coming out of the south, and like them, I guess I hoped we'd escape it.

We didn't. But first we had some luck. We were on a shaggy ridge, boulder-studded with grassy openings dominated by giant flowering zolocuahuil trees. The dogs ranged ahead, when suddenly the eldest and most experienced of the pack, a black bitch named Sombra—Shadow—opened up with a confident note in her beautiful bell-clear voice. She was below us on a lava pitch dotted with smokebrush. I spurred Pony toward her and presently saw what she had found—the carcass of a little cat-killed whitetail doe.

The kill was maybe two days old, and the liver, kidneys and part of the loin had been eaten. Her neck was broken and there were deep claw marks on the muzzle and withers. Pancho got down and scouted for sign. The dogs were also scouting. The latter didn't find anything. The cat scent had been sun-dissolved. But old Pancho found what he claimed was a track. Maybe it was a track. It was in lava scree and I couldn't see it. Neither could Policarpio or Tomás. But then they were in my class, nontrackers.

"It is the *tigre* of Santa Rita," Pancho asserted solemnly, glancing over his shoulder as if he feared he might be overheard by the cat. "I would know his track anywhere."

This left me only one thing to do, because there was always the chance that the guy might be right. I didn't think he was. I would have made book that no tracker could have identified that misshapen depression in the lava scree. Moreover, I still didn't believe that the *tigre* of Santa Rita existed except in the mind of Sierra farmers. But still. . . . "You people take the dogs and go on down the ridge a mile or so and make camp," I said. "I'll take a stand here maybe until sundown. Expect me when you see me."

If I sound like all the stuffy White Hunters in the world, that isn't the way I felt, believe me. Because as I finished speaking, a hard gust of wind howled through the jungle and rain slashed across my face. There may be worse, more dispiriting, forms of hunting than to sit alone in the rain on a tropical ridge, with gnats biting you, watching a bait in the silly hope that a mythical cat will arrive and allow itself to be shot, but I can't imagine what they might be. The migration of bugs and parrots had vanished. My only company were some green-tailed jays and an outsize black-and-white iguana that lay draped across a rock, regarding me with an eye as cold as that of a bank examiner with a sheaf of phony figures. The rainfall became a cloudburst. The wind made Igor Stravinsky sounds among the rocks. I sheltered my buckshot-charged muzzleloader as best as I could with the tail of my shirt, and told myself bitterly that this, holy Moses, was ***adventure***, just the kind of thing to read about while snug and dry before an open fire, with one's feet on a hassock, one's pipe drawing well, and a highball within reach.

Then, on the slope below me, barely visible through the sheets of driving rain, something moved. I was sixty yards above the deer carcass, safely crosswind. At first I thought it was a weaving bush. Then I thought one of the dogs had got loose and returned to make another try for the cat that had killed the deer. Then, in a lull between rain gusts, I saw what it was—a pair of coyotes. They were long-legged mountain coyotes, looking almost black on account of their rain-soaked coats, and they were plenty nervous. I suppose they knew they had come upon a cat kill, and of course the place was still loaded with man, dog, horse and mule scent. But they wanted the meat. The slope below them was steep, a lava slide on a forty-degree pitch. They milled about, trying the wet wind, obviously fearful of an ambush. They sniffed at the carcass, and licked their chops. Next, working together as if they had rehearsed the act, they took hold of the carcass and backed down the slope with it. The carcass rolled, and the next thing I knew, they were out of my view and so was the carcass.

At this point I achieved one of those important decisions that hunters sometimes have reason to boast about but more often try to forget. Two hours had passed since my little band of valiants had ridden on to make camp. I was cold, wet, tired and hungry. The day was waning. So I told myself, what the heck, I would ease down the ridge side and kill a coyote, then beat it to camp, wherever camp was, with at least a coyote scalp to show for the day's travail. Accordingly, I headed down through the mess of brush, boulders and jungle trees. It was an easy stalk, what with the hammering rain and the eldritch sounds of the wind. I reached the top of the lava-slide and, from the cover of a snaky-twisted clump of organ cactus, peered about for the two coyotes and the deer carcass. What I presently beheld made my hair lift. Between two red lava boulders, fifty feet distant, appeared a *tigre.* I didn't have time to lift the muzzleloader. A man's reflexes are only so fast. But I saw that it was a *tigre* to write home about. It looked a dozen feet long, and in the split second before it passed out of sight behind the second boulder, I saw that it was limping.

Right then I was a believer. I had never seen a bigger *tigre.* I was convinced that the *tigre* of Santa Rita existed. I could even have been convinced, against all reason, that old burrohead Pancho had recognized its track.

This was an emergency, no occasion for an Injun-type stalk. This was a time to throw the book away. At any moment the *tigre* would get the rain-softened man, mule, horse and dog scent, and vanish as only a *tigre* can. A *tigre* simply disappears in a now-you-see-him-now-you-don't performance. It had happened to me too many times. In addition, I freely admit that I was at the moment probably the most chagrined hunter in Mexico, and therefore not thinking at my sharpest. I had been certain that the deer kill had been made by a puma, because it looked to me, with the broken neck and the claw marks on the withers and muzzle, like a puma kill. A *tigre*, using its superior weight, simply bears a deer down and either tears its throat out or grabs it by the back of its neck and crunches bone and muscle the way a terrier shakes a rat to death. It doesn't wrestle, not even with a 1,000-pound steer. A puma does a lot of fancy claw work and uses head-holds that would make a black-belt judo champion jealous. So, adjusting myself to the fact that I had been a dope, I made a slipping, sliding run down the pitch.

Gentlemen, you should have seen it. I rounded a lava cornice in time to see the *tigre* make an anyhow twenty-foot bound at the two coyotes who were engaged in making a meal from the deer carcass. They also saw him sailing through the air at them, and departed. I let go with the muzzleloader, holding on the *tigre*, I hoped. But it was a situation of maximum confusion, and I never claimed to be a Jimmy Robinson with a scattergun. When the smoke cleared there was no *tigre* lying dead. Instead, a poor old coyote lay kicking against the side of a boulder. I reloaded, taking it slow and easy on account of the rain, and went down for a look. The coyote had taken the full charge of buckshot. There was no sign of the *tigre* or the other coyote. I peeled off the coyote scalp and went back up the slope to where Pony was tied under a zolocuahuil tree, tightened the cinch, and rode along the ridge until, half-an-hour later, I smelled woodsmoke and came to the camp.

"Did you kill the *tigre*?" asked Tomás, Pancho and Policarpio practically in concert.

I told them not to ask embarrassing questions, and poured myself a cup of scalding-hot, bitter Mexican coffee from the pottery pot stone-propped over a bed of hardwood coals. Later, in dry clothes and sprawled with the *paisanos* under a sheltering tarpaulin, bare feet comfortably extended to the fire, I recounted my bizarre experience and declared rashly that, in the circumstances, we would stay on the trail of the putative *tigre* of Santa Rita until we harvested its pelt or I died of old age. Nobody replied. I gathered that it wasn't a popular decision. My buddies manifestly figured that old age would be the deciding factor. They figured that if they wanted to gather their monthly checks, which they did, they would have to reconcile themselves to spending a good part of their lives in this ghastly wet, windy, inhospitable wilderness. I rolled up in my blanket and went to sleep.

We turned out in the morning at what would have been daybreak if there had been any sun. We worked the dogs all day and found only a fat black opossum, which we took in for dinner. Down there the camp cooks singe an opossum and scrape off the burned hair to the white skin, the way good Eskimo cooks prepare a harbor seal. It was still raining. We hunted five days and the rain continued to fall. Mold formed on our boots and other leather goods. The salt and sugar turned to liquid. Dry washes became rivers. Pony, my old friend, tried to bite me one morning when I put a wet saddle blanket on his back. Sombra, the dog I had trained from an awkward pup, came into heat and hated me because I kept her on a leash. Nobody spoke to anybody else unless it was absolutely necessary. We were really a congenial outfit.

Then came the big break. It came in the middle of the night. The *tigre* of Santa Rita didn't want for us to find him. He moved in on us.

I woke when Sombra whined.

There was a desperate sound in her voice which I at first mistook. Half asleep, I thought that on account of being in a mood for love she simply wanted me to release her from the handicapping chain. The other dogs weren't making a sound. Pony and the horses were quiet. But from long habit of trusting the senses of my animals, I sat up with my hand on the breech of the muzzleloader, trying to see through the flapping mosquito net.

If I live to the age of eighty, and some newspaper reporter asks me to what do I attribute my old age, I will certainly inform him that I attribute it to the confidence I placed in the animals that worked for me.

Because I now beheld a shadow moving across the open campsite toward Sombra. I knew from the way it moved that it was a cat, and a big one! There are two American cats that will come into a man's camp with murderous intentions. One is the tricky, treacherous *onza*; the other is the *tigre*. Neither does it often, but they do it, and I could rally a small army of witnesses.

Secure behind my wall of gauze, heaven help me, but awake, I felt to make certain the percussion cap was seated on the firing nipple of the muzzleloader, and rolled clear of the mosquito tent. At the same instant two things happened.

There was a small eruption beside me as Pancho got out from under his net, stumbling in the dark and yelling the ancient war cry "*Ay Chihuahua!*" and Sombra howled. I had a flashlight, and thumbed the button. Sombra was down and the *tigre* of Santa Rita had her by the neck. Pancho loped into my field of fire, his machete raised, the long blade shining in the light. I yelled for him to get out of the way. The whole camp was awake, men shouting, dogs bellowing, horses screaming, Pony yodeling the way a scared mule does. I saw Pancho swing the machete, then I shoved him aside and dropped the muzzle of the scattergun into line and fired. I needn't have bothered. Tomás and Policarpio arrived with additional lights, and there the cat lay, its head half machete-sliced from its body, and Sombra lay beside it, her hunting days over forever.

If the cat wasn't indeed the *tigre* of Santa Rita, it almost certainly was the *tigre* that had tried to rob Pancho's pigpen, because it bore a half-healed machete wound on its shoulder, evidence that Pancho, in addition to killing his boar hog, had also struck the cat. We built up the fire, quieted Pony, the dogs and the horses, and took off the *tigre's* pelt. It measured ten feet, six inches over pegs. Daylight came. We ate breakfast, buried Sombra, and headed back through the sheets of rain to Cuyutlan. There had been nothing in the *tigre's* stomach. It had been old, its teeth were blunted and it was wounded. After the little whitetail doe, it probably hadn't been able to make another kill, therefore it had pounced on the chained Sombra.

I gave the pelt to Pancho to display as evidence that the *tigre* of Santa Rita was no longer of this world, and trusted that Pancho's good wife and the redoubtable Doña Rosario would no longer harass us regarding the animal.

With the spotted skin across his saddle bow, Pancho shifted his machete belt and said, "Perhaps now nobody will again call me a burrohead." I assured him that only a jackass would dream of doing so.

The Damnedest Duck on Earth

How are you s'posed to reckon with
a critter that should like water—and doesn't;
shouldn't roost in trees—and does?
This wily bird runs like a deer on stilts, with what
I'll swear is an educated brain.

"Kill one of those genius tree ducks if you can," Dámaso wheezed like a stranded bottle-nosed porpoise. "*Ojalá*, kill them all. But me, I am going to sit here in the shade, smoke a cornshuck cigarette, and let the ashes fall on my shirt as a good *caballero* should." He sat down heavily under a leafy, blossoming zolocuahuil tree. "I will laugh and laugh—sympathetically, of course, because, in this matter my future well-being is also at stake—while you go chasing fruitlessly across the countryside again. They tell me," he said, mopping sweat off his big, TV-type face, "that death by sunstroke is sudden and painless. I pray to Santa María del Rosario that it will prove so in your case." He reached for the makings.

"Chicken," I said.

"Go right ahead, sucker," Dámaso panted complacently. Dámaso is a very smart Mexican, a little overweight, maybe a little too cautious, but he is a hunter who always knows what time it is and when to blow the whistle.

Dead ahead, 200 yards distant, in a feather-headed oil-nut palm standing in a grassy opening that was reminiscent of a green piece of Wisconsin, except for the palms, the orchids and the legions of land crabs, were perched three black-bellied tree ducks. They just sat there where no normal, non-psycho ducks should have been sitting. They didn't appear nervous. They didn't seem to be watching me. But nobody was fooled. We all knew better. My giant bewhiskered hound Snowser knew better than any of us that the birds were the most cussed and deceitful of ducks. The Irish wolfhound's tongue was hanging out and his sides heaving; he wanted to join Dámaso under the zolocuahuil tree.

"Chicken, too, are you?" I said. "On the ball, Cuchulain."

With that, the reluctant Hibernian hound at my heels, I made an Indian-opera stalk across the heat-pounded greensward. I thumbed back the hammer of my muzzleloading shotgun that I carry because I like the weapon, and checked to make certain the cap was in place. Probably I was gritting my teeth. Unless you have hunted the incredible, long-legged, black-bellied tree duck in the coconut plantations of this latitude (20° North) you will have no idea until you finish this article how competently they can shatter the morale of an otherwise tranquil-minded gunner.

These three specimens let me approach to within ninety yards, which I figured was the ultimate killing distance of the muzzleloader when charged with No. 2 shot and FFFG rifle powder. I was using this powder today because I needed maximum range and performance from the gun.

The tree ducks took off, in their typical maddening fashion. They hopped around the front butts of the palm, and with the tree's bole and some thick sack-of-potato-sized clusters of oil nuts between them and my gun, headed thataway. These ducks are big. In the air they look, to an eager scattergunner's heated vision, as if they had the wingspread of a Piper Cub. One of the three pretenders lacked flying space. He was crowded to the left, into the open, and, oh boy, I swung on him and pulled. With the percussion-cap muzzleloader—which Mexican hunters call a "wait-a-bit" gun—there is a nerve-racking time lag between the instant you pull the trigger and the firing of the charge. You just keep leading the target until something happens. Plenty happened.

Except in dire emergencies, never load a muzzleloading shotgun with rifle powder. The gun boomed, fire flashed and the recoil kicked me back three feet. I fell over something and landed with a Richter Scale seven jolt on my hip pockets, a billow of smoke fanning out in front of me and obscuring everything. I crawled dazedly sideways out of the smoke and saw the long-legged duck on the ground, running, with Snowser in pursuit. Traveling at astonishing speed, the wounded duck disappeared over the brow of a slope below which, I knew, was the arm of a freshwater lagoon margined by thorn jungle. Snowser was only a couple of yards behind the bird when the two flashed out of sight.

On the other side of the hill, Snowser let out an agonized, high-pitched scream of surprise and pain—and Snowser is not a dog that sounds off without excellent cause. I got busy pouring in powder and shot—more FFFG powder—without measuring it, and tamping it with coconut fiber. I didn't have anything else, except my shirttail, that would serve as a wad, and I'd already used so much of my shirttail that I could barely keep it inside my pants.

I couldn't imagine who or what had ambushed Snowser. Here in this backwoods section of Colima, Mexico, he could have encountered any of a long list of hostile beasts, reptiles, or duck-coveting humans who had no respect for a hardworking Irish wolfhound. While I was loading the gun, Dámaso hove on the scene. He had a purty little .38 auto in his hand and looked like all the angry valiant Mexican *caballeros* in the republic since Miguel Hidalgo.

"Well, let's go and find out what happened," he hollered as I rammed down the ultimate wadding. "Who's chicken now?"

I disdained to reply. I was plenty shook and out of coherent phrases. In my experience the best thing I've learned to do in such a situation is to maintain a dignified silence. This isn't always too easy when one's been powder-banged dizzily to the ground and one's favorite dog is in mysterious difficulty over the immediate horizon.

Which, I think, is a strategic spot for me to explain how this hunt for black-bellied tree ducks began.

I was drinking black Mexican coffee which was just below the boiling point and strong enough to hold a spoon upright, and eating a slab of wonderful, aromatic rose-colored papaya that you can get occasionally in the tropics, while sitting in the sunny, open-sided restaurant of the Hotel Fénix in Cuyutlan, Mexico. Pacific surf was crashing 100 yards distant and webs of bright-winged seabirds were crying. I was wholly at peace with myself and the world when, as the saying goes, things went to hell in a hand-basket.

Doña Rosario had arrived on her calculated morning rampage. Doña Rosario, widow of a hunter and mother of hunters, owns the hotel. She is maybe forty-five, has fine Spanish eyes, the shoulders of a good welter-weight and the deliberately assumed voice—in the morning—of a veteran muleskinner. She cracks down because she is a good businesswoman and knows her people and her country; she raises holy hell with her help and her multitudinous animals. She can hit an errant pig or a hopeful prowling dog in the ribs with a cobblestone at sixty feet. I see her do that and better every morning.

When she figures that her hotel is in order, she relaxes with a pot of coffee and for the rest of the day displays one of the truly golden hearts on this coast, and her voice becomes that of a dove. But it is prudent in the early morning to keep your head down until the cobblestones cease flying.

This morning she sounded especially formidable. The trouble began in the kitchen. The cook, a pretty eighteen-year-old Mexican-Aztec girl named Trinidad, was in tears. Doña Rosario bellowed, "Don't you know what day this is, *tonta*? It is October 7, the day of my saint, Santa Rosario. I intended to have a duck dinner. And how many ducks have you bought? Hah! Three ducks for the fifteen persons I have invited. Were you on a *rumba* last night? Heaven protect our stomachs, are you in love again? I tell you now," she said ominously, "I need twelve more ducks." Doña Rosario strode to the door, picked up a cobblestone, and hit a hairless black pig named Curly squarely in the short-ribs. The pig had it coming—he was closing in on a brood of young turkeys.

Sharing my table was Dámaso, thirty-year-old son of Doña Rosario. I said, keeping my voice low, "What kind of ducks does she want?"

He replied, his voice also hushed, "She wants some of those big, long-legged, black-bellied tree ducks that roost in the palms. And although she hasn't said so yet, I will have to go shoot them."

I said, "*Ay, Dios*, tree ducks? You ever try to kill one?"

Dámaso said, "Yes, to my sorrow—with small success. But if I do not bring home twelve tree ducks today, it will be prudent for me to remove to Guatemala."

"My friend," I said, "I will join your cause. I will accompany you to kill these tree ducks or go down trying. I, too, have been exposed to the Doña Rosario's wrath. But I fear the worst. I mean, even Guatemala is a doubtful haven."

Well, I've told you that Snowser was in mysterious trouble, bellering his head off, and that Dámaso had arrived on the scene, panting as if he had used up all the oxygen for yards around, with a .38 auto clutched in his hand. I do not know why Mexicans are in love with handguns. Dámaso was also carrying a 12-gauge double, which for close-range work I would prefer to any weapon in the world. But typically his trust, for whatever lay ahead, was in the pistol.

We loped over the rim of the hill. Snowser was still hollering for help, and he seemed to be somewhere in the depth of a gray-green thorn patch. Approaching the place cautiously, we saw him. He had crawled in under the low branches of the thorn trees and had caught and killed the tree duck. But fishhook-like thorns had snagged his flesh, and he couldn't back out—and to make matters worse he was on an anthill. The little insects were busily eating him alive, and there was nothing he could do about it but yell for assistance. I had a machete. I always have a machete. We cut through the thorn branches to Snowser, salvaged the duck, and together picked the wicked soldier ants off the Irish hound's flinching carcass.

"We're doing fine," I said. "It's noon and we've got one tree duck. Which practically makes certain that Doña Rosario's party will be a bust. Nobody will insure our futures hereabouts."

I must explain that the 365 saints on the calendar are seriously celebrated by those who bear their names, so that no matter what other important matter may be taking place, every day in Mexico is a day of fiesta. One of the most humiliating things that can happen to anybody is to have a saint's day fiesta turn sour.

"We could hunt along the water," Dámaso said without enthusiasm, eying the mineral-green inlets we would have to wade or swim, the thorn patches and the tule jungles.

"Whoever saw a tree duck in the water?" I said, and got no answer.

But we headed down the pond and some fulvous tree ducks got up. We knocked down a couple. The ones we killed were fat, their crops bulging with rice they had looted from some farmer's fields. But they weren't black-bellied tree ducks. We were working back toward the road and the beat-up hotel truck, when some more fulvous ducks rocketed out of the tules. We shot, and Snowser went out and got them. I told myself that if this was my saint's day and I had a choice, I would rather have fulvous tree ducks than black-bellied ones any old time.

We threaded a way through thorn jungle to the road, and Dámaso said with spurious cheerfulness, "They tell me that in Guatemala the people are really amiable, and that the girls are beautiful."

At which point we heard a motor approaching. It was a car, but such a car as I had not seen since I was a youngster—an old high-seated Lincoln coupe. It *belonged* in a museum, but at the wheel sat

Doña Rosario, a shotgun leaning against her shoulder. Dámaso looked about wildly, as if seeking an avenue of escape. Snowser, a dog acquainted with emergencies, crowded against by leg. The Lincoln came to a bucking stop and Doña Rosario stepped out, reaching back for the shotgun. She took a long look at the lone black-bellied tree duck and the four others.

"We did not expect you, mamá," said Dámaso.

"Hah!" she said, then smiled. When Doña Rosario smiles, the world lights up. She gave us both a cigarette, and said to me, "The great hunter.... When I was a girl, the man I married—Don Jesús—took me hunting one day. There is a lake not far from here where the tree ducks come to water. He took me to it. I will now," she said, "if you two gentlemen are not too fatigued, take *you* to it."

I crossed my fingers as we departed for this lake of Doña Rosario's girlhood, the Lincoln in the lead, its engine singing a low note of power. The road was a stub road. It deteriorated. It became a green tunnel through exotically flowered jungle growth. I was thinking, Holy Cats, I would have to use the machete to get us out of here. If we proceeded much farther it would mean a weekend of chopping. We busted through a skein of lianas and a barricade of plants with leaves the size of a breakfast table, and there was the lake. I don't know how large it might have been, but I could see maybe twenty acres of it, blue-glowing like a good sapphire. On the water were rafts of coots and fulvous ducks, loafing and unafraid.

Doña Rosario took control, for which Dámaso was manifestly grateful because it relieved him of responsibility. As for me, I was both relieved and curious. You ever see a trimmed-down Tugboat Annie walking confidently ahead of you with a shotgun?

We crossed a sandy opening, maneuvered through some thorn jungle, came to a grassy place where cattle or horses had grazed—and there, peacefully sitting, all in a huddle, were anyhow 200 tree ducks, all within range. They got up like kites in a slow wind. In the palm trees they were experts, but here they couldn't get off the ground for sour owl steaks. I killed one with the muzzleloader, and of course was out of business. Dámaso—how could he miss?—brought down two.

But Doña Rosario carried a beautiful old-model autoloader. In this country plugs have never been heard of, and she blasted the full magazine of six. Two tree ducks dropped. She stuffed in more shells while keeping her eyes on the birds. I was, as usual, pouring powder without measuring it and fumbling for wadding, shot and caps, while Dámaso was picking shells out of his handsome safari-type hunting jacket. The tree ducks circled. They came back over us. Don't ask me why. Despite the scientists, sometimes I do not think that they are ducks. I think that they should be classified as upland birds. Anyhow, they came back over us, maybe 100 feet high, the most wonderful targets you ever saw. Here were the black-bellied tree ducks, a sky full of them.

All the rest of my life I will wish that I might have known Don Jesús, who taught his bride where to find tree ducks and how to shoot. He has been dead for sixteen years, but he would have been proud of the lady's performance just now. Dámaso and I each killed one. But Doña Rosario's auto sounded like rimshots by a top trap drummer, and three ducks dropped.

Going home I rode in the ancient Lincoln, and took opportunity to say, "In case nobody ever told you before, you are a fair hand with a scattergun. I wish I might have known your husband."

Doña Rosario said, with one of those luminous smiles, "He always said that I was much better with a cobblestone."

Hell in Catskin

I don't know who let that steel-clawed ghost out,
but when the party was over, they rewrote the definition of wild!
I still shudder when I hear church bells ring.

"Gawdamighty, I never hoped to see sech a Donnybrook as this," Grandpop Lovett whooped delightedly as the spotted *mohocoan* cat (ocelot) and the six bellering cat hounds plowed into the mob of celebrants jamming the Fénix *cantina* in Cuyutlan, Colima, Mexico. "Go it, cat. Go it, hounds. HAPPY NEW YEAR, EVER'BODY."

"Get behind something," I hollered back. "This is going to be rough." There were maybe 100 persons in the *cantina*, and two *mariachi* bands. I mean, the place was loaded. Not ten square feet of spare space anywhere. Moreover, it was hard on midnight and everybody, including decorous *señoritas* and their *dueñas*, had taken many drams of holiday punch or more potent brands of good cheer. I grabbed a chair with some notion of crowding the *mohocoan* into a corner. But the cat went over the service bar and up the side of some display shelves heavily laden with bottles. The Mexican carpenter who had made the shelves hadn't anticipated such an emergency, anyhow, so the bank of shelves and their bottles crashed down across the bar and onto the bongo drummers, who were too startled to dodge. One crawled away combing broken glass out of his hair, while the other leaned against the bar, hands clasped, eyes tightly shut, and lips moving a silent litany against disaster.

Grandpop Lovett was carrying a fancy striped silk blazer over his arm, the tropical evening having gotten warm. I grabbed it.

"Where did she go?" I yelled at him above the uproar. "Dammit, that's *my* cat."

"Powder River," hollered Grandpop Lovett as the six cat hounds slammed past us, also trying to locate the *mohocoan*. "This is the real way to make a cat hunt."

I don't know who coined the phrase, "A scene of indescribable confusion," but he should have seen what was going on here. A *marimba* overturned with a Wagnerian chord. Dámaso, the bartender, was throwing bottles at the hounds and shouting unintelligible oaths. *Señoritas*, who in other circumstances would have faced a *tigre* with a machete, were trying to outdo one another in the matter of shrieking. A local policeman had drawn a .45 and was waving it, about to shoot something but not quite sure what. And the cat hounds, tough, sierra-trained and single-minded, were telling the world at the top of their voices that they had a *mohocoan* bayed—they hoped. But the *mohocoan* was nowhere in view.

Dámaso came out from behind the bar, wading through fallen bottles, and caught my arm. "I think she went that way," he bellowed, pointing upward at the open breezeway to the second story.

It sounded reasonable. I grabbed the pack leader of the hounds, a black bitch named Sombra, and headed for the stairs, the other dogs crowding joyously past us. Behind me I heard Doña Rosario, the formidable widow who owns the hotel, shout, "*Dios de mi vida*, the entire hotel will be ruined." Sporting *caballeros* among the guests, realizing belatedly that this was an honest-to-gosh cat hunt with hounds, if in a unique setting, joined the safari. Magically, all produced pistols. In this country a pistol is as much a part of a gentleman's dress as his pants. In fact, if he had to choose between the two, I think he'd leave his pants home.

As we reached the top of the stairs, the hounds were baying "treed" around the bend of a dark corridor. Vaguely I heard the church bells clamor. It was midnight, 1960. Grandpop Lovett shrilled, "Happy New Year ever'body." Then, from the direction of the hounds came a crash of glass, crockery and other falling objects that beat anything I had heard since Fibber McGee last opened his fabulous closet. I remember thinking dolefully that Doña Rosario was right, the whole doggoned hotel would be wrecked before this was over.

Here I must explain how this New Year's cat hunt in a hotel came about. The *mohocoan*, as I said, was mine. I had captured it for Tom Snowden, a Memphis, Tennessee, banker, who wished to present it to the Memphis zoo. Tom is an old and valued friend, and I wish to state emphatically that I would not attempt to take a *mohocoan* alive for anybody except an old and valued friend. But anyhow, I had this one, and arrived at Cuyutlan with it in time for the New Year's celebration. I didn't have a cage for the cat. It was swathed in fish netting and trussed to a pole, so furious that I feared it might die if I didn't let it move about some. Doña Rosario solved this problem. She had a spare room which contained nothing but some sacks of dried corn for tortilla meal. The one window was barred and covered with heavy screen. She said she would put a pan of water in the room and we would simply turn the *mohocoan* loose in it. It *sounded* like a good idea.

I don't know who opened the locked door. Probably one of the hotel servants. But as nearly as I could reconstruct the crazy affair, the *mohocoan* had streaked for the open, and encountered my pack of cat hounds which were relaxing in the front yard. Whereupon the cat had beat it back through the hotel and blundered into the *cantina*, with the hounds in hot pursuit. To capture it the first time, I'd had enough adventures to last me for quite a while. Grandpop Lovett had helped—and he had been a problem, too, but a lovable one.

Take the slate-gray, mist-curtained morning on remote Cerro Indio when circumstances convinced Grandpop that he had developed a powder-load for his .30-06 that the War Department ought to know about immediately because it made nuclear fission seem as ineffectual as a kid's cap gun.

Paisanos had assured me that there were *mohocoans* on this mountain. Just exactly how I was going to capture one alive, I was not yet certain. But the hounds had hit a hot scent, and with Sombra leading them were heading through a horrible tangle of live oak and stunted pine, sounding off for all the world to hear. I didn't have much confidence in the outcome. You can't explain to a cat hound that you want a *mohocoan*, not a *tigre*, puma, margay, jaguarundi or whatever. All you can do is go along with them until you find out what cat it is they are chasing.

It can be a discouraging business. I didn't crowd the packtrain much. We had three men, six horses and my black saddle mule Pony. I didn't aim to let the outfit knock itself out in wild pursuits unless I had good evidence that we actually were on the trail of a *mohocoan*. It looked to me as if it were going to be a long hunt and perseverance would be the deciding quality.

Ahead, a white-tailed buck bounced out of a thicket and stood looking over his shoulder at us. He was a dope, a setup. And we needed fresh meat. I told Grandpop, "Take him. We'll find out later what the dogs are chasing, maybe." Grandpop is a spry, wiry little chap with a goatee, bright blue eyes and what easily could be mistaken for an ingenuous attitude toward life. But he had been around; a cowpuncher, a cotton buyer, a colonel in the Army and a banker. He was a poker-playing, julep-drinking friend of Tom Snowden, for whom this hunt was being made. He carried a Springfield and loaded his own shells, experimenting tirelessly. After looking over some of his notes, I will never understand why he hasn't blown himself and the Springfield up long before this. Grandpop dismounted and slid the rifle out of its boot. Thunder was growling over the sierra and a wind had begun to moan through the rocks. Grandpop fiddled with the sight. More thunder banged as the storm approached. I could barely hear the dogs now. I wished the hell he would hurry. The buck just stood here. You could have assayed his type for brains without finding a trace in a carload.

Grandpop leveled the Springfield and fired—at the same time lightning forked down from the sky and hit an oak snag 200 yards beyond the buck. The deer went down kicking, and for the next few minutes I was busy getting the packtrain back under control. Sierra-bred horses are scared to death of lightning. They've had experience. When everything was back to normal, I rode over to Grandpop, who was examining the Springfield with an awed look on his face.

"Y'know," he said with bated breath, pointing at the fallen deer and the smashed, smoking oak snag, "that last batch of shells I loaded have really got it. I gotta get in touch with the War Department as soon as I remember where I wrote down the formula."

But it was Grandpop Lovett who figured out how to take a *mohocoan* alive. Today's strike with the dogs didn't amount to a hill of beans. Sombra brought the dogs back, looking apologetic, and we pitched camp in a slashing, noisy thunder-and-rain storm. In the morning, however, we made a better strike. This time it was a *mohocoan*. The dogs were below us on the bare ledges of a *barranca*, and I saw the cat with my glasses, loping along with its tail in the air, stopping to look back, obviously sore as heck. I hung my spurs in Pony's ribs and put him down the pitch, letting the rest of the outfit take care of themselves. By taking shortcuts, I caught up with the dogs and was with them when the *mohocoan* went up a tree at the base of a purple lava cliff. It was quite a tree and belonged in a botanical garden. Actually, it was a crossbreed. A wild fig, the jungle strangler, had taken over a primavera, using its trunk and branches to spread itself over a quarter of an acre. I saw the *mohocoan* forty feet up and could have shot it. In view of what happened, I should have.

The outfit came pounding up, with Grandpop Lovett riding straight and easy, not a visible rock or branch wound on him, which was a relief. I held consultation with Policarpio, my three-quarters Aztec *segundo*.

The only idea I had was to climb the tree and try to rope the cat. It seemed a sour idea even as I mentioned it. I am no champion with a *reata*, and I doubt whether even the best roper could sit perched in a tree and catch a *mohocoan* through intervening foliage. But I was about to try when the cat resolved the situation. One side of the mixed-up tree touched the purple lava cliff, and we saw the *mohocoan* go across a hammock of vines lightly as a squirrel and leap to the rocks. Then it was gone. We found a way up the cliff, and Sombra picked up the trail again, only to lose it at the base of another cliff. The sun was now rolling down the western sky and it was time to make camp.

"Y' know what I'd do to catch one of those cats in a tree?" said Grandpop Lovett. "I'd get me a dog catcher's net with a long handle and haul him in as easy as spitting up a stump."

I said, "Grandpop, out of the mouths of children, bankers and geniuses—and I know where we can get some fish net."

I asked Policarpio to ride to a place called Madrid, on the Armeria River, where a friend of ours fished commercially for the silvery perch-like *mojarra* fish, and buy or beg from him a few square yards of fish net.

Box traps, snares or steel wouldn't work. Like the dogs, traps weren't selective. We'd have harvested everything from squirrels to opossums, and could have spent our lives out here and not laid hands on a live *mohocoan*. The only hope I'd had, and it was forlorn, was to take one with my *reata*. If anybody has ever roped a *mohocoan*, I'd like to hear about it. I would about as soon depend on trying to drop a loop over a bolt of greased lightning. Anyhow, I also asked Policarpio to put the word out through the sierra grapevine that if anybody sighted a *mohocoan*, I wanted to know about it and would pay for the information.

Policarpio didn't ask me where we'd be when he returned. It would have been beneath his woodsman's dignity. He figured he could find us.

Policarpio was gone three days. During his absence, we killed a puma and lost a dog. Sombra and her pack bayed the puma on a narrow rock ledge fifty feet above a streambed. The cat couldn't climb any higher because above it there was only bare, backshelving rock, and there was no avenue of escape to right or left. It crouched there, snarling demoniacally, lashing its long tail. It was a dead cat, and maybe it knew it. But while Sombra stood back out of the cat's leaping distance, the other five dogs clustered at the base of the rock pitch, clawing at it, yelling hysterically, daring the puma to come down and fight. They were not good dogs. They were a motley crossbred collection picked up from ranchers because they had made a few cat hunts. You can't get good dogs down here, and even if you could, they would be too expensive because they don't last long. In any case, these five knotheads were endeavoring noisily to climb up to the puma and take the cat apart cell by cell, they hoped.

Sombra was standing back looking worried.

I had to kill the cat. Down here it is a public duty to destroy a puma because of the inroads they make on stock. But beneath this one there were the leaping, yammering dogs. If I shot the cat and only wounded it, a dog or two was certain to be killed when it fell. It was impossible to call the dogs back. They were at the moment stone deaf. They had a puma bayed and were all heroes. Grandpop Lovett wanted to shoot the cat with his .30-06, but I told him no, with one of those new cartridge loads of his he might start a chain reaction that would dissolve the cliff in an Apocalyptic blossom of flame. The truth was, I felt the muzzleloader, at this distance, was by far the deadlier weapon. Moreover, I didn't know how well Grandpop Lovett could shoot. Plenty of men can hit a deer like a champion, but a bayed puma and excited hound music do things to a man's adrenal glands.

I held on the cat's head and pulled. Maybe you know how it is with a muzzleloader. There is the long hammer fall, then the cap busts, the fire strikes down through the firing tube, and finally the charge catches. Meanwhile, you just keep holding on your target. Mexicans call my muzzleloader the "wait-a-minute" gun. I will always believe that this desperate puma was in the act of jumping. At any rate, I caught him a little too far back, in the neck and shoulder, and he came down screeching among the waiting dogs. Actually, he had to be dead, but his reflexes were still working. He was kicking, biting and clawing. When the smoke of the black powder blast cleared away, Sombra had the puma by his neck, backing away from him, and a dog named Payaso lay dying on the rocks with his guts spilling out of a torn belly.

Policarpio rode into camp at first light next morning, looking gaunted, his pinto was leg-weary and heavy-headed, but he had a fathom or so of *mojarra* net and some news. He said he had cut *mohocoan* sign on his way to our camp. Only ten miles distant on a high plateau, he said, a *mohocoan* had killed a *choncho*. The tracks were plain, and the scent should still be strong. I must explain that the *choncho* is the crested guan, a turkey-size bird that makes strange sounds in the jungle. The *mohocoan*, Policarpio said, had eaten only a few mouthfuls of the *choncho's* breast, so obviously it had killed out of sport on a full belly, and no doubt would return when it became hungry. Grandpop Lovett unrolled the fish net, cut saplings, and presently came up with something that looked like an oversized butterfly net. By this time we had broken camp and had the pack animals loaded.

Sombra picked up the *mohocoan's* scent at the carcass of the *choncho*, and within minutes the pack was in full beller, heading out across the low-jungled plateau. I don't know what mixture of breeds may have been in Sombra, but she was a good cat dog. She was coal black except for a white blaze on her chest, and looked like an oversized, deep-chested greyhound with mule ears that tipped over halfway up. She could outrun anything in that country, had a good nose, telescopic eyes and plenty of brains in her head. Less than half-an-hour had passed when she belled "treed." We hacked our way through the jungle to an open space. There, on the shore of an emerald-green pond, stood a tall, skinny *retama* (Jerusalem thorn) snag. Partway up, on a broken limb, was crouched a *mohocoan*.

"When we get back to civilization," declared Grandpop Lovett, "I'm gonna feed that black dog the biggest beefsteak I can find."

What happened thereafter will remain forever in my scrapbook of dramatic hunting memories. Nobody except a steeplejack could have climbed the snag, and no steeplejack I ever knew could have captured the *mohocoan* alive in such a situation. The *mohocoan* is not big enough to do dire damage to a dog or a man, but for its size it gets my vote as being the fastest and bravest of all jungle cats. It is a ghost with steel claws. Any cat dog who has tangled with a *mohocoan* instinctively drops his ears and becomes wary when he hits the scent of one. It would take a stroboscope-fitted camera to catch one's movements. A *mohocoan* will cut up a whole pack of dogs and escape, leaving them battling one another. I call them "hell in catskin."

But we had this one. The *retama* snag leaned toward the jungle pond. I told Policarpio and one of his assistants to cut the tree down so it would fall into the water. They got busy with their broad-bladed machetes. The cat, with the vibrations of the machete blows in his paws, climbed higher. As the snag fell, the *mohocoan* jumped, but too late; it landed in the water, and Sombra was after it in a flash. Most jungle cats don't swim so well, but Sombra swims like a seal. She herded the *mohocoan* back toward the shore, nipping at it, and snapping the other dogs that got in her way. Grandpop Lovett waded out to meet them with his net, while I stood by with the muzzleloader, just in case.

As the beach party neared shore, Grandpop made his pass with the net, and so help me, I couldn't tell at first whether he had got a dog or the *mohocoan*, but he hollered, "Powder River," and came ashore towing something. It was the *mohocoan*, all right.

We fought the dogs off, and I thought, "Okay, Tom Snowden. Okay, Memphis zoo. Here comes your cat." But I thought, "Oh boy, if he asks me for another *mohocoan*. . . ."

We trussed up the little cat and headed for Cuyutlan, crowding the outfit because the New Year celebration was coming up and nobody wanted to miss it.

Well, I've told you what happened on New Year's Eve in the Hotel Fénix at Cuyutlan, to the point where the *mohocoan*, our safari of celebrants and the cat hounds reached the second story and there was a world's-end crash just around the bend of the corridor.

Sombra broke away from me and disappeared in the direction of the unholy sound. I got there as fast as I could. There was a room, the door of which was open. I knew the room. In it Doña Rosario kept her bric-a-brac treasures. They had been artistically arranged on a mahogany table with an Irish linen cover. Many of the items were of glass, I suppose priceless, but I am no expert. Anyhow, they were now on the floor. The *mohocoan* had jumped onto the table, and from it to a ceiling beam. My screwball hounds had overturned the table. With Grandpop Lovett's silk blazer wrapped around my left arm for protection, I waded into the fray and began throwing dogs toward the door. Dámaso, the bartender, caught them with outfielder precision and heaved them into the corridor. Downstairs, the *señoritas* were still trying to outdo one another screaming. The church bells were sending their season's greetings across the countryside.

I was wondering what to do when Doña Rosario arrived. She is a woman acquainted with many emergencies, having reared sons and survived a revolution. She caught my arm and pushed me into the corridor. Only the *mohocoan* was left in the room. "Leave the cat there," she said. "No more damage can be done. So far as I can see, everything breakable has been broken—and the window has bars and a screen. The cat cannot get away, because I will lock the door and this time," she said, "I will keep the keys in my pocket."

We trooped toward the stairs. Grandpop Lovett and Sombra were beside me when we reached the *cantina*. "If there is anything left unbroken to do it with," Grandpop said, "I wish to give you, the Memphis zoo, and all present a heartfelt toast to a happy New Year."

Doña Rosario said with feeling, "*Amén*."

Coyote-Wolverine War

. . . how much more punishment could we take?
We were beat-out refugees from a
Coyote-Wolverine War.

"Fer gawd's sake, hurry up an' shoot," Tex hollered as we stood there half frozen in the inky shadows of our wolverine-wrecked combination storehouse-meat house at Old Matanuska. "The varmint is fixin' to jump on me!" He had to shout to make himself heard above the clamor of the eight excited Malamutes outside who were trying to drag the heavy-loaded Yukon sled through the doorway so they could join the party. "Get busy with that gun," he implored.

"I will when you hold the light steady," I said. "You're waving it around like a railroad brakeman."

"I'm sh-shivering," Tex hollered back.

Ten minutes earlier everything had been swell. We were trail-weary and frostbitten, but had no problems that the comforts of a warm cabin wouldn't take care of in a hurry. "Jest think," Tex had said through his icicle-fringed beard, "We ain't gonna have no more wolverine trouble fer a while anyhow." He gestured toward the scattered lights of town shining through tall cottonwoods. "On account of we are now, by gosh, enterin' the precincts o' civilization—an' that's a relief, I tell ya."

I didn't reply. I was worried about my nose, which was either freezing or already frozen. Tex claimed that the temperature was down around fifty below, and with my numb nose and the cold striking through my caribou fawn parka practically to my bones, I believed him. It was bitter, a brute of a night, but beautiful. The aurora was doing a multicolored scarf dance from horizon to horizon where the giant silver Chugach peaks leaned over us, sawing at the sky. Our sled runners wailed musically on the wind-drifted powder snow as the team of long-legged siwash Malamutes lunged powerfully into the harness to cover the last quarter-mile home as rapidly as possible.

"Home" was a single-room, sod-roofed log cabin on a short hillside above Spring Creek. Below the cabin, where the creek flats began, stood a ten by twelve-foot frame shack—now the meat house-storehouse—which had been our first headquarters in town until we were compelled to admit that in winter it was too cold for human occupancy. Tonight we were arriving from a trapline on upper Knik River, to get the wrinkles out of our bellies, as the saying goes, and rest up a while. We had a rest coming to us. We were beat-out refugees from a coyote-wolverine war, the only wildlife war of its kind that I ever heard of, and I hope I never have to run traps in the midst of another.

"Hold 'em up a coupla minutes," Tex said as we drew alongside the meat house-storehouse. "I wanta git a haunch o' sheep meat to hang by the stove so's hit'll be thawed by mornin'."

I stepped on the brake and the dogs halted resentfully. They yowled and yammered and milled about until I had to bang a whip threateningly over their heads lest they tangle their traces and start a bloody battle royal. Meanwhile, Tex was at the plank door of the shack with a flashlight, fumbling in his pockets and complaining profanely that he couldn't find the doggoned padlock key and his hands were freezing. He asked me if I had it. I searched, found the key in my watch pocket and went over and unlocked the padlock for him, figuring that by this time his fingers were too cold for the task. Tex shouldered the door open and we stepped inside with the flashlight beam dancing ahead, only to halt abruptly, staring. The place looked as if a typhoon had spent a weekend. It was a spectacular shambles.

"Hell's afire," Tex moaned in disbelief. "Another wolverine? Here in town? Hit ain't possible."

Gear that we had carefully stowed was wildly scattered. The fat goat, sheep and black bear carcasses which, three months ago, we had quartered and left hanging from meathooks, were on the floor, gnawed, and thoroughly fouled with dung and frozen urine. The shack was filled with a musky animal odor—the odor of every wolverine I had ever pelted. But, like Tex, I couldn't understand how a wolverine had happened to pass this way, or how one of the larcenous, ever-hungry animals had managed to get into the tightly constructed shack.

"Wolverines don't carry padlock keys," I said, arguing with myself as I tried to massage some circulation back into my nose. "And without a key one couldn't have got in here, holy Moses."

"Go ahead an' be funny," Tex said in the grief-stricken voice of a lifelong meat-eater about to turn vegetarian. "But hit was a wolverine that done this. I know because I always git a headache when I smell wolverine stink, an' I'm gettin' one now." At this point I realized belatedly that the yelling dogs weren't simply registering annoyance because of the delay so close to the home cabin. They were telling the countryside that an enemy animal had been brought to bay. But there had been no wolverine trail in the snow outside. If there had been, I would have seen it. Therefore it followed.... I yanked my right mitten off with my teeth and clawed for the .22 auto I carried under my parka.

"Watch yourself," I said urgently. "I think the wolverine is still in here. The dogs say it is."

"Yeah. I jest figgered that out my own self," Tex said. "I think the cuss lives here, because my headache is gettin' real bad. But where is he at?"

I backed against a wall and with a fast-freezing hand poised the deadly little .22. Tex wasn't carrying a belt gun, and our rifles were on the sled. Tex quickly swung the flashlight beam over the room again. No wolverine. Only the ruined supply of meat, a tumbled heap of assorted saddle gear, a couple of claw-torn balloon silk tents, a handsome white goat pelt which we had been drying for use as a bunk cover and which had been ripped off the wall and now lay in tatters, some bales of dog salmon torn open and the dried fish largely distributed over the floor, and ten gallons of honey-colored black bear fat that we had painstakingly rendered out and stored in glass jugs. Every jug was broken; the fat was filthy and bound to be loaded with glass splinters.

When Tex saw the broken jugs, he exploded in righteous rage, for he was passionately fond of black bear fat. He used it as shortening when he made bread, enriched stews with it, greased the hotcake griddle, and often ate it in lieu of butter. He maintained, moreover, that, rubbed on, it was a wonderful hair tonic and a sovereign remedy for rheumatism, colds in the chest, snowshoe cramps, and other maladies.

"The cussed varmint ain't in here after all, he gritted when he had once more played the flashlight over the room. "But come morning I'll find his trail. If I have to, I'll foller him plumb to the Arctic Ocean an' kill him on the ice. I've had me a gutful o' wolverines. I—what in heck was that?"

Somewhere inside the shack, during a brief lull in the uproar of the dogs, an animal had snarled—a peculiarly vicious, rasping snarl, one I had heard a hundred times before—the snarl of a desperate wolverine. The animal was above us. Tex tilted the flashlight, sweeping the rafter supports and the heaps of trapline and hunting camp gear piled on planks laid across the peeled-spruce beams. In a moment he had located our Injun devil. The wolverine—a big one—crouched in the shadow of some sacks of wild hay that we kept for moccasin filling. I cut down on its head as Tex steadied the light, but felt a qualm despite the confidence I had in the vicious little high-speed .22 slugs. A wolverine is almighty hard to kill, and when wounded is absolutely no animal to be associated with in close, crowded quarters. Not even an ornery, 100-pound Susitna king wolf cares to come to grips with a berserk wolverine in a spot where he can't protect himself with fast footwork.

But I squeezed the trigger, the gun barked, and the wolverine jumped—straight at Tex. Having anticipated this, Tex leaped backward, but tripped over a packsaddle and came down heavily across a couple of kegs of salted king salmon. The flashlight smacked the floor and went out. At the juncture, while I was reaching for my match safe, trying to locate the wolverine in the darkness, and requesting Tex to get back onto his feet in a hurry and switch on the torch if it was still functioning, the Malamutes broke the towline and came surging through the doorway.

Just before the avalanche overwhelmed us, I heard Tex say in a hoarse voice that didn't sound like his, "Dear friends an' gentle people."

Here I've got to explain how we became involved in the war between the coyotes and the wolverines, and what that war was all about. We were running forty miles of traps, operating out of a cabin on Friday Creek at the edge of the two-mile-wide, desert-like Knik bars, taking lynx mostly, when suddenly, almost overnight, the timber had filled with wolverine trails, more than either of us had ever seen before. The animals took over the trapline. For two weeks they killed and ate every lynx we trapped, which hurt because this year—a good rabbit year—there were plenty of lynx in the valley and their pelts were bringing the all-time high price of $80.

Ordinarily a marauding wolverine would have been no problem. Tex and I used to say, show us a wolverine trail and we'll show you the animal's pelt. In fact, I subsequently put myself through the University of Washington chiefly with wolverine pelts. We got many a laugh out of dire tales of the terrible Injun devil, the destructive and almost supernaturally clever beast that couldn't be trapped and would harass a luckless trapper plumb off his line and back to town. But now it was different. We were the victims, and there were just too many wolverines to cope with.

"Where in blazes are they comin' from?" Tex asked. "There ain't that many wolverines in Alaska, dang hit."

We found out a few days later where they were coming from. We had been hearing coyote songs out on the windswept bars, a strange sound here because coyotes were new in the north, and today we had spotted a pair of coyotes drifting out toward the frozen river. Making a stalk for them under the cover of some dwarf cottonwoods, we presently beheld an enlightening bit of wilderness drama. At the edge of the river, on a strip of sand bar which the eternal glacier winds had blown clean of snow, a wolverine was digging industriously. We knew what he was digging for. Here in the Knik country, the sizable wolverine population subsisted almost entirely on the myriad salmon that, dying when spawning was completed, were washed ashore and sanded under. We hadn't trapped much out here. It was difficult to keep traps working in such a windy, open area; wolverine pelts weren't worth much anyway; and Tex shied away from trapping wolverines anywhere because he always got a headache when exposed to their scent.

It now appeared that the wolverines had tough competition for the rights to their ancient feeding ground. As we watched through our glasses, out of effective rifle range, the two coyotes, reddish-brown ghosts in the blue winter light, came upwind to the wolverine. Spotting them, the wolverine sat up like a bear, and then, when they came on, made a head-down, fairly fast rush at them. I could practically hear his buzz-saw war snarl. He and his fellows were the titular bosses here. The salmon burial grounds had been the freehold of their ancestors since time out of mind. Probably their rights had never been seriously challenged. The timber wolves weren't interested in digging out dead salmon. The bears, black and grizzly, were all asleep in their snow-masked dens. But the immigrant coyotes, the "little wolves" of the Indians, with inherited guile and knowledge of survival in deserts, mountains and tropical jungles, were a new breed of sophisticated claim jumpers, and it became evident that they had a taste for the rotten salmon interred in the iron-hard sands of the Knik.

At the wolverine's savage charge, the two coyotes floated apart, light as wind-drifted leaves, to let the wolverine slam between and past them. Then one coyote expertly set his teeth in the wolverine's rump and threw him off balance. When the wolverine recovered himself, spun on his short legs and charged again, the second coyote grabbed him by the rump and sent him sprawling again. That was the pattern. It was the infallible technique that had cost the Knik wolverines their immemorial rights to the tons of salmon frozen in the snow-patched gray bars.

"So now we know why the timber is full o' wolverines," Tex said as we cased our glasses. "The coyotes chased 'em off the bars, an' now, instead o' eatin' salmon, the stinkin' flat-eyed so-and-so's are makin' a free lunch of our trapline."

We couldn't get any closer to the coyotes, so we returned to camp. In the morning I set out to run the line, not taking the dogs because Tex needed them to skid in wood logs. It was the same maddening story. We had caught two lynx and what maybe had been a fine cross fox, but the wolverines had killed and eaten them, leaving only scraps of fur and splintered bones. The lynx had died hard—there was wolverine fur on the snow, too—which was some satisfaction. As the short day waned, I shot a young goat who stood poised on a rocky point above the glacier, presumably contemplating the sunset, gutted the carcass, loaded it onto my packboard, and went on to a line shelter known as the Tea Camp. We had been out of fresh meat for several days, and the prospect of sweet, fat roast ribs and a brisket stew was welcome indeed.

The Tea Camp was no luxury bivouac. It was a framed eight by ten-foot tent on a drifted bar under a cliff, wind-tattered, equipped with a rusted Yukon stove and two pole bunks. There was no cache. I ate most of the goat liver, washing it down with black trading post tea, then dragged the goat carcass inside the tent for security, and turned in. Coyotes were singing far out on the river bars. They sounded triumphant.

A three-quarter moon rose above the peaks, flooding the tent with soft radiance, and I covered my head to keep the light out of my eyes and went to sleep. Some time later, partially awakened by a sound that wasn't the glacier wind, I uncovered one eye and observed a curious phenomenon. The goat carcass was moving out the open door. The head and shoulders were already outside, and the hind quarters were just passing me. With no idea as to what was causing this, but unwilling to let a prime carcass depart without active protest, I reached out and grabbed hold of the nearest hind leg. I was still half asleep and could easily have persuaded myself that the whole thing was a fantastic dream, the result of too much fried liver. But when something tugged powerfully at the carcass and a threatening snarl sounded, I came wide awake in a hurry, leaped out of the bunk, and snatched up my rifle.

There in the moonlight just outside the pole-framed canvas door were two wolverines, their teeth fastened in the neck of my goat carcass. Apparently unafraid, they were still trying to make off with the carcass when I brought up the .30-06 and shot one of them in the face. The other fled toward the timber, and in the tricky light I missed it. Since there was no way to lock the door, and the ancient canvas would have been only a token barrier anyway, I didn't sleep much the rest of the night. Next morning I mushed back to Friday Creek headquarters, toting the goat carcass and the wolverine pelt, and told Tex what had happened. He cuffed his frazzled muskrat cap to the back of his head and assumed the expression of a martyr while the fagots were being piled.

"We gotta pull the traps," he declared. "The St. Louis Fur Exchange is tough enough to work for. But I sure as shootin' ain't gonna tend no more traps fer a mob o' thievin' displaced wolverines, especially now that they've started comin' right into camp at night." He wrinkled his nose. "An' take that pelt outside, will ya" I'm already gettin' a headache from hit."

"Maybe the wolverines will leave," I said.

"They won't as long as we string traps to feed 'em," he said. "The thing to do is get outa here a couple weeks. We'll go back to Matanuska, by gosh, an' live high whilst they starve, or eat one another, or fight with the coyotes some more, or depart fer more promisin' regions."

Here I must tell you that we did not as yet know how to trap coyotes in these special Knik conditions. It took us a couple of years to learn, and then we didn't use traps, but snares. Moreover, we had no idea of how to deal profitably with a mass invasion of wolverines. One or two wolverines at a time were absurdly easy to kill, because the wolverine, regardless of his gaudy publicity, is really a pathetic animal, a creature that nature double-crossed. His temperament and continual hunger can lead to his downfall. Although biologically he is a member of the weasel family, the largest member, I believe—in effect he is a small bear that has been denied the boon of hibernation. He cannot take refuge in sleep during the long, barren winter months when there is neither vegetation nor easy prey, but must hunt in competition with swift, winter-adjusted killers such as the lynx, the fox and the timber wolf. For him, winter is a terrible time. Because of his short legs he is clumsy in deep snow, unable successfully to pursue the fleet prey animals. He is always starving.

I once figured out that a wolverine—except the formerly lucky Knik wolverines with their wind-cleaned salmon bars—was fortunate if he got two full meals a month. His reputation as a glutton comes from the fact that when he does find a quantity of food, usually a winter-killed moose, sheep or caribou, he stuffs himself—who wouldn't? His black reputation as a robber of caches and traplines stems from the same reason. He is forever hungry, forced to travel constantly on an empty stomach, so that food, no matter whose or where it is, is bound to be the most important thing in his universe, something to obtain at almost any cost and something to fight for. No epicure, he will eat a greasy dishrag, the babiche filling of snowshoes, or even a porcupine with its quills if the going is truly rough.

To trap him, you wire a large bait, preferably a moose head, in a rock crevice or between the roots of a tree, and set a battery of traps around it. It isn't necessary to conceal the traps. The wolverine is no dope and will discover the traps no matter how well concealed. He will cat-foot through the battery of traps and take hold of the wired-down bait. Unable to move it, his temper flares and he forgets his feet and the traps. When you next run your line he'll be there, probably with traps on all four feet. But how to deal with a gang of wolverines was something we did not know. I guess Tex, being allergic to the animals, didn't want to know.

Well, I've told you about our homecoming. There we were in the utterly dark storehouse-meathouse, Tex down among the pack-saddles and kegs of salt salmon, the flashlight out, and the eight bellowing Malamutes in the act at last. With stiffening fingers I broke four matches before I got one lighted. Tex was getting to his feet, belt knife in his hand. The wolverine was six feet up on a shelf which we had once used as a lamp stand, lips curled back to show his teeth, eyes glaring. I couldn't tell how hard he was hit, or even if he was hit. Lining the .22 as best I could in the feeble light of the match, I let go the full clip, and as I did so, Tex threw his knife. Then the match went out and the wolverine fell among the waiting Malamutes.

Later, when we had fetched a gasoline lantern from the cabin, we discovered how the wolverine had gotten into the shack. He had torn the tar-paper roofing from what had been the stovepipe hole and jumped down into the room. Probably he hadn't yet found a way to get back out, if he wanted to. I asked Tex if he thought the animal was one of the displaced Knik wolverines. "Sure I do," Tex said. "The varmint was smarter than the others an' lit out first, that's all."

We went up to the cabin, unharnessed the dogs, and built a fire in the cast-iron stove. Tex peered sharply at me, and said, "Holy smokes, didja know yer nose is froze?"

I said, "Uh-huh. We can maybe blame that on the Injun Devil, too. But look what it all got him—he's dead."

Mad Coyote

The word spread like scorched tracings from a hot iron—RABIOSO. Any shadow might conceal the slashing, foam-flecked jaws.

Just before the police siren wailed behind us, Lucky Hal was saying, "What we got this time is a routine assignment. The museum wants some ghost bats, a pair of those purty yellow mulatta birds, a red-faced hawk, and a dwarf jungle whitetail deer. Up to now the deer is just a rumor. It may not exist."

This was in the state of Colima, Mexico, on a cold, gray tropical autumn afternoon, and we were barreling south on the federal highway in Lucky Hal's prairie-schooner type truck, heading for the mouth of the Armeria River. Lucky Hal is a museum collector, an amiable giant who always needs a shave, and whose trademarks are an outsize, wondrously battered black Stetson and a .45 Peacemaker stuck in the waistband of his jeans. With his three Mexican assistants, he hunts and lives like a timber wolf and apparently has given up sleep as a bad habit. I had joined him for the present hunt because his operations are so rough they fascinate me. Although none of us knew it yet, this was to be the meanest, deadliest, most urgent hunt we had made together—a hunt to date time from.

The police siren hit. Lucky Hal braked down and reached resignedly for his identification papers as the highway patrol car slid alongside. But the cop who came over to us waved the papers aside. "You two," he said, with a glance that took in both of us, "are needed at Four-Winds Rancho. Immediately. It is an emergency—and a direct order. Do you know the way there, or do you want me to lead?" We knew the way, and the government could give Lucky Hal orders because he worked for the government as well as for his museum and a university. The cop said he didn't know what kind of emergency it was. All he knew was that he had received instructions by radio to sort us out of the highway traffic and send us to Four-Winds.

"**O**kay, okay, officer, we'll go," Lucky Hal grumbled. "We were headed thataway anyhow." He put the truck in gear and tromped on the gas.

We turned into a dirt road that wound through dense, low jungle, and began passing groups of armed men, afoot and on horseback. "Looks like a combat zone," Lucky Hal said. "Countryside must really be in an uproar." The buildings of Four-Winds came into view, red tile roofs and pastel walls, brilliant with massed bougainvillea blossoms. Woodsmoke was rising from the great chimney of the main house. Don Basilio, the owner, an old friend of mine, came out with his daughter Trinidad to greet us. Don Basilio is a gorilla-shouldered, bald-headed chap who looks like a retired heavyweight wrestler. Usually he is smiling and has a joke for all occasions. Today he looked grim. Trinidad, husky and green-eyed, as pretty as her father is homely, achieved a smile, but it was brief.

"I sent for you," Don Basilio told us in a bass rumble, "because we have a rabid coyote on the ranch and it is attacking people. If it isn't killed at once, other coyotes will be infected. Then the stock. Nobody, nothing, is safe here until the animal is destroyed." He passed a hand over his big face in a gesture of weariness, then motioned for his *secundo*, a lean Indian type named Nacho, to join us. "Tell them what happened," he said to Nacho.

Nacho told us. They had been clearing land for a cornfield on a hillside above the river, ten men working with machetes, their horses picketed on some grass, two mongrel dogs from the ranch curled up asleep in the cold sunshine, everything serene and peaceful. Then a horse snorted, and the two dogs bounded up, bristling. Out of the jungle wall came a wildlife apparition. It was a big mountain coyote, long-legged and gaunt, with glaring eyes and foam-flecked jaws. Its shoulders were bare of hair, and the exposed skin was blue. Moving erratically, jerking its head from side to side, it trotted toward one of the workmen. The man yelled and raised his three-foot machete. The coyote snarled, ropes of saliva spilling from its mouth as it showed its teeth. It sprang toward the man, stumbled

louise
lopina 96

and fell, but had regained its feet to make another rush when the two dogs attacked. They weren't fighting dogs. They circled the coyote, popping their jaws and squalling. The coyote backed against a felled tree. As one dog bored in, the coyote slashed the hapless beast's hip. An instant later, the second dog was bitten.

"By now we all knew, *señores*, that the coyote was *rabioso*," Nacho told us, "and, in truth, we were afraid. You understand we had no guns, and no animal in all the jungle is more dangerous than a mad coyote. This one was not only crazy; he wanted to fight. We could have killed him with our machetes, but undoubtedly someone would have been bitten. So we retreated to our horses. Mounted, with our *reatas* in hand, he would have been no problem. He followed us, snapping at the dogs when they came too close, but then he turned off and went in among the jungle vines, to disappear."

That was early yesterday morning. The men abandoned their work and returned to the ranch, where Don Basilio ordered them to kill the luckless, almost certainly infected dogs. Since then Four-Winds had been an armed camp. Nobody ventured outdoors without a gun. Work had practically ceased. Country Mexicans, with reason, have an utter horror of rabid animals. Their folklore is filled with tales of them, with accounts of the ghastly deaths of persons who had been bitten. The more superstitious claim that rabid animals are bewitched and sent to harass people by hostile *brujos*—witch doctors. But, educated or primitive, nobody down here wants to be in the same area with a *rabioso* beast. And of all rabid animals, they consider the coyote to be the most deadly to humans.

"**Y**ou men are professional hunters," Don Basilio said. "Kill this mad coyote for us, and we will be indebted to you the rest of our lives."

Lucky Hal's three hard-case Mexican assistants had emerged from the covered back end of the truck and were awaiting instructions. I whistled, and my black cat hound, Sombra, leaped out. Everybody at the ranch knew her and respected her ability. She looks like a deep-chested, heavy-boned greyhound, only I understand that there are no black greyhounds. She can run like the wind and think like a man, and she is a killer. "They have brought Sombra," somebody said. "But that is wonderful. She will soon find the *rabioso* beast." And I thought, no you don't, brother; I'll never put Sombra on the trail of a rabid coyote. I would almost as soon be bitten by one myself.

Lucky Hal looked up at the late afternoon sky, the cloud-hung peaks, and said it was too late now to do anything about the coyote. He would go on to the river and make camp, set some bat traps and return tomorrow morning to start a campaign against the coyote. I told him I would stay here. Blundering about in heavy river jungle on a black night setting bat traps is my idea of a hard way to make a living. Besides, I need a reasonable amount of sleep. Lucky Hal and his crew seem to have learned to do without it. I tied Sombra under a mango tree in back of the house, and fed her. It was a dispiriting evening, everybody tense and uncommunicative.

In the morning I borrowed a horse and some gear. Then I waited. Nine o'clock came and no Lucky Hal. The day was coming in overcast and cold, so cold the ranch hands were going about hunch-shouldered and swathed in serapes. I decided to take off alone and work the countryside with my glasses, and I was heading for the corral when I saw a Mexican family, mounted on burros, coming toward the ranch. There was a man, a woman, and a boy; the man was holding a child in his arms.

Trinidad called to me from the ranch house gallery, "Wait. Something has happened."

She must have had a psychic flash, because indeed something had happened. The family rode into the dooryard, and the man stepped down, weeping. The girl child he held was maybe four years old, plump and pretty, with her hair cut in bangs like a *kachina* doll. Her right leg was bandaged with strips apparently torn from a white shirt. As a crowd gathered, the man told us what had taken place. The child's name was Conchita, and this morning when her brother went out to bring in the family milk goats, she had followed. She lagged behind and was out of her brother's view when a coyote burst out of some brush under a mesquite tree, bit her and dragged her down. She screamed, and her brother came running back, a rock in each hand. The coyote departed. The boy said that the animal had no hair on it shoulders, and that it was slobbering. The family, living in an isolated spot, had not heard about the rabid coyote, and nobody had thought to warn them. But the man knew, from his son's description of the animal, that Conchita had been bitten by a *rabioso*.

"She will die," the woman moaned. "We are riding to the priest at Armeria."

"She will not die," boomed Don Basilio, who had arrived in time to hear most of the story. "Somebody bring my car. There is a doctor in Armeria, too. We are going to him first." He looked at me, his eyes like gun muzzles. "You see? Kill me that coyote, please. Pronto."

Five minutes later they were on their way, Don Basilio driving like a wild man. Now I knew what I had to do. I went around the house to the mango tree and slipped Sombra's collar. I told her we had a tough job and hoped it would turn out all right. She looked at me with her dark intelligent eyes and made the *wooo-ooo* sound in her throat that meant good morning, she loved me and would do her best. I headed for the corral again and was saddling the borrowed horse, a tall steel-dust gelding, when Trinidad joined me. She was booted and spurred and wore bullhide chaps. In her hand she carried a .30-30 carbine. "I am going with you," she said. "I know where the place is. You would only waste time finding it." She took a rawhide *reata* from the corral fence and tied onto a buckskin, making her cast over the heads of three other horses, snubbed the animal down and put her rigging on it as handily as any *vaquero* could have.

"I know how you feel about this," she said as we loped up the trail, Sombra running ahead. "But you would feel worse if you didn't use her."

We came to a palm-thatch hut, with a couple of udder-heavy milk goats blatting in the dusty yard. We rode a wide circle about the hut, and suddenly Sombra halted, carefully investigating the scent trail she had struck. Her back hair rising, she sneezed, followed the scent a few yards, walking stiff-legged, then looked back at me, trying to tell me what I already knew—that this was a sick animal. But I got down and joined her, to make certain, and after a moment, on a bit of 'dobe ground, found coyote tracks. Feeling plenty grim about it, I told her to get going, to chase the coyote down and bust its neck. She regarded me as if wanting confirmation, then accepted the order and lined out on the trail. I have never known a dog as fast as Sombra on a scent. She was over a ridge and belling in some jungle before I got back onto my horse.

This coast country is no area for riding to hounds. There are thickets no horse could get through. You don't see the cliffs and rimrocks until they are practically under your mount's front hoofs. You detour and follow openings that lead you astray. Lianas snare you. Most of the foliage is either sharp-edged or has thorns. Many a northern hunter has come down here with his dogs, taken one look and thought nothing doing, not for me. Trinidad and I got fouled up in a mess of lava slides and bullthorn brush, and for a half-hour we didn't know whether Sombra was ahead of us or behind us. Finally we heard her beautiful, carrying voice below us where a ravine fanned out into a valley filled with giant vine-laced trees. I had been so busy that I hadn't paid any attention to the weather. But now, as we started down the ravine, a gust of wind hit us and I felt rain on my face. By the time we reached heavy timber on the alluvial fan, it was raining steadily and a hard wind was crying in the treetops.

Sombra sounded off close ahead, and when we caught up with her she was circling, having lost the coyote's scent on the wet ground. She picked it up, lost it again and repeated her circling tactic. By now the rain was coming down in sheets. Muddy creeks ran in the *arroyos*. The 'dobe soil underfoot was turning to slippery gumbo. Sombra was still trying, but I said the hell with it and whistled her in. Soaking wet, we made for ranch headquarters. Trinidad, her shirt sticking to her as if it had been pasted on, her glossy hair hanging in strings, said, "How long does a rabid coyote live?" I suppose she was hoping that the animal would die before Sombra had to tackle it. "I don't know," I told her. "I never made a study of rabies. But I'm going to when this is over."

We came to a stub road, and there was Lucky Hal's truck, parked under an oil-nut palm. Somebody shouted from a hilltop—one of Lucky Hal's assistants. He said the others were scattered out at various high spots taking the region apart with their glasses. After running bat traps most of the night, they had begun their campaign for the coyote at sunrise without returning to ranch headquarters. Trinidad told him emphatically to tell Lucky Hal and the others to come on in and dry out in a warm place before they all caught pneumonia. We went on and found Don Basilio at the house. The little Conchita, he said, was under the doctor's care and her course of rabies shots had been started. The medic had seemed optimistic. I changed into dry clothes and was in the kitchen drinking a mug of fortified black coffee, Sombra curled up at my feet, when Lucky Hal and his crew came in and joined me.

"And I said this was going to be a routine hunt," Lucky Hal said. "Holy suffering, all night out there in the boondocks I kept looking over my shoulder expecting that damned coyote to bust out of the brush and grab me. Had me a real swell case of creeps."

All the rest of the day and all night rain crashed on the roof tiles and wind moaned under the cornices like a lost soul, but toward morning the storm ceased. I dressed and went down to the gallery for a look at the sky. It was clear from horizon to horizon. The Southern Cross, its four stars white and brilliant, was hanging on a sierra crest, and the new moon was straight overhead. After a while Trinidad came out wearing a blue robe and a scarf around her head, bearing a pot of coffee and cups. I said, "Did I ever tell you that you would make some hunter a swell wife?"

She poured coffee and replied, strictly on formula, "I might, if he proved he could kill a *rabioso* coyote." A few minutes later it happened, as if the conversation had been a cue. From a low, black ridge crest a half-mile distant lifted a hoarse, ragged parody of coyote song. I'll bet I have heard 10,000 coyotes howl in my time, but never before or since have I heard one howl like the one on the ridge. In the sound was torment, despair and the terrible knowledge of approaching death.

Trinidad whispered, "It is the *rabioso*.

"There'll be shooting light in less than an hour," I said. "I'm going to start up there with Sombra now." Like Trinidad, I figured it was the *rabioso*.

I went upstairs for my rifle and gear, and when I came down Trinidad had dressed and was getting into her chaps. "I am coming, too," she said. "No argument, please."

Trinidad looked up from fastening the last snap of her chaps and said, "Lucky Hal left with his crew an hour ago. I made coffee for them." Which ended that.

We rode eastward toward the ridge as great whorls of pink and saffron light grew ahead of us. Trinidad knew a cattle trail to the ridge crest, and we took it and came out on top as the light strengthened and the boulders and trees about us began to take form. Sombra scouted ahead. Then her bell-toned voice started echoes bouncing from the gullies and cliffs. I hung my spurs in the steel-dust's flanks, and hoped he was a lucky horse and wouldn't pile us up at the bottom of a rimrock. Sombra was below us somewhere, and she was telling me that this time she had the coyote cinched. With Trinidad's buckskin a *reata* length behind, the steel-dust plowed through barriers of tangled vines, slid down lava pitches and hurdled washes, traveling like a spooked deer. We came out on a point above a clearing that had once been a cornfield, and I saw Sombra, then the coyote.

They were maybe 200 yards distant. I got down fast and tried to pick up the coyote with my sights, but in this light, and against the background he had, he blurred. I knew I couldn't hit him, but I wanted to try. To be able to say afterward that I had, I guess. There wasn't time. Sombra, floating over the rough ground, covering yards to the coyote's feet, closed with the animal. There was a flurry of action too fast to follow, then Sombra had the coyote by the throat and was shaking him savagely. Trinidad and I rode down to them and I was thinking that if Sombra had been bitten, making it necessary to shoot her, I would get the bloody hell out of these tropical jungles and never return. The coyote looked dead, but I put a slug through his head to make certain.

Sombra came to me and I petted her and told her what a great dog she was, after which I looked her over, inch by inch. There wasn't a mark on her, not a drop of blood that wasn't coyote blood. Trinidad, pale and wide-eyed, crossed herself. I bundled the coyote carcass into a slicker, tied it behind my saddle, and we returned to the ranch house. The carcass had to be put on display, I knew, because otherwise the more primitive folk hereabouts would never believe that the animal was dead. Don Basilio came out and shook hands solemnly and said that there was a prime steak in the kitchen he had intended to eat for his own breakfast, but that he was going to give it to Sombra, *Dios* guard her. It was still cold—it seemed to me I had never been colder even in Eskimo country—so we went inside and built up a fire in the fireplace. After an hour or so Lucky Hal and his men came in. They had heard Sombra's voice and the shot and had concluded that the hunt for the mad coyote was over.

"So now," Lucky Hal said, "we can settle down to some routine hunting for a change. And believe me," he added, "after this experience it will be welcome."

I said, "Amen."

The Gotch-eared Bull of Toonakloot

When I first met Lucky, he was a wobbly-legged calf floundering around in a beaver pond. We were friends from the start, till one of us turned a kind of Judas.

"He's coming in," whispered amiable, white-headed Harvey, the newest pilgrim visitor at Toonakloot rancho. "You got him fooled. Dog my cats if you haven't. And with the wind in his favor." He eased onto one knee and slipped the safety latch of his elegant .300 magnum.

I hoped he was right. I earnestly hoped he was right. We were on the brink of a gravel cutbank overlooking the stream from which my homestead took its name. Across the creek was a triangular flat, autumn-painted and wonderfully jungled with cranberry brush, alders, high redtop grass, and skinny foxtail spruce. Somewhere in this formidable subarctic growth was the bull moose I had been talking to with a birch-bark horn for the past forty-five minutes. We could hear him grunting and had caught glimpses of him, and he seemed to be carrying a trophy-size set of antlers. But he was a spooky, suspicious so-and-so. He didn't quite believe me when I kept telling him with the horn that I was a lone, romantic and willing cow moose in dire need of companionship. Only he didn't quite disbelieve me, either. I put the horn to my mouth, and feeling silly, as I always have when using one of the things, let out a warlock, wailing moan, ending it with a petulant squeal as an added fillip. That should have fetched him, but it didn't. He began a circle to get our wind, and presently we heard him splash across the creek on the far side of a bend.

"Dammit, he's gonna play cute again," Harvey whispered. "I don't believe he's a sure-enough, red-blooded Alaskan bull moose. Must be a freak or something."

Harvey had never killed a moose. He was a retired truck-transportation chap who, he said, had spent his life making money and dreaming about hunting and fishing. We had hunted three days and seen only cows and mulligan bulls. Now we had this supposedly trophy bull located within easy packing distance of the cabin, less than a mile, and he was playing games with us. Harvey carried a water canteen on his belt. I reached over and unhooked it. Unscrewing the stopper, I held the canteen high and spilled its contents onto a rock as noisily as I could. Then I sounded off again with the horn, putting plenty of elemental schmaltz into it, I hoped. The bull appeared in the heavy shadows of some birches, directly downwind, but I still couldn't see both of his antlers. As he started in among the birches, I whistled to stop him. To my inexpressible surprise, he came galloping toward us. I had my glasses on him and the head looked good, a flat spread with wide palms and a slew of points. I said, "Take him," and the .300 boomed. I saw hair fly from the point of the bull's shoulder. There was the solid smack of the bullet striking through bone and flesh. The great, dark beast dropped as if clobbered by lightning, his head in a patch of fireweed, one polished antler blade gouged into the gravel.

"Be doggoned," Harvey said happily. "Be absolutely doggoned. Waited my whole life to do that." He fumbled a cigarette out of his pocket and broke two matches lighting it. "But I guess," he said, "that you probably don't remember what it's like, killing your first moose."

I could have told him a fairly dramatic story in that connection, but didn't. We went over to the kill, and I was getting out my steel tape when I had my first good look at the bull's ears. They had been gotched with a knife, an old-time, cattle-country mark. I took a seat on the bull's shoulder and asked Harvey if he had another cigarette. He gave me one and lit it for me. "You look like you'd seen a ghost," he said jokingly. "Rabbit jump over your grave place?" Unwittingly, he was almost right, at that. I was seeing a lot of ghosts, the ghosts of a lost period, of men, animals and events in a brave, colorful kind of life that could never again be duplicated on this earth. To me the gotch-eared bull had been a prime symbol of the closing years of that era.

We first met at the edge of an old burn above a beaver pond, on a sunny spring day when the perfumed cottonwood buds were bursting and the sky was clamorous with northbound geese and cranes. In company with iron-maned, green-eyed, venerable Tex Cobb, I was returning from a winter-long trapping expedition into the Talkeetnas. Tex and I crossed the beaver dam, slipping on peeled aspen sticks, teetering under the weight of our packs, and climbed, sweating, up a bank to the rim of the burn. Something moved in the shadow of a brush clump. As I turned, thumb on the safety of my rifle, a moose calf stood up. Completely unafraid, staring at us with big, liquid eyes, the calf came to me at a wobbly-legged trot. He couldn't have been more than a few days old.

"Purty little bugger," Tex said. "But let's git the heck away from him, on account of mamma ain't fur off."

Hardly had he finished speaking when there was a ringing snort close downwind. A windfall broke like a rifle shot. It was mamma, advertising her presence and warning us away. Unfortunately, she was between us and where we wanted to go. As I tried to spot her, the calf crowded up against me. I moved away, having heard that if you left your scent on a moose calf, the mother would disown it. The calf followed, snuggling against me again. Then here came the cow. She was huge and gaunt, and her sunburnt-looking spring pelt was practically red-roan. She slammed straight at us, ears laid back, pounding the earth with her great splayed hoofs. Maybe she was bluffing, but you couldn't depend on it. I had seen a cow moose stomp the living daylights out of a black bear who had murderous designs on her calf.

Anyhow, Tex and I took no chances. As a single man, we dropped our packs and fled back onto the beaver dam. Something hit the water at my heels, and thinking it was the cow, I spun on the perilous footing to shoot.

It was the confounded calf. The misguided little beast had joined our wild retreat down the bank, only to tumble into the pond. It couldn't swim worth a doggone, but it was floundering toward me. The cow wasn't in sight. I had no idea where she was. While Tex stood guard, I waded in, got hold of one of the calf's legs and hauled it onto the dam. It lay there panting and coughing. Still no glimpse of the cow. Suddenly sore, I said, "This is ridiculous." I took the calf in my arms and headed back to our packs.

Tex was amused. "You figger to shoot pore old mamma if she gits tough?" he inquired. I told him that I would stand on the Fifth Amendment. It was only some three miles to the Toonakloot cabin, and after being away all winter, I wanted to get home. What happened in the next few minutes was strictly up to the cow.

I put the calf down where we had first seen it. We shouldered our packs and set out for home. But we hadn't covered 100 feet when I looked over my shoulder and saw the calf following. We shouted at it to go back; we made large, threatening gestures; I fired my rifle into the air. No dice. The calf joined us, looking up at me trustfully, and leaned against my legs. What could you do? The country was full of black bears. If the cow would not accept the little critter again, and we abandoned it, it wouldn't live 24 hours. Besides, even if we had wanted to, there didn't seem to be any way to desert it. In short, it appeared that we had a moose calf on our hands. We went on, the calf tottering behind. During the last mile, it began to stumble and fall. So Tex took part of my pack, and I carried the tuckered-out youngling the rest of the way.

By now we had named the calf Lucky, chiefly because it didn't seem that he was. At the cabin we fed him diluted condensed milk sweetened with canned honey. He ate it ravenously, and slept. In the morning we built signal fires in the dooryard—three fires in a row, banked with wet moss to make plenty of smoke—and a passing bush pilot saw them and landed. Tex went to Anchorage in the plane to sell our catch of furs, to consult a veterinary regarding the care and feeding of a young moose, and to bring back my hard-boiled Doberman pinscher Hey-You, whom I had boarded out during the winter. When he returned, he said that the vet had searched his reference books in vain, but had, by guess and by gosh, worked up a formula consisting of powdered mild, cod-liver oil and various vitamins. It must have been a good formula, for the calf thrived. Better yet, he and the tough Doberman became friends. This, as much as anything else, preserved the calf's life. The first run of salmon was in the creek, and the bears were on hand to meet them. Hardly a night passed that Hey-You didn't hurraw one out of the clearing. Any one of the shaggy nocturnal visitors would have been overjoyed to vary its diet with a fat moose calf.

Then, one midsummer afternoon, a family of Susitna-Denna Indians dropped in to pass the time of day. We were sitting under a dooryard birch, drinking tea, when the patriarch of the family, one Wasilla Stepan, let out a surprised grunt and reached for his rifle. Our Lucky was ambling across the clearing toward us. I knocked the rifle down and explained that the calf was a pet. Maybe the Indians believed me. Maybe they didn't. But when they had gone, Tex declared that Lucky had to be marked, and I agreed. So we threw the calf, and Tex swallow-forked his hears with his belt knife—the gotch mark of Texas cattlemen. Henceforth, anybody

who encountered the animal would realize, if he had a brain in his head, that it wasn't an ordinary moose. During his first summer Lucky did not see another moose, since the Toonakloot herds had departed on their annual migration to the foothills. He played with Hey-You, learned to browse willow and aspen shoots and grew at an astonishing rate.

With freeze-up and the first of the little snows, the herds returned, and as usual a dozen or more of the moose hung around the clearing to feed on slash we had piled up. I think they also liked the place because here they were reasonably safe from the huge, ever-hungry Susitna wolves. A barren black cow at once adopted Lucky, and with that he became a member of the herd in good standing. These were the good days in our part of Alaska. Most of the Susitna country was as wild as it had been at the dawn of creation. There were almost no settlers. The streams were full of fish, and there were moose, bears, grouse, ptarmigan and rabbits without end. Fur-bearers were plentiful. One could live in peace here. You were your own man. But it was too good to last. War drums were sounding. When we turned on the radio at night, the news from all over the world was grim. Then, suddenly, Pearl Harbor was bombed. Then Dutch Harbor.

Everything happened too fast. I found myself in the Aleutians as a war correspondent. After that came Guam, Okinawa, battles at sea and battles in the air. When it was over, I got aboard an aircraft at Shanghai and returned to Toonakloot as rapidly as engines and wings would carry me. This was in February and there were eight feet of snow. Moose had yarded up in the clearing, but Lucky was not among them. I asked the Indians about him. They had seen him, off and on, and had heard tales about him. They did not believe that he had been killed. He had, they said, a charmed life. His medicine was strong. For instance, he had wandered into the dooryard of an Alaska Railroad section house and gotten a clothesline wound around his antlers. The section foreman's wife, alone in the house, telephoned frantically up and down the railroad for help, asserting that a bull moose with weird ears was making off through the timber with her week's washing. The clothes, I gathered, were recovered, but the vengeful section foreman failed to catch up with Lucky.

From Forty-Mile Porter, a sourdough friend who stopped in at the cabin en route to the Deshkah country by dog team where he planned to lay out a beaver, trapline, I had another rare account of the gotch-eared bull. Forty-Mile said he had spent the summer up on Bacon Creek, to the north, trying to find gold where there wasn't any, and was returning to civilization in September when Lucky threw a scare into him from which, he feared, he never would recover completely. "I was mushing down that so-called trail that follows the creek bank," he related, "head-high grass on both sides and alders all around, carrying eighty pounds, swatting white-stocking flies and worrying about what was I going to use for money to finance a winter's outfit, when I heard a moose grunt off to one side in the alders. I didn't pay much attention. The rut was just starting, and up there you heard a lot of ambitious bulls bragging to cows about how big and tough and handsome they were—and how about a date? I just kept mushing on. Then, by gosh, there was a loud crashing in the alders, and out galloped an absolutely *huge* moose. I tell you, he looked as big as an elephant, his horns with the sun shining on them were wide as a barn door—and he was headed straight at me.

"Now you know as well as I do," Forty-Mile said, "that a bull moose in the rutting season can be an almighty dangerous animal. Worse even than a grizzly? Fact is, I believe, without any proof, that a lot of the men who disappeared in the boondocks and were thought to have been killed by grizzlies, actually were killed by rut-crazy bull moose. Anyhow, I took no chances. I just left my pack hanging in the air and leaped off the bank into the creek. I landed in an eddy, ice water up to my brisket, at the same instant that this bull reached the spot I had just vacated. I looked up at him and he looked down at me. That was when I saw that he was gotch-eared and knew he was your damned pet moose. I told him to go away, please; I reminded him of one time when I fed him some salt right here at this cabin; I explained I wasn't exactly comfortable and the eddy was trying to carry me out into midstream, where I would surely drown.

"He shook his horns and gritted his teeth, then looked over his shoulder to the patch of alders we had come out of. Maybe he had a cow back there and was worried about her. Anyway, he beat it, and boy, was I delighted to see him go. I tell you," Forty-Mile concluded, "that moose hasn't got any fear of humans at all. You spoiled him rotten when he was a calf."

I was living alone at Toonakloot. Tex was somewhere in the Nelchina country running a trapline, and he had taken Hey-You with him. But being alone was good after the ghastly business of war. I shoveled snow, kept the cabin clean and cut firewood. I reread my library of books and listened to the radio. It was pure anodyne. The only company I had was the local herd of moose, around twenty of the animals, which made the clearing their headquarters.

I knew them all by sight and had names for them. In the night I would hear them stomping about and snipping off frozen willow and aspen twigs, sounding like a battery of hedge clippers. They ruined my snowshoe trails by sleeping in them. The heat of their bodies would thaw bathtub-shaped holes in the trails, and when the snow crusted, it was like traveling over a boulder field. You had to be careful or you'd break more snowshoe frames than you had time to repair. The herd had a social system based on power and orneriness. Its current tyrant was a rawboned, coffee-colored character, who didn't seem to like any of his fellows. He didn't molest the pregnant cows and young stuff, but the bulls got out of his way when they saw him coming—or else. I named him Wild Bill.

One bitter night of a million blazing stars when the temperature had dropped to forty below zero, I heard a terrific commotion just outside my bedroom window. Grunts, wheezes, groans, and the sound of thudding hoofs. I got up and scraped enough frost off the windowpane so that I could see out. Two bulls were fighting. They were only a few yards distant, and I was able to recognize one of them as Wild Bill. The other seemed to be a newcomer. He was winning the battle. As I watched, he reared high and came down to drive his hoofs with pile-driver force onto Wild Bill's spine. Then, like a range stallion, he set his teeth in the hapless tyrant's neck and shook him. It was an educational demonstration of brute strength and savagery. Wild Bill managed to break free, but he'd had enough fighting. He galloped pell-mell off into the timber, with the other bull biting his rump at every jump.

I stoked the heating stove with chunks of green birch and went back to bed and was soon asleep. But it was destined to be an eventful night. Along in the small hours, I woke up with the unhappy knowledge that it was necessary to visit the outdoor privy. Cussing, I pulled on my moccasins, belted on a bathrobe and sprinted out to the small, peak-proofed structure set in a circle of aspen trees. It was plenty cold for a scantily-dressed man. Aurora banners flapped across the sky. Down on the creek bank the freezing birches were popping as loud as pistol shots. Presently, as I sat there, shivering all over, I heard a moose approaching and hastily slammed the door and latched it. The animal halted in the trench-like trail I had shoveled out, not ten feet distant, and snorted. I shouted threateningly at it to depart, but it snorted at me again and stayed where it was.

Desperate, thinking that this was a hell of a way for a sourdough to freeze to death, trapped in his own privy, I pounded on the plank door and did some more hollering. The moose didn't leave. At last I had an idea. I peeled off at least a dozen yards of toilet paper, wadded it into a tight bundle and felt in the pockets of my robe for matches. By luck I had some. I set fire to the paper, and when it blazed up, I jerked the door open and threw the ball of fire at the moose. Its light gave me a good look at the beast. It was a bull, a big one, antlerless, of course, at this season. Eyes shining, he stood there a split second gazing at me. His mule-like ears were turned forward—and they were gotched. It was Lucky. He wasn't hostile. He knew me, I figured later, and had just come out to bid me welcome home. But if he wasn't hostile, I was.

Leaning against the front of the privy was a six-foot length of two-by-four, left over from the construction of the edifice. I pried the piece of timber out of the frozen snow, as Lucky fled back down the trail a few yards and then turned again to watch me. Every northern woodsman has heard about moose charging men, but I'll bet that this was one of the few instances of a man charging a moose. Lucky tried to climb out of the trail into the moose yard before I reached him, but I succeeded in breaking the two-by-four over his backsides before he made it. I threw the pieces after him, then hastened back into the cabin to thaw out. The process required half-an-hour and a whole pot of black coffee. In the morning when I got up, suffering from chilblains in parts of my anatomy where I had never before had chilblains, the identity of the bull who had defeated Wild Bill soon became evident. Lucky was the new boss of the herd. He was running the show typical moose fashion, letting the other bulls know where they could feed, and threatening all and sundry if they came too close to the cabin.

After breakfast, I put some salt out for him. I sat on the doorstep and talked to him as I had when he was a calf. I really believe that he was glad to see me, to be back with me again on the homestead. As for myself, I was happy indeed that he had come home. He was a part of the good days before the world went mad, a part of a way of life soon to vanish forever.

The northern spring came. Patches of bare ground began to show on the southern slopes. I was trying to decide whether or not to put out a beaver trapline, when a telegram came requesting me to go to Hollywood. I flew to that remarkable place and from there to New York. What with one thing and another, I spent the entire summer in the States. Returning in September, I met Harvey, the retired transportation man, in Anchorage, and agreed to take him moose hunting. During my absence the metamorphosis of

Alaska had begun. Anchorage was booming, with two skyscrapers planned. Settlers were swarming north. Organized colonies had their sights set on the Susitna valley. The lost, lovely lakes of the valley had become priority targets of families who wanted private wilderness lodges as status symbols and as retreats where, the saying goes, they could get away from it all. Bush pilots had hit a pay lode flying in lumber, sheet iron, boat sections and household furnishings. All this in one summer.

When Harvey and I reached Toonakloot, the stream bars were littered with beer cans and assorted garbage typical of cheechako visitors. Where once a strange boot track would have been a matter for much speculation, there was now an untidy campsite at least every 100 yards. Somebody had shot the cabin's stovepipe full of holes. Some lumber I had left stacked in the yard had been carried away, probably for firewood. Two handsome birch trees under which I had often set up my writing table had been ringed for their paperlike bark and were dying. There is small point in endeavoring to explain how I felt, except to say that it was clear I had outlived the true wilderness and no longer belonged here. But Harvey thought that everything was just wonderful. To him there was nothing incongruous about moose tracks amidst tin cans, candy-bar wrappers and discarded egg cartons. We hunted three days, but saw only cows and young bulls.

Then, as I have told you, we took a stand on a cutbank above the sun-spangled creek, and I went to work with a birch-bark horn and a bull came to us, and Harvey killed it. I sat a while on the bull's shoulder, seeing twenty years of my life at Toonakloot gone down the wind in anticlimax. I measured Lucky's antlers. They were sixty-nine inches, a top head for the Susitna country. On the Kenai they run bigger. They are bigger in the Rainy Pass. Nobody has explained this. The Susitna valley is probably the world's most populous moose range, but something in the forage or water here limits the spread and weight of the bulls' antlers. Perhaps, I thought, the vitamins and cod-liver oil I had fed Lucky when he was a calf had given him an advantage over the other bulls.

"Did you notice," Harvey said, "that when this moose got our scent and you whistled at him, he came straight toward us instead of taking off into the timber? It was almost as if he knew you."

"We were acquainted," I said. "Maybe sometime I'll tell you about him."

Kill or Starve

Burned out: a phrase that strikes terror in the hearts of wintering woodsmen. As zero temperatures sap men's strength, they turn to the animals' code—KILL or STARVE.

"Holy cow! Do you see what I see?" With a forkful of sourdough hotcakes halfway to his mouth, my partner, old Jack Filce, was staring past me at something he had spotted through the cabin window. We were at breakfast, comfortably bivouacked at our trapline headquarters on the upper Wood River, on the northern slope of the Alaska Range. It was nine o'clock of a mean, sullen November day—a fateful day for us, it turned out. "Standing there in the snow big as life," Jack added, his voice unconsciously dropping to a whisper. "And boy, we can use him."

I swiveled around and craned my neck for a look. I don't know what I had expected to see, but certainly the animal I now beheld was a thundering surprise. It was a taffy-colored Toklat grizzly, the short-headed, roly-poly, humpless type that must have been the model for all the toy teddy bears in the world. Apparently a long-yearling, he was about a 300-pounder, fat as a prize pig. He was at the edge of the surrounding wall of spruce timber 200 feet distant, gazing dubiously at the cabin. I didn't hesitate to ponder on the phenomenon of a grizzly being at large in November. I just grabbed my rifle and prayerfully started easing the door open. Both Jack and I were fond of fat bear meat, as winter provender. Of course we preferred black bear meat, but grizzly meat would do, it would do nicely indeed.

The door creaked. I have never known a cabin door that didn't creak when I was trying to open in quietly. I couldn't see the bear, but Jack was watching at the window, and he said urgently, "There he goes." I flung the door open and ran outside, in time to catch a glimpse of the grizzly's rump disappearing into the spruces. Jack came out and helped me cuss our luck. We were still in our red flannel underwear, with worn-out moccasins on our feet in lieu of house slippers, because it is a dumb idea to wear trail clothes when cooking in a warm cabin. Your clothes get sweaty, and later you pay for it. Anyway, the point is, we weren't clad at the moment to pursue a grizzly in the snowy boondocks. "Well, shucks," Jack said, "he ain't reely spooked. We can track him down. We got the whole day ahead of us. But let us get started." He turned and stalked back to the cabin.

Forgetting breakfast, we changed into trail gear. I shoved a camp ax into my packboard, filled my tobacco pouch, and made sure I had matches and a whetstone. I closed the dampers of the Yukon stove. By now Jack was ready, waiting outside. When I joined him, he pulled the door shut and stuck a birch pin through the metal hasp to lock it. We were leaving everything shipshape and copacetic—we thought. The bear's trail led upriver, and the animal hadn't been running, so he wasn't spooked, only distrustful. There wasn't enough snow for the use of webs. The big snow winds hadn't come yet, and the river wasn't even completely frozen. For trappers it was the worst time of year, a time of waiting and preparing. We had been doing plenty of both. At Fairbanks we had arranged for Frank Dorbandt, the bush pilot, to fly a winter's outfit in when the river froze. We had walked in from Healy Station on the railroad, our idea being to cut wood, kill some meat and perform other necessary chores until the plane came and it would be time to string traps.

But game was scarce. The caribou hadn't arrived, and the famed bands of Wood River sheep were holding forth elsewhere, probably over on the Yanert side of the range. This fat Toklat long-yearling grizzly was the first meat-bearing critter we had laid eyes on.

"We'll catch up with him soon," Jack said. "He isn't going anywhere. He's just fooling around."

Jack spoke authoritatively. A little, white-headed guy with a Santa Claus beard, tough as whang leather, he was one of the original Yukon sourdoughs, and he probably knew as much about Alaskan bears as any man living. But he could make mistakes. We followed this Toklat grizzly for three hours without getting another look at him. The bear may have been just fooling around, but he did it energetically. Shortly after midday, he made a wide swing around a blowdown area and turned back downvalley toward our camp flat. Jack and I sat down for a rest. We were tired, cold and hungry. We hadn't expected to be gone more than an hour or so. The sky had turned gray, and you could see snow clouds moving down the bleak mountainsides. While we were sitting here, a thread of smoke caught my eye. Pale and wispy, it was rising from our camp flat. I nudged Jack, and pointed. Jack said, "We got company, hey?" Then, with sudden alarm in his voice, "Or have we?" The smoke was changing color. In a moment it was black, the smoke of burning birch bark. The roof of our cabin, beneath its insulating layer of earth, was waterproofed with birch bark shingles.

"Gawdamighty," Jack moaned, "the cabin's burning."

Two hours later, completely winded, we burst out of a jack spruce thicket onto the camp flat. The cabin was what is described in newspapers as a total loss. The roof and walls had fallen in. The dry spruce logs made a large, lovely bonfire. Already the short subarctic day was merging into purple twilight. Snow feathered out of the north. Neither of us had any good idea as to how the fire had started. Maybe the homemade safety flue was faulty. Maybe a spark had flown out of the stove while I was cooking breakfast, falling unseen into the kindling pile. At any rate, we were suddenly homeless and practically destitute. Our immediate chore was to make camp for the night. While Jack cut spruce boughs, I climbed into the stilt-legged cache and took inventory. The cache hadn't even been scorched, but its contents weren't reassuring. There was a ten-foot-by-twelve-foot tarpaulin, our snowshoes, a couple of caribou hides, bundles of traps, bottles of trap scent, a crosscut saw, some empty five-gallon cans, a few pounds of rice, a roll of snowshoe babiche and a pair of Mackinaw pants with a sizable hole in the seat.

I threw down the stuff we would need tonight, and we pitched the tarp lean-to fashion, where it would catch heat from the mound of coals and chunks of burning logs. For supper we had rice soup boiled in a can without sugar or salt. Later, Jack lit his pipe, whereupon I fired up mine, too. The only tobacco we had was that in our pocket pouches, and it was a cinch that if Jack ran out first, he would borrow from me, so there was no point in being conservative.

"If anything goes wrong and that airplane doesn't arrive, it's gonna be a long, tough winter," he said. "I been burned out before," he said, but never so doggoned thoroughly. We ain't even got an extra pair of socks between us."

"Listen. If you had your choice," I said "just one choice, what food-getting tool would you choose for a pair of sad characters in the kind of predicament we're in?"

"Oh boy, that one again," he said. "I've seen it kicked around in anyhow 500 magazines and books. But I'll tell you. I'd choose one that the boys always overlook—a beaver trap. And if I had me a beaver castor to go with it for bait, that sure would be a big help."

"Senile decay hasn't got you yet," I complimented him. "Not entirely. We got the traps, and I found some castors in the cache. Have a comfortable night's sleep, with sweet dreams. Tomorrow we go beaver trapping."

In the morning snow was sifting through the spruces, a steady, light fall of powder-dry flakes, the kind that stays until spring. We ate more rice soup and took off for a beaver pond we had passed yesterday. It was no great shakes of a beaver pond, just a dammed streamlet in against the mountainside where a stand of young aspen was available, with a new black-earth lodge humped up in the middle of it. At the pond's outlet there was open water, and here a beaver had crawled out last night and gnawed down a sapling. Judging from the size of the chips and the height of the stump, he was quite a beaver, no doubt an ancient blanket-sized customer, who had gotten weary of his relatives and moved out to enjoy a solitary existence.

During my life and times I had made a slew of beaver sets, and Jack had made more, but I'll bet that neither of us had ever taken such elaborate pains with one as we did this morning. Close at hand there were plenty of green saplings for bait—willow and alder and such—but I climbed the hill for a length of aspen, on account of, for reasons that they alone could explain, beavers are plain crazy about aspen bark.

I peeled the four-foot stick halfway down, letting the attached ribbons of bark hang free, so they would blow in the wind. I split the top of the stick and wedged a slice of castor into the cleft. This last was to frustrate any birds that might have a taste for castor. I gathered a double handful of the beaver's own chips, rubbed them with castor and tossed them out to float on the black water. By now Jack had chopped an underwater shelf into the bank, some twenty-inches below the surface, and arranged a trap on it. He toggled the trap chain to a spruce windfall, and we drove sharp deadwood guide sticks into the bank on both sides of the trap, underwater, to force the beaver to come straight into the pan. Then I stuck my scented bait stick into the frozen moss a couple of feet back from the set, where the beaver would see and smell it the moment he came out from his lodge and surfaced. He would think that a strange male beaver was moving in and, fighting mad, would hasten ashore to investigate. It was a hind-foot set. A beaver caught by a front foot will sometimes escape by wringing the foot off.

"It's okay," Jack said. "We'll have us a fine, fat beaver come morning. About a forty-pounder, I figure."

We had brought several traps, and I asked Jack if he thought we should go on to the next beaver pond, some three miles upvalley, and make other sets, or return to camp and construct a more comfortable shelter. He looked at the blank, snow-filled sky, laughed without humor into his tobacco-stained Santa Claus beard and replied that he voted wholeheartedly for the latter idea. He hadn't yet, he said, thawed out from last night. Partway back, a cock spruce grouse boomed up to alight on a limb thirty feet distant. It was a temptation, a gosh-awful temptation, but we had only twelve cartridges between us, and they would be precious when the caribou and sheep came back from wherever they were. We went on, the grouse cackling idiotically after us. At camp we gulped more rice soup from our five-gallon tureens and got busy building a barabara.

The barabara was developed by the sea-people who fringe the bitter Aleutian Islands with their misery. It is a sort of yurt, a round framework of poles covered with sod, earth or whatever is handy—inelegant but efficient, a place to crawl into when snow winds howl, and to dream wistfully of more sumptuous shelters. We drove willow saplings into the ground to form a circle ten feet across, bent the tops together and tied them with snowshoe babiche. Lacking a spade with which to cut sods, and fearful of risking our one ax in the rocky soil, we thatched the framework with spruce boughs and wild redtop hay and added a final covering of moss. This forest moss could be peeled off the ground in thick, blanketlike strips, and it made good temporary insulation. With a fire burning close outside the entrance, it wasn't so bad. Moreover, we now had the tarpaulin for bedding. Nightfall was upon us by the time we had dined on another bait of rice soup and smoked a pipeful of tobacco apiece.

"Tomorrow, with some beaver meat in our bellies, things will look a whole hell of a lot better," Jack said. "You wait and see."

I told him I could hardly wait. Toward midnight it ceased snowing, a million stars blazed in a black sky, pale aurora ghosts flickered, and the temperature dropped to a discouraging degree. I got up to replenish the fire. I felt rocky. My shoulders were stiff, my rice-abused stomach seemed to be adhering painfully to my backbone. Shivering, I went out beyond the firelight to drag in part of a snag we had cut. A shadow moved between me and the timber, and as I stared at it, a rasping snort rang across the flat. I sprinted back to the barabara, snatched up my rifle and threw some pitchy kindling twigs on the coals of the fire. When they flared up, I saw the green shine of a pair of eyes. In an instant they were gone. There had been no opportunity for a shot. Jack came surging out of the barabara, demanding to know what was going on. He had heard a bear snort, he asserted. Or was it me? I replied that I almost never snorted in bass, and carrying a blazing torch stick, we went out for a look. In the loose snow were bear tracks, heading toward the mountain, the tracks of a small grizzly. After making the appropriate profane comments, we built up the fire and went back to bed.

"Something mighty seldom about that bear," Jack grumbled. "Seems attached to this flat. I think maybe I am getting an important idea about him."

"He's an insomniac. Like you," I said. "Go back to sleep. So I can."

Next morning, in the first wan glow of light over the jagged eastern crests, we arose and sat glumly by the fire, thawing the frost out of our bones, while a can of rice soup boiled. It was snowing again, but still there wasn't enough on the ground for webs. A pair of ravens circled us, bonk-bonking musically, and went away. They knew a hungry camp when they saw one. Jack chewed on the stem of his pipe. Today, he said, he was going to gather aromatic red willow bark and mix it with the tobacco he had left. He had never smoked red willow bark, he said, but the Injuns smoked it, and he could do anything an Injun could do, watch him prove it. I took a searching, hopeful look at the pink-flushed mountains. No sheep trails yet. Or anyhow, I couldn't spot any. I sorely missed my binoculars, which were somewhere in the ashes of the cabin.

We ate, and took off for the beaver pond, slogging drearily through the dry snow, not talking. A rice diet, I thought, was rough on the morale of northern meat-eaters. Beyond the camp flat we cut the bear's trail. He had come downvalley to the flat straight as a surveyor's line, as if he had known exactly where he was going and why. Then, holy Moses, we sighted a porcupine. Yellowish, medium sized, it was climbing a slanting spruce windfall the top of which was lodged in two tall river birches. At the moment it was only a few feet above the ground, but it had seen us and was clawing for altitude.

Jack said emotionally, "Hallelujah—the hungry man's banquet," and broke into a stumbling run. "I never knowed it to fail," he said, throwing glances right and left as we bore down on the windfall. "When you need a good club, there ain't one within five miles."

Not that it mattered. When we arrived on the scene, the porky was twenty feet up on the snag, back humped, quills erect, peering defiantly down at us. I didn't want to throw my ax at him. I was afraid it would fall on a rock. So, when Jack had last found a club and was standing ready, I began hitching myself up the snag. It was icy and ridged with snow. Before I was midway to the porky, I feared that I was going to suffer severe frostbite where I had never suffered it before. The snag creaked and shuddered under me. This was likewise ominous, but I ignored it. The porky, confronted by a barricade of spike-tipped broken limbs, now elected to fight. Turning his back to me, he lashed his quill-armed tail threateningly. I was almost close enough to clobber him with the ax. I hitched myself cautiously closer. At this point the snag sunfished under me, there was a loud splintering sound and a warning yell from Jack.

I threw the ax away from me; nobody wants to fall twenty feet onto an ax blade. Then the snag fell, and I rode it down. It was a fairly rough landing. I hit so hard that I could swear that I bounced. A shower of limbs and the broken top of the snag followed. Next, the snow that had collected on the two birch trees followed, and there was plenty of it. There was so much snow in the air that you couldn't see anything. Into this white smother charged Jack. He was hollering, "Where is he? Where did he go?" I know that I don't look like a porcupine, but just then I didn't want to attract attention to myself. I'd had enough trouble for a while. Ahead of me, Jack's club swished and connected with an unmistakable, solid whump. Jack cried triumphantly, "Hah! Gotcha!" I lurched up and staggered blindly into the clear.

Jack appeared carrying the porcupine by a front paw. "Boy, we sure were lucky he didn't get into another tree," he gloated. "I think he's fat, too. An' bound to be tender," He paused. "What's the mater? You hurt or something?"

I informed him that I would never be the same again, and asked him to hurry and skin his doggoned porcupine, because I would surely refrigerate if I didn't start moving. It was a young porcupine, fat, and nearly all white meat, the kind of porky that old-timers like Jack called a chicken porky. Jack stowed the meat, with the heart, liver and kidneys, in his packboard, and we mushed on to the beaver pond. Here we encountered disappointment. A wilderness drama and feast had occurred, at our expense. We had caught a beaver, true, but the rich, life-giving meat of the critter had alleviated other appetites. The snow roundabout was paw-padded to ice. In the confusion of sign it was difficult to tell exactly what had happened. The certain thing was that a big blanket beaver had put a hind foot down on the pan of the toothed No. 14 trap, as planned, had climbed out onto the bank to take stock of the dire situation in which he found himself, and had unluckily wound the trap chain around a spruce root, so that he couldn't get back into the water. After that, a lot of things had taken place. I tried to figure it out and deferred to Jack. He filled his pipe and lit it with one of the twenty-odd matches we had left.

"Well, the way it looks, our grizzly friend et most of the meat," he said. "You see the tracks he left. But he had a mob of co-culprits. There was an otter here, an' a fox, an' about one hundred shrews, an' some ravens, an' gosh knows how many whiskey jacks. I think the grizzly killed the beaver. Or maybe it was the otter. Anyhow," he said, "we got the porky. So let's eat some of him."

We built a fire and broiled the hams and the loin on willow stick, and the tender white meat was wonderful. Full of juice and flavor. We broke the bones and sucked out the marrow. We licked the grease from our fingers. I felt, or imagined I could feel, a wave of new vitality and strength run through me. Jack said, "I've been thinking seriously about that bear." He shoved his beat-up muskrat cap to the back of his head and gazed into the little fire, eyes half closed. Jack had lived for years with the Indians. He was a member of the very exclusive Denna Bear-Killer clan. He had the right to wear the claw necklace, a privilege extended to not more than a half-dozen white men in all the north. He could, when he wanted to, put himself inside a bear's thoughts. I had seen him do it.

"That damn bear is an ex-mamma's pet," he said. "He hibernated with her because she didn't breed last spring. Now he yearns to join her den again, but she won't have him. She figures it's time for him to find his own den. So he's just hanging around waiting for her to start pounding her ear good. Then he'll sneak in an' cuddle up alongside, like before. He hopes." Jack was silent a moment, after which he said, "And where do you think that den is?"

"Tell me, Maestro," I said. "You're the guy who can think like a bear."

"It's on that rocky slope right above our camp, of course. "That's why sonny boy keeps coming back there. Such being the case, leave us go at once and kill us a few hundred pounds of grizzly meat. Not to mention the thick warm pelts, which surely will be a comfort."

That was jake with me. What he had said made good sense. I wondered why I hadn't thought of it myself. We returned to the place where I had seen the bear last night and took his trail. It led up through thickets of dwarf spruce to a rimrock. There was an overhang, with a dark cave entrance at the back. At the cave mouth, I saw movement. It was the long-yearling, but before I could line my sights, he ducked back in out of view. Jack put a hand on my arm. He had a faraway look in his eyes. He was thinking like a bear again. "Y'know," he said, "she might have had twin cubs, and took the runt into hibernation with her. In fact, I think she did. Let's go find out." He headed up to the overhang, a gaunt old man, Santa Claus beard blowing in the snow wind, rifle ready. When we were close enough, I pitched a rock into the cave.

Things happened. It was as if the mountain suddenly erupted bears. There were three of them all right, and they came out of that hole in the rock like woolly missiles. The long-yearling came first, with mamma biting at his rump, giving him the grizzly heave-ho, the old bum's rush. I don't think she suspected that there was a human in the valley. Behind her came an undersized long-yearling, proving Jack's thesis. It wasn't much of a shooting chore. As Jack said later, the only real danger was that we'd get trampled in the rush. At any rate, when the blasting was over, the three grizzlies lay dead on the snowy slope below the rimrock. Well, we had meat, and grizzly hides for bedding, and a barabara for shelter. During the day it had occurred to me that we could salvage salt from the burned cabin. I remembered where the salt sack had been. Let her snow, let her freeze. We could start stringing traps anytime. . . .

Two weeks later when Frank Dorbandt landed his Pilgrim on the river ice, he climbed out with a big grin on his weather-beaten face. "You trappers have the real life," he said. "No problems. Strictly back to good old nature."

"But it's a tough dollar," Jack said. "A very tough dollar. Break out the smoking tobacco, will you?"

Snowblind!

It was like looking into the jagged, white-hot flame of an icy furnace.
Yet nature is cruel, and a blind man
must live up to the rules—or pay with his life.

"He's a killer grizzly," whispered Olga, the Susitna-Denna girl lying beside me on the ten-foot-deep, heavily crusted spring snowdrift. "I think that in just a moment he will charge us."

I had to take her word for it—I was playing this one by ear. Snowblind! Never in my life had I felt more helpless. It was in Alaska, in the ragged, phantom-white Talkeetna range, in the narrow valley of stream flowing westward to the great Susitna River.

I could hear the bear moving about, his heavy claws rattling on the crust. I heard him snuffle and then blow out his breath in a sharp *whoosh* as he analyzed our scent. I knew, as well as if I could see him, what he was up to and why. He was out of hibernation too early, perhaps routed from his den by a snowslide, and was hungry and in an explosively savage temper. He had, Olga told me, found the carcass of a winter-killed moose. He was guarding it and wanted to feed undisturbed. As professional hunters will testify, a grizzly bear in the snow in spring is perhaps the orneriest beast native to the continent. He is sore at the whole world. His feet are tender, and the crystallized snow abrades them. Probably, because he hasn't eaten for some five months, he has a bellyache. I had handed Olga my .30-06, telling her, if she had to shoot, to hold on the bear's nose. The animal was about 100 feet distant.

"Here he comes," the Indian girl said, her voice high, but steady.

Blowie! went the .30-06. The grizzly bawled. I couldn't tell whether he was down or still coming at us. I reached for my belt knife. This, I told myself, was a hell of way to cash in, after all the bears I had dealt with in my time. But, if possible, I aimed to put eight inches of Swedish steel into the bear when he swarmed onto me. Olga worked the action of the gun to chamber another shell. *Ka-wham!* went the shot, and Olga wailed desperately, "He will not stay down."

"I've got to interrupt here to tell you how we happened to be in such an unlovely predicament. A few days earlier Jack Filce and I had flown into the Talkeetnas by chartered plane to trap beavers. Jack was a wiry, ageless little old-timer, one of the original Yukon sourdoughs, and a master hand at taking beavers through ice. But our project had been ill-starred from the beginning. The bush pilot we engaged put us down on a round timberline lake under the peaks, and when the plane came to a halt, its skis broke through overflow ice into a foot of water. At the pilot's frantic command, Jack and I unloaded our gear, whereupon, full-throttle, the guy began rocking the plane violently, splashing cascades of water over us and our outfit. The prop wash blew my fur cap a quarter-mile down the lake. By the time the pilot horsed the plane out of the overflow, Jack and I were sheathed in ice—and so was our gear. We stood there, knee-deep in slush, freezing, and watched the plane take off and disappear over the saw-edged mountain horizon.

"**W**e're in the wrong business," Jack gritted. "That daggoned pilot is warm and dry. An hour from now he'll be home, sittin' by the fire with his slippers on, guzzlin' a hot drink, happy because he's got another hundred bucks in his pocket—an' here we are." He surveyed the forbiddingly bleak lake shore. "You see any trees that look like they might make firewood?"

This last was a rhetorical question, because we didn't have any choice. The only trees on the lake's margin were a couple of dozen wind-tortured cottonwoods, but some of them were dead, with loose bark that could be pulled off in slabs to make first-rate fuel. We pitched our tent on fifteen feet of snow, set up the Yukon stove on the heads of spikes driven into green logs (the spikes served to prevent the log foundation from catching fire), changed into dry clothes, put a five-gallon can of snow on the stove to melt, packed the remainder of our ice-armored outfit to camp, rustled enough wood and bark to last through the night, and ate supper as the sun rolled down in a vast world's-end flare of saffron and crimson light.

With the coming of night, the temperature dropped, and a congealing wind sucked down the canyons, whirling sheets of snow dust against the straining tent walls and rattling the stovepipe wildly. As we got into our sleeping bags, we congratulated ourselves on having equipped them with inner mattresses of moosehide. The hollow hair kept out the cold as down filling, compressed by our bodies, never would have.

I said to Jack, "Have yourself a big medicine dream about lodges crowded with blanket beavers ready and eager to step onto a trap pan."

"Yeah. That would help," Jack said seriously. "But the trouble is, I got a pessimistic feelin'. My gosh, you ever see so much snow? Musta snowed day an' night up here the whole daggoned winter."

Next morning we left camp at first light to scout for beaver sign. Jack took the east side of the lake and I took the west side. As the snow crust was thick enough to support my weight, I carried my six-foot siwash webs over my shoulder. By noon I had covered about ten miles of country and had found only five beaver houses—hooded mounds stained yellow on top by the breath and body warmth of the beavers inside—all of them strung out along the lake's outlet in a rough, steep-sided canyon. It didn't look so good. I mean, unless Jack was having better luck, the area was no beaver bonanza. Heading back to camp, I struck the deep-wallowed trail of a bear. Probably a quarter of a ton heavier than I, he was breaking through the crust at every step. His trail led toward the lake, and half-an-hour later I sighted him. He was a fair grizzly, the color of light mahogany, long-snouted and with a big, ugly-looking head. He had heard me, and presently reared up, staring. I shucked off my right mitten, and with the .30-06 ready, began a cautious detour around the animal.

As I came abreast of him, at a distance of fifty yards, he dropped to all fours and roared at me. I should explain that I knew he was a male because of the placement of urine sign I had seen in his trail. I said, "Look, big stuff, I don't crave any trouble. I've got enough of that, and so have you. So how about taking it easy?"

I didn't want to kill him. We didn't need the pelt or the meat. Beaver meat is better than grizzly meat any old day, at least until you get plumb tired and sick of it and begin to smell like a beaver yourself. The bear whuffed and snorted, and humped himself over into the tops of some half-buried spruces, where he stood peering balefully at me. I went on. But I should have killed the shaggy cuss. Because he, or his twin, was to cause me some outrageously bad trouble. I reached camp toward sundown, and Jack was there drinking black tea Indian fashion, a lump of sugar held in his mouth, and looking unhappy. He had found only three beaver lodges.

"An' I ain't sure one of 'em is a beaver house," he said. "Could be it's a boulder. This," he said, crunching the lump of sugar and taking another gulp of tea, "is a hungry piece of country we got into, sure enough."

In the morning Jack decided to take some grub and traps and move over onto the next watershed to the north, because apparently there weren't enough beavers hereabouts to make trapping profitable for two men. As was customary with old-timers, he departed without ceremony, only saying that he'd see me at the railroad or maybe in town.

I spent the next three days shoveling snow, chopping and chiseling ice and putting out traps—setting the No. 14 tooth-jawed jump traps on the pond bottoms and using aspen poles as bait because, for some reason known only to themselves, beavers prefer aspen bark to any other. While thus engaged, I took five pelts, three of which would grade as blankets. One of the beaver carcasses I carried to camp for fresh meat; the others I left where I skinned them. I was doing all right, making around $50 a day. But on the fourth day, fate hauled off and kicked me in the head. The preseason grizzly, which I soon wished I had killed when we first met, precipitated a ghastly chain of events.

Angling down into the canyon shortly after daybreak one morning, I found that the grizzly had run the line ahead of me. He had killed and eaten a trapped beaver which had climbed onto the ice to avoid drowning and had thriftily carried away the carcasses I had left. It was a cinch now that he would hang around, that I was likely to encounter him at any time and that he would be dangerous. A grizzly protecting meat that he considers rightfully his can be a most unreasonable and aggressive beast. Toward midday, at the last trap, I pelted another good beaver, lashed the skin on my packboard and started climbing out of the canyon. This was a south slope, and the sun had been on it a couple of hours; as a result the crust wouldn't support me. I had to wear my webs. Making a steep climb on webs is a laborious, exasperating chore, especially when there are no brush or trees for handholds. Panting and cussing, I sat down to rest a dozen yards or so short of the top. In the distance I could see the broad Susitna valley, bare of snow, green with budding leaves, like another, happier world. I was regarding the prospect wistfully when, suddenly, I smelled bear.

There was no mistaking the scent. During my woodsy career, I had skinned out close to 100 bears. But the mountain breeze was eddying so trickily against the canyon wall that I couldn't tell where the scent came from. I resumed climbing, and just under the crest, got hold of a limb sticking out from a fallen spruce snag. As I was pulling myself up the final few feet, reaching for an overhanging alder top, the grizzly shoved his head over a wind-carved snow cornice so close above me that I could have hit him with my hat. In his mouth he held part of a beaver carcass, the guts dangling. Manifestly I had blundered upon his combination lookout and meat cache and had unfortunately arrived at mealtime. He dropped the mess of beaver flesh and innards and let out a bellow that could have been heard for a mile roundabout. My rifle was slung over my right shoulder. Certain that the bear was going to jump on me, but hoping he would demonstrate a bit first, I took the gun in my right hand while hanging onto the spruce limb with the other, thumbed the safety latch, shoved the muzzle practically into the bear's face and fired.

Everything happened. I saw hair and part of the bear's left ear fan into the air. At the same instant, my webs went out from under me, so that all my weight was on the spruce limb. The limb broke, and the bear either jumped at me or, dazed by the .30-06 slug, fell. Handicapped by the webs, the packboard and the rifle, I didn't have a prayer to operate. I rolled, pinwheeled and bellywhopped down the glassy slope. I caught glimpses of the bear, who was doing better, but not much better. The packboard kited over my head and one of the shoulder straps sawed into my Adam's apple, trying to break my neck. The snowshoe hitchings were up around my knees. I banged into a drift on the canyon floor with a bone-wrenching jolt, and sat up, dizzy, with all the wind belted out of me, to see the bear toboggan into another drift a biscuit-toss distant. He shook himself and lined out down-canyon without even looking back. When I was able to, I took inventory and concluded that, while I had lost some skin and gained some wonderful bruises, I wasn't badly hurt. I cut a limb from an aspen top and poked the snow out of the .30-06's barrel. I retied the snowshoe hitchings. I told myself that I had at least put my mark on the bear, and that if I ever met the gotch-eared so-and-so again, I would endeavor to do a better job of shooting.

At this point I missed my snow glasses.

It took a moment or so for the import of this to sink in. I didn't have an extra pair, and here in the high country, with the spring sun beating down, a man without protection for his eyes could quickly find himself in serious trouble. I had already suffered snowblindness twice and had been told by competent medics that if I fell victim to the malady again, I should place myself in the care of an eye specialist at once, or else. I searched an hour for the glasses, toiling back to the canyon rim, covering every foot of the route I had taken in my wild, tumbling descent. No luck. At last, giving up, I made for camp. My failure to include extra snow glasses in my personal gear had been, purely and simply, a boner. I knew better. It was just one of those mistakes that a man makes and pays for. By the time I reached the lake shore, I had a headache. The storm of light on the lake and the circling hills was a phenomenon difficult to describe. Mirage-like, the glare swirled and flowed, blotting out terrain features, making it difficult to tell an angle of depression from one of elevation. If you can imagine such a thing, it was like looking into the eye-piercing brightness of a furnace flame without heat. When I limped in through the lone stand of cottonwoods to the tent, I felt feverish and nauseated.

The symptoms were familiar. I was going snowblind again. Hoping that it was only a minor attack, I got into my sleeping bag and covered my head with the flap. Night fell, and I managed to sleep. When I awoke in the morning, I didn't need a medic to tell me that I was in a grim plight. My eyes felt as if they were full of sand. My vision was blurred. A single glance at the snow outside the tent flaps sent a stabbing pain through my head and brought on a gagging, retching spell. "This time, son," I told myself, "you've bought it. Fifty wilderness miles from nowhere and going blind. Somebody will find your wolverine-gnawed bones out here and wonder how a sourdough ever managed to get himself into such a stupid fix." I covered my head again and did some high-powered thinking. The way it added up, I could stay here in the tent until the grub ran out and then, if my eyes were still bad, starve. Or I could blindfold myself to shut out the light and try to make it to the railroad.

With some snowshoe babiche and a wool sock, I contrived a blindfold. Then I built a fire in the Yukon stove, made tea and boiled a beaver tail. Finishing the meal, I remembered that when I was a youngster on the fur trails, some of the old-timers had claimed that burning dried beans in a frying pan and letting the smoke rise into your eyes would cure snowblindness. It sounded ridiculous, but having nothing to lose, I tried it. Nothing happened except that I coughed and wheezed for a quarter of an hour, tears streaming down my face and my eyes ached worse than before. I got back into my sleeping bag and, eventually, slept. In the morning I decided to find out if I could hold an approximately straight course across country with my eyes blindfolded. I believed that I could. I wouldn't have to detour around thickets and blowdown, because those hindrances to travel were snowed under. By lifting the blindfold now and then to orient myself, I thought, I ought to be able to fumble my way to civilization. But I needed to make a check first.

It proved to be an educational experiment. Stepping clumsily into the hitching of my webs, and taking a bearing from the tent, which was pitched facing north, I set out westward. An aspen pole I had cut for beaver bait served as a staff. The moment I left the tent, I began losing confidence. I couldn't balance myself on the webs. I had the feeling that there was a drop-off just ahead of me and had to fight back a desire to lift the blindfold. I began to sweat. After ten minutes, I knew that something had gone very wrong. Instead of encountering drifts, hummocks and the exposed tops of trees, I was on smooth, level snow. I sat down and tried to pull myself together. After a while, I lifted the blindfold and opened my eyes. There was an instant of shocking pain before I replaced the blindfold, but through the red-shot, whirling dazzle, I had seen the tent. It was only about sixty feet distant. While doing my best to maintain a straight course, I had walked a half-circle, bearing to the left. I made for the tent, missed it the first time and had to lift the blindfold again.

I stoked the stove with cottonwood bark and stretched out on my sleeping bag. I was more resigned than scared. I had taken my last shot, and it had failed. There was nothing to do now, I told myself, but wait for the payoff. I want to make it clear that I was acquainted with the various touted methods of fending off snowblindness, such as blacking one's face with charcoal, wearing slitted, wooden "spectacles" which theoretically shut out reflected sun glare but enable one to see after a fashion and so on. I had tried most of them on occasion, and for me they didn't work. The likeliest anti-snowblindness device I had ever seen was one I picked up in a Japanese hut during the battle of Attu. It was a close-fitting mask made of fine, black-enameled screen. I didn't have opportunity to try it out, but I believe it might have been superior even to colored optical glass. There would be no danger of breaking the mask, and certainly it wouldn't fog.

After making some more tea and drinking it, I dozed off. Some time later, the barking of a dog woke me. At first I thought that it was a dream. But then, scrambling on my hands and knees to the tent entrance, I heard the clatter and squeal of a sled on the crust and human voices. Indian voices, speaking in the Susitna-Denna tongue. I recognized them. They belonged to Talkeetna Tom Stepan and his teenage daughter Olga. I just sat there leaning against the tent pole, listening to the two talk as they came in off the lake and thinking that no composer ever wrote music half as beautiful.

"Whassa matter you eyes?" Talkeetna Tom said by way of greeting. "You catch some snowblind?"

I told him that I had indeed caught some snowblind, that I was delighted beyond expression that he had dropped in and that I needed somebody to steer me out to the railroad. I explained why Jack wasn't here and told him about the grizzly and how I had lost my snow glasses. "Just get me out of here," I said. "For your trouble you can have this outfit and the trapline, such as it is."

Talkeetna Tom sat down beside me without answering. I understood what his trouble was. He was an old man, almost the last of a fading clan of Susitna-Denna. His squaw had died two years ago and his only son was a cripple, a polio victim. Spring beaver trapping was his main source of revenue. If he missed even a part of the season, he'd be on short cash the rest of the year. "I've got to get to a doctor," I said. "Maybe it's too late now. I don't know."

"We gonna take you to dat doctor," Talkeetna Tom said. "Don't worry no more about dat. But maybe it's better Olga goes with you. She knows all dis country well as I do. Me, I like to stay here. I gotta catch some beavers if I can. We figured mebby so plenty blankets up here where nobody traps. Same like you, I guess."

I said okay, I would certainly buy his proposition. Olga was a woods brat, a slender, clean-striding, high-breasted part Russian, whom I had known for most of her sixteen years. Pretty and animated, she customarily wore jeans and a red shirt, moosehide moccasins with knee-high, striped, mattress-ticking leggings and a caribou-fawn jacket, decorated with dyed porcupine quills. I wished that I could see her now.

She was one of the last sure-enough tribal girls of her people.

"You gonna have to walk," Talkeetna Tom said apologetically. "I got only one dog and a single-runner sled."

I assured him that there was nothing wrong with my legs, that all I needed was somebody to keep me headed in the right direction.

"You rest now," Olga said. "I think it is more better we start at midnight when there is no sun and the crust is strong."

I said okay, okay and maneuvered back to my sleeping bag. It was a long day and a longer night. I was just starting to pound my ear when Olga shook me and said it was time to start. She had some breakfast ready, and when we had eaten, she made up two light packs, and we set out, Olga leading me at the end of a cottonwood limb. It was easy going, and we made good time. I could feel the sun on my face when we slanted down into what Olga said was a narrow stream valley. Suddenly, in a tangle of spruce tops, she halted, and I heard her draw in her breath sharply.

"There is a bear somewhere ahead of us," she said. "His claw marks are here in the crust." She left me a moment. "There are some spots of blood," she added when she returned.

"You know how to use this rifle?" I asked her. She said that she did, and I handed her the weapon. I heard her lift the bolt to make sure the gun was chamber-loaded. "If you sight the bear," I said, "tell me fast how far away he is and what he is doing."

We mushed on, and I was thinking that, holy Moses, it was fantastic that with all of Alaska to roam around in, this one particular grizzly had to keep crossing my trail. The blood spots, of course, made it practically certain that the bear ahead of us was the one I had bullet-grazed back on the canyon rim. Probably, since I had stopped providing beaver meat for him, he was heading for the lowlands to take on a diet of green stuff. We had traveled another hour and were in timber now, with the sound of open water somewhere near, when Olga halted again and put her hand on my shoulder with a warning squeeze.

"I see the bear" she whispered. "It is close, feeding from a dead moose. A winter-killed moose. One that my father and I saw when we came in." She was silent for half a minute. Then, "The bear has winded us. He is standing up on his hind legs, and he is angry."

I took Olga's hand and pulled her down to the snow. "Easy," I whispered. "Don't start anything. But if he charges, hold on his nose—and keep shooting. Feed him every slug in the gun."

Well, as I told you at the beginning, the grizzly made his rush, and Olga opened up on him and then said, sounding frightened, that he wouldn't stay down. I had my knife ready, intending to sell out as dearly as possible. The .30-06 blasted again, and the bear uttered a strangled bellow that ended in a kind of sobbing whine. I could no longer hear the animal's claws on the crust. Olga fired twice more, "He is dead," she said between her teeth. He is plenty dead now."

I said that I hoped so, but that we should wait a while. I fished some shells out of my parka pocket and gave them to her. She reloaded. When it was certain that the grizzly was finished, I asked Olga to do me a favor. We couldn't take the hide with us, I said, but

I wanted a trophy from this troublemaking, hard-boiled lout of a bear. I asked her to cut out the animal's genital bone. I wanted to have it made into a pen holder, I explained, so that every time I wrote anything, I would remember what the confounded bruin had done to me, and what it had got him.

Olga laughed and said to wait. When she returned with my pen holder, she said that heretofore she had thought that only Indians really understood revenge, but now she had changed her mind.

We continued on, and after a while Olga said that the sun was going down. We made camp on bare ground beside a free-running stream. I could smell ferns and new grass. After a supper of rice, bannock and bacon, washed down with tea, we unrolled our sleeping bags and turned in. The fire sounded good. A wolf howled. A horned owl hooted his spooky warning that he was hungry.

I said, "If you had a pocketful of cash, what kind of present would you buy for yourself in Anchorage?"

Olga thought a while, then said, "Why, all my life I have wanted a pair of shoes with high heels behind."

I said, "What color?"

She thought some more. "Red," she said. "Oh, yes, red."

I told her it was an admirable choice. Before I went to sleep, I heard a locomotive whistle, far and lonely across the springtime flat.

Eighteen hours later we were in Anchorage. I asked Olga to tell old Jack's cronies at the Sourdough Club that he would come to town sooner or later, and that I hoped he was pelting a slew of blanket beavers. An eye specialist worked me over and said that I was lucky. With treatment, he said, my eyes would be all right in a few days, but if I was ever so careless or unfortunate as to become snowblind again, it might be for keeps. Olga was waiting in the corridor. I asked the medic to excuse me because I had something important to do downtown. He wanted to know, making conversation, if I were going to sell some furs. I said that that wasn't it.

"I am going to buy," I said, "a pair of shoes with high heels behind. Red ones, because a girl can always walk faster in red shoes."

Waiting for the Caribou

In the old days, Jack and his Indians would knock off twenty-five or so animals and sell meat to trappers.

"Well, dammit, we can't wait much longer," Buck said. "In fact, I think we've waited too long already. Maybe the caribou aren't coming this year."

He hitched up his suspenders and gazed without enthusiasm at the gray late-October morning sky, at the rocky waste of river bars, at the brilliant, frost-painted cottonwoods and willows that were already dropping their leaves.

"I wish," he said solemnly, "that Caribou Jack's ghost would walk tonight."

"You ever see a ghost?" I asked him.

"No. And I never yearned to. But I'm all set to welcome Caribou Jack's spook, if he'll just pay us a visit."

This cultural exchange was taking place outside the long-abandoned Rhone River trading post in Alaska, some 200 miles from civilization. Buck and I were at the tag end of a monumental pack trip. Since May we had been on the trail with a string of ten horses, threading our way westward from Mt. McKinley National Park through the beautiful Alaska Range wilderness, exploring, fishing nameless lakes and streams, having fun in a large, primitive way. In September we had killed bear, sheep and moose. Now we wanted to take a caribou trophy before beating a hasty retreat back to the railroad. It was a ticklish matter, because if heavy snowfall caught us, we would be in bad trouble. Like Buck, I thought that perhaps we had waited too long. The rabbits and ptarmigan were turning white. Aurora banners flamed in the night sky. Even the wind, combing through stripped branches and frost-killed grass, had an ominous, threatening sound.

"It isn't just that I want a Rhone River caribou trophy," Buck explained for the dozenth time. "I want to see a real caribou migration, the kind the old-timers yarn about. It could be I'll never get another chance."

I was sympathetic. Since the buffalo ceased thundering across the Sioux prairies, our greatest wildlife spectacle has been the dramatic annual march of the caribou hosts. Once, when I was a youngster and Caribou Jack was operating this trading post, I had watched the caribou gather here. You understand it was back in the bad days of the caribou-salmon economy, the days of fantastic slaughter. There came an October morning when an Indian employee awakened us with the glad shout, "They come—the caribou!"

We had been nervously awaiting them for days. Everybody along the 1,000-mile migration track was waiting, the inhabitants of the lost, forlorn villages, the trapping camps, the missions, the trading posts. When the caribou came, there was food aplenty and skins for clothing. If they didn't come, famine and death were certain.

While they waited, the Indian and Eskimo shamans made medicine day and night. The mission priests prayed. The hard-boiled, bearded sourdoughs worried, grew silent, kept their eyes on the stream bars and the autumn-colored passes. Most remembered grim years when, unaccountably, the caribou had changed their migration route, and petitioned various gods, saints and demons to prevent it from happening again.

"They come—the caribou!" the Indian yelled, sprinting to the wide front door of the post.

We had heard him the first time and were dressing, snatching glances out of one window or another while pulling on pants and boots. At first it was only a trickle of caribou, the point of the migration, a few small bands merging on the gray gravel bars—maybe 500 animals. But they made a brave, thrilling sight, with their polished antlers and snowy capes agleam in the early sunlight. It put a shot of adrenaline into your bloodstream, sent a primordial shiver up your spine. They plunged across the fretwork of muddy channels, swimming high, buoyed by their coats of hollow hair, and slanted across to the deep, timber-fringed pea-vine flat on which the trading post stood.

Caribou Jack at this time had ten Indians working for him. He had, I must explain, married a pretty Kuskokwim Denna girl, and when her immediate family, together with assorted uncles, cousins and nephews, moved in joyously to share her new-found bounty, he put them all to work on a no-work, no-eat basis. They cut timber and built the trading post for him, after which the greater number of them became discouraged and moved on, anathematizing Jack as a tight-fisted slavemaster who had no proper feeling for kinship. But he had ten able-bodied tribesmen left, and this morning he deployed them like a general.

"Three of you hide in the bushes at the far end of the flat. The rest of you stay here," he rasped.

He was a short, easy-moving man, built like a good, lightweight fighter, with eyes as bright and hard as blue knife steel.

"Let 'em come up out of the water. You hear? Don't nobody start shooting until I do. And use those sights. That's what they're for. The trouble with you Injuns is, you get excited and think you're still using bows and arrers."

The caribou came lunging up a cutbank onto the lawnlike pea-vine sod, antlers clattering, hoofs clicking. They made the ground shake. They were so close, 100 yards, that you could smell them. At Caribou Jack's order, we had lined up, kneeling, along the front of the main building. The caribou knew we were here, and as they topped the cutbank, they rolled their eyes and grunted. But they held their tight formation, as traveling caribou always will when they can, because they believe that their safety is in numbers and the judgment of their leaders. As proof of the latter, I once saw part of a migration slam through the frozen streets of Fairbanks, ignoring gunfire, cheering citizens and a mob of hysterical sled dogs, all because the ribby old bat of a cow leading them had decided in a moment of lunacy that she was on the correct route north, and the devil with the consequences.

Caribou Jack held his fire until the herd passed us. Then he raised his long-barreled .30-06 and dropped a bull in a kicking half-somersault. In a second everybody was shooting. The caribou fled pounding across the flat, whereupon the three Indians concealed in the bushes there stood up, firing and yelling. The herd turned, milled in confusion, then ran the cross-fire gauntlet to the closest timber.

When it was over, twenty-five caribou were down. I saw cripples among the spruces. A wounded yearling got up with guts dragging, ran until its feet tangled in them, and fell again. The Indians were whooping and laughing. Now would come the knife work, the skinning and gutting, and the chore of hanging the carcasses in the big-platformed meat cache.

Tonight there would be a feast: red meat, marrow bones to crack, raw liver with a touch of gall on the knife point to add flavor. Later, when snow winds blew and mushers came toiling in over the mail trail from salt water and the far reaches of the Yukon, Caribou Jack would supply meat for them and their dogs, at fifty cents a pound. We had, Caribou Jack said, done all right for a start, but he hoped the weather would turn colder before we made another killing. Meat was expensive, he said, and he hated to lose it. Most folks didn't realize how much ammunition ten Injuns would burn to knock down a measly twenty-five caribou.

Well, all that was ancient stuff, mossy historical color that probably no historian would ever write. Buck and I, sweating out the caribou and our special weather-logistics problem, ate breakfast in the bat-haunted trading post kitchen, then saddled up and rode east on the old Rainy Pass trail.

Two bull moose, their wet coats black, trotted ahead of us to shake their antlers belligerently before vanishing into the timber. Buck spotted some white rams on a crag above Dalzell Creek, and we watched them a while with our glasses.

Finding no caribou sign, we turned back. Buck was plenty durable, a hard pilgrim to discourage. Hailing from Tennessee and weighing 140 pounds, all whalebone and rawhide, he had hunted big game all his adult life, had spent five years with me in Alaska and Mexico. He could take it. But this morning he was sunk in black pessimism.

"I hate to say so," he declared, as we rode back with the rain whanging against us, "but if Caribou Jack's ghost doesn't appear tonight, we're licked. This rain could turn to snow any minute."

He had heard about Caribou Jack's ghost while we were foregathered one afternoon with the Hootlinana Kid, an Ophir Creek miner, in a bootleg home-brew parlor in Anchorage. Things had been getting tough for Caribou Jack, the Hootlinana Kid said. Times were changing too fast for him. The age of aviation had dawned with a bang over Alaska, and such pioneer pilots as Frank Dorbrandt, Joe Crossen and Matt Neiminen were flying freight and passengers pretty well all over the north. It was rumored that they would soon get the mail contracts. If they did, 100 trading posts on the mail trails would abruptly go out of business.

Jack stubbornly refused to believe that such a thing would ever happen. The airplane, he asserted, was only a fad, and a dangerous one. He himself was betting on the Malamute sled dog, and the proved ways that had made this territory what it was. He still had his Indians, a dozen or so now, and he dog-freighted trade goods in, put up salmon and sheefish, killed caribou and bought furs. Of course the Indians were getting to be a problem. Some of them could read and write nowadays—the work of the missions—and they kept wanting to be paid in cash for their work, instead of in credit on the trading-post books. But everything was all right. Times were going to get better and better.

"He was a friend of yours," the Hootlinana Kid said to me, highballing a waiter for another round of home brew, "so you know that in his last years Caribou Jack was going off his rocker. You heard about the dimes?" he asked Buck. "Well, in the early days the sourdoughs hated small change. They would accept a quarter sometimes, but nothing smaller. Shucks, I've seen two-cent postage stamps sell for a quarter at Fairbanks. Caribou Jack especially loathed dimes, don't ask me why. When he had to accept them, he took them out of circulation by tossing them into a five-gallon kerosene can he kept under the counter. He told me that sooner or later he'd have every dime in Alaska. Then he would heave the lot of them, he said, into the river. I know that when he at last went completely haywire and killed himself, he had at least three gallons of dimes in that confounded can. I never heard who salvaged them. Anyhow, he was going batty, and that was the autumn he killed 150 caribou.

"I was there," the Hootlinana Kid said, "waiting for some of his Indians to freight an outfit into the Stony River country for me, and what happened was the kind of thing a man wakes up at night remembering. The little family bands of caribou were funneling down from the high summer pastures, from the Rainy Pass, from Ptarmigan Valley, from the Holitna and the Hoholitna, from the Rhone headwater and from clear over in the Happy River country. They were gathering out in front of the post, and I suppose their ancestors had since the beginning of time. Ten, twenty, 100 animals in a group. The rut wasn't quite over, and they were making a big party of it, getting acquainted, fighting, making love, choosing leaders, squaring away for the long trek north. Caribou Jack waited. He didn't trust the weather. For a week he didn't kill a caribou, and he wouldn't let the Indians make a kill. He had to have freezing temperatures, so the meat would keep. Finally he was satisfied, and he and his Indians maneuvered the herd onto the Rhone River pea-vine flat. These Indians, after some years of Jack's training and hard discipline, had become competent mass slaughterers.

"Of course, probably the buffalo hunters, the hide peddlers, the bastards who shipped barrels of pickled buffalo tongues to eastern markets, would have done better—if you look at it that way—because they had the cold North Atlantic blood. Their race invented the rifle. But Caribou Jack and his tribesmen put down, as I said, 150 before the herd of maybe 10,000 swung back onto the river bars and made its getaway. Then Caribou Jack's troubles began. The Indians wanted to divide the carcasses, half and half, and began building a meat cache of their own. Jack bullied them out of it. They still respected him, you see, but mutiny was in their hearts. They dutifully hung the carcasses in his cache, all right, and Jack gave them some credit on his books for their work, as he always had.

"That night, though, the Indians gathered at a fire at the other end of the flat. They roasted marrow bones and some heads, and there was singing and drumming. Quite a lot of drumming, with sticks on a spruce plank that two men carried on their shoulders around the fire, and the songs weren't mission hymns. They were still at it when I dropped off to sleep. Before daylight I was awakened by a sound I hadn't expected to hear until spring—rain on the roof. A hard, lashing downpour. Caribou Jack was up, cussing his head off. Raving. 'Those damned Injuns did it,' he shouted as I joined him in the lamp-lit trading room. 'They were drumming for rain. You heard them. Now the rain's come, and they've all pulled out, my wife with them, blast her eyes. And as soon as the weather turns cold again, I've got to kill at least another 150 caribou. Maybe with no help. Because, you know, there's going to be a lot of business come in over the trail this winter, mister.' He was pacing up and down, gesturing, his long hair tangled, moccasin strings dragging. He hadn't put on a shirt, but was wearing that old caribou fawn jacket with the dog-rib, porcupine-quill patterns on the sleeves, the one he claimed had always brought him luck.

"I think it was then I realized he was really crazy," the Hootlinana Kid said. "'Another 150 caribou,' he shouted, 'because there'll be a slew of hungry mushers and dogs to feed this winter. The country is booming—booming. People don't understand.'"

"I went back to bed. When I got up, it was still raining. I headed for the kitchen and made some coffee. There was nobody around. While drinking the coffee, I thought about the tragic loss of all that caribou meat—the rows of carcasses in the platform cache, souring. Food for the ravens and foxes. A senseless sacrifice. Or some sort of wilderness judgment. You name it. I stepped out for a look at the sky. There wasn't much light yet, but suddenly I saw something suspended from the cache that hadn't been there before. Something hanging from a beam, turning slowly in the rain-wind. I ran toward it, hollering for help. Nobody heard me. There was nobody to hear. Well, Caribou Jack had climbed up the cache ladder, put a slipnoose of babiche around his neck, tied the other end to a beam and kicked the ladder over. He was as dead as the caribou carcasses above him.

"Well, everybody knows the story," the Hootlinana Kid said. "The trading post was abandoned after that. The Indians never came back. Traffic over the trail had ended—poof—just like that. Airplanes were carrying the mail, the freight, the passengers. They had been all summer. Oh sure, a few hunters—sportsmen—made the place their headquarters for a week or so in the fall. Some claimed they saw Caribou Jack's ghost, and that when it walked, the caribou came the same day. Me, I dunno. I'm no authority on ghosts. I've never seen one. . . ."

Buck and I rode down off the Rainy Pass trail to the trading post flat, and in the last timber a flock of sharp-tailed grouse got up with a fine roar of wings and scattered to alight in their typical fashion, each in the very top of a spruce. I don't know why they do this. No other grouse does it. You would think that evolution would have eliminated the habit or the species, because it makes them so vulnerable. You can see a sharp-tail as much as a half-mile distant when it is thus idiotically perched in a treetop. But, as the saying goes, it was no epidermis off my posterior. I was all for it. Buck and I needed fresh meat. We each carried a .22 and just rode from grouse to grouse, as they waited in happy imbecility, and banged away until we had enough for supper. They were fat young birds, and their crops were crammed with fermenting blueberries. There may be more savory provender than broiled breast of blueberry-fed sharp-tail grouse, but I don't know what it is. I'm not even interested. Buck and I went onto the trading post, changed into dry clothes, cooked our epicurean meal, and ate while twilight came on and a rising wind cried under the eaves.

There were some twenty-year-old magazines in a cupboard. We lit candles and read a while, getting a kick out of the illustrations and the advertisements, then turned in. I heard the rain cease and the wind die. I woke up briefly when silver moonlight poured through the window. Some time later, one of the horses snorted. That is a sound that will jerk a wrangler awake quicker than the best alarm clock ever invented. I was on my feet fumbling for my boots, I'll bet, in two seconds flat. I found the boots, picked up my rifle and headed for the front door. This was grizzly and wolf country, and while it is rare indeed that these big predators will attack horses, they will stampede a string so thoroughly that assembling it again becomes a major project. As I hurried through what had been the trading room, I saw that Buck was up ahead of me. Indistinct in the wash of moonlight from a window at the far end of the room, he was mumbling to himself.

"Now I gotta kill another 150 caribou," I heard him growl as I went out the door.

I thought, what the hell, that's Tennessee humor for you, and turned to say something or another, but then a couple of horses snorted and hobble chains rattled, so I went on. The string was at the rim of the timber, facing upwind, alert and spooky. Talking to them, calling them the five-fingered names that wranglers apply affectionately to scared horses to make them feel secure, I got hold of the halter of my saddle mount. I had it made then, no matter what happened.

The horse was a tall bay gelding named Moose, and he was trying to inform me that something terrible was off yonder in the moon-dappled timber, about to descend upon us. I told him it couldn't be that bad, and would he hold still, please, until I got his hobbles unbuckled. Presently, with the hobbles over my arm, I swarmed aboard him, and started the string back onto the flat. I saw Buck walking toward the ruins of the old meat cache. He was wearing, I thought, my caribou fawn jacket, one I had bought a decade ago at Fort Norman, Canada, because it was decorated with the prettiest dog-rib quill designs I had ever seen—a better jacket by a long shot than the one Caribou Jack had been so proud of. I was framing a sarcastic comment to the effect that Buck could afford to wear his own clothes, since Tennessee cotton had sold for a fancy price this year, when Moose pivoted on his hind feet and came down trembling all over.

Then I saw them. Caribou moving out of the timber, moonlight on their capes and antlers, and more caribou on the bars. It was the migration. I hazed the horses to the trading post, tied Moose and

Buck's mount. As I was wearing only boots and underwear, and it was cold, I hurried inside to dress. When I passed Buck's room, a match flared from the darkness.

"What's goin on?" Buck wanted to know.

I pushed the door open. He was sitting up in his sleeping bag. He was wearing a ridiculous pair of bright green flannel pajamas he had bought in Seattle because, he insisted at the time, it had been scientifically proved that green was a restful color. He lit a candle, and I went in and sat down on his bunk, my knees suddenly weak.

"You got insomnia or something?" he said. "You look kind of funny."

I said it was natural. The doctor, I said, had remarked on it when I was born. Then I beat it into my room. My dog-rib jacket was where I had left it.

Returning to Buck, I said, "Have you been outside tonight?"

"Well, once," he said. "I had to get up. Drank too much tea, I guess. Why?"

I ignored that one. "Come out and have a look at the caribou," I said. "We are practically surrounded." And I was thinking that I ought to get in touch with the Society for Psychical Research.

There really isn't much more I can tell you. When there was shooting light, Buck killed a nice caribou. We packed up and beat most of the snow to the railroad. It got tough in Highway Pass, but we headed north out of the mountains and made it through in good condition to Healy Station. I didn't tell Buck what I had seen and heard at the trading post. No guide wants the reputation of being a guy who sees ghosts. Besides, maybe it was Buck in his green pajamas that I saw. Moonlight is tricky. Anyway, when you come north for your caribou hunt, why don't you try the Rhone River flat? It's a swell spot for caribou. But don't expect me. I'm pretty sure I won't be there.

Long Hunter, Alaskan Style

Sports Afield's *favorite storyteller begins a two-part tale on Tex Cobb—famous hunter and woodsman who became a legend in his own time.*

PART ONE

The ragged, hay-colored, high-jumped old sow grizzly was on the warpath, kill-crazy, as savagely hostile as an Alaskan grizzly can get without tearing something apart, a log or a bush if it can't do worse. I had her and her two brown spring cubs full in the field of sixteen-power glasses and she was, this pretty July morning, the very type portrait of bruin frustration, a natural killer with a mad on and nothing to kill. Nothing she could get hold of, that is. Her slat-thin sides heaved. Foam dripped from her flews. She was trying to glare in seventeen directions at once.

My partner, old Tex Cobb, was the presumably innocent cause of her spectacular tantrum. At the moment Tex was hunkered behind a boulder some 100 feet up the steep, alder-jungled mountainside from her, endeavoring to resemble a piece of the scenery. He didn't have his rifle—it was standing against a sapling back where the drama began. He had been carrying an ax, but had abandoned it as a mere encumbrance, since his strategy was based on mobility. Besides, there is nothing in the records to make anybody optimistic about battling a grizzly with an ax.

I have no idea what grievance the bear had against Tex. He claimed later that he hadn't molested her in the least. Perhaps the cubs had spooked and squalled when they got his scent. Or perhaps the enraged sow and Tex had met before in circumstances that she remembered and resented. Anyway, when the fracas began, he had been cutting a trail up through the alders from the gravel bars of Hunter Creek to a high Chugach pass we hoped to use as a pack-horse route come the next sheep and goat season. I had gone down to the mouth of the creek for a pack of grub and was sweating it back up the bars when, high above me and across the roaring, milk-white stream—a good 800 yards distant—I was astonished to see Tex soaring down over the alder tops. There is no other word for it; that is what he was doing—soaring.

The alders here are tough, tangled and interfretted, bludgeoned down by the weight of winter snows they have borne, a growth so dense that often a man caught in it can't see more than the length of a riffle ahead. Standing about five feet high and covered with glossy green foliage, this jungle is the curse of the north, the bane of honest woodsmen. Ordinarily, the technique of coming downhill through such alders is to back down, pushing with your legs to force a way. You cover maybe a half-mile an hour. But Tex, being in a great hurry because of the grizzly, had improved on the old, slow method. As I watched, he would leap outward from the nearly vertical mountainside and, arms spread, toboggan—all right, soar—down over the brush tops until he broke through. When I first spotted the grizzly, she was right behind him and gaining fast. I guess Tex realized she was gaining. At any rate, he changed course and technique abruptly. Scuttling on his hands and knees, following what appeared to be a goat trail, he headed around the mountain on a contour line. The bear blundered past him, busting through the brush like a woolly tank, until she realized that Tex was no longer ahead. It was here that she put on the tantrum I have described. Finally she got smart and started searching back up the slope, and at this point, Tex took to the alder tops again

I dropped my pack and tried several shots, holding as fine and carefully as I knew how, but aware that I couldn't have hit the bear at that distance, in that brush, in 100 years. I doubt that she even heard the shots above the thunder of the creek. If she did, they didn't faze her. She was a grizzly with one thought in her head this morning. I watched the bizarre decathlon with my glasses until Tex went out of sight over the brow of a ravine, the bear tearing after him, the two fat brown cubs bringing up the rear. Then, abandoning the pack of grub, I sprinted up the stream bars toward where I estimated he would eventually appear if the grizzly didn't catch him. Passing our tent camp and the bridge we had constructed, I rounded a bend below the ravine's mouth, and here I found Tex. He was on this side of the creek, sprawled with his back against a rock, panting like a spent draft horse. He raised a hand in greeting, a big, rawboned man, craggy-shouldered, bearded, with swamp-green eyes and a mane of iron-gray hair that swung almost to his shoulders. I don't know how old he was then. I never really did know how old he was. Give him fifty-five or sixty.

"Honest, I was jest choppin' alders," he panted. "Mindin' m' own business. Enjoyin' the sunshine. My rifle thirty feet behind me against a saplin'. Then all of a sudden here comes that damn bear swarmin' outa the brush, foamin' an' bellerin'. So," he said, "I went away from there. Lost m' hat. Lost m' pipe. Lost m' ax. But, by gad, I lost the damn bear too, blast her lights an' liver."

True, the bear seemed to have gone elsewhere. I couldn't spot her. I was about to comment on Tex's unique method of getting through alders in a hurry, or rather over them, when I observed that he wasn't wet. Of course he had somehow forded the creek, since he was on this side, an incredible feat, considering that a horse couldn't have crossed it at this time of year, but still you don't ford any fast stream without getting wet. I sat down and did some thinking. It didn't get me anywhere. At last, the pressure becoming too great, I said, "All right, I'll bite. How did you get across the creek?"

Tex's gaze followed mine to his bone-dry pacs and pants. He registered bewilderment, or expertly counterfeited it. "Why, be daggoned if I remember. Things were kinda busy. Musta flew across, huh?"

I couldn't supply a better theory just then. Later, however, I discovered that around the next bend close upstream there were some huge, tumbled boulders in the creek that a man could cross on by leaping from one to another, assuming he was desperate enough, and obviously Tex had been. But it was typical of him—a part of his woodsman's mystique—to make a good yarn of it. Tex possessed all the qualities of a great long hunter. He was powerful, with the lean stamina of a timber wolf; he could think fast in an emergency; he thrived on solitude; he was a close, accurate observer; and he had a natural sense of terrain and weather. But I think that it was chiefly his humor that brought him close to the status of an Alaskan folk hero. Men who never knew him spun campfire tales about his exploits, some of them doubtless invented on the spot, most of them tall, all of them funny. Even his death at the age of ninety had the stuff of legend in it. It was the newspapers,

Louise Lepina ©96

incidentally, that put his age at ninety, not me. But it's a good, round figure.

One autumn we signed up two New England sportsmen for a sheep hunt, and in advance of their arrival, backpacked some grub and gear into the towering jumble of glaciered peaks near the headwaters of Carpenter Creek, in the Chugaches. It was raining when we reached our camp with the first packs, an icy, dismal downpour driven by mean gusts of wind. Across the creek, at the first line of cliffs above a tilted blueberry meadow, a band of six Dall rams were bedded down. We were out of fresh meat. We were cold, wet, tired and hungry. I don't know about Tex, but I had that what-in-hell-am-I-doing-here feeling. Tex put his glasses on the sheep, intermittently visible through the rain, and spoke with sudden forceful decision. "What we need," he declared, "is a fat brisket stew an' some barbecued ribs. So if you will pitch the tent an' rustle a little wood, I will sashay over there an' kill the makin's." He picked up his rifle, floundered across the moss-slippery rocks of the brawling creek and disappeared into a willow wash downwind from the sheep.

I got busy making camp. After a while I heard Tex's long-barreled Mauser boom. Then I saw him coming down the tilted meadow, dragging a sheep carcass. He had some trouble at the creek. With the carcass across his shoulders, he slipped on a rock and went to his knees in the battering current, but managed to regain his feet and come on across, towing the carcass. "Kind of a funny-looking sheep," he said, as he dropped it at the tent, "but I reckon hit's edible. Fat enough, anyhow."

I looked at the carcass and couldn't believe what I saw. It apparently was a Dall ram, about a five-year-old, in good flesh. But it was sky-blue. Now in those days nobody knew exactly what fauna existed in the unmapped, wildly glaciated, largely unexplored coastal wilderness. There were strange rumors—rumors of white sheep with black tails, of the mysterious, shaggy, sheeplike *tebay* of the Indians, of the Alaska ibex. To give you an idea, an outdoor magazine had recently offered a reward of $1,000 for the hide, horns and bones of one of the storied ibex.

But a blue sheep topped all the tales, and here we had one, a specimen in good condition. Overwhelmed, I broke a half-dozen matches trying to light my pipe in the rain-wind. Tex was singularly calm, as he sweetened the edge of his knife preparatory to butchering the kill. Too calm, too suspiciously calm even for him.

Presently I got it. He had dragged the carcass down through a quarter-mile of ripe blueberries, the wet berries hanging thick as grapes in a vineyard, and then had inadvertently dunked it in the creek. Naturally it was blue. Tex cut his eyes slantwise at me, read my mind and let out a bellow of laughter. I knew then that I would never hear the end of the episode. I never did. I am still the straight man in the campfire yarn of the blue sheep of Carpenter Creek.

"Aw, well, blue or polka-dotted, hit still looks edible," Tex chuckled. "Let us find out."

As a rifleman, Tex was no great shakes—in my opinion. I saw him miss too many important shots for no reason that I could understand. But he was a maestro with a shotgun. No man I have ever known could beat him at downing waterfowl, and that includes Jimmy Robinson and Nash Buckingham. When we lived at Old Matanuska, we used to salt down ducks and geese for winter use. We would take a packhorse down to the tidal grasslands, which we called the Hay Flats, and walk the birds up from the puddles, or shoot from passes in the bordering tall cottonwoods, banging away with the tawny flats all to ourselves until the pack panniers were filled. We split the plucked birds down the back and pounded them flat with a cleaver, then salted them in kegs, skin side down. To freshen a salted bird, you placed it in fresh water with the skin side up. They were wonderful roasted in the oven of the Yukon stove when winter winds howled and snow drifted deep around the cabin. But I did most of the shooting for ducks and geese, because Tex liked to shoot jacksnipe. The elusive, corkscrewing little spooks fascinated him. He would bet with himself, a dollar a shot, and at the end of a day would declare happily that he had come out winner and maybe could afford to buy himself some cigars tonight.

Then, bless us all, the Bureau of Biological Survey wrote some game laws—they were distributed on mimeographed sheets—and appointed Frank Hoffman, the local Deputy U.S. Marshal, to act as game warden. There was a bag limit on waterfowl, of course, and a shooting season. It looked to us as if the brave, carefree old days were coming to an end. One brilliant autumn morning after a hard frost, as we were eating breakfast, we heard geese in the sky. They were Canadas, the first big flight of the season. Tex grabbed his shotgun, a cherished Parker 12, and dashed outside. The cabin was on a little rise of ground above a spring-fed creek, and the geese were coming in low from the north, slanting down to the great Hay Flats, their ancient stopping place here. They passed directly over us. Well, for Tex it was easy. Without thinking of consequences, he let go with the Parker and feathers flew from the leading honker. The bird was hard hit, but it set its wings and staggered through the bright air toward Matanuska Village, which lay between our cabin and the flats.

Frank Hoffman, our brand-new game warden, was digging potatoes in his backyard garden plot when the stricken goose plummeted down within a few yards of him. Tex and I ducked back into the cabin. The goose season wasn't open. It wouldn't open until the day after tomorrow. Tex hadn't thought of that. I hadn't thought of it. We weren't yet conditioned to game laws.

"Now we're in trouble," I said. "That Hoffman would put his own brother in jail for any reason at all. In fact, I heard he did it once."

Tex said, "Well, he ain't got us yet. Let's go on down there. I'll do the talking." Feeling already convicted and sentenced, I followed him through the cottonwoods to Hoffman's blue-painted frame house. The goose lay on the doorstep, Hoffman stood in the doorway, looking grimly official. He was a big man, gone to fat but still tough, and hell on wheels when it came to law enforcement.

"Mr. Hoffman," Tex said, "you ought to get that goose out of sight. The whole daggoned town heard the shot an' saw the goose fall into your garden. Of course, ya jest didn't remember the season is still closed. But ya know how people are—an' you got your job to think of."

Hoffman turned purple. "I didn't shoot the confounded goose," her roared. "I was digging my spuds, and there was a shot and the goose fell practically on top of me. But I'll find out who. . . ." He paused, eying Tex with hard speculation. The two often tangled in poker games. They respected each other. "So that's the way it is," he said presently. "Well, you're right, I'd never be able to prove anything, and the bird did fall in my yard. And I do know how people are. So will you please," he shouted, "get out of my sight and take the goose with you, before I run you both in on general principles." We departed, Tex carrying the evidence.

"All that hullabaloo over one goose," Tex grumbled, as we headed back through the cottonwoods. "I tell ya, this country is goin' plumb to the dogs."

Tex was also a fair hand with a belt gun, both fast and accurate, and he claimed he was a whole lot better as a young man. "But I knew when not to crowd my luck," he used to say. "There were some awful rough pistoleers around in those days. Shoot you to see which way you'd fall." He told me that when he was twenty-odd, he had an experience in the Indian Territory that taught him, once and for all, the value of prudence. The Dalton brothers, then the most notorious outlaws in America, were hiding out in a little border town, posing as farmers. Tex rode into the town, a big, handsome Longhorn with a white-handled gun and his hat on the side of his head, met Flo Dalton, sister of the outlaws, and took her to a dance. He brought her home a bit late, to find two of the Dalton men on the front porch waiting for him. One of the supposed farmers pointedly consulted his watch and allowed that maybe Tex ought to explain how come he was bringing their sister home three hours after the dance closed.

"Never was much on explainin'," Tex told them. "Besides, here's the gal, right side up an' all in one piece. An' here I am—so if you hayshakers want to start somethin', jest turn your wolf loose any time you feel lucky."

To Tex's enormous surprise, the two men on the porch burst into laughter. They laughed until they had to cling to each other, out of breath, tears streaming down their faces. They were still laughing when Tex, bewildered and wondering if they were crazy, left for his hotel. Next morning an acquaintance told him in strict confidence who the "farmers" were. "I headed north right after breakfast," Tex said, "an' I kept goin'. Those Daltons were pizen mean, and if they hadn't took to laughin', they most likely would have shot me to doll rags."

Like one or two other great hunters I have known, Tex seemed to be able to read a wild animal's mind. On occasion this was downright uncanny. For example, there was the time on Knik River when information he got from a wolf helped us kill our winter's meat almost in camp. We had come upriver in late November and had started putting out a line of lynx traps. It was a cold morning, five sundogs in the gray sky and a bitter wind whining off the glaciers, the river ice grumbling, a morning when it was hard to believe that there was warmth left anywhere in the world. With our parka hoods pulled snug to our eyes, bent under the weight of traps we were carrying, we left the cabin at first good light and prospected through the spruces bordering the mile-wide snowy bars. We were hunting fur sign, and also meat, one being as important as the other, since as yet we had sighted no goats or sheep on the mountain faces, no moose in the valley thickets. We came to a point of timber that thrust out into the white bars, a prime spot for a lynx set, and had dropped our packs to scout the place when, a quarter-mile distant, coming straight toward us, we sighted a wolf. It was a sizable wolf, dark gray, a six-footer, maybe $150 worth of wolf if we could put a rifle slug into it.

The wolf was coming across the wind to the point, floating over the crusted snow, manifestly unsuspicious. We sat down, checked our sights and waited. The wolf was almost in range, when suddenly it halted, staring. It whirled on its back trail, then hesitated, visibly trying the wind, not wanting to leave, but afraid to come on. It couldn't have seen or heard us, and the wind told it nothing, yet after a moment of indecision, it loped back the way it had come, out of our ken, 150 pretty bucks going with it.

"Big cuss must have a college education," I said. "How in hell did he know we were waiting to bushwhack him?"

Tex put a gauntleted hand on my shoulder and motioned for silence. He was gazing narrow-eyed into the packed skinny spruces behind us. There was nothing to be seen. No movement or sound. Just nothing, not even a bird. Then Tex stood up, shucking off his right glove, and as he did so, a bull moose stepped into view so close that I could have hit it with a snowball. The Sauer blasted, and the bull dropped with a broken neck. Eight hundred pounds of moose, within sight of camp.

"Daggoned wolf didn't see us," Tex said. "He saw the moose, but he wasn't dead sure hit was a moose, an' he knew we were in the valley, so he played hit safe an' lit out."

Tex was the last sourdough working woodsman. There are some sourdoughs left, a dwindling handful, and of course there are plenty of smart, new-style woodsmen operating in Alaska, but Tex was the last of the old, indomitable, hard-boiled breed who lived exclusively by trap and gun, following the game and the fur trail into mountains and forlorn wilderness valleys that then had no name, staying out on a long hunt until, as the saying went, calico began to look like silk and you'd wake up some morning to find that a field mouse had built a nest in your navel. He was born in Carrizo Springs, Texas, in 1872, as nearly as I can figure it, and came north as a young man because, according to him, a drastic change of climate and scenery was clearly indicated if he wanted to continue healthy and at large. He had worked as a professional hunter in the Southwest, supplying government survey crews with meat, and he had learned the difficult trick of getting along with Indians. These two assets served him well when he arrived, a raw cheechako, in the Susitna country of eastern Alaska. I have no idea what year that was; he always insisted he couldn't remember.

The Denna Indian people liked him. No sentiment was wasted on either side, but he and the tribesmen had a live-and-let-live understanding that was rare in those days. He stayed off their trap-lines, and they stayed off his. If an Indian had a salmon net in an eddy, Tex found another eddy, and vice versa. Due to the fact that the Indians trusted him, we became involved one autumn with what today would be called, I suppose, an abominable snowman. I have since heard and read a great deal about the abominable snowman. I have seen the photographs of those tracks in the snow on a Tibetan mountain, and to me they are simply the tracks of a man with gunnysacking or some other cloth wrapped around his feet as protection from the cold, climbing slewfooted because the slope was steep and he had no crampons. But when I was a youngster roaming the north with Tex, we had never heard of the abominable snowman. We had, however, heard much about Gilyuk, the shaggy cannibal giant sometimes called The-Big-Man-With-The-Little-Hat.

Our adventure with Gilyuk occurred while we were camped in a pretty spruce park on Yellowjacket Creek, south of Tyone Lake. We had spent the entire summer on this mountain-girt Nelchina plateau, wandering about in aimless nomad fashion. Tex said we were prospecting and looking for fur sign. Maybe we were. He always had to have an excuse for enjoying the country, a commercial excuse if he could think of one. Anyway, it was now late September, the beautiful time, no mosquitoes, the land ablaze with color, the fish and the meat animals summer-fat, the caribou horde gathering, and we were footloose and free as perhaps men can never be again. This morning Tex was making coffee, and I was down at the creek cleaning a mess of grayling for breakfast, when six Indians filed in through the timber. They stood a moment solemnly regarding our four horses. To them a horse was a rarity, a mysterious animal. They called them McKinley moose, because McKinley was the only president they had ever heard of, and the horses were as big as moose. I followed them to the camp.

"Have you eaten?" Tex asked them in Denna.

They said they had eaten. Chief Stickman was with them. I had seen him once before, at Eklutna Village. A squat, square-faced man, very dark, with long hair and quick moving obsidian eyes, he was the Denna boss of this entire area, and his reputation was bad. But now he had trouble that he couldn't handle. He told us about it, and as he talked, he kept standing first on one leg, then the other, balancing himself with the moccasined sole of the free foot against the knee of the supporting leg. I don't know whether it was habit or a medicine trick to ward off evil spirits, or both, but it was disconcerting. He had come into this area two days ago, he said, with some of his people to kill and cache caribou for winter use. But they had discovered that Gilyuk, the shaggy giant, was hanging around. They had found his sign yesterday. And of course everybody knew that Gilyuk wasn't interested in caribou. Gilyuk ate men.

"What kind of sign?" Tex asked.

"We will take you to see it," Stickman said. "It is not far."

After breakfast we followed the Indians upstream a couple of miles to a burned flat on which a nurse crop of aspen and birch had grown. In the center of the flat stood a ruined birch sapling. It had been about four inches through and maybe ten feet tall. Something had twisted the sapling as a man would twist a match stick. The wood had separated into individual fibers, the bark hung in tatters. Stickman and his hunters stood back, while Tex and I looked the site over. Moose often ride a sapling down to get at the tender upper twigs. So do caribou. But no moose or caribou had done this. This had been done by something with hands. It had happened yesterday, because the leaves of the sapling had not yet completely wilted. It wasn't the work of lightning—no burns. A freak whirlwind hadn't done it, because trees and brush a few yards distant were undamaged. The hard ground showed no tracks. We found no snagged hair in the brush. Absolutely nothing except the incredibly twisted birch sapling. It was without question the eeriest sight I ever beheld in the wilds.

Stickman said, "It is Gilyuk's mark. We have seen it before."

I wish to make clear that to the Denna people Gilyuk was no legendary creature their grandfathers had told them about. He was reality, and they spoke of him as they spoke of the bears and wolves. They saw his sign, and they saw him. He was a shaggy giant who wore a little hat and ate men. "We want to ask you to camp with us until we have killed our caribou," Stickman said. "Gilyuk doesn't molest white men. Perhaps he will not molest us if you are in the camp." Stickman had already told us that he was bivouacked on the shore of a pothole lake two hours to the eastward.

Tex said all right, we would move to his camp in the morning. As he spoke, he was still looking at the twisted sapling, his green eyes narrowed in thought. I couldn't take my gaze off it either.

Stickman said, "Thanks, Kosaki," a strange word of respect, held over from the old Russian Cossack, and we parted company with the Indians.

Next morning I brought the horses in at daybreak. We ate, broke camp and were putting on the packs, when here came the Indians, all of them—all, that is, except Stickman. An old man told us that they were returning to their town on Tyone Lake. Stickman was dead, he said. Gilyuk had taken him. The chief had got up in the night and gone down to the lake, perhaps for water, but nobody knew. A squaw with a birch-bark torch found his red flannel underwear on the gravel beach. It had been torn off him. There may have been tracks, but the entire hunting party had swarmed over the beach, and by daylight no tracker on earth could have made sense of the jumble.

Well, until the day of his own death last July, while on a sentimental journey to a fateful spot in Cook Inlet, Tex was convinced that the cannibal giant Gilyuk killed Stickman. When asked if he believed in the existence of abominable snowmen, Tex would reply that he didn't think there were any around in Alaska nowadays, but that they had existed, at least one of them, a couple of decades back. That is good enough for me. I go along with it.

Long Hunter, Alaskan Style

Further adventures of the author and his sagacious backwoods partner, Tex Cobb. In this, the concluding part, Russ and Tex roam Alaska in search of game, adventure and gold.

CONCLUSION

Tex was the ultimate in hard-nose professionals, had been one, apparently, since he was belt-high to a graining block. I do not believe that he ever heard the terms "hunting tricks" and "camp kinks," so popular today among our sportsmen, most of whom train and dream and research assiduously eleven months of the year in preparation for their vacation month in the wilds. But he had the damnedest collection of tricks, kinks and shortcuts that ever contributed to a tenderfoot's education. They worked; they were practical. He used them as unconsciously as he laid a diamond hitch or made certain his match safe was in his pocket in the morning.

Very often they were a source of huge embarrassment to me when I was serving my woodsman's apprenticeship under him.

There was the rainy autumn afternoon on Sheep Creek, in the Talkeetnas, when he showed me the easy way to gut a moose. I was seventeen, alone in the trapline cabin except for our Malamute lead dog, Peluk. Tex had gone out to kill us some meat, he hoped, on account of we were currently reduced to a diet of beans and sow bosom, which is tiresome provender at best.

Lying on the big split-pole bunk, I was struggling with a book concerned with the origin of the species when a hoarse, gagging sound interrupted. I assumed that Peluk was sick, hastily opened the door and ordered the dog outside. But, standing in the open doorway, I realized that Peluk wasn't guilty—the sound was ventriloquial; it seemed now to be coming from down in the creekside birches. *Aghr-r-r uh!* It was a bull moose, a rutting bull telling himself and the world how tough he was and what dire things he would do to any rival bull, just give him an opportunity.

I got a line on the sound, ordered the bewildered Peluk back into the cabin and beat it down into the birches with my rifle. The bull was standing on the creek bank, still bragging, swinging his heavily antlered head this way and that, when I located him. I wanted to shoot him in the neck to save meat, but was afraid to take the chance. He was 100 yards distant and the light was bad; and if I missed, I would never live it down. So I put the 220-grain slug into his shoulders and he went down, coughed and presently died. Congratulating myself, I set about dressing him out. With a moose this is always an onerous chore. You can't turn the critter onto his back, not without block and tackle anyway, and to get at some of the guts, you practically have to crawl inside.

Well, the carnivorous little whitestocking flies had found me, and they were terrible, biting chunks out of my hands and face, and the cold rain drove in gusts across the painted birch flat. With my knife I sliced through the neck muscles of the carcass and, using an antler as a lever, managed by a wrist-spraining effort to break the vertebrae and remove the head. I cut off the legs at the knees. I skinned out the top side of the carcass. Shucks, let us face it, I was stalling. We had just arrived here and all my clothes were new. I was wearing an expensive, chromatic squaw-catcher shirt, and my underwear was the new silk-wool stuff. I just plain hated to get all bloodied up so early in the season. To kill some more time, I put a new edge on my knife, and then reluctantly was about to open the carcass and start wrestling with the barrelful of guts when I saw movement out of the corner of my eye. Here came Tex. He was grinning happily, as he always did when meat was down, big and black-bearded, a man who walked with the snowshoe swagger in his legs, lank wet hair swinging in the wind, green eyes sparkling.

"Fat, too," he said. "Ain't been in the rut long. But let's git those guts afore we drown in this rain."

I stood back. He was the expert. Let him get plastered with blood to his ears this time. I would watch him, I thought, like an eager student, and save myself half a day washing clothes. As it turned out, I was a student all right. I learned a hunting trick I have never seen in the books. Tex took his ax off his packboard, straddled the carcass and with several slashing chops, severed half the ribs close to the spine. He then, with his knife, made two cuts that separated these ribs from the others. He pulled the rack of ribs outward and folded it down, thus exposing the innards. What he had was a sort of window that he could work through without pulling and hacking blindly to get at the diaphragm, lungs, windpipe and heart, as I in my ignorance had always been forced to. Furthermore, the carcass would cool faster, and if he wanted to close it later, all he had to do was sew the rack of ribs back in place with some twine.

"You got here just in time," I said, "to save my purty squaw-catcher shirt."

"I wish the hell," he complained, ignoring my statement, "that you would learn to shoot a moose somewheres besides in the shoulders. Lookit all the fine steaks you ruint."

Another time, in midwinter, we mushed up King River to a nameless lake under the snowpeak where there was supposed to be a concentration of marten. A Denna Indian, sick and coming down from the Chickaloon country for treatment at the government hospital, told us about the marten. Maybe he was sicker than he knew, to the point of seeing things. Or maybe he was a natural prevaricator. Anyhow, there weren't any marten.

But we didn't know this when we arrived at the lake. It was around nine o'clock, colder than a witch's nose, with a slow wind out of the north, a million big stars blazing and the aurora doing things that could not be described (nobody would believe it anyway unless he saw it). We unharnessed the dogs, tied them and pitched the tent. Tex said that he would gather the night's wood if I would cut a water hole. That made me sore, but I managed to keep my mouth shut. There was plenty of good dead wood around, spruce snags all over the place. All he had to do was drag some to camp. But chopping a water hole in the ice of a lake, the ice maybe four feet thick, when you were tired and hungry, working in the dark, the polar cold congealing the marrow of your bones, was another matter.

I got busy chopping ice. As usual, I didn't start the hole big enough and had to enlarge it when the ax handle began banging against the rim. I scooped out ice chips with my hands, chopped some more, scooped out more ice chips, chopped, cussed, shivered and asked myself in a real red-headed temper if Tex thought I was his camp boy or what. I had got the hole down about two feet when Tex came out across the ice.

"What's the trouble?" he asked gruffly. "The sooner we get some water, the sooner we can boil some tea."

I stood back. "You chop a while," I said. "Or melt some snow for water, either way you want it. This isn't like dragging in a couple of wood snags."

Tex stared at me a moment in the weird flare of the aurora and let out a shout of laughter. Shedding his right glove, he stood over the hole I had laboriously chopped and fired his rifle into the ice. Water spurted up, under pressure, and in a few seconds filled the hole.

"All right, all right," I said, as humiliated as I had ever been. "So I'll be a tenderfoot all my life."

"Aw, don't say that," Tex chuckled. "Don't give up so easy. Wait a few years an' we'll find out."

And there was an interesting piece of ingenuity the old gent displayed one autumn in the Kashwitna country. We had taken a visiting sportsman upriver in September for a moose hunt, making the trip by chartered airplane, utilizing a sand bar as a landing strip. While scouting for a suitable trophy bull, we came across a good deal of fur sign, beaver, mink and otter, and Tex and I decided to return after freeze-up with traps and an outfit.

The hunter, a pleasant chap from Seattle who sold mining machinery, made his kill in dramatic circumstances. We were awakened at first light by the sound of antlers clashing a few hundred yards back in the timber from camp. Two bulls were fighting. Hastily getting into our clothes, we made for the scene of the fray. The morning sun had just topped the snow-patched eastern peaks when we came to the edge of a natural clearing and saw the huge, dark animals going at it hammer and tongs. It was a thrilling scene, primitive and blood-stirring, straight out of the mists of time. But we were here to take a trophy. The heads were pretty evenly matched, but Tex thought one had better brow antlers, and whispered for the pilgrim to take him. The chap did so, neatly, with a single shot.

"Y' know, this would be a good spot for a trapline cabin," Tex said, gazing about with appreciation, as we took off the head and cape. "Good cabin timber. Plenty of dead stuff for wood. We better salt down as much of this meat as we can. Hit'll come in handy later."

I thought, holy Moses, the old guy is beginning to slip. He's in his dotage sure enough. While we had a good supply of salt—you always need a lot for curing trophies—there wasn't a barrel or keg

within a week's hard travel. Not that his idea wasn't a good one. To me the grimmest part of trophy hunting in those days was the necessity of leaving good meat for the ravens and wolves. You could eat only a fraction of the meat you killed, and except in rare cases it was impossible to transport the rest of civilization. For example, we were going to walk out, having dismissed the airplane, and the trophy itself would be burden enough. Anybody who has ever sweated a set of moose antlers through fifty miles of brush and blowdown will understand what I mean.

The pilgrim had been taking photographs. Now he leaned against a tree and took a long, contemplative look at both of us. Maybe he thought we were balmy. If so, you couldn't blame him. He was no dope; he knew you needed a barrel to salt meat. We skinned out the moose and took the trophy and the liver and a tenderloin to camp. Then Tex lashed a sack of salt onto his packboard, and we returned to the scene of the kill. Here the pilgrim and I received a first-class lesson in the ancient and difficult art of woodcraft. Tex spread the moosehide flat on the ground, flesh side up, and piled chunks of meat onto it, lean meat only, no fat or bones, maybe 150 pounds of it. He salted the meat heavily, then cut holes around the rim of the hide and threaded a strip of rawhide through them as a drawstring. When he pulled the drawstring tight, the salted meat was in a safe, waterproof container. With the pilgrim and me helping, he hoisted the sack of meat into a tree and suspended it from a stout hangman's limb. The birds couldn't get at it, wolves couldn't reach it; the only danger was that a talented wolverine might climb the tree and chew through the rawhide line. And that was a remote chance because there weren't many wolverines hereabouts.

"Well, I'll be damned," said the pilgrim. "You professional woodsmen are really clever. When you were talking about salting meat without a barrel, I thought you must be crazy. I apologize."

Me, I didn't say anything.

Tex never was greatly interested in money, although before he died, he amassed a considerable amount. When we were together, roaming the north in high, carefree fashion, he only wanted to make enough to pay for grub, clothes, gear and ammunition. Mostly we depended on furs, and we had good seasons and bad ones, some very bad ones. In the spring when we had pulled our traps, Tex would say, "I'll divide the pelts into two piles, and you take your pick. Or you divide them and I'll take my pick. King Solomon couldn't have come up with a fairer method—except that Tex knew infinitely more about furs than I did. But I was getting a wilderness education. Thanks to Tex I learned enough about furs to grade them in a New York loft. Tex never worked a day in Alaska for any man. He only wanted to wander, enjoy the wilds and shoot. And of all the shooting available then, he preferred to shoot hair seals.

I think he had something, because hunting hair seals is the most fascinating kind of varmint hunting. There is nothing comparable. It is exciting, difficult, sometimes dangerous; and besides, we used to get paid for it, $2.50 for a seal's scalp. You load an outfit into an outboard-powered dory and cruise down Cook Inlet, for example, to one of the big, unspoiled bays, where in late spring the sun is swinging north and there's light nearly twenty-four hours a day, and make yourself a camp near a trout stream and calm beach. When the tide ebbs and vast mud flats are exposed, hair seals haul out on the mud to bask in the sun—hundreds, even thousands of them. They are always just beyond easy rifle range. At the first sight, scent or sound of danger, they flounder pell-mell into the water. Getting at them is a task as complicated as military strategy. It teaches a man to make a stalk, and it teaches him to shoot. We never profited much from our sealing expeditions, but we burned a lot of ammunition and had some golden, marvelous adventures. In my opinion seal hunting is one of the best, and certainly the most neglected, of sports.

We were running across to Kenai one day in June, a storm threatening, big, ugly gray waves tossing the dory every which way, when the outboard motor began to buck and sputter. I didn't know what was wrong with it, but it sounded serious. Off to port was the southern tip of Kalgin Island. We headed for it, Tex steering, while I nursed the sick motor. Tex's dog, a giant Chesapeake named Sport (Tex was now naming all his dogs Sport—to save himself the trouble of thinking up new names, he said) had been curled up at my feet in the bilge, about as miserable and discouraged as a dog can get. He scented land as we headed into a stretch of wave-beaten beach, raised his head to give us a grateful look, and feebly wagged his tail. It was a bad landing. We hit a rock going in, the pin sheared, a wave caught us and the dory broached. Sport swam ashore and, while Tex and I salvaged the dory and our soaked outfit, the dog fled straight into the timber. That was the last we saw of him for a couple of hours.

"Confounded dog has abandoned us," I said. "What's wrong with him?"

"Well, he's seasick, he's constipated on account of seal meat doesn't agree with him, he drank some salt water out there and he's afraid we're going to put to sea again. Otherwise he's just fine."

We made camp and dug a bucket of butter clams in a blinding rainstorm. We repaired the motor. It was a wildish day and a wilder night, but morning broke calm, sweet and innocent as the dawn of creation. Out front a great tidal eddy swung counterclockwise in the red, early light. The eddy was full of salmon and seals, and above it, diving and screaming, was a canopy of gulls. The heads of seals gleamed like polished bronze. We didn't bother with breakfast. We each made a stalk, took a stand and began shooting. I think I averaged one seal in five shots. The range was about sixty yards, and the bronze heads of the seals rose and fell unpredictably in the swells. For a man who likes to shoot and at the same time do some good for the economy of his country, and get paid for it in the bargain, shooting salmon-killing hair seals in such a setup is a dream come true, a varminter's heaven. When the eddy died with the changing tide, we harvested our seals, broke camp, and stood out again for Kenai.

"I like that place," Tex said, gazing back over the stern. "I got a feelin' about hit. Sport liked hit too, an' not jest because he's a dry-land dog that hates the water. Yes, sir, I got a feelin' that we'll camp there again."

Thus through fate a man's life is arranged. Sport didn't make it back to Kalgin Island, but Tex did. As he said, he had a feeling. I'll tell you presently about Tex's return.

He was a man who followed his hunches, and he had some real stem-winding dandies. We spent part of one summer prowling about on the high, broken plateau north of the Talkeetna River, short of grub, our diet consisting chiefly of caribou meat and the wild mushrooms that covered the earth there. We were supposed to be hunting a lost mine. Some characters had come out of this country years ago, Tex explained, burdened with free-milling jewelry-type gold ore, all they could carry, and had unfortunately drowned trying to ride a raft down to Susitna Station. Since they all died, nobody was left to reveal the source of the jewelry rock. But Tex said it had to be right around here somewhere, and maybe we would find it if we had any luck. I'll bet we had covered 300 miles, walking. Our clothes were worn out, and my belly was cleaving to my backbone, so that I had to punch a new hole in my belt practically every day. Calluses caused by the straps of my packboard were themselves growing calluses, before Tex allowed regretfully one morning that perhaps we ought to go down to Stepan Lake and loaf for a spell. Some good fishing there, he said, and he sure was hungry for a mess of fried trout or grayling.

That certainly was all right by me. I never was fond of caribou meat—I don't like the taste of it—and I never saw a fat caribou in my life. As for wild mushrooms, they may contain nourishment—people keep saying that they do—but I'll go to my grave doubting that there is a calorie in a carload. Anyway, for breakfast we drank some caribou-and-mushroom soup, ate a couple of stringy caribou steaks apiece, shouldered our packs of gear and caribou meat and lit out for Stepan Lake. The lake is named for the tribe of Stepan Indians, whom Tex called the Stewpan Indians.

When we came down through the timber to the outlet, around noon of the second day, we found a group of Stepans camped there, five men and a woman. Old Chief Talkeetna Tom Stepan was with them, and the woman was his wife, name of Christine. They had a little wall tent pitched in a meadow and were sitting around a fire talking.

With willow sapling poles and caribou bait, we caught some fish, rainbows and Dolly Varden, fried them and ate while the Indians watched. After a while Talkeetna Tom came over and asked Tex if he would like to play some poker. Tex replied that he would indeed. He always enjoyed a friendly game of poker with old friends, he said, especially if the stakes were high enough to keep things interesting. I have no idea as to how good Tex was at poker—I'm no expert—but whenever he played with Indians, he won, although they kept trying as long as they had any money or collateral to put in the pot. I mean they liked to play, and they weren't chicken. But this particular game was doomed from the beginning. The Stepans were drinking sourdough, a villainous beverage, and the woman Christine was hostile. Somebody, probably Talkeetna Tom, had blacked one of her eyes. She looked as dangerous as a grenade with the pin pulled. The game took place in the tent, and Christine sat on a rock just outside, glowering. Tex kept glancing sidewise at her. Finally, when he had played a couple of hands, Tex announced abruptly that he had just remembered something and we had to leave.

Fifteen minutes later we were on our way, the lake and its wonderful fat fish behind us, heading back to more skinny caribou meat and wild mushrooms. With as much restraint as I could command, I asked Tex if he would mind telling me, just to satisfy my curiosity, of course, why the hell we were departing.

"I got a hunch," he said. "There's gonna be a heap of trouble back there, an' we don't want no part of hit. That woman Christine is a chief's daughter. She's gonna pay somebody off for her black eye."

Some hunch. When at last, a pair of ambulant scarecrows, we arrived at Old Knik, the news was there ahead of us. Christine had indeed taken bloody vengeance for her black eye. She came out from Stepan Lake alone, and told a U.S. Marshal that the five Stepan men had badly mistreated her, and that while they were playing poker after Tex and I left, she cut the tent ropes, then walked onto the fallen canvas with the camp ax and vigorously chopped everything that stuck up. There were no survivors, she testified. As far as I know, Christine was not sent to jail. Her plea was self-defense, and nobody then was vitally concerned over what happened to a few Indians.

I am told that a couple of years ago a handsome new hunting and fishing lodge was erected there. Anyway, I have never since eaten caribou meat and wild mushrooms, and during the rest of the time we were together, when Tex announced that he had a hunch, I was deeply and respectfully interested.

There never was anybody like the shaggy, green-eyed old gent; there never can be again. Because, besides being very special, he was the product of an era gone forever. He did things with a flair, with a certain color and gusto that caused belly laughs all over Alaska, that will be the substance of campfire yarns, I believe, as long as men foregather on northern hunting trails.

There was the time he got into a fight with a fur buyer at McGrath, and was arrested and sentenced by the new U.S. Commissioner to thirty days in jail. The trouble was that McGrath had no jail. But the commissioner solved that by confining Tex to his tent, under guard. When he was released, Tex sued the town and the commissioner for the use of his tent, $10 a day for thirty days, and collected.

There was also the time at the Richardson roadhouse in the Rainy Pass when he tried in vain to sell 500 pounds of frozen salmon eggs to some tenderfoot mushers for dog food. They were tightwads and wouldn't pay the price Tex asked. So that night, when everyone was asleep, he turned their sleds around so that they pointed back toward Salt Water, from whence the mushers had come. Next morning, stumbling out half asleep in the bitter mountain darkness, the cheechakos hooked up their dogs and traveled fifteen miles in the wrong direction before they realized that something must be wrong.

Well, I left Tex to go to college, returned and left again to go to war. During my absences, Tex established a salmon fishery at the south end of Kalgin Island, the place he had a hunch about. He made, I understand, a good deal of money; but he continued to trap, to wander the wilds and to prospect in his fashion. Last summer, in July, he went back to Kalgin, to the big salmon and seal eddy, with another dog named Sport, and there he died, quite suddenly. He was a man who hated to say good-bye. So I'll just say . . . hail and farewell.

Louise Lopina

Joys and Sorrows of a Wrangler

It's a good life. Honest it is.
You may not travel at airplane speed,
but you get fresh air and lots of exercise—
and trouble, trouble, trouble.

The tubby pilgrim in the fire-engine red shirt and pants and pacs so obviously new that he could have been an escapee from a sporting-goods window display, gazed at our packtrain with raw, undisguised covetousness. "What I wouldn't give," he said, "for some of those horses. All my life, gentlemen, I have been seeing horses—in the movies, at the track and pulling beer wagons and whatnot—but never until today did I realize that the horse is absolutely the most wonderful, useful and beautiful beast in the whole world." He made a gesture that took in the wide, frost-painted Alaska valley and its jagged upsweep of peaks. "In the whole world," he repeated almost tearfully, "but especially, dammit, right here, where I desperately need some horses."

The guy had reason to be emotional. The previous morning he had eaten breakfast in Seattle, after which he had flown to Anchorage. His guide met him at Anchorage, and today a bush pilot had flown them and their outfit to this remote upper Tonzona valley, where it busts out of the towering, snow-topped Alaska Range. They landed on a gravel bar east of the pounding river, the plane departed and they had finished putting up camp when Gunn Buckingham and I came upon them. Now the Tonzona is prime hunting country, hard to beat—moose, white sheep, caribou and grizzly bear—but it is a big area, and the river slices it in half. The sheep and bear inhabit the west side, while most of the moose and caribou hold forth on the east side. The river can be forded by a man on foot in the early mornings when the water is low, if he knows how to handle himself and doesn't mind bone-chilling cold and spending the day in wet clothes. But he can't get back until the next morning.

With horses, of course, the place is a gut cinch, no problem at all. But getting in and out by packtrain is a slow, time-consuming business; and our red-shirted pilgrim who had eaten breakfast in Seattle yesterday had craved fast action and so had bet on wings instead of hoofs. Now, having sized up the valley and the river, he saw that he was in for an unnecessarily tough, onerous hunt; that he was in fact going to spend most of his time foot-slogging drearily back and forth across the valley and floundering about in ice water and trying to get his clothes dry for more of the same tomorrow. "But I've seen the light," he told us. "I catch on fast. From now on it's strictly horses for me." Buck and I wished him well and went on. We were heading for another valley to the east, a place we had scouted the year before. I remarked that I was sorry for the chap.

"Yeah. Me, too," Buck said. "But I'd like to talk with him after he's spent a month or so hoorawing a string of knotheaded cayuses across the country. He'd really be moaning."

Too well I know what he meant. Packhorse travel is great, the best way to see and appreciate a northern hunting range; but packhorses themselves can be, and too often are, a severe and localized pain to their long-suffering wranglers. Take something that had happened only the other morning. We were camped in a spruce-rimmed meadow on the bank of a fast creek plunging out of the peaks. The sky was clear, although rain had fallen all night, a cold, miserable downpour with rowdy gusts of wind behind it. I got up in the false dawn, built a fire, started coffee and went out to look for the horses. No horses. Sometime during the night all ten of them had departed. This was nothing unusual, for packhorses are a wandering lot; but I was sore because I wanted to make an early start. I took out after the string through head-high redtop grass that was so wet that I got a shower bath at every step. The lead horse wore a Kentucky bell around her neck, but there was a thrush in the region whose call duplicated the bell's middle G note so closely that you needed an ear like Leonard Bernstein's to tell them apart. The sun came up in a shivering fan of colors; and I battled through a mile of brush and grass, casting this way and that, before I knew I was hearing the bell and not a bird.

The close-hobbled horses were huddled on a strip of barren sand bars halfway across the creek, heads hanging, looking sorry for themselves. Don't ask me why horses would leave a lush meadow and kangaroo-hop a full mile, hobbled, to stand on a sand bar in a creek. It is one of the mysteries of the equine world. If I knew why horses do such things, maybe I would be a happier man. It reminds me of the guide and his client who came out to town after a long hunt in the back-of-beyond, and somebody asked the pilgrim what they had been hunting. The pilgrim replied, "Horses, mostly." Anyhow, I waded across to the bar, slipping and stumbling on mossy rocks, up to my crotch in liquid ice, and eased toward the bell mare, a pretty little maple-sugar character with yellow mane and tail, named Pixie.

She let me approach within a couple of yards, then threw up her head with a snort, staring at me in wild affright, as if she had never seen me before. At once the entire string slammed into the water and fled, splashing and blowing, back to the other side. I waded after them, the refrigerating current up around my belt again, teetering on the slippery rocks, hostile enough to club hell out of the screwballs but trying not to show it because if they spooked it might take hours to herd them to camp. I used to have a many-splendored profane vocabulary, and I yearned to use it in a loud voice. Instead I summoned a falsely ingratiating smile and spoke softly.

"Pixie, take it easy," I said pleadingly between my teeth as I climbed out of the water. "You and I have always been friends, huh? Just hold still, and I'll give you a whole handful of sugar, damn you, as soon as we reach camp."

She looked interested. I had a bridle, and holding it behind me, I closed in and got hold of the bell strap. I put the bridle on her, took off her hobbles and stuffed some moss into the bell to stop its clamor. I was shivering so violently that I had trouble lighting a cigarette, but I felt cheerful as I swarmed aboard the mare. It was just a routine morning after all, I told myself. Just ordinary packstring difficulties, the kind of morning that lets a wrangler know he is earning his money. We headed in through the spruces, and I could smell woodsmoke and frying bacon in the wind, so Buck was up cooking breakfast. Swell. It was going to be a good day.

Like blazes it was! The packhorse in the lead, a husky Oregon paint, boggled suddenly. It was a flock of spruce grouse, a big flock of spruce grouse, maybe fifty of them, on the ground ahead of us. The birds took to the air, flying crazy, wings roaring, whipping past the horses' heads as they clawed for altitude. Of course the horses had seen grouse before; they were veterans. They knew all about grouse, but the noisy flock was an excuse.

Pixie came unglued when a big bay crowded her. She squealed and sank her head, went up high and came down hard, spun and tried to sunfish; but caromed off the big bay's rump and crashed into a spruce snag, off balance, with my leg between her and the tree. A spike-tipped limb hooked my pants leg, high up, and ripped it to the cuff. I came back on the Spanish bit, and she reared. Afraid she would fall on me, thinking my leg was broken and that was enough for one day, I belted her between the ears with the heavy chain hobbles. She grunted and went to her knees. I got hold of the cheek of the bridle, pulled her head around so she couldn't pitch any more and talked to her. The other horses were stampeding toward camp as if pursued by all the demons in the north. Pixie cooled off presently, and we followed. It appeared that my leg wasn't actually broken, anyhow I could move it; but it hurt like the devil and my pants, my best pair, were a total loss.

Buck was sitting by the fire in the cinnabar-and-orange sunrise flare, drinking coffee. The horses were over against the timber. "The string seems to be full of peas and vinegar this morning," Buck said conversationally. "Gave you some trouble, I see."

I told him they had crippled me permanently. Only the fact that it was a hard ten days back to civilization, I said, prevented me from shooting them outright and continuing the hunt afoot. Buck looked shocked. He thought that I meant it. And maybe I did, at the moment.

There is something in the heritage of the sporting subspecies of *Homo americanus* that convinces him that he is a horse-oriented fellow, with a natural talent for diamond hitches, *reatas* and bronc-stomping that needs only a bit of practice to blossom spectacularly. An experience I suffered with the late Fred Hollender is a case in point.

Fred, a perennial dude, had hunted everywhere and was a pack-train aficionado. He never could understand why some sportsmen used airplanes. One autumn I took him over into the Kantishna country to meet the caribou migration, renting six horses from Mt. McKinley National Park for the occasion. Since there were only the two of us, Fred insisted on doing a share of the work. This was all right with me, except that I like to make up the packs myself. I like to know that the panniers balance within a pound or so; and it is important to me to know what they contain, so that it won't be necessary to remove the lash ropes and mantles from a half-dozen packs, for example, to locate a roll of film or a carton of cigarettes in case somebody runs out on the trail. But Fred fancied himself as a packer, and it pleased him to help. Thus, in the interest of peaceful coexistence, I didn't object when he took part in the morning chore of making up packs, although as it turned out I damn well should have.

We topped Clearwater Pass in a savage hailstorm, and as we angled down toward the headwaters of Moonlight Creek, I got fouled up in a mountainside alder jungle thicker than hair on a dog's back. There wasn't even a rabbit trail through the mess. The hailstones hammered down; I couldn't see twenty feet in any direction, including up; and the horses were mutinous and wanted to stampede, only they didn't know where to stampede to. Finally I got down with the camp ax, cutting a trail of sorts while Fred held the string back. By sheer luck I chopped myself into a caribou-moss opening that led toward the creek bars, and I started back to inform Fred of the good news. I needn't have bothered, because at approximately this moment Fred's alarm clock, which supposedly was not functioning, went off in one of the panniers he had made up. That was all it took. Here came the string of horses in a disorderly scramble, squealing and kicking, packs banging against the tough alders. The packhorse in the lead was a tall, ewe-necked sorrel, a snorty so-and-so with too much white in his eyes. I stepped in front of him, arms spread.

My intentions were praiseworthy. I aimed to grab the shank of his halter and quell the insurrection before it got out of hand. But as I stood there with hailstones whanging against my slicker, the oncoming sorrel only a few yards distant, the alarm clock jangling somewhere behind, I saw something that sent a chill jittering up my spine. The long blade of the camp butcher knife had cut through the canvas of the sorrel's right pannier, which Fred had also made up, and was aimed at me like a lance point. I had always stowed the knife in our plywood lunch box, but Fred had omitted to do this. Leaping backward as the knife blade sliced the spot I had just vacated, I stayed under cover in the alders until the horses, Fred and the clamoring alarm clock had passed. The string ran until it reached the creek bank spruces. By the time I got the hair on the back of my neck to lie down again, Fred was hollering for me. Rejoining the outfit, I secured the butcher knife and searched through three packs before I found the now silent alarm clock.

"What we need," I said, employing some psychology in the rough, "is a fair division of labor. You're a top hand with horses.

So if you will wrangle the string to camp in the mornings, I will make up the packs. All of the packs." Fred agreed, and it proved a good system. I recommend it for other eager-beaver, horse-oriented pilgrims.

The common garden-variety diamond hitch is just one of many pack hitches. To name a few, there are the three-point diamond, the double diamond, the one-man diamond, the squaw hitch, the military hitch, the barrel hitch, the prospector's hitch and something from Oregon called the Goldendale tangle. An expert, with his side packs and top packs made up in advance, and a good offside man helping, can pack a horse in about one minute and a half. But it is no task for an amateur when time, efficiency and the horses' backs are considerations. For wilderness country—no trails, and ford the rivers the best way you can—I seldom load more than 150 pounds to a horse and figure on a five-hour day. It is plenty, and the pack has to be put on right. A crease in a saddle blanket, a pack off balance by as little as five or six pounds, a sharp-cornered object in a pannier can in the course of a day make a sore on a horse's back that may take months to heal. Those white marks you see on the withers and kidney areas of many packhorses are the scars of injuries caused by carelessness or ignorance in packing.

Personally, I like double-rigged sawbuck saddles with breeching and breast straps, and leather-reinforced canvas panniers sized to take wooden gasoline cases as liners. The cases add a bit of weight, but they protect your outfit and are easy on the horses. Also, when they are available, I use Humboldt pads for the same reasons. These felt-stuffed, slat-framed pads make it possible to screw a pack down tight so it will ride pretty, come whatever. Some old-timers, set in their ways, scorn the so-called "hurry-up" cinch buckle, preferring to tie the latigo in the ancient manner. But a latigo knot will eventually put a sore on a heavy-packed horse's ribs, and in an emergency when you've got to re-cinch or maybe unload the pack—a horse stuck in a bog or upside down off the trail—the latigo knot is exasperatingly difficult to get at, whereas the "hurry-up" buckle will never gall a horse and is so low on the animal's barrel that it is always handy. The old-time buckskin westerners were rough on their horses, because replacements were cheap and plentiful. Today's wranglers appear to take better care of their horses than of themselves.

The above is purely background information, since the modern sportsman usually deals with an outfitter who supplies both horses and rigging, giving the hunter little if any choice except in the matter of personal gear. One thing I earnestly recommend in the latter connection is a duffel bag that zippers down the side. For years I used the old drawstring-at-the-top bags; and invariably when I wanted an item, the hobgoblins of fate caused it to be at the very bottom, making it necessary to dump the works. If you expect wet weather on your next trip or will have to ford rivers, I suggest that you buy a number of waterproof sacks in which to stow flour, salt, sugar and so on. Your outfitter may have some, but he can always use more and will bless you for bringing them. And don't forget a saddle slicker. This garment is ankle length, split down the rear like a swallowtail coat and a joy forever when you get caught in a rainstorm. Chaps are mighty useful, too, not just foofaraw—leather for brush, angora for warmth. If you are going to act as your own outfitter, you ought to have a complete checklist of grub and gear and personally inspect every item before leaving a supply point. I once flubbed a checkout; and after a month on the trail, when the horses began throwing shoes, discovered that instead of standard horseshoe nails the hardware store had sold me Shetland pony nails. We finished the trip with our horses wearing caribou-hide boots to protect their rock-abused hoofs.

There used to be a glib saying that Alaska was a swell country for Swedes and bears, but hell on horses. I wish to amend that. Alaska is also hell on horse wranglers. Of course dudes are spared the grief incident to packhorse travel. Often they aren't even aware that it exists. They are too busy enjoying the scenery and the game, dreaming happily about blue-chip trophies but an unkind fate takes malign pleasure in kicking the poor wrangler in the groin every time he turns around. To give you an idea, who else but a wrangler would have the lousy luck to fall off a 5,000-foot mountain pass in a blizzard with nine horses on top of him, as I once did? This happened at the head of Healy River in June, and immediate cause of the misadventure was a hard-boiled, roman-nosed, snake-eyed, long-eared strawberry roan named Hungry because he always was.

Gunn Buckingham and I were going to make a spring grizzly hunt in the Wood River country and then spend the summer prowling eastward along the north slope of the Alaska Range, with the idea of reaching Canada before freeze-up. We lined out of Healy River in pretty spring weather, plenty of new grass, cottonwood buds bursting, geese flying, the ptarmigan and rabbits caught short and only partly changed into their summer colors. We had shipped our ten horses north from Oregon, and although I had painstakingly checked every animal, we had an outlaw in the string, the aforementioned Hungry. I don't know how this happened, unless somebody switched horses on us when I wasn't looking. Maybe on the boat coming north. At any rate, we were stuck with Hungry; and he was a stem-winding s.o.b. He refused to carry a pack. He would buck, throw himself backward, roll, slam full-tilt into trees and boulders, anything to get rid of his load. Naturally this was hard on gear and poison to packtrain discipline. So what happened? So I had to take the animal as my saddle mount. It is an old custom. When a horse is too cussed mean for any other use, the wrangler gets him.

On the third day out, we tackled a nameless pass cutting through the range that separates the Healy River and Wood River watersheds. A misery of snow was blowing when we topped the summit, powder-dry flakes riding an enormous gale of icy wind. It was a grim, blank, surrealistic spot. Fangs of black rock stuck up out of weirdly sculptured drifts. The wind sounded like a training camp for banshees. It was hard to believe that below us, on both sides of the pass, the valleys were green, sunlit and hospitable. I had head-and-tailed the packhorses—each horse's tail tied to the halter shank of the horse behind—and was in the lead, with Buck bringing up the rear. Buck had put on his saddle slicker to break the wind, but I hadn't yet found opportunity to put mine on. I was wearing a pair of black angora chaps, the stovepipe variety, so the lower half of me was all right; but from my belt up I was snow-plastered and freezing. It was exactly the kind of day to make you think that perhaps the airplane boys had something after all. As we started down the Wood River side, skirting the top of a vast drift, I figured we had it made and reached behind my saddle and untied the rolled slicker.

Up to now Hungry had behaved well, for him. He had shied violently a couple of times at rock shapes; but I couldn't blame him for that, because they looked spooky to me, too. And once he had snaked his head around and tried to bite my foot. I anticipated this move, however, and gave him a mouthful of sunflower-roweled spur instead. Perhaps he had forgotten to be really tough because he was awed by the pass and the storm. Or maybe he was waiting for the main chance. In any case, I had my arms halfway into the sleeves of the wind-whipped slicker when he suddenly came unstuck like a ton of T.N.T. Nobody needs to tell me that it is a risky thing to put on a slicker when aboard a mean horse. I knew that. I had known it since I was head high to a stirrup fender. But by the same token, I am a professional wrangler and I will, by gosh, put on my slicker and take it off when I please; and if the horse doesn't like it, that's too bad. The trouble was that in the present case, it turned out too bad for all concerned. I had taken a couple of turns around the horn with the bell mare's lead rope and tucked the free end of the rope under my leg. A mistake.

When Hungry bawled and plunged down the slope, trying to buck and run at the same time, hoofs banging on the icy, iron-hard shale, the rope snapped taut and yanked him off balance. He fell, twisting to the right; and the rope across my thigh held me in the saddle. I remember thinking that probably never in the tortuous course of human history had a wrangler been in a worse predicament.

We landed in soft snow at the top of the drift, the rope still fouled on the horn and the screaming bell mare coming over onto us; and behind her the rest of the string falling in the wild tangle of packs and horseflesh. After that the details are pretty vague. I only know that we rolled to the bottom of the great drift and that I was underneath as often as on top. Somewhere along the way I lost one leg of my chaps, my hat and a cherished belt gun. We piled up in some alders at the edge of bare ground, and I was astonished to find that I was still alive and apparently had no broken bones. Buck came down to me; and in time we got the horses onto their feet, straightened the packs and went on to the first timber at the head of Cody Creek and made camp. I believe that the episode scared the cold whey out of Hungry, because he never got especially rough with me again, although I rode him every day the rest of the season and made a practice of putting on my slicker every time I thought about it. Buck's comment regarding the classic tumble down the side of the pass was typical.

"I was real worried there for a while," he said. "I sure thought we had crippled some horses."

River crossings cause a wrangler some first-class headaches, because few horses are good in water, and dudes are generally unreliable due to lack of experience. Take the time Harvey Dodson and I forded the American River, over in the Kantishna country. Before we started across, I briefed Harvey carefully. I would lead the way, I explained. His job was to crowd the pack animals into the water after me. Once the horses were lined out, I emphasized, he should keep his eyes on the opposite bank, letting his horse have its head. If he looked down at the rushing water, I told him, it would make him dizzy and he might actually fall off. I had seen it happen. Harvey said okay, he read me loud and clear; and we started across. He was riding a keg-bellied, cold-blooded appaloosa gelding, not excitable and with plenty of water savvy, the favored high-swimming kind of mount we used to call a sea lion. So I figured he was all right, as safe as anybody could hope to be in a wilderness river crossing.

Everything went well until the unexpected happened. An uprooted cottonwood came down the muddy current, limbs waving like the arms of drowning men. You could see that it would miss the packtrain, but probably would hit Harvey and his horse. Harvey didn't even see the thing. He was sitting ramrod-stiff in the saddle, eyes glued on the far bank. But his horse saw it, and being no dope, headed straight downstream and off the riffle. The last glimpse I had of Harvey for some time, he was steaming grandly around a bend, still staring at the shore as if hypnotized. I tied the horses in a stand of spruce and went looking for him, hollering and firing my rifle. When I at last located him in the strawberry-and-opal glow of sundown, he was plodding forlornly along the bank of a muskrat slough. I asked him with some heat where in the devil he thought he was going, taking off downstream like that.

"Don't ask me," he retorted. "Ask the horse. I did exactly what you told me to do."

But it's a good life. Honest, it is. You don't travel at airplane speed; but you get a lot of fresh air and healthful exercise, and you feast your eyes on the best scenery. And boy, you sure do meet some interesting people. See you on a pack trip someday.

The High Price of Moose Meat

"A single cartridge will buy a man his winter's supply of prime meat," said Tanana. It may if you discount plane crashes, smashed rifles and the depredations of marauding bears.

Just before fate kicked us in the teeth, we were gliding in for a landing on a gravel bar between the milky, rock-studded Kahiltna River and a wall of towering cottonwoods, engine idling, wheels about to touch. I was up front with Leon, the pilot. My venerable, white-headed sourdough partner, "Tanana" Stewart, sat in back. Suddenly Tanana yelled, "For Gawd's sake, look out for that bear. We're gonna land smack on top of him." At the same instant Leon fire-walled the throttle and horsed back on the stick.

I hadn't seen any bear. I had been gawking out the window, looking for a campsite. But now I saw the animal, holy suffering. It was a grizzly, one of those ugly, long-legged, grotesquely churn-headed grizzlies that you find in this area and nowhere else. He was galloping down the middle of our narrow landing space. At the near end of the gravel bar a small clear-water creek spilled out between red cutbanks crowned with overarching willows. Silver salmon spawned and died in the stream, and apparently the bear had been in the water catching himself a mess when he became aware of the approaching plane. Spooking, he had bounded up onto the gravel bar where, I suppose, he thought he would outdistance us handily. Due to the willows, Leon hadn't seen the bear until it materialized, as in a bad dream, exactly where he intended to put the wheels down.

Engine screaming, the heavily loaded plane lifted, then shuddered and dropped like a brick. But we had hurdled the bear. The last glimpse I had of the misguided beast, he was streaking for the cottonwoods, looking back over his shoulder at us in slack-jawed dismay. After that, such was the press of events, I forgot about him for the time being. When the plane hit, a tire blew with a report like a shotgun's blast. We bounced, hit again and slewed toward the timber, Leon fighting the controls. Piled along the first rank of massive gray-brown cottonwoods was a driftwood jam, relic of the Kahiltna's spring floods. The ground loop we were in took us careening at the jam; and I was braced for a bad crash, when I saw something more spine-chilling than the solid mass of driftwood.

From the top of the jam, aimed at us like a lance, thrust a weather-whitened spruce snag, its limbs broken off by running ice, its four-inch top splintered to a sharp point. The plane quartered into it, and with a rending assortment of sounds, impaled itself. The snag drove through the right side of the fuselage, missing me, and through the right rear seat, missing Tanana, who occupied the left seat—proof that the age of miracles had not passed. A large silence prevailed, broken by Leon as he spoke for all of us.

"That's what happens when a man's luck turns sour," he said. "Grizzlies jump up in front of him, and he can't win for trying."

It's the truth, whoever says it isn't. Tanana and I had flown to the Kahiltna from my homestead to make our annual October moose-meat hunt. An hour before, while we were stowing our gear in the plane, Tanana had been very optimistic. "This is the life, boys," he burbled. "A single rifle cartridge buys a man his whole winter's supply of prime meat. I sure do pity those city cheechakos."

Now we were in trouble before we had even seen a moose. We pitched camp; and Leon worked on his plane the rest of the day and, by lantern light, most of the night. Because I had helped bring the kid up, he wasn't charging us for the use of the aircraft. But we had agreed to pay all expenses. In the morning Leon told us he thought he could take the plane off, and it ought to hold together long enough to reach Anchorage. He would return for us and our moose meat, he said, sooner or later. After one of the roughest take-off runs I had ever seen the plane staggered into the air and disappeared over the spruce-fringed horizon, leaving only the fading sound of the engine in bright October sky.

"Let us now," Tanana said, "fare forth, by gad, and kill the biggest, fattest moose on this watershed. A bad start always brings a good ending. That's my motto."

Behind camp the land pitched up steeply, alder-covered, to a tawny high tundra dotted with islands of brush and stunted spruce timber. We set a course toward a burnt-over island a half-mile ahead and were toiling over the mattress of yielding sphagnum moss, sinking ankle deep at each step, when we saw a flash of movement where the tundra ended and the island brush began. It was the newly polished antlers of a bull moose. Without glasses, we saw that the bull was bedded down at the base of a low rib of green rock, legs tucked under his body, outstretched head resting on the moss in the manner of a dozing dog, supporting the weight of his antler spread. He may have been asleep and dreaming, but his marvelously sensitive big ears were working, moving this way and that as they picked up sounds of the Alaskan morning. If we had snapped a twig the size of a lead pencil, the sound would have registered visibly.

We had the wind, but otherwise the setup was tactically bad. The bull was too far away; we couldn't see enough of him to score with any but the luckiest of lucky shots. There was no intervening cover, not so much as a rock or a clump of grass. Our only hope was to walk toward him and try to cut the distance to effective rifle range before he heard us. Tanana, his whisker-stubbed face creased in a wide neon grin, stepped in front of me to supervise the approach. Tanana was one of the original sourdoughs, a member of the durable clan of old-timers who still called the Klondike the Reindeer River. Moose hunting was his favorite occupation, just as moose meat was his favorite provender. We practically tiptoed over the springy sphagnum; and despite the odds against, might have been successful, if some willow ptarmigan hadn't got into the act. The birds, a half-dozen of them, appeared from nowhere, running ahead of us; and a mottled cock began sounding off hysterically in his loud Klaxon alarm voice. At once the bull was on his feet. Blanket ears turned alertly forward, he stared in our direction, trying to figure out what was happening and whether it concerned him.

He was a fine bull, who hadn't yet run his fat off chasing cows. His new fall coat was sleek and quite dark, with chunks of pale sphagnum from his bed clinging to it. That he was young, perhaps a five-year-old, was evident, because he sported a "bell" at his throat instead of the "muff" that betrays advanced years. He carried a fair set of antlers, around sixty inches, pennants of velvet fluttering from them; but while they were his current pride and many hunters would have coveted them, they interested us not at all. What we wanted was a couple of fat carcasses to hang in the meat house for steaks, roasts, stews and mooseburgers when winter winds howled and the big snows drifted the cabin eaves under, We probably could have put lead into the bull at this distance, but it wouldn't have been a placed shot. So we stood motionless, waiting for him to make the next move. Once you have followed a gut-shot moose across miles of tough country, camped cold and hungry on the blood trail and found the soured, bloated carcass at last only when the ravens have led you to it, you thereafter try hard to make clean kills if you have a conscience.

The cock ptarmigan continued to squawk, warning the countryside of our presence, and suddenly the bull believed him. Shaking his antlers, he pivoted like a quarter horse and trotted into the brush. "Well, what of it?" Tanana said. "He ain't going nowhere. That island don't cover more than twenty acres. We can sort him out of it easy if we don't make any mistakes."

The island bristled with an outrageous combination of waist-high redtop grass, raspberry thickets just tall enough so you couldn't see over them, diabolically concealed down timber and standing snags whose crooked, brittle limbs caught and held with the efficiency of fishhooks. A good many moose had been hanging around here. There were beds everywhere on the rim, and piles of fresh dung pellets. Tanana plucked a tuft of hair from a spike-pointed limb and handed it to me. It was autumn hair, smooth and clean, without the reddish sunburn and kinked tips that mark summer hair.

Then, somewhere to our left, a bull grunted his war challenge. As always, the sound was ventriloquial. I didn't locate its point of origin even approximately. We froze, waiting, and after a moment the hoarse, chesty grunt was repeated. This time, holy Moses, it seemed to come from a spot a good twenty degrees to our right. Thus my hearing was haywire, or the bull had the extraordinary ability to move silently through the terrible raspberry jungle. Or, happy thought, there were two bulls. I glanced at Tanana, who shrugged. He didn't have the answer. We waited ten minutes that dragged past like an hour, but there wasn't another sound. So, since the bull, or bulls, wouldn't talk, I reluctantly concluded that I should.

We found a fallen tree and climbed onto it, which enabled us to see over the screening raspberry brush. I then made some moose talk. As a youngster, I was taught by Nikolai Chickaloosun, one of the most expert hunters the Moose-Eater Denna Indians could boast. I learned the various calls, when and how to use them, and spent much time practicing on moose when I could see the animals and note their reactions. The call most likely to get action here, I figured, would be that of a cow moose in heat. It is a difficult call, and Nikolai had insisted that to make it properly you had to think like such a cow moose, to put yourself in her place. Otherwise you wouldn't get the requisite appeal, desperation and where-the-hell-are-you into your performance. I have no doubt that he was correct. After all, he was a maestro. But I found it embarrassing when I had a hunting companion. I was always afraid the guy would read my mind and laugh, and I would have to invite him to do battle. But anyway, while Tanana stood by with his thumb on the hammer of his rifle, I made with the eerie, banshee moans and wails of a really lovesick cow. I didn't need a birch-bark horn. A horn is a foofaraw, for photographs. I just thought the way I thought an eager cow thought, and vocalized accordingly. Nikolai, I felt, would have been proud of me.

Dead ahead, sixty yards distant, a stand of raspberry brush weaved against the wind; and I caught a brief glimpse of brown hide. The moose was coming toward us, but sneaking, playing it cute. It wanted to get a good look before committing itself. Okay. I took a deep breath and let out an impassioned moan that ended in a quavering soprano squeal. That did it. I mean, that *forever* did it. Into a grassy lane, so close that I could see the shine in her eyes stepped a trim, leggy, little brown heifer. Tanana gurgled, then suffered a violent paroxysm of what he later claimed was asthma or something, and collapsed off our perch. The heifer gazed speculatively up at me, waggling her ears, a question in her limpid eyes. I made threatening gestures. I wished she was in hell and I had never known Nikolai Chickaloosun. Finally, obviously puzzled, she gave her head a toss and tripped back into the brush. With that, I slid off the windfall, assuring myself that I wouldn't try to call moose again even if I lived 5,000 years surrounded by the brutes. Our remaining bet was to stalk the bull that had grunted, or the two bulls, however it turned out. So I headed for the place where the last challenge had seemed to come from. Tanana, red-faced and choking, fell in behind.

I must explain that in a populous moose range, when the rut is just beginning, the animals often herd together, bulls, cows and young stuff. This, we shortly discovered, was the case here. As I eased into a particularly mean brush patch, using the top of a crooked snag as a navigation marker, I saw that the thicket was festooned with yellow jackets' nests. Probably because of a bumper crop of the sweet wild raspberries, these social wasps had colonized the place. Their round, gray paper nests, football size, hung all about me. By this date the wicked little assassins should have retreated to the underground castles where their honey was stored. But I assumed that they knew their business. At any rate, here they were, in residence. What happened next was my fault. I have vast respect for yellow jackets and should have been more careful. But I was concentrating on my footing, keeping track of the wind, trying to see through the brush and grass and listening for any sound that would reveal a bull's whereabouts. The result was that I inadvertently joggled a nest.

Out swarmed a fighting squadron of yellow jackets. I wasn't stung. I departed in great haste when the first one zinged past my ear. But Tanana, three or four paces behind, was a cinch target. He uttered a howl of anguish when the red-hot stingers jabbed into him, and tried to flee, only to trip over a grass-hidden log and plunge, in bad order, out of sight. He was flailing about and bawling piteously for help, but there was nothing I could do for him. Besides, the racket he was creating had solved the problem of where the moose were. They were all around us. Tanana's bellering had stampeded them, and they were plowing through the bush in every direction, snorting, breaking branches, knocking over spruce snags. It sounded like a herd of twenty or more. A dark bull with a bell tore past me, visible only for a split second. Even if I had been expecting him, I wouldn't have had time for an aimed shot. I thought, however, that he looked like the bull we had tried to kill at the island's rim. So I ran after him. Everything considered, it seemed as good a chance as any.

When, some minutes later, I busted out of the brush to the edge of the tundra, I had lost part of my shirt and sundry patches of skin, and was panting as if all the oxygen in the atmosphere had been used up. The bull was nowhere in sight. I had no idea where he was. It had been my belief that I was following him, or some other bull, but apparently that was a delusion. I was all alone. Out here the luminous autumn day was innocent and peaceful; and if you hadn't known better, you might reasonably have thought that there wasn't a moose within miles. I sat down and reached for a cigarette. At this juncture there was a slight sound behind me. I turned to behold the dark, bell-equipped bull walking out of the brush fifty feet distant. He hadn't seen me. He never did see me. Without getting up, I laid my .270 on his neck and shattered a vertebra. He went down on his brisket, in the same position he had been in when we first saw him, dead instantly.

Tanana arrived. His face was so swollen that it looked like somebody else's, and he was manifestly hostile. He had broken the stock of his rifle, a cherished .375 H&H Magnum with an antique scope that he had bought away back when the caliber first became popular. Holding the splintered stock in one hand and the rest of the weapon in the other, he gave me a shaggy scowl and rasped accusingly, "I never thought you were the kind to run off and leave a partner in the fix I was in. All those damn yellow jackets trying to kill me. Why, I oughta—" He saw the moose carcass. A painful smile contorted his face. "Well, now," he said in a changed voice. "Well, whaddya know? Fat, too, huh? And like I said, with just one shot."

I wanted to point out that the price of moose meat wasn't so doggoned low this year. We already had racked up an airplane repair bill and the cost of a new rifle stock, and the hunt was only half over. We were spending money like it was going out of style; and if anything else expensive happened, we would be on a diet of moose meat and beans until spring. Maybe short rations of beans. But I didn't have the heart. I said that he was right and we sure were lucky, and that we should get busy dressing out the carcass.

We took our time at this important task. When we finished and the meat was stacked on the hide, it was as clean as butcher shop meat. And that is the way a carcass ought to be treated. A man sitting down to do justice to a mulligan stew, say, has a right to be everlastingly griped if he finds it necessary to skim moose hair, grass seeds and other nonedible debris off the top in order to get at the stew. We made up our packs, hung our shirts on poles beside the meat pile in the hope they would discourage carnivorous fauna until morning, and set out for camp.

Partway across the tundra we cut the trail of a grizzly bear. You couldn't see clear individual paw prints, but the way a grizzly oversteps makes his trail distinctive on tundra moss. It resembles the marks made by a wide-runnered sled or a man on skis. This trail looked fresh, and I thought it almost certainly was that of the bear that had caused Leon to crack up his plane. I had a sudden bad hunch about the animal. When you've got meat down and no bearproof cache handy, it pays to be wary of the entire bruin tribe, even if there isn't any warning sign. Presumably this bear had dealt us one mess of trouble, and I had a hunch he was just naturally bad medicine and we were going to run afoul of him again in an unpleasant way. My hunches are sometimes pretty accurate.

At camp, after building a meat rack, we repaired the .375 with birch splints and rawhide. The job wasn't much for pretty, but it was all right for stout. If Tanana didn't fall on it again, the gun would do until he could replace the offended member. Turning out next morning in the tall flare of a wild-rose sunrise, we resumed the chore of packing meat; and by late afternoon it was all on the rack and covered with netting to protect it from birds and bugs. Tanana and I then had a mild argument. What with one thing and another, the old gent had had two rough days. His wasp-stung face looked feverish, and you could almost hear his joints creak. So I suggested that he stay in camp and guard the meat, starting tomorrow, while I scouted for another moose rendezvous. Tanana didn't buy it. His pride was hurt. He wanted it understood, by gad, that he was a moose hunter from who laid the chunk, and nobody's camp tender.

"If you're worried about that big-headed bear, forget it," he said. "He was heading for the hills. Right now he's probably in his den, tucked in for the winter. Never worry about hibernating bears until next spring. That's my motto."

Well, it was no pansies off my grave. In the morning we sallied out again and hunted three long days without making a kill. Although the region was cut up with fresh tracks, we saw only two moose, a yearling moping all forlorn on a ridgetop because, one gathered, his mamma's tough new bull-friend had given him the heave-ho, and swaybacked, ineligible veteran bull whose age could have been arrived at only by a Carbon 14 test.

Then, on the fourth day, bless us all, everything happened. It began with a steel-gray, pregnant sort of morning, a cold wind crying out of the north and Mt. McKinley looming above us like the frozen watchtower of the world. We hunted up the timbered valley of a nameless creek that wound through low hills patched with ivory caribou moss. Flakes of wet snow were riding the wind when, in a park back from the creek, a bull grunted.

We made our stalk and sighted the animal 100 yards distant. He was an alp of a bull, around 1,400 pounds, with a roan coat and wavy, malformed antler palms from which sprouted a bizarre array of crooked points. At the moment he was engaged in a tribal ritual. With his big front hoofs, he was pawing a hole in the ground, throwing the moss and earth back over his rump. Occasionally he paused to glare about him and utter a thudding, belligerent grunt. At last, when the excavation appeared to suit him, he squatted over it and urinated, after which, kneeling, he ground both antler blades and his shoulders into the mud.

"He's got it bad," Tanana whispered. "Love among the moose sure is edifying, huh?"

Neither of us wanted to kill the animal. He looked old as the hills, and we figured his meat was bound to be tough. While a happenstance tough steak or roast is nothing to dismay a man, a winter-long diet of leathery, unchewable meat is a frightening prospect. But still, we hesitated to pass up the critter, a moose in hand being worth a slew of moose somewhere else. We stuck around. The bull was making loud war talk, and we hoped it would attract another, likelier candidate for the meat house. Having anointed himself, the character was now fighting an alder bush, whacking it with his antlers and rearing to strike pile-driver blows with his front hoofs. He curvetted, plunged and bucked. He was a real Fancy Dan having a big time for himself at his age, and the devil take his blood pressure. Suddenly he had company. In the timber a challenging grunt sounded, and a second bull swaggered into a view. Behind him, dun shadows under the javelin spruces, I saw at least three cows. This newcomer, we were delighted to note, was an authentic Grade-A meat moose, full-bodied, obviously in his prime and wearing the dark, slick coat typical of the good ones.

Bristling, the two bulls made for each other. They sparred, then slammed together with a resounding clash of antlers, to struggle mightily for the chance to deliver a maiming thrust. It was dramatic, a savage bit that would have drawn a paying crowd anywhere; but I had seen it before and was here for a more practical purpose than watching a moose hassle. I glanced at Tanana. He had the battered .375 at his shoulder, but clearly was enjoying the fight too much to end it. So I nudged him. He sighed, lined his sights and pulled. Our meat bull, when the 300 grains of metal crashed through his head, ear to ear, dropped so abruptly that the leverage of his locked antlers dragged the elderly bull to his knees.

The latter wrenched free, and after a wild stare toward us, galloped into the timber. The cows joined him. He was a fortunate old bull. His life had been spared, his antagonist lay dead, and with almost no effort, he had gained a harem. When I mentioned this, Tanana chuckled.

"That's the way it oughta be," he declared. "The young bucks have got no license to win all the time."

By the time we had skinned, gutted and cut up the kill, snow was coming down pretty good. It took Spartan fortitude; but we put our shirts on display again to give meat thieves pause, then struck out for camp with a hindquarter and a side of ribs. I had the hindquarter, which I later found to weigh 130 pounds, a fair load for a packhorse or a Chilkat Indian. This wasn't bravado on my part, but simply the consequence of a bad guess as to the weight of the quarter. I presently had the uncanny feeling that I was growing shorter, my feet flattening and my spine telescoping. Tanana was in the lead when we reached the ancient bankside game trail that follows the Kahiltna from source to mouth. He halted, pointing wordlessly. In the snowy trail, holy smokes, were the tracks of a grizzly. The bear was traveling toward camp and was maybe five minutes ahead of us. My hunch was in full force; and I knew, as surely as I knew that the sun would come up the next morning, that trouble was about to slug us. Burdened as we were, a man doesn't hurry, but we tried. Snow sifted between our thin undershirts and the packboards and melted. The icy packstraps galled. At length, winded and beat out, we came to the end of the gravel bar on which camp stood. Or rather, had stood. Both the tent and the meat rack were down.

Through the blowing snow we made out the vague form of the bear, lying on the pile of fallen meat. At the instant we saw him, a revealing thing occurred. The wind, sweeping uninterrupted across the open bar, got under the tent and ballooned it. The bear must have thought that the flapping cloth threatened him. Anyway, he was on the tent in a flash, biting and striking. I think it quite likely that he had the same motive for pulling the tent down in the first place. And I think that the incident explained, at least in part, why bears have wrecked other tents I have pitched in the wilds.

The animal made a poor target. He was 250 yards distant and moving, and gusts of snow kept blotting him from sight. But we dropped our packs to try for him. In my case this was a mistake. I should have kept my pack on. I'd had enough years of experience. The moment the weight was off my shoulders, by balance left me. I staggered like a Saturday night drunk, and it took concentration to keep from falling backward. I felt fantastically light, unballasted, and could no more have put a bullet into the big-headed bruin than I could have hit him with a snowball. Tanana, however, was fit, ready and eager.

The .375 boomed, and the bear spun to face us. I didn't think he was hit. A second afterward, I knew he wasn't. As Tanana worked the bolt, the animal bounded back to the meat pile and grabbed a hindquarter between his jaws. He was humping for the cottonwoods with his loot when Tanana fired again. This time the old gent did himself proud. The softnose broke the bear's spine. When I saluted him, Tanana's weather-arroyo-ed face let up so it should have been visible several miles downriver. The sourdough had vindicated himself. Our tent was the biggest casualty of the raid. It was a treated silk job, custom-made for me in Seattle, a status tent that had cost plenty. Now it was ruined, useful only as tarpaulin material, and a damned poor tarp at that.

Tanana contemplated the dead grizzly. "This time the nonhibernating s.o.b. bought himself the big sleep. All meat bandits like him oughta be dead. That's my motto."

Well, we set about our chores, of which there were a formidable number. During the night the snowfall ceased. Three days later, Leon came in; and by afternoon we were back at the homestead, hanging our moose meat in the meat house—the most expensive meat the structure had ever sheltered. Which, I guess, ends this. See you up north some day on a meat hunt. But don't forget your checkbook. Unless luck loves you, you'll have to put out more than the price of a single cartridge.

Louise Lopina

In the Moon of the Drunken Bears

How was I to know that the bear was looped, sozzled, plastered, stewed to the eyeballs? To me he looked like any other autumn-fat Alaska black bear, except that he was a mite bigger than most, in the 300-pound class or close to it. Gunn Buckingham and I were riding across a terraced blueberry meadow above Indian Creek, on the Kenai Peninsula, when we jumped the animal. This was early of a vivid, optimistic September morning, full of cold sunshine and frost colors; and we were hoping to spot some bull moose in the scattered timberline spruces below us and maybe kill one whose antlers would make the book of record heads. The bear apparently had been asleep in a clump of painted, Indian-yellow willows and hadn't heard us until we were practically on top of him.

As I tried to get a good look at the animal, he lined out through the brush and redtop grass, grunting hoarsely and veering this way and that in most erratic fashion. During his first bounds, he relieved himself of an amazing lot of digested blueberries that spurted forth explosively, as if under high pressure. It was comical, but Buck didn't give me time to enjoy the laugh the sight merited.

"I could use another black-bear pelt," he declared, "but I want to be damn sure it's a good black-bear pelt." Sliding his rifle out of its boot, he waited for me to pass judgment. Over the years Buck had collected fifty or sixty heads and skins in various parts of the world, and had developed an almost irrational aversion to spending money for the taxidermy of any but first-rate trophies. I mean, the guide had to guarantee that a specimen was very good, or Buck wouldn't shoot. Which, of course, was his privilege. He was laying out the dough.

I figured that this present bruin no doubt had a typical autumn pelt, short, thick and silky, with no rubbed spots or patches of unsightly dead summer hair; but I couldn't prove it. I was catching only glimpses of the animal, all from the same side. So I concluded that my safest bet was to stall. There were plenty of black bears around, probably more than in any other hunting range on earth; and sooner or later we would meet one that I could size up at leisure with my glasses.

I was about to say something to this effect when the bear saved me the trouble. He climbed a tree. It was the only tree within a quarter-mile, a shaggy-barked balm-of-Gilead cottonwood, standing in lonely grandeur like an anchorite of the arboreal world. The bear had no valid, tactical reason for climbing the tree. There was plenty of cover from this point on, and all he had to do was keep going in any direction. But up the tree he went. When he reached a thick, hangman's limb that stuck out thirty feet above the ground, he sat on it, clinging to the bole of the tree with his forepaws and gazing over his shoulder at us. He was panting; and it seemed to me, as we spurred over to the spot, that he was unsteady on his perch, weaving from side to side.

"What do you think?" Buck asked.

He was no amateur, and his eyes were as good as mine. He was just putting me on record, from long habit. I told him that the pelt appeared to be exactly the same as was being worn at that moment by every healthy adult black bear in Alaska, give or take a few hairs per square inch. But to make dead certain, I said, I would ride around the tree and inspect the animal from all sides. This turned out to be my blue-ribbon error of the season. As I started around the tree, the bear turned his head to keep me in view. He had swiveled his neck hoot-owl fashion to what must have been the breaking point when suddenly he belched, hiccuped loudly, lost his balance and, holy Moses, fell.

Violent things happened. I was riding a snorty pinto gelding, named South America because he had on his near shoulder a large spot shaped like that continent. We had bought him from a homesteader, and he had proved to be too crazy to be trusted with anything as valuable as a pack of groceries or camp gear. Therefore, by custom, he had become the guide's mount—my mount. When the bear, clawing the air desperately, toppled to the ground, South America came unglued.

The pinto was a big horse as hunting horses go, 1,200 pounds, and was powerful, but not fast or tricky. Ordinarily I could have cut him to size without much trouble. But I was handicapped. I was trying to keep track of too many things simultaneously. Anyhow, that's my alibi. The witless wonder of a bear was fifteen feet distant of my right side, in a sitting position, the way he had landed, mouth hanging open, moaning. To my left was Buck, trying to get in a shot. Manifestly, he was no longer hypercritical as to the quality of the bear's pelt. He just wanted to put a slug into the animal where it would do the most damage. But the pitching, end-swapping South America and I kept getting in the way. Buck's horse was a trustworthy, cold-blooded, paddle-footed buckskin that probably would have held still in a typhoon; but a lot was happening even for him, and besides, he hated bears. He was beginning to dance. I didn't want to get shot, and I didn't want to fall into the bear's embrace.

"Get the hell away from here," I hollered at Buck. "Give me room."

At this point I lost a stirrup and felt myself daylighted. Then the cantle hit me a pile-driver whack on the hip pockets, as South America came up in another twisting jump. I made a quick pass at the well-known safety knob, missed it and went over the pinto's head in bad order, to land on the back of my neck with a bone-rattling crash. Dazed, seeing all manner of stars and comets, my head ringing like a burglar alarm, I rolled over and sat up. So there we were, tableau, the bear and I, flat on our fannies, facing each other at such an intimate distance that I could have counted his whiskers.

I have never considered the black bear to be a particularly dangerous animal. But the Indians, who ought to know, claim that on occasion he can be a fearsome beast, that he will disassemble a man completely, spending hours at the chore, whereas a grizzly or brown bear will likely wallop a guy a few times, bite and shake him and then beat it. That is what I was thinking about as I looked at the bear and he, visibly trying to break through the stupidity barrier, looked at me. Then his stomach rumbled seismically, he uttered another "Hic!" and began getting his feet under him. This seemed an excellent idea, and I was doing likewise when Buck's .30-06 hammered behind me.

The top of the bear's head exploded, blood, brains, bones and hair spraying out over the yellow cottonwood leaves. I stood up and leaned against the tree. "I am going to get out of this business," I informed Buck solemnly. "I'm going home and sit on the front porch in an old Boston rocker."

Instead I rounded up South America, who had bucked my rifle out of its boot and was now standing on the reins, wild-eyed and trembling all over, his jaw cut and bleeding from yanking against the Spanish bit. When I came back, Buck was laughing. He had opened up the bear's carcass. The stomach contained, I'll bet, five gallons of blueberries. They were fermented berries, and they smelled like the inside of a winery vat. Frost and sunshine, and maybe his own body temperature, had turned their sugar content to alcohol. The bear had been thoroughly, gloriously drunk.

"Anyway, it's a good pelt," I said, "Front, back and sides. As your taxidermist will be delighted to hear."

That was just a sample. I have lived for many years in the world's most outstanding bear pastures, and always after the first of the little frosts, when the blueberries, currants and high-bush cranberries are fermenting, my bruin neighbors begin doing strange things. Visiting sportsmen usually attribute their fey acts to eccentricity or pure cussedness. But I am convinced that in most cases off-beat bears are drunk or, quite possibly, suffering from hangovers.

In early autumn the bears are putting on fat as fuel for the coming seven months of hibernation. They gorge themselves, feeding day and night; and if the available food happens to be berries, and the berries have been frosted and contain alcohol, it follows that until this natural berry wine turns to vinegar, the animals stay fairly well looped. And not only the bears. The grouse become erratic lushes. The geese, feeding on tundra flats covered with crowberries, often find themselves too soused to straighten up and fly right.

A tipsy, arrogant, brawling oaf of a mountain grizzly just about ruined my venerable friend Chief Wasilla Stepan, master snowshoe maker of the Susitna-Denna Indians, one fine autumn afternoon. I had been up at the Montana Creek falls repairing the roof of a trapline cabin, and on my return was approaching Wasilla's place intending to spend the night with him, when three fast rifle shots echoed off the hillsides. A few minutes later, perhaps a mile ahead, a dense column of black smoke billowed up from the timber. As nearly as I could tell, the smoke came from the site of Wasilla's ancestral log dwelling, a barn-like relic of the days when the Susitna-Denna were numerous and powerful and needed large houses. Since I was traveling light, I broke into a trot. The trail wound through acres of high-bush cranberry shrubs, on which the wine-smelling fruit hung in clusters like grapes, and presently opened onto a white-birch flat with the opal glitter of a lake beyond.

I found Wasilla sitting on a windfall, bare to the waist, shoulders slumped, gazing at the blazing remains of his house. Just off the trail in front of him lay the carcass of a fat, high-humped, long-snouted, coffee-colored grizzly. The grizzly's back hair had been burned off to the skin. Wasilla's face, arms and torso were smoke-grimed and blistered. He had opened the grizzly's paunch and rolled out the fat-sheathed innards. The stomach had been crammed with fermenting high-bush cranberries, which now lay spilled onto the bloody, trampled grass. The chief looked up at me and shrugged wearily.

"He was drunk," he said. The Denna people use the same word for "drunk" and "crazy"—*gistun*. In this case, with the berries as evidence, I gathered that he meant literally that the bear had been barrelhouse drunk.

Dropping my pack, I sat beside him on the windfall; and while we watched the gaunt old tribal house burn, he told me what had happened. It was a wildish tale.

He had been alone in the house, he told me, at peace with himself and the world, working on part of a consignment of snowshoes which the Army had ordered to use as pilot models for mass-manufactured webs, when he heard a sound at the open doorway forty feet distant. He looked up to see the grizzly shoulder its way in. It was such an extraordinary happening that at first he simply stared. During his lifetime in the wilds, he had known black bears to enter an occupied house, but had never heard of a grizzly doing so. Grizzlies were too smart, or too spooky.

But this one came in as if he owned the place, rattling his claws across the plank floor, turning his big head from side to side, blowing. Wasilla's rifle stood against the wall halfway down the long room, the bear closer to it now than he was. So that was out. As he tried to think of some way to frighten the bear back through the door, his gaze fell on some heavy, granite river rocks that he used as weights in shaping snowshoe frames. He scooped up one of the rocks and, yelling, sent it thundering over the planks at the animal. The result was unexpected and horrifying. The bear jumped aside with a snarl, and the rock struck the door, slamming it shut.

With that, Wasilla fled. He went up the ladder to the loft with a squirrel-like agility which, he said, he had not known he possessed. It was only a half loft; planks laid across the ceiling beams, used as storage space for grub and gear and for seasoning birch snowshoe timber. From this vantage place he watched the trapped bear wreck his home.

Roaring, froth dripping from his flews, the animal smashed the cast-iron stove, pulled down the kitchen shelves, reduced a table to splintered planks, hammered the water bucket flat, ruined a cherished gasoline lantern. Three pairs of Wasilla's light, beautifully made snowshoes, newly shellacked and ready for the Army, stood in a corner. The bear slapped them to the floor, bit the frames, ripped out the babiche foot-filling. The house had only one window; and it was curtained with trading-post calico, a conceit of Wasilla's absent squaw. The bear ignored it. Probably, Wasilla thought, he didn't recognize it as a possible exit. Or maybe it occurred to him, but he just didn't give a damn. The chief had now concluded that the bear was drunk. He could smell fermented berries.

The grizzly began tearing bunks apart; and while he was thus engaged, Wasilla made his way across the ceiling beams to the far end of the house and managed, with a length of snowshoe birch, to open the door. Feeling that this was one of the major triumphs of his life, he returned over the beams and prodded the bear with the piece of timber. His idea was to goad the animal toward the door. Instead of seizing the opportunity to depart, the bear knocked the timber out of his hands with a lightning pawstroke and then reared high, reaching for the beam on which Wasilla was crouched.

At this juncture, Wasilla's judgment went sour. He had begun to suspect that in addition to being drunk, the animal was perhaps a medicine bear. After all, the door was wide open, yet the bear didn't seem to want to leave. It continued to roar and rage about, tearing up a mattress, shredding a lynx-skin sleeping robe that, when new, had been worth $1,000. Maybe it was the lynx robe that did it. Anyway, Wasilla took partial leave of his senses. In the loft was a five-gallon can of kerosene. He slopped a generous amount over the bear's back. Then, as the animal roared savagely, he lit a match and, hoping for the best, dropped it.

His aim was good. Its whole back suddenly ablaze, the bear screamed and slammed out the door like a flaming missile. Wasilla at once swung down from the loft, snatched up his rifle and ran after the animal. He fired three times as the bear plowed into the brush, and was sure he had scored. Following cautiously, he found the bear twenty minutes later, lying stone dead beside the creek bank trail. He opened its belly to confirm his belief that it had been full of fermented berries.

Only then did he see that his house was burning. Apparently some of the kerosene had spilled onto the floor and had also ignited when he set the bear afire. In his haste to lay hands on his rifle and wreak bloody vengeance on the bear, he hadn't noticed it. Well, it was an old house and the spruce logs were tinder dry. Wasilla hadn't been able to save anything. Actually, there wasn't much that could have been saved. The bear had been quite thorough.

"Maybe he really was a medicine bear," Wasilla said. "A drunken medicine bear. I can't think of anything worse."

The old snowshoe maker sighed. "Maybe you will lend me some money to buy grub and a new shirt, huh? It looks like it's gonna be a long, cold winter. And I gotta do that work for the Army."

I think that bears suffer from hangovers. Otherwise, I don't know how to account for some of their actions. Take an episode that occurred at the Metal Creek cabin in the Knik country. With "Starvation" Smith, an ageless bean-pole sourdough who occasionally packed for me, I had just returned from a very rough thirty-day sheep hunt in the jungle of peaks and glaciers to the east. We were both dog-tired, completely beat out, and this morning we slept late, not even bothering to make coffee. Around nine o'clock, when the sun topped the range and its light streamed in the open doorway, Starvation got up, cussing the necessity, and stepped outside. In a moment he was back, his whisker-stubbled face split in a wide grin.

"Whopping big old sow grizzly and two cubs out there," he said. "If you want to, we can kill her easy."

Starvation was eager because he hated bears, especially grizzlies. They picked on him, he claimed, went out of their way to give him trouble. They were damned nuisances, stumbling blocks to progress; and the government, by gosh, ought to put a bounty on the varmints. I told him I wasn't interested. I had no use at all for a grizzly. All I wanted was to soak up a lot of rest, and skinning a grizzly and then fleshing the pelt and stretching it added up to work. So would he please go back to sleep, or go somewhere, because I yearned to resume the pleasant business of resting.

But his excitement was contagious; and I presently got up, stiff and sore in every joint, checked my rifle and went outside for a look. She was a typical Knik grizzly, a long-legged, hog-snouted old bat with a cream-yellow pelt. Followed by two roly-poly, mustard-colored spring cubs, she was coming down off the mountainside that sheered up directly behind the cabin, heading for the creek.

The first fifty yards of this slope were very steep and covered with short, frost-killed grass. Beyond, reaching clear to the naked talus pitches and stringers of permanent snow, was a vast serviceberry thicket whose tons of berries attracted bears from far and wide at this season of the year. When the grizzly reached the almost vertical belt of grass, she did something that I had never before seen any bruin, black, white, blue or brown, do. She laid down on her belly, and with a kick of her hind feet, pushed off. The grass was so slippery, you could have made a ski run on it; and in a moment she was shooting toward the creek at astonishing speed. A stone's throw from the cabin, she soared over a ten-foot rimrock, turned half a somersault and, with a magnificent splash, landed on her back in the icy, silt-gray water.

While her less impulsive cubs picked their way down the slope, mamma enjoyed a cold bath. She rolled, ducked under repeatedly, snorting and groaning, and sat on the bottom with only her head sticking out. At last she waded ashore and stretched out on the gravel. There was something pretty familiar about all this. I mean, it was a routine that I recognized. Starvation got it, too. "Ugly old so-and-so acts like somebody hurting from the morning after the night before," he whispered. "You sure you don't want to shoot her? Might be a favor, the way she seems to feel."

I told him to forget it, that bears were an asset to the country and besides, when I left home I had promised my parents that I would never shoot a bear with a hangover. We went back to bed. Some thirty minutes later there was a great rattling of tin cans in the garbage pit, followed by the muffled wailing of a cub. So we got up again, to behold a curious and revealing bit of drama. One of the mustard-colored cubs had got its head stuck in an empty, five-gallon can that had held Lubeck's dried potatoes—the so-called varnished potatoes of the early days—and, squalling frantically, was running toward mamma, on instruments, so to speak.

The sow heaved to her feet and stared at the oncoming cub. I could imagine what went through her mind. She had been resting peacefully after her cold bath, maybe had even been asleep, and now this unseemly, nerve-jangling uproar. She took two steps toward the cub and swung at the can. It was a mighty wallop, and whether it was intended to punish the cub or remove the can, I have no idea. It accomplished both.

The luckless cub sailed a dozen feet through the air, parting company with the can en route, and landed upside down against a boulder. Whuffing angrily, the sow belted the can again, then shambled off upstream with her offspring, no doubt in search of more tranquil parts. I got busy building a fire for coffee. When the birchbark and spruce kindling caught, I asked Starvation if he really thought that the bear had been hungover.

"Of course," he said. "She had a hangover big enough for all of us. She'd been stuffing herself with frosted berries." He piled a handful of coffee into the pot. "Doggoned if I ain't got a good notion," he said wistfully, "to climb that mountain and eat a couple of gallons of those berries myself. It's been a long time."

One of the most memorable bear stories I ever heard involved Gordon Bettles, the Hootlinanna Kid and a black that presumably was under the influence. The two sourdoughs had spent the summer prospecting in the Alaska Range wilderness and, in early October, were heading back down the Tonzona River to civilization, ragged, footsore, short of grub and almost out of ammunition. While plodding through a riverbank bog one pretty afternoon, slapping white stocking flies, cussing the life of prospectors and wishing they were somewhere else, they sighted a black bear in a narrow canyon that slashed back into the mountainside. It was the first meat-bearing animal they had seen in a week; and although it was out of rifle range, both men at once had mouth-watering visions of fried chops, roasted ribs, steaks and broiled liver.

"I'll go up and kill him," Gordon said. "When you hear me shoot, come on and lend a hand. Oh boy, oh boy, our luck has turned, by gad. Tonight we eat." He started up the bed of the canyon, a limping scarecrow light-headed on account of a long diet of beans and bannock, but wonderfully cheered by the prospect of red meat. The bear turned in to a side canyon walled at its upper end by a hanging glacier and went out of sight among some huge boulders. Gordon stalked it patiently. He had only two cartridges for his battered .405 and was praying that nothing would go wrong.

He rounded a lichen-encrusted, cabin-size boulder and saw the bear 100 feet distant. Taking a rest, he cut down carefully on the bear's head and pulled. There was the click of the hammer. Nothing else. The shell had misfired. The bear heard the sound, but apparently didn't see Gordon. As Gordon, dismayed, jacked the remaining shell into the chamber, the bear came galloping hell-bent back down the canyon bed. It was a most unorthodox thing for an animal to do, a complete tactical boner that no normal bear should have committed; and it was such a surprise to Gordon that he almost blew his chance to make a kill with his final shot.

He held on the bear's head again, and the heavy slug went inches wide, only creasing the skull, but fortunately entering the animal's body at the base of the neck. Gordon always maintained that the bear wasn't charging, but the effect was the same. Only a dozen feet distant when shot, momentum kept it coming the rest of the way; the route through the fallen boulders was narrow, and Gordon was too tired and slow of foot to sidestep. The next thing he knew, he was down, with the bear on top of him. His head had struck a rock and he felt consciousness flickering out, but by an effort of will drew his belt knife and split the bear's belly from one end to the other.

The Hootlinanna Kid, when he arrived on the scene some minutes later, was horrified. Gordon had blacked out and was just coming to. The bear, naturally, was dead. "Take it easy, old pal," the Kid said shakily, as he eyed the blood and guts covering Gordon's midsection. "Maybe we can wash 'em off and stuff 'em back in. Then we can sew you up with some fishline, and you'll be as good as new—I hope."

Gordon looked at the intestines and up at the Kid. "What in hell are you talking about?" he shouted. "They ain't mine; they're the bear's." He began fumbling under his shirt. "At least, I think they are."

When it had been decided that the innards were indeed the bear's, the Hootlinanna Kid sniffed pointedly. "I smell blueberry wine," he said in phony accusation. "Found a cache, and didn't save any for your pore old partner. That's how come the bear got you down, huh? Jest plumb stinking dunk." Finding relief in argument, the Kid pretended profound disbelief when Gordon protested that it was the bear who had been drunk, not himself.

A harassed black bear, who no doubt was carrying high voltage due to having feasted on fermenting berries, once did me a favor. It was unwitting on his part; but nevertheless it was a favor and I was grateful, although unfortunately I had to kill the animal. This was when I was in charge of forest-fire prevention for the General Land Office in Alaska, my beat extending from the southern coastal forests to the ultimate timber on the Arctic slope, a sizable piece of territory, considering that I had no permanent assistants.

Toward the end of September I was in Anchorage, closing up shop for the season, when word came that a large fire was burning near Caribou Creek, in the upper Matanuska country. Since no laborers were available, I got permission from the governor to impress the ten current occupants of the local jail, including the jailhouse cook. I then requisitioned some packhorses, got a camp outfit together and set forth with my jailbirds by special train for the railhead at Chickaloon.

Although I had no way of knowing it then, the expedition was foredoomed to frustration. There wasn't just one fire; there were a score of them. A Denna shaman, returning from Eklutna to his village on Tyone Lake, had set a fire in the trail every few miles to prevent the demons of civilization from following him home. Some shaman!

Anyway, four days later we made camp on a narrow, timbered point jutting into a nameless lake under the Matanuska snowpeaks. It was coming dusk, and a crown fire was burning a quarter-mile across the lake. The whole world seemed to be drowned in smoke. I didn't know how big the fire was. I didn't know where to start work. I suspected that my crew was planning to desert at the first opportunity. In short, I had problems.

I was sitting on a boulder, doing some high-caliber worrying, when somebody sighted an animal swimming across the lake toward us. At first I thought it was a beaver, but as it drew closer, I saw its ears and realized that a beaver's ears don't stick up. The animal was a bear, black. My firefighters, cheechakos all, who probably had never seen a wild bear, gathered at the water's edge and joyously began throwing rocks at it. I protested, but to no effect. After all, there was no law against throwing rocks at a bear. Besides, in the circumstances, my authority was kind of limited. I didn't want to crowd my luck by getting tough.

But it griped me. The bear was tired and wanted to come ashore. He couldn't turn back, because the whole countryside over yonder was afire. Yet each time he tried to head in, my gang of stalwarts would shower him with rocks. They followed him up lake and down lake, whooping like Indians at a potlatch, having themselves a wonderful time. Big deal. Finally, coming back to the point, the bear was directly in front of camp again, swimming wearily, when he must have decided the heck with everything. At any rate, here he came swarming out of the water. The yelling conscripts bounced another barrage of rocks off him, then fled incontinently up the point to camp.

On the beach were five hobbled packhorses, and they joined the retreat. The bear brought up the rear. It was a nice camp, neat and trim, silk tents pitched Forest-Service style, gear and rigging stacked according to the book. Within thirty seconds it was a shambles. The damage that ten men, five horses and a bear will inflict on a camp while stampeding through it cannot be adequately described. It is something that must be seen.

My sympathy was wholly with the bear, but I now had to take action. My rifle was beside me on the boulder. I picked up the bear with the sights as he galloped across a fallen tent, and more by good luck than good shooting, dropped him. The hard-case crew was overjoyed. For them it was a great adventure. It became even greater when one of them, opening the bear's mouth to examine its teeth, got a strong whiff of berry whine. "Hey, men!" he hollered. "Whaddya know? This bear is been hitting the jug. He's a wino."

Later in the evening, when we had cleaned up most of the wreckage, one of the men, a tough redhead from San Francisco, came over to me and said, "Everything is okay, boss. We were gonna pull out tonight and leave you all by your lonesome. But hell, this is fun. Drunken bears and everything." So they stuck around, and we did our best for the General Land Office, and eventually it rained and the rain put out the fires, as usually is the case.

Which, I guess, winds up this chronicle. See you up north in a berry patch some autumn in the moon of the drunken bears.

BIBLIOGRAPHY

"Fiesta of Fins," .... *Sports Afield*, March 1957
"Life in the Big Frost," .... *Sports Afield*, May 1957
"Horse Hunt in Caribou Land," .... *Sports Afield*, July 1957
"Adventure with Makos," .... *Sports Afield*, September 1957
"Buck Fever Can Happen to Anybody," . . *Hunting Yearbook*, January 1958
"Trophy Hunt in *Mañana* Land," .... *Sports Afield*, July 1958
"Grudge Grizzly," .... *Sports Afield*, September 1958
"Big Luck at Cuyutlan," .... *Sports Afield*, October 1958
"Trouble at Erickson Creek," .... *Sports Afield*, November 1958
"Death of a King Wolf," .... *Sports Afield*, January 1959
"Pete's Educational Bear Hunt," .... *Sports Afield*, February 1959
"Adventures of a Mexican Mutt," .... *Sports Afield*, May 1959
"Long Hunt for a Water Dog," .... *Sports Afield*, September 1959
"Captain Sharkbait's Triumph," .... *Sports Afield*, November 1959
"The Curse of the Chonchos," .... *Sports Afield*, February 1960
"The Mysterious *Onca*," .... *Sports Afield*, April 1960
"The Shootingest Characters," .... *Sports Afield*, December 1960
"The Craziest Cat Hunt," .... *Sports Afield*, January 1961
"Ladies...with Guns," .... *Sports Afield*, February 1961
"*Chubasco*," .... *Sports Afield*, April 1961
"When the Fish Went Nuts," .... *Sports Afield*, May 1961
"Storm Ducks with Crocs," .... *Sports Afield*, August 1961
"The *Tigre* of Santa Rita," .... *Sports Afield*, October 1961
"The Damnedest Duck on Earth," .... *Sports Afield*, December 1961
"Hell in Catskin," .... *Sports Afield*, January 1962
"Coyote-Wolverine War," .... *Sports Afield*, March 1962
"Mad Coyote," .... *Sports Afield*, October 1962
"The Gotch-eared Bull of Toonakloot," .... *Sports Afield*, November 1962
"Kill or Starve," .... *Sports Afield*, February 1963
"Snowblind!," .... *Sports Afield*, April 1963

ADVENTURE IS IN MY BLOOD

"Waiting for the Caribou," . . . . *Sports Afield*, June 1963
"Long Hunter, Alaskan Style, Part One," . . . . *Sports Afield*, July 1963
"Long Hunter, Alaskan Style, Conclusion," . . . . *Sports Afield*, August 1963
"Joys and Sorrows of a Wrangler," . . . . *Sports Afield*, January 1964
"The High Price of Moose Meat," . . . . *Sports Afield*, February 1964
"In the Moon of the Drunken Bears," . . . . *Sports Afield*, March 1964